THE

CREATOR AND THE CREATURE,

OR,

THE WONDERS OF DIVINE LOVE.

BY

FREDERICK WILLIAM FABER, D.D.,

PRIEST OF THE ORATORY OF ST. PHILIP NERI.

Ού γὰρ πάριγγον δεῖ τοιεῖσθαι τὸν Θεόν.

PYTHAGORAS.

FOURTH EDITION.

TO

ST. MATTHEW,

THE APOSTLE AND EVANGELIST

OF THE INCARNATE WORD,

THE PATTERN OF OBEDIENCE
TO DIVINE VOCATIONS,

THE MODEL OF PROMPT SUBMISSION
TO HOLY INSPIRATIONS,

THE TEACHER AND THE EXAMPLE
OF CORRESPONDENCE TO GRACE,

WHO
LEFT ALL FOR GOD,

SELF AND THE WORLD AND WEALTH,

AT GOD'S ONE WORD,

WITHOUT QUESTION, WITHOUT RESERVE,

WITHOUT DELAY,

TO BE FOR EVER IN THE CHURCH

THE DOCTOR, THE PROPHET, AND THE PATRON,

THE COMFORT AND THE JUSTIFICATION,

OF THOSE WHO FOLLOW HEAVENLY CALLS

IN THE WORLD'S DESPITE,

AND WHO GIVE THEMSELVES IN LOVE,

AS HE GAVE HIMSELF,

WITHOUT LIMIT OR CONDITION

AS CREATURES TO THEIR CREATOR.

PREFACE.

It appears necessary to trespass on the reader's patience for awhile by giving him the history of the composition of this Treatise. Books, reviews, conversation, personal experience, and the phenomena forced upon our notice in dealing with souls, seem to concur in showing that it is almost a characteristic feature of the present age, at least in this country, to have harsh, unkindly, jealous, suspicious, and distrustful thoughts of God. It is not so much that men do not believe in Him, as in past times, or that they are irreverently inquisitive, as they have been in other days. Infidelity and intellectual impiety are unfortunately common enough; but they are not, as compared with other times, the characteristic sins of the day with us. We find in their place abundant admissions of the existence, and even of the excellence, of God; but joined with this, a reluctance, which hardly likes to put itself into words, to acknowledge His sovereignty. There is a desire to strip Him of His majesty, to qualify His rights and to abate His

prerogatives, to lower Him so as to bring Him
somewhat nearer to ourselves, to insist on His
obeying our own notions of the laws of morality,
and confining Himself within such limits of justice
and equity as are binding on creatures rather than
on the Creator. There is a tendency to turn religion
into a contract between parties, very unequal certainly, but not infinitely unequal, to object to whatever in God's Providence betokens a higher rule
than the rule of our duties towards each other, and
to revolt from any appearance of exclusiveness,
supreme will, and unaccountable irresponsibility,
which there may be in His conduct towards us.
This appears to be the attitude of the day towards
God. The acknowledgment of Him is conditional
on His submitting to be praised and admired, as
other than the God whose own will is His sole
law, whose own glory is His necessary end, and
who by virtue of His own perfections can have no
other end, rest, or sufficiency, than His own ever·
blessed Self.

If this were simply a mitigated form of infidelity belonging to the nineteenth century, and
affecting those only who are immersed in worldliness, the present Treatise would not have been
written, inasmuch as it is purely practical, and
addressed only to believers. But the epidemics of
the world are never altogether unfelt within the
Church. The air is corrupted, and in some much
milder form the souls of believers are affected by
the pestilence which reigns without. So is it in
the present case. In the difficulties through which

men have to force their way, by the help of grace,
into the One True Fold, in the obstacles which
hinder others from advancing in the ways of
holiness, in the temptations which tease, if they
do not endanger faith, in the treatment of religious
controversies, in the sides men take in ecclesiastical
politics, in the tendencies of their theological views,
and even in the common exercises of daily devotion, we find indubitable traces of an attitude
towards God, caught from the fashion of the day,
and which seems to betoken some obliquity in the
mind, logically working itself out in the worship
and obedience of our souls. It is not that believers
believe wrongly about God, but either that they do
not understand, or that they do not realize, what
they most rightly believe.

It has thus come to pass, from various circumstances which need not be detailed, that the composition of this Treatise has been a work of charity
towards souls, almost forced upon the writer in
consequence of the position which he occupied,
and the work into which such a sphere as London
introduced him. The result of much thought on
the subject led to the conclusion, that it is possible
for the intellectual inconsistencies of men to realize
that they have a Creator without realizing, what is
already involved, that they themselves are creatures, or what is actually implied in being a creature; and further, it seemed that this very inconsistency explained and accounted for the phenomena
in question.

The Treatise therefore, will be found naturally

to divide itself into three parts. The First Book, consisting of three chapters, is the statement of the case, and contains a description of the phenomena around us, a detailed account of what it is to have a Creator, and of what follows from our being His creatures. The result of this inquiry is to find, that creation is simply an act of divine love, and cannot be accounted for on any other supposition than that of an immense and eternal love. The Second Book, consisting of five chapters, occupies itself with the difficulties and depths of this creative love, which have been classified as answers to the following questions, Why does God wish us to love Him, Why does He Himself love us, How can we love Him, How do we actually love Him, and how does He repay our love. Here, in other times, or in another country perhaps, the Treatise might have concluded. But the course of the investigation has started some grave objections, which the Third Book, consisting of four chapters, is occupied in answering. If this account of creative love be true, if God redeemed us because He persisted in desiring, even after our fall, to have us with Him as participators in His own eternal beatitude, salvation ought to be easy, even to fallen nature. If it is easy, then it might appear to some to follow that at least the majority of believers would be saved. If these two questions are answered in the affirmative, then a fresh difficulty rises to view. How are we to account for what is an undoubted fact, that these relations of the Creator and the creature are not practically acknowledged by creatures? The answer to this objection is found in the nature, the power, and the prevalence of worldliness. The flesh and the devil will not adequately account for the way in which men behave towards God, and the attitude in which they put themselves before Him. Worldliness is the principal explanation of it. But then the conclusions, which may be drawn from an inspection of worldliness, seem to dishonour, if not to destroy, the previous conclusions about the easiness of salvation and the multitude of the elect. How is it that so many can escape, how is it that they do escape? By personal love of the Creator, by a religion which is simply a service of love, by a love which brings them within the suck of that gulf of the Divine Beauty, which is our holiness here, as it is our happiness hereafter. And thus the creature secures that enjoyment and possession of the Creator which was His primary intention in creation; and so the Treatise ends.

Although it seems occupied with very simple truths, and might almost be regarded as a commentary on the catechism, the composition of it has been a work both of time and labour. It stands to the Author's other works in the relation of source and origin. It has been this view of God, pondered for years, that has given rise to the theological bias, visible in the other books, as well as the opinions expressed on the spiritual life. Difficulties which may have been found in the other books, respecting the Sacred Humanity, the Blessed Sacrament, our Lady, Purgatory,

Indulgences, and the like, will for the most part find their explanation here; for this treatise explains in detail the point of view from which the Author habitually looks at all religious questions, of practice as well as of speculation.

It should also be borne in mind that the Treatise is a whole, and keeps sedulously to its one subject. Hence, unless the book were loaded with repetitions, a cursory reader may easily meet with statements, against which grave objections may seem to lie, whereas those very objections have been met or provided against in some other portion of the work. The Author trusts it is no want of humility to say, that, after the careful thought and deep reading of years, he should refuse to trouble himself with criticisms, which shall not bear upon them the impress of a careful study of his book, at least proportionate to the care he has expended upon its composition.

The Author cannot allow his Treatise to go forth to the public, without acknowledging the obligations he is under to the Rev. Father Gloag, the librarian of the London Oratory, who has spared no pains in verifying quotations, in seeking for passages in voluminous works to which other writers had given incorrect references or made vague allusions, and also in bringing under the notice of the Author some important passages of which he was not aware himself, especially with reference to the Baian Propositions. As the work has been written for the most part in ill-health,

and under the pressure of other duties from which
he could not be dispensed, the Author is the more
anxious to acknowledge thus gratefully a coopera-
tion, which circumstances rendered peculiarly valu-
able, and which, tedious and troublesome as it
was, has been proffered with such a graceful kindness, as to make the sense of obligation a pleasure
rather than a burden.

In truth though all appears so plain and smooth,
the composition of the Treatise has in reality led
the Writer along a very thorny and broken path.
The ground of creation, of the natural order and of
the supernatural order, is, as theologians well
know, strewn all over, as if a broken precipice had
overwhelmed it, with Condemned Propositions, the
theology of which is full of fine distinctions and
insidious subtleties, and, not unfrequently, of apparent contradictions. Nowhere does the malice
of error more painfully succeed in harassing the
student, than in this matter of Condemned Propositions. The utmost pains however have been
taken to secure accuracy. The best theologians
have been collated, even to weariness; and if the
book had been allowed to exhibit in notes or ap-
pendices the labour which it has entailed, it would
have swollen to an inconvenient bulk. It has
moreover, been submitted to two careful and minute
revisions by others, in whose ability and theological
attainments there was good reason to confide. But
the author cannot now entrust it to the thoughtful
charity and kindly interpretations of his readers,

PREFACE.

without also submitting it in all respects, and without the slightest reserve, to the judgment of the Church, retracting and disavowing beforehand any statement which may be at variance with her authorized teaching, who is the sole, as well as the infallible, preceptress of the nations in the ways of eternal truth.

Sydenham Hill,
Feast of the Dedication
of the Basilica of St. Peter and St. Paul.
1856.

CONTENTS.

BOOK I.

BOOK II.

BOOK III.

THE CREATOR AND THE CREATURE:

OR,

THE WONDERS OF DIVINE LOVE.

BOOK I.

THE CASE STATED BETWEEN THE
CREATOR AND THE CREATURE.

THE CREATOR AND THE CREATURE.

BOOK I.

THE CASE STATED BETWEEN THE CREATOR AND THE CREATURE.

CHAPTER I.

A NEW FASHION OF AN OLD SIN.

"Quid ad me si quis non intelligat? Gaudeat et ipse dicens: Quid est
hoc? Gaudeat etiam sic, et amet, non inveniendo invenire potius Te,
quam inveniendo non invenire Te."--*S. Augustin.*

LIFE is short, and it is wearing fast away. We lose a
great deal of time, and we want short roads to heaven,
though the right road is in truth far shorter than we
believe. It is true of most men that their light is
greater than their heat, which is only saying that we
practice less than we profess. Yet there are many
souls, good, noble, and affectionate, who seem rather
to want light than heat. They want to know more
of God, more of themselves, and more of the relation
in which they stand to God, and then they would
love and serve Him better. There are many again
who when they read or hear of the spiritual life, or
come across the ordinary maxims of Christian perfection, do not understand what is put before them. It
is as if some one spoke to them in a foreign language.
Either the words are without meaning, or the ideas

are far-fetched and unreal. They stand off from persons who profess to teach such doctrines, or to live by them, as if they had some contagious disease which they might catch themselves. Yet they are often very little tainted by worldliness; often they are men who have made sacrifices for God, and who would lay down their lives for His Church. Their instincts are good; yet they seem to want something; and whatever it is that they lack, the absence of it appears to put them under a most mournful disability in the way of attaining holiness. In other words, there are multitudes of men so good that it seems inevitable that they must be much more good than they really are, and the difficulty is how so much goodness can continue to exist without more goodness.

This is a phenomenon which has at once attracted the attention and excited the sorrow of all who love the souls for which Jesus shed His Precious Blood. It may not be true that any one solution of the problem will meet or explain all the difficulties of this distressing experience. Much lies deep in the manifold corruption of our hearts. But there is one fact which goes far towards an adequate explanation of the matter, and which is at the same time rightly considered, a profound mystery. It is that men, even pious men, do not continually bear in mind that they are creatures, and have never taken the pains to get a clear idea of what is involved in being a creature. Hence it is true to say, even of multitudes of the faithful, that they have no adequate or indeed distinct notion of the relation in which they stand to God, of His rights, or of their obligations: and when trial comes, their inadequate idea betrays them into conduct quite at variance with their antecedents.

Forgetfulness of God has been in all ages the grand evil of the world: a forgetfulness so contrary to reason, and so opposed also to the daily evidence of the senses, that it can be accounted for on no other hypothesis than that of original sin and the mystery of the fall. This forgetfulness of God has been far more common than open revolt against Him. The last is rather the sin of angels, the first the sin of men. Yet every age of the world has its own prevailing type and fashion of iniquity; and in these latter times it appears as if the forgetfulness of God had taken the shape of forgetfulness on our part that we are creatures. Men may realize that they are creatures, imperfect, finite, and dependent. This truth may be continually coming uppermost in books of morals, in systems of philosophy, and in the general tone of society. And yet, with all this, God may be set aside and passed over, almost as if He did not exist. The world simply does not advert to Him. Who that has read certain philosophical and scientific books of the last century does not know how men could write of creation without their thoughts so much as touching or coming in contact with the idea of the Creator? To such writers creation seems the end of and answer to all things, just as the Most Holy Trinity is to a believer. They speak of creation, investigate creation, draw inferences from creation, without so much as brushing against a personal or living Creator even in their imagination. Creator is to them simply a masculine form of the neuter noun creation, and they have a kind of instinct against using it, which they have probably never perceived, or never taken the trouble to explain even to themselves. It is not on any theory, or any atheistical principle, that God is thus passed over. He is unseen, and hence is practically considered as absent; and what is absent is easily forgotten. He is out of mind because He is out of sight. There is no objection to giving God His place, only He is not thought of. This is one phase of the world's forgetfulness of God.

Then again there have been times and literary schools, in which God was continually referred to, and His name used in an impressive manner, sometimes reverently and sometimes irreverently. He has been a fashionable figure of speech, or an adornment of eloquence, or the culminating point of an oratorical climax. Or there has been a decency in naming Him honourably, as if it were burning a kind of incense before Him. It soothes the conscience; it gives an air of religion to us, and it enhances our own respectability, especially in the eyes of our inferiors. And yet this word God has not in reality meant the Three Divine Persons, as the Gospel reveals them to us. It has been an imaginary embodiment or a vague canonization of an immense power, of distant majesty, and of unimaginable mystery; a something like the beauty of midnight skies, or the magnificent pageant of the storm, elevating the thoughts, quelling and tranquillizing littleness, and ministering to that poetry in our nature which is so often mistaken for real worship and actual religion. The ideas of duty, of precept, of sacrifice, of obedience, have been very indistinctly in the mind, if they have been there at all. It is the notion of a grand God, rather than a living God. The multitude of His rights over us, the dread exorbitance of His sovereignty, the realities of His minute vigilance, of His jealous expectations, of His rigid judgments, of His particular providence, of His hourly interference, these things have not been denied, but they have not been part of the idea wakened

in the mind by the word God.   The close embrace
and tingling pressure of His omnipresence, as theology
discloses it to us, would have made the men, of whom
we are speaking, start away in alarm or in disgust.
The God who demands an account of every idle word,
and measures His penalties to each unbridled thought,
and before whom all men are simply and peremptorily
equal, is a different Being from the poetical sovereign
who reigns over the Olympus of modern literature, to
keep our inferiors in check, to add gravity to our rebukes,
to foster our own self-respect, and, in a word, to " point
a moral or adorn a tale."   This God is rather our creature than our Creator ; He is the creature of moral respectability, the necessity of a dissatisfied conscience, the
convenience of a social police, the consolation of an unsupernatural sorrow, and the imagery of a chaste and
elegant literature.   Yet the atheism of this is not
explicit: it is only implied.   No revolt is intended.
A false God has slipped into the place of the true one ;
and because their faith had failed, men did not see the
change, and do not see it still.   This is another common form of forgetfulness of God; but it does not seem
to have the peculiar characteristics or particular malice
of the form which we suppose to belong eminently to
our own days.   For in the form, of which we have been
speaking, the name of God was a necessity just because
men did not forget that they were creatures.   Nay, it
was respectable and moral to speak slightingly of
human nature, its weaknesses, and its vagaries, and to
say great things of the far-off God.   Men's notions of
God wanted correcting and purifying, enlarging and
heightening ; above all, they wanted to be made real,
and brought home to them, and laid as a yoke upon
them.   Nevertheless they remembered they were crea-

tures; only, because they had lost the true idea of the Creator, they made the weaknesses of the creature an apology for his sin, and so went desperately astray.

But if we mistake not, the characteristic malice of these times takes a somewhat different direction. God is certainly ignored; but He is rather passively than actively ignored, rather indirectly, than directly. Men do not look at His side of the question at all. They do not pass Him over, even contemptuously. Still less do they look at Him, and then put Him away. They are otherwise engaged. They are absorbed in the contemplation of themselves. Theories of progress and perfectibility throw so much dust in their eyes, that they do not see that they are creatures. They do not know what it is to be a creature, nor what comes of it. Hence the idea of God grows out of their minds: it is thrust out of them, extruded as it were, by the press of matter, without any direct process or conscious recognition on their parts. Their minds are purely atheist by the force of terms. They are the proprietors of the world, not tenants in it, and tenants at will. They hardly suspect that there are any claims on them. God was a fine thought of the Middle Ages, and religion an organized priestcraft, which was not always simply an evil: but which has now outlived any practical utilities it may ever have had. God is subjective: He is an idea, He is the creature of man's mind. If there be any real truth in religion, it must be looked for in the direction of pantheism. But the world is too busy to think much even of that. This is practically their view, or would be, if they took the trouble to have a view at all. What it comes to is this. Men are masters. They begin and end with themselves. Humanity marches onwards with grand strides to the magnificent goal of social perfectibility. Each generation is a glorious section of the procession of progress. Liberty, independence, speed, association, and self-praise, these compose the spirit of the modern world. The word creature is a name, an affair of classification, like the title of a genus or a species in natural history. But it has no religious consequences: it entangles us in no supernatural relations. It simply means that we are not eternal, the remembrance of which is salutary, in that it quickens our diligence in the pursuit of material prosperity.

All phases of civilization have a monomania of their own. Certain favourite ideas come uppermost, and are regarded with so much favour that an undue importance is given to them, until at last the relative magnitudes of truths and duties are lost sight of, and the ethics of the day are full of a confusion that only rights itself in the failure and disappointment, in which each age of the world infallibly issues at the last. Then comes a reaction, and a new phase of civilization, and a fresh monomania; and either because the circle looks like a straight line, because we see so little of it at a time, or because the living world, like the material one, really advances while it revolves, we call these alternations progress. Now we generally find that each of these monomanias, with its cant words, its fixed ideas, and its onesided exaggerations, transfers its temper and characteristics to the view which it takes of God. The ideas of liberty, progress, independence, social contracts, representative government, and the like, colour our views of God, and influence our philosophy. No one can read much without seeing how the prevailing ideas of the day make men fall into a sort of unconscious anthropomorphism about God. Indeed nothing but the magnificent certainties and unworldly wisdom of

catholic theology can rescue us from falling into some
such error ourselves.[*]   At the present day particularly
we should be careful and jealous in the view we take of
God, careful that it should be well ascertained, and
jealous that it should be according to the pattern showed
us in catholic theology.[†]

In whatever direction we turn we shall gain fresh
proof of the want of this true view of God, and fresh
evidence that the peculiar forgetfulness of God in these

---

[*] The gibe of Voltaire is after all full of bitter truths; depuis que Dieu a
fait l'homme à son image, l'homme le lui a bien rendu.

[†] There are two views of God in theology, the Scotist and the Thomist.
The Scotist seems to bring God nearer to us, to make our conceptions of Him
more real, to represent Him as more accessible to our understandings, even
while He remains incomprehensible. St. Thomas carefully observes the
mean : Nullum nomen univocè de Deo et creaturis prædicatur; sed nec
etiam purè equivocè, ut aliqui dixerunt : and again, Aliqua dicuntur de Deo
et creaturis, analogicè, et non equivocè pure, neque pure univoce, ι. q. xiii.
5 and 6. The Thomist view, by driving us away from many of the analogies
on which the other view rests, or by regarding these analogies as more
equivocal, seems to put God further from us, and to thicken the darkness
which is round His throne. But, if the Scotist view seems more directly to
lead to love, it is exposed to much greater philosophical dangers than the
Thomist, and may more easily be pressed into the service of anthropomorphism, perhaps of pantheism. Thus the Thomist view is safer. " You ought
to know," says Malebranche, (Huitieme Entretien sur la Metaphysique, sec. 7.)
" that to judge worthily of God, we must attribute to Him no attributes, but
those which are incomprehensible. This is evident, for God is the infinite
in every sense, so that nothing finite is congruous to Him, and that which is
infinite in every sense is in every way incomprehensible to the human
mind." So also Tertullian adv. Marcion, i. 4. Summum Magnum, ex defec-
tione æmuli solitudinem quandam de singularitate præstantiæ suæ possidens,
unicum est. So it has been well observed by Simon in his beautiful but
insidious work on natural religion, (Religion Naturelle, 48) that we almost all
of us start from the Christian idea of God, as author of the world, and land at
the pagan idea of God like ourselves. All beings, except God, are in a system.
It is their nature and condition. He alone is outside of and above all system ;
and thus by applying to Him our principles, we run into contradictions, and
by attributing to Him our faculties, we become entangled in impossibilities.
Thus a clear and intelligent view of God is one of the first requisites for all
of us at this day ; and it is just this view which the catholic catechism
gives, and which all the wise men of the world seem so unaccountably
to miss.

times consists in the forgetfulness on our own part that
we are creatures. For, think in what this forgetfulness
consists. It is the new fashion of an old sin. Nothing
offends our taste more than disproportion, or unseemli-
ness. We like things to be in keeping, and when proprieties are violated, we have a sense of being wounded.
If a servant puts on the manners and takes the liberties
of a son, we are angry with him because he forgets
himself, and a whole string of moral faults is involved
in this forgetfulness. The manners, which befit the
members of our own family, are unbecoming in a guest;
and the demeanour and address of a stranger differ from
those of an acquaintance. Our taste is annoyed when
these things are confused, and the annoyance of our
taste is only the symptom of something far deeper in our
moral nature. So is it in the matter we are discussing.
The propriety of man as man, his moral and religious
propriety, consists in his constantly remembering that
he is a creature, and demeaning himself accordingly.
The bad taste and vulgarity (to use words which may
make the meaning clearer) of his not doing so are in
reality sin and irreligion, because the contempt, presumption, and affectation, fall upon the majesty of the
Most High God. Yet is not this forgetfulness quite a
characteristic of the times in which we live?

Look at politics; and may we not read evidences of
this spirit everywhere? How little has religion to do
with questions of peace and war? We go to war to
avenge an offence, or to push an interest, or to secure a
gain, or to cripple a hostile power, as if there were no
God of Hosts. We do not ask ourselves the question
whether it is God's will that there should be such a
war. The whole action of diplomacy is as if there were
no special providence, and as if God having retired from

the management of the world, we must take up the reins which He has let fall from His wearied grasp. Since the balance of power was substituted for the central unity of the Holy See, we have come more and more to act as if the world belonged to us, and we had the management of it, and were accountable to none. On the most solemn subjects, even those of education, and religion, and the interests of the poor, how little of the tone and feeling of creatures is exhibited in debates in parliament, or in the leading articles of a newspaper. It would seem as if there were nothing we had not the right to do, because nothing we had not the power to do. With far less of intentional irreligion than would have seemed possible beforehand, there is an incalculable amount of forgetfulness that we are creatures. What else is our exaggerated lust of liberty? What else are even the vauntings of our patriotism? What else is the spirit of puerile self-laudation into which our national character seems in the hands of an anonymous press to have already degenerated, or to be fast degenerating?

The same tone is observable in our poetry and elegant literature. Everywhere man is his own end, and the master of his own destiny. Subordination and a subject spirit are not virtues, neither in works of fiction do the meek inherit the earth.* Still more strongly does this come out in systems of philosophy. Humanity is a person with a unique destination and perfectibility. Man is complete in himself. There is neither wreck nor ruin about him. The natural stands off, clear and self-helpful, from the supernatural. Accountableness

* E. G. see Kingsley's Two Years Ago, a work by an Anglican clergyman, propounding what the Saturday Review satirically termed a " *muscular* Christianity !"

is not a necessary part of selfgovernment. There is no need to call in the idea of God in order to explain the situation of man. His duties begin and end with other men or with himself. Philosophically speaking, things can be managed at Berlin without God.

But of all things the most amazing is the innocent, childlike, simple-hearted atheism of physical science. The beginning of matter, the elements into which it may utimately be resolvable, how the cycles of the heavenly bodies first began, the unspeakable intricacy of their checks and counterchecks, the secular aberrations and secular corrections of the same, the secret of life, the immateriality of the soul, where physical science ends,—all these questions are discussed in a thousand books in a spirit and tone betokening the most utter forgetfulness that we are little creatures, who got here, God help us! not by our own means, and are going, God help us! where He chooses and when. We read sentence after sentence, expecting every moment to light on the word God, or to come across some allusion to the Creator. And the writers would not omit Him, but would speak good words of Him, if it came to them to do so. But it does not. They are not unbelievers. Nay, they would loudly profess themselves to be creatures and to have a Creator, if they were asked. They would be lunatics if they did not. But the double sense of His creation and of their createdness (to coin a word) is not in all their thoughts, and has not mastered the current of their intellectual activity. They left God at church yesterday, and are closeted with matter to-day. So many secondary causes are waiting for an audience that their time is fully occupied. Besides, is there not one day in the week fixed for the reception of the First Cause, and the

acknowledgment of His claims? But, to be serious,
no one we think will say that modern science, at least
in England, is profane and irreligious. Really it is
most creditably the contrary. It is ourselves whom we·
forget: we forget that we are creatures. Our error
about God comes from a mistake about ourselves.

There are many persons in these days who do not say
they are not Christians; yet who write and speak as it
were from without, as if they were at once Christians,
and not Christians. They have not taken the pains to
formulize a positive disbelief; but they do not see how
progress, and perfectibility, and modern discovery, psychological or otherwise, comport with that collection of
ancient dogmas which make up the Christian religion,
and their instinct would be to give up the dogmas rather
than the discoveries, and that with a promptitude worthy of modern enlightenment. With such persons the
dignity of man is a matter of prime consideration, while,
in their view, his assent to the doctrines and practices
of the Church is as degrading to his intellectual nobility,
as his obedience to them is superstitious and debasing.
The pope and theology, the Blessed Virgin and the
Saints, grace and the sacraments, penance and purgatory, scapulars and rosaries, asceticism and mysticism,
combine to form a perfectly distinct and cognizable
character. They give a tone to the mind and a fashion
to the conduct, which is indubitable, and which it is
difficult to mistake. In the Church such a character
is held in honour. It is the catholic type of spiritual
beauty. But the men, of whom we are speaking, are
far from holding it in esteem. To them it appears
mean, weak, tame, contemptible, cowardly, narrow,
pusillanimous. It wants the breadth and daring of
moral greatness, according to their view of greatness.

Nothing grand, lasting, or spreading will come of it.
But let us put out of view for the moment the undoubted agents in the formation of this character, the
pope and theology, the Blessed Virgin and the Saints,
grace and the sacraments, penance and purgatory, rosaries and scapulars, asceticism and mysticism. Let us
take the character as we find it, without enquiring into
the process of its formation. Granting that there is a
God, eternal and all-holy, granting that we are His
creatures, created simply for His glory, dependent upon
Him for all things, and without any possibility of
happiness apart from Him, granting His perfections and
our imperfections, is not the behaviour, the demeanour,
of a catholic saint, precisely what would come of a
wise and reflective apprehension of the fact that he is a
creature and has a Creator? Does not Christian sanctity with inimitable gracefulness express to the life the
modest, truthful, prevailing sense that we are creatures,
standing before the eye and living in the hand of our
everlasting Creator? And are not the selfsufficiency,
the daring, the vainglory, the speed, the unhesitating-
ness, the reckless manners, which many esteem to be
moral and intellectual bravery, just so many evidences
of forgetfulness that we are creatures? Are they not
vagaries and improprieties, which, to put out of sight
their falsehood and their criminality, are as if a worm
would fain attempt to fly or a monkey to ape the manners of a man? It is not true that the practices and
devotions and sacramental appliances of the Church
introduce something which is incongruous and out of
keeping, something to be added to our human life, but
still an addition easily discernible, and not dovetailing
into our natural position. On the contrary the manners
which they form are simply the most perfect, the most

graceful, the most sensible and self-consistent exhibition of our indubitable condition, that of finite and dependent creatures. The supernatural grace, of which these practices are the channels, at once completes and restores our nature, and makes us eminently and winningly natural. If Christianity were not true, the conduct of a wise man, who acted consistently as a creature who had a Creator, would strangely resemble the behaviour of a catholic saint. The lineaments of the catholic type would be discernible upon him, though his gifts would not be the same.

This forgetfulness that we are creatures, which prevails in that energetically bad portion of the world which is scripturally called *the world*, affects multitudes of persons, who are either less able to divest themselves of the influences of old traditions and early lessons, or are happily less possessed with the base spirit of the world. It leads them to form a sort of religion for themselves which singularly falls in with all the most corrupt propensities of our hearts: a religion which in effect teaches that we can live two lives and serve two masters. Such persons consider that religion has its own sphere, and worldly interests their sphere also, and that the one must not interfere with the other. Thus their tendency is to concentrate all the religion of the week into Sunday, and to conceive that they have thereby purchased a right to a large conscience for the rest of the week. The world, say they, has its claims and God has His claims. Both must be satisfied; God first, and most scrupulously; then the world, not less exactly, though it be indeed secondary. But it is not a "reasonable service" to neglect one for the other. God and the world are coordinate powers, coordinate fountains of moral duty and obligation. He is the really religious

man who gives neither of them reason to complain.
We must let our common sense hinder us from becoming over-righteous. Men who hold this doctrine, a
doctrine admirably adapted for a commercial country,
have a great advantage over the bolder men of whom
we spoke before. For they enjoy all the practical laxity
of unbelievers, without the trouble or responsibility of
disbelieving; and besides that, they enjoy a certain
good-humour of conscience in consequence of the outward respect they pay, in due season and fitting place,
to the ceremonies of religion.

Hitherto we have spoken of classes of persons in whom
we take no interest, further than the sorrow which all
who love God must feel at seeing Him defrauded of
His honour, and all who love their fellowmen in seeing
so much amiability, so much goodness, with a millstone
round its neck which must inevitably sink it in the
everlasting deeps. Let us come now to those with whom
we are very much concerned; and for whom we have
ventured to compose this little treatise. Errors filter
from one class of men into another, and appear in
different forms according to the new combinations into
which they enter. We are all of us more affected by
the errors which prevail around us than we really
suppose. Almost every popular fallacy has its representative even among the children of faith; and as when
a pestilence is raging, many are feeble and languid
though they have no plague-spot, so is it in matters
of religion. The contagion of the world does us a
mischief in many ways of which we are hardly conscious; and we often injure ourselves in our best and
highest interest by views and practices, to which we
cling with fatal obstinacy, little suspecting the relationship in which they stand to widely spread evils, which

we behold in their naked deformity in other sections
of society, and hold up to constant reprobation. The
forgetfulness that we are creatures, which produces the
various consequences already mentioned, is an error
which is less obviously hateful than a direct forgetfulness of God, and consequently it wins its way into holy
places where the other would find no admittance, or
scant hospitality. Good Christians hear conversation
around them, catch the prevailing tone of society, read
books, and become familiarized with certain fashionable
principles of conduct: and it is impossible for their
minds and hearts not to become imbued with the
genius of all this. It is irksome to be always on our
guard, and from being off our guard we soon grow to
be unsuspicious. When a catholic enters into intimate
dealings with protestants, he must not forget to place
his sentries, and to act as if he was in an enemy's
country; and this is unkindly work, and as miserable
as it is unkindly. Yet so it is. When newspapers tell
us that catholicism is always more reasonable and less
superstitious when it is in the immediate presence of
protestantism, they indicate something which they have
observed, namely, a change. Now if our religion be
changed by protestantism, we can have little difficulty
in deciding whether it has changed for the better or
the worse. All this illustrates what we mean. The
prevailing errors of our time and country find their
way down to us, and corrupt our faith, and lower our
practice, and divide us among ourselves. This un-
startling error of forgetting that we are creatures is
thus not without grave influence upon conscientious
catholics; and it is to this point that we are asking
your attention.

It is beyond all question among Christians that there

are such things in religion as the counsels of perfection, and that the true way of serving God is to do so out of love. No one doubts but that a saint is a man who loves God ardently and tenderly, who attempts great things for His honour, and makes painful sacrifices to promote His glory. No one imagines a saint to be one who does no more than he is obliged to, and who, having just avoided mortal sin, is careless about venial faults, and takes his ease and liberty outside the verge of strict and certain precepts. The Church possesses a whole literature which is occupied with nothing else than teaching these principles of Christian perfection, as they are called. Many of these books, such as the Imitation of Christ, are in such repute that it would be rash and presumptuous to question what they teach; and there are others of the very highest spirituality, such as the works of St. Theresa and St. John of the Cross, to which the Church has given her most solemn approval. Persons accustomed to the perusal of these books regard the axioms on which their teaching is based as almost selfevident. They know on the authority of the church that there ought not to be two opinions on the matter; but even independently of that, they cannot conceive as a matter of common sense how there can possibly be two opinions about it. Even if men *might* go wrong on such a question, how *could* they do so in point of fact?

Nevertheless, there are numbers of catholics, who, strange to say! see the question in a different light. The teaching of spiritual books and the doctrines of perfection, as laid down by the most approved writers, do not recommend themselves to them. They consider that, unless they are under the vows of some monastic order, they should aim at nothing more than the avoiding of mortal sin, and giving edification to those around them. They are good people. They go to mass; they aid or start missions; they countenance the clergy; they are kind to the poor; they say the rosary; they frequent the sacraments. Yet when any one talks to them of serving God out of personal love to Him, of trying to be daily more and more closely united to Him, of cultivating the spirit of prayer, of constantly looking out to see what more they can do for God, of mortifying their own will in things allowable, of disliking the spirit of the world even in manifestations of it which are short of sin, and of living more consciously in the presence of God, they feel as if they were listening to an unknown language. They have a jealousy, almost a dislike, of such truths, quite irrespective of any attempt being made to force such a line of conduct upon themselves. If they are humble they are puzzled: if they are self-opinionated, they are angry, critical, or contemptuous, as the case may be. There are many others to whom such views are simply new, and who with modesty and self-distrust are shaken by them, and to some extent receive them. Still upon the whole such doctrines have a sound in their ears of being ultra and extravagant, of poetical and fanciful, or peculiar and eccentric.

Now it must be beyond a doubt to any catholic scholar that such persons are completely out of harmony with a considerable and important part of the catholic system, that they think differently from the saints and holy men, and that a great deal of what the church has approved is new, startling, and perhaps displeasing to them. This is a very strong way of putting it; but we do not see that it goes beyond the truth. They do not view it in this light themselves. God forbid! but this is what it comes to in effect.

In speaking of unbelievers, we pointed out that the character formed by the peculiar doctrines, devotions, and practices of the catholic church, was not something monstrous, or exotic, or unnatural, as they are too often in the habit of considering it. We maintained that it rested on the undeniable common-sense view that we are creatures, the creatures of an Almighty Creator, and that a man who acted consistently (if unassisted nature could do so,) as a creature, would not be unlike a catholic saint: always excepting the practice of voluntary mortification, and all the shapes of love of suffering, for these are ideas peculiar to the kingdom of the Incarnation, or to such false religions as retain in distorted shapes great portions of the primitive tradition which prophesied of the expiation of sin by the vicarious sufferings of a Redeemer. So now we would call the attention of the good people, of whom we are at present speaking, to a similar fact. The doctrines of Christian perfection and the teaching of approved spiritual books do not rest upon any peculiarity of any school of theology, or upon any special spirit of a religious order, or on the idiosyncrasy of any particular saint, or upon any unusual and miraculous vocation, but simply on the fact of our being creatures. Even the practices of voluntary penance or of acquired contemplation, though not of obligation, at least rise naturally and easily out of the relations in which we every one of us stand to God as our Creator. There is nothing in the whole range of asceticism, which does not turn out at last, to be a natural and logical result of our position in the world as the creatures of a Creator: and hence there is nothing in such practices fanciful, eccentric, or intrinsically indiscreet:

though wrong time, wrong place, wrong measure, can make anything indiscreet.

From this fact we draw two inferences. The first is that the strangeness of the doctrines of spirituality to these excellent persons is attributable, without their knowing it, to the prevailing forgetfulness that we are creatures. They are unsuspectingly influenced by the very evil which gives its tone and colour to the unbelief and worldliness of the times. They have no distinct conception of the relation in which their being creatures places them with regard to the Creator, nor of what comes of it in the way of practical religion. It has probably never occurred to them that it was a subject which needed study. Hence, unprovided with antidotes to the poison they were compelled daily to imbibe, an imperceptible change has passed upon them, or the poison of the error has been beforehand with the truth, or, in the case of converts, it has troubled the processes of conversion, and stopped them short of their legitimate completion: for almost all enter the Church only half converted, and several remain so to the last. Thus they have come as it were by instinct to rise up in arms against a claim which is urged in behalf of God. Next they have jealously examined His claims, in a commercial spirit, and with a bias towards themselves. Then they have put limits to His service, made a compromise with Him, reduced Him from a Creator to a Being, who is to tax and to tythe, and no more, for He is a constitutional monarch and not despotic, and they have come to regard notions of perfection with disfavour as an unconstitutional aggression on the part of God or His executive. Now every one of these six processes says as loudly and plainly as it can, "I am not a creature. There is

some such sort of equality between God and myself,
as that I am entitled to come to terms with Him.''
Moreover the spirit in which all this is done is equally
incompatible with the modest position of a creature.
It is as if they were the judges, as if they possessed
some inalienable, indefeasible rights of their own.
There is no diffidence, no self-distrust.   They see
their way more clearly, and assert their supposed
liberty more positively, than they would do in matters
which concerned the claims and interests of their fellow-
citizens.   It would make a great change, we will not
say how great, in them, if they realized and clearly
comprehended the relation in which a creature necessarily as a creature, stands to his Creator.

My second inference is, that, as the doctrines and
practices of spirituality rest mainly on our position as
creatures, and entirely on our position as redeemed
creatures, the common evasion that they belong to the
cloister, and are peculiar to monks and nuns, will not
hold good and cannot be maintained.   A monk is not
more a creature than a soldier or a sailor, a billiard-
marker or a jockey, and no more comes out of his
relation to the Creator than out of theirs.   There may
be questions of degree in the amount different men
may do for God; there surely can be none as to the
principles on which and the spirit in which He is to be
served.   Monks and nuns have given up their liberty
by the heroism of vows.   They are obliged to the practices of perfection, or to apply themselves to the acquisition of them.   Theirs is a glorious captivity in which
supernatural charity has bound them hand and foot,
and handed them over to the arms of their Creator.
They have used the original liberty He gave them in
the grandest of ways, by voluntarily surrendering it.

All then that distinguishes the Christian in his family from the monk in his community is his liberty. If he is to serve God at all it must be on the same principle as the monk. There are not two spiritualities, one for the world and one for the cloister. God is one; God's character is one; our necessary relation to Him is one. There are many distinct things in spirituality to which people in the world are not bound, many which can with difficulty be practised in the world, many which it would be unwise for most persons to attempt to practise in the world, and some which it would be actually impossible to practise there. But whatever differences there may be in the amount done for God, or the manner of doing it, or the obligations under which it is done, there can be no difference in the principle on which it is done. God must be served out of love. This is the first and great commandment. No one is condemned except for mortal sin; but any man who starts professedly on the principle that he will do no more than avoid mortal sin, and that God shall have no more out of him, will infallibly not succeed in his single object; that is to say, he will not avoid mortal sin. Though he is not bound to do more than this in order to secure his salvation, yet because he has gone on a wrong principle, it will, just because it is a principle and not merely a mistake or a negligence, carry him far further than he intended, and end by being his ruin. He will fail in his object, because he made it exclusively his object. Love is the sole principle of the creature's service of his Creator, however remiss that love may be. Thus then, if it be true that the doctrines and practices of Christian perfection are simply based on God's love of us and our love of Him, that is, the relation between the creature and the

Creator, it is either true that monks are more God's creatures than we are, or that, *in our measure and degree*, the principles of perfection are as applicable to ourselves as to them.

We are not going to write a book on perfection. Very far from it. But we believe that the ruling spirit of the age is rather a forgetfulness that we are creatures, than a forgetfulness of the Creator, that many more persons are infected with this evil than have any suspicion of it, that it lies at the bottom; of all the objections men make to the doctrines of spirituality, and furthermore that many more persons would try to serve God, would frequent the sacraments, avoid sin, and be ordinarily good catholics, if they had a clear view of the relations between themselves and God, as creature and Creator. Hence we are undertaking what may seem a childish, or at least an unnecessary, work. We wish to explain, or to state rather than to explain, the first elements of all practical religion, the A B C of devotion. We want to write a primer of piety ; and to do so in the plainest, easiest, and most unadorned style. The experience of the priesthood has led us to think that we shall serve souls by putting forward what every one thinks he knows already, and what he will say he knew before as soon as he reads it. Nevertheless these common-places are not so well known as they should be. Their very commonness leads men to overlook them; and we trust that not a few readers, if they will follow us patiently, will find that both head and heart will have learned not a little in the study.

All our duties to God, and to ourselves no less, are founded on the fact that we are creatures.* All reli-

* Since the publication of the first Edition of this work the following notice has appeared in the Cronaca Contemporanea of the Civiltà Cattolica

gion is based on the sense that we are creatures. Our responsibilities mean that we are creatures. The foolishness of this simple truth will bring to nought the pride of the wise world. It will be as the plain stone of the common brook against the might and bravery of the giant of modern misbelief. We speak to simple-hearted believers. We put no high things before them, but rather the lessons of a village dame. We draw no conclusions, and urge no definite duties. We only ask our dear readers to try to put together with us a few obvious matters of fact about our heavenly Father, and then leave it to grace and our own hearts what is to come of it all. We will therefore ask each other some such questions as these—What is it, as children express themselves, what is it to be a creature?—What is it to have a Creator?—Why does God wish us to love Him?—Why does He love us?—How can we love Him?—How do we repay His love of us?—How does He repay our love of Him?—Is it easy to be saved?—And what becomes of the great multitude of believers?

What, if when we put our answers together, something new and striking comes of it all? What if it warms our hearts, and moistens our eyes? Anyhow it

for October 17th, 1857, p. 240, No. clxxxii. Mgr. (now Cardinal) Pietro de Silvestri, Dean of the S. Rota, maintained an erudite argument before the Accademia di Religione Cattolica, intorno alla domma di Creazione. He shewed how, at the introduction of Christianity, the Apostles' Creed began by proclaiming the dogma of Creation; and that, while many and new errors arose to combat the divine revelation every heresy was in fact contained in Gnosticism, which, nato d'orgoglio &c...had in these days assumed its latest form, Pantheism. Whence he inferred that as Gnosticism nacque dallo sconoscere il vero della Creazione, così ancora per combattere i moderni increduli razionalistici panteisti si dee dagli scrittori cattolici fare ogni sforzo per mettere in sodo cotesto domma importantissimo in vece di perdersi in questioni secondarie. It was naturally a great pleasure to me to find the views of this chapter expressed by an authority so much higher and more competent than my own.

is very sweet to talk of God. There is no holyday in the world like it. So, dear readers, take this weary and disagreeable chapter as a preface to something better, something easier, simpler, heartier and more loving; and let us begin, as little children, at the very beginning.

CHAPTER II.

WHAT IT IS TO BE A CREATURE.

Si homo mille annis serviret Deo etiam ferventissimè, non mereretur ex condigno dimidiam diem esse in regno cœlorum.—S. Anselm.

LET us sit down upon the top of this fair hill. The clear sunshine and the bright air flow into us in streams of life and gladness, while our thoughts are lifted up to God, and our hearts quietly expand to love. Beneath us is that beautiful rolling plain, with its dark masses of summer foliage sleeping in the sun for miles and miles away, in the varying shades of blue and green, according to the distance or the clouds. There at our feet, on the other side, is the gigantic city, gleaming with an ivory whiteness beneath its uplifted but perpetual canopy of smoke. The villa-spotted hills beyond it, its almost countless spires, its one huge many-steepled palace, and its solemn presiding dome, its old bleached tower, and its squares of crowded shipping—it all lies below us in the peculiar sunshine of its own misty magnificence. There, in every variety of joy and misery, of elevation and depression, three million souls are working out their complicated destinies. Close around us the air is filled with the songs of rejoicing birds, or the pleased hum of the insects that are drinking the sunbeams, and blowing their tiny trumpets as they weave and unweave their mazy dance. The flowers breathe sweetly, and the leaves of the glossy shrubs are spotted with bright creatures in painted

surcoats or gilded panoply, while the blue dome above
seems both taller and bluer than common, and is
ringing with the loud peals of the unseen larks, as the
steeples of the city ring for the nation's victory. Far
off from the river flat comes the booming of the cannon,
and here, all unstartled, round and round the pond, a
fleet of young perch are sailing in the sun, slowly and
undisturbedly as if they had a very grave enjoyment of
their little lives. What a mingled scene it is of God
and man! And all so bright, so beautiful, so diversified, so calm, opening out such fountains of deep reflection, and of simple-hearted gratitude to our Heavenly
Father.

What is our uppermost thought? It is that we
live, and that our life is gladness. Our physical
nature unfolds itself to the sun, while our mind and
heart seem no less to bask in the bright influences of
the thought of God. Animate and inanimate, reason-
ing and unreasoning, organic and inorganic, material
and spiritual—what are these but the names and orders
of so many mysteries, of so many sciences, which are
all represented in this sunny scene? We, like the
beetles and the perch, like the larks and the clouds, like
the leaves and the flowers, like the smoke-wreaths of
the cannon and the surges of the bells, are the creatures of the One True God, lights and shades in this
creature-picture, kith and kin to all the things around
us, in near or in remote degree. How did we come to
live? Why do we live? How do we live? What is
our life? Where did it come from? Whither is it
going? What was it meant for? All that the sun
shines upon is real; and we are real too. Are we to
be the beauty of a moment, part of earth's gilding, to
warm ourselves in the sun for awhile and glitter, and

add to the hum of life on the planet, and then go
away, and go nowhere? The beautiful day makes us
happy, with a childish happiness, and it sends our
thoughts to first principles, to our alphabet, to the
beginnings of things.

But we must commence with a little theology, before
we can fall back upon the simple truths of the catechism.
We are not on safe ground, although it is such simple
ground. Baius, Jansenius, and Quesnel have contrived
so to obscure and confound and divorce the orders of
nature and grace, that we cannot treat at any length of
the subject of creation, unless we start with some sort
of profession of faith. Theologians, in order to get
a clear view of the matter, consider human nature as
either possible or actual in five different states. The
first is a state of pure nature. In this, man would
have been created, of course without sin, but also without sanctifying grace, without infused virtues, and without the helps of a supernatural order. None of these
things would have been due to his nature regarded
in itself. He would have been obnoxious to hunger and
thirst, to toil, diseases and death, because his nature
is compound and material, and contains the principles
of these inconveniences within itself. He would have
been subject also to ignorance and to concupiscence,
and his happiness would have consisted in his knowledge and love of God as the author of nature, whose
precepts he would have observed by means of what is
called natural grace. This natural grace requires a
word of explanation. What is due to nature we do
not call grace; in a certain sense God is bound to give
it to us. But He is not bound so to combine secondary
causes that the right thoughts and motives, requisite
for us to govern ourselves and controul our passions,

should rise in our minds at the right time, or even if
such assistance were due to nature in the mass, it would
not perhaps be due to it in the individual. Nevertheless we suppose such an assistance to be essential to a
state of pure nature, and as it is over and above what
our nature can claim of itself, we call it grace, but
grace of the natural, not of the supernatural order. In
the time of St. Thomas some theologians held that Adam
was created in this state, and remained in it for a time,
until he was subsequently endowed with sanctifying
grace, and raised to a supernatural end. This is now
however universally rejected. Both angels and men
were created in a state of grace. The orders of nature
and grace, though perfectly distinct and on no account
to be confused, did as a matter of fact start together
in the one act of creation, without any interval of time
between. This state therefore was possible, but never
actual.

The second condition of human nature is the state of
integrity. Baianism and Jansenism regard this as identical with the state of pure nature ; but catholic theology
considers it as endowed with a certain special perfection,
over and above the perfections due to it for its own
sake : and the twenty-sixth proposition of Baius is condemned because it asserts that this integrity was due
to nature, and its natural condition. It consists in the
perfect subjection of the body to the soul, and of the
sensitive appetite to the reason, and thus confers upon
man a perfect immunity from ignorance, concupiscence,
and death. It inserts in our nature a peculiar vigour
by which this glorious dominion of the soul is completed
and sustained, while the tree of life, it is supposed,
would have preserved the material part of our nature

4   †

from the corroding influence of age.*   Of this state also
we may say that it was possible but never actual;
because, while it is true of Adam as far as it goes, he
never was, as a matter of fact, left to the possession of
his integrity without the supernatural addition of sanctifying grace.

The third condition of human nature is the state of
innocence.   By this, Adam in the first instant of his
creation, or as some say immediately afterwards, had
the theological and moral virtues, and the gifts of the
Holy Ghost, infused into him, inasmuch as he was
created in a state of grace, and elevated to the supernatural end of participating in the beatitude of God by
the Beatific Vision.   He was likewise endowed with
such a perfect science both of natural and supernatural
things, as became the preceptor and ruler and head of
the human race; and a similar science would have been
easily acquired by his descendants in a state of innocence, though as they would not have been the heads
of the race, it would probably not have been infused
into them from the first.   This innocence is what we
call original justice, to express by one word the aggre-
gate of gifts and habits which compose it; and what
constituted man in this state was the one simple quality
of sanctifying grace, by which the soul was perfectly
subject to God, not only as its natural, but also as its
supernatural author.   This is the teaching of the
Church; whereas the heresies of Baius and Jansenius

---

* Here theologians differ. Some include the immunity from disease and
death in the state of integrity; as Billuart. Others refer it to the state of
innocence; as Viva. The difference is not of consequence to our present
purpose. See Billuart. Praeambula ad tract. de gratia: and Viva de Gratia
Adamica in his Trutina thesium Quesnellianarum. See also Ripalda's Dispu-
tation on the Baian Propositions, which Dr. Ward of St. Edmund's College
has published in a separate form.

hold that the grace of Adam produced only human merits, and was a natural sequel of creation, and due to nature on its own account.* This state of innocence, or original justice, was that in which, as a matter of fact, Adam was created.

The fourth condition of man is the state of fallen, while the fifth is that of redeemed nature, to which may be added the state of glorified nature, and the state of lost nature, in which ultimately the other states must issue. Our present purpose does not require us to enter upon these. We will only stop to point out a very beautiful and touching analogy. Just as the separate orders of nature and grace were by the sweet love of God started in the same act, so the promise of the Saviour and the actual operation of saving grace followed at once upon the fall, and fallen nature was straightway placed upon the road of reparation and redemption. Thus is it always in the love of God. There is a pathetic semblance of impatience about it, an eagerness to anticipate, a quickness to interfere, an unnecessary profusion in remedying, a perpetual tendency to keep outstripping itself and outdoing itself; and in all these ways is it evermore overrunning all creation, beautifying and glorifying it with its own eternal splendours.

What then we must bear in mind throughout is this, that the orders of nature and grace are in reality quite distinct, that God must be regarded as the author of both, and that we must continually bear in mind this distinction, if we would avoid the entanglement of errors, which have been noted in the Condemned Propositions. At the same time we shall speak of God

---

* The 21st and 14th Propositions of Baius.

throughout as at once the author of both these orders, and of creation as representing both, because as a matter of fact they both started in creation, in the case both of angels and of men.* Out of this significant fact, that God created neither angels nor men in a state of mere nature, our view of God materially proceeds. It is a fact which reveals volumes about Him. It stamps a peculiar character upon creation, and originates obligations which greatly influence the relations of the creature to his Creator. Creation was itself a gratuitous gift. But, granting creation, nothing was due to the natures either of angels or men but what those natures respectively could claim on grounds intrinsic to themselves. It was to have been expected beforehand that

---

* See Propositions xxxiv. of Quesnel and i. of Bains, also xxxv. of Quesnel and xxi. of Bains. It will be observed that we carefully avoid the controversy about the condemnation of the xxxivth proposition of Baius, on the distinction of the double love of God, as author of nature and author of beatitude. Suarez and Vasquez quote Cardinal Toledo, (who was sent to Louvain on the subject by Gregory XIII. and may therefore be supposed to have known the pope's mind,) as saying that some of the propositions of Baius were only condemned because of the bitter language used of the opposite opinion. Billuart and others are very vehement against this. On the xxxivth proposition in particular Vasquez and De Lugo take one side, and Suarez, Viva, Ripalda, and the Thomists generally the other. See Vasq. 1. 2. p. Disp. 195. cap. 2. De Lugo de Fide disp. 9. n. 11-13. The controversy does not concern us, because we are regarding the two orders of nature and grace throughout as starting simultaneously in creation, distinct yet contemporary, and are also studiously regarding God as the author of both. We have therefore nothing to do with the question whether in order to a true act of love we must explicitly regard God as the author of the supernatural order. In order to avoid multiplying notes, the reader is requested not to lose sight of this fact throughout the whole treatise. Van Ranst, in commenting (page 29) on the proposition of Baius, quotes the following passage of St. Thomas from his commentary on the first Epistle to the Corinthians. Amor est quædam vis unitiva, et omnis amor in unione quadam consistit. Unde secundum diversas uniones diversæ species amicitiæ distinguantur. Nos autem habemus duplicem conjunctionem cum Deo. Una est quantum ad bona naturæ, alia quantum ad beatitudinem. Secundum primam communicationem ad Deum, est amicitia naturalis. Secundum vero communicationem secundam est amor charitatis. *Ad 1 ad Corinth. xiii. 4.*

God would have created them in a state of perfect
nature. It is a surprise that it was not so. On the
very threshold of theology we are arrested by this
mysterious fact, that rational creatures came from their
Creator's hands in a supernatural state, and that in
His first act the natural never stood alone, but it leaned,
all perfect as it was, upon the supernatural. It was
as if God did not like to let nature go, lest haply He
should lose what He so dearly loved. This one fact
seems to us the *great* fact of the whole of theology,
colouring it all down to its lowest definition, and marvellously illuminating, from beneath, the character and
beauty of our Creator. It is a hidden sunshine in our
minds, better than this outer sunshine that is round us
now. O surely to be a creature is a joyous thing ; and
even our very nothingness is dear to us, as we think of
God ; for it seems to be almost a grandeur, instead of an
abasement, to have been thus called out of nothing by
such an One as He.

We are creatures. What is it to be a creature ?
Before the sun sets in the red west, let us try to have
an answer to our question. We find ourselves in existence to-day, amid this beautiful scene, with multitudes
of our fellow-creatures round about us. We have been
alive and on the earth so many years, so many months,
so many weeks, so many days, so many hours. At
such and such a time we came to the use of reason ;
but at such an age and in such a way that we clearly
did not confer our reason upon ourselves. But here we
are to-day, not only with a reason, but with a character
of our own, and fulfilling a destiny in some appointed
station in life. We know nothing of what has gone
before us, except some little of the exterior of the past,
which history or tradition or family records have told us

of. We do not doubt that the sun and the moon, the planets and the stars, the blue skies and the four winds, the wide green seas and the fruitful earth, were before our time; indeed before the time of man at all. Science unriddles mysterious things about them; but all additional light seems only to darken and to deepen our real ignorance.

So is it with the creature man. He finds himself in existence, an existence which he did not give to himself. He knows next to nothing of what has gone before; and absolutely nothing of what is to come, except so far as his Creator is pleased to reveal it to him supernaturally. And thus it comes to pass that he knows better what will happen to him in the world to come, than what will be his fortune here. He knows nothing of what is to happen to himself on earth. Whether his future years will be happy or sorrowful, whether he will rise or fall, whether he will be well or ailing, he knows not. It is not in his own hands, neither is it before his eyes. If you ask him the particular and special end which he is to fulfil in his life, what the peculiar gift or good which he was called into being to confer upon his fellow-men, what the exact place and position which he was to fill in the great social whole, he cannot tell you. It has not been told to him. The chances are, with him as with most men, that he will die, and yet not know it. And why? Because he is a creature.

His being born was a tremendous act. Yet it was not his own. It has entangled him in quantities of difficult problems, and implicated him in numberless important responsibilities. In fact he has in him an absolute inevitable necessity either of endless joy or of endless misery; though he is free to choose between

the two. Annihilation he is not free to choose. Reach
out into the on-coming eternity as far as the fancy can,
there still will this man be, simply because he has been
already born. The consequences of his birth are not
only unspeakable in their magnitude, they are simply
eternal. Yet he was not consulted about his own birth.
He was not offered the choice of being or not-being.
Mercy required that he should not be offered it; justice
did not require that he should. We are not concerned
now to defend God. We are only stating facts, and
taking the facts as we find them. It is a fact that he
was not consulted about his own birth; and it is truer
and higher than all facts, that God can do nothing but
what is blessedly, beautifully right. A creature has no
right to be consulted about his own creation: and for
this reason simply,—that he is a creature.

He has no notion why it was that his particular soul
rather than any other soul was called into being, and put
into his place. Not only can he conceive a soul far more
noble and devout than his, but he sees, as he thinks,
peculiar deficiencies in himself, in some measure dis-
qualifying him for the actual position in which God has
placed him. And how can he account for this? Yet
God must be right. And his own liberty too must be
very broad, and strong, and responsible. He clearly
has a work to do, and came here simply to do it; and
it is equally clear that if God will not work with him
against his own will, he also cannot work without God.
Every step which a creature takes, when he has once
been created, increases his dependence upon his Creator.
He belongs utterly to God by creation: if words would
enable us to say it, he belongs still more utterly to
God by preservation. In a word, the creature becomes
more completely, more thoroughly, more significantly

a creature, every moment that his created life is continued to him. This is in fact his true blessedness, to be ever more and more enclosed in the hand of God who made him. The Creator's hand is the creature's home.

As he was not consulted about his coming into the world, so neither is he consulted about his going out of it. He does not believe he is going to remain always on earth. He is satisfied that the contrary will be the case. He knows that he will come to an end of this life, without ceasing to live. He is aware that he will end this life with more or less of pain, pain without a parallel, pain like no other pain, and most likely very terrible pain. For though the act of dying is itself probably painless, yet it has for the most part to be reached through pain. Death will throw open to him the gates of another world, and will be the beginning to him of far more solemn and more wonderful actions than it has been his lot to perform on earth. Everything to him depends on his dying at the right time and in the right way. Yet he is not consulted about it. He is entitled to no kind of warning. No sort of choice is left him either of time or place or manner. It is true he may take his own life. But he had better not. His liberty is indeed very great, since this is left free to him. Yet suicide would not help him out of his difficulties. It only makes certain to him the worst that could be. He is only cutting off his own chances; and by taking his life into his own hands he is rashly throwing himself out of his own hands in the most fatal way conceivable. One whose business it is to come when he is called, and to depart when he is bidden, and to have no reason given him either for his call or his dismissal, except such as he can gather from the character of his master—such is man upon earth; and he is so, because he is a creature.

Is it childish to say all this? We fear we must say something more childish still. We must not omit to notice of this creature, this man, that he did not make the world he finds around him. He could not have done so, for lack of wisdom and of power. But it is not this we would dwell on. As a matter of fact he did not do so; and therefore, as he did not make the world, it is not his world, but somebody else's. He can have no rights in it, but such as the proprietor may voluntarily make over to him in the way of gift. He can have no sovereignty over it, or any part of it, unless by a royal grace the true sovereign has invested him with delegated powers. In himself therefore he is without dominion. Dominion does not belong to him as a creature. Dominion is a different idea, and comes from another quarter.

Furthermore—and we do not care whether it be from faith or reason, or from what proportion of both—this creature cannot resist the certainties that there is an unseen world in which he is very much concerned. He is quite sure, nervously sure, that there are persons and things close to him, though unseen, which are of far greater import than what he sees. He believes in presences which are more intimate to him than any presence of external things, nay, in one Presence which is more intimate to him than he is to his own self. Death is a flight away from earth, not a lying down a few feet beneath its sods; it is a vigorous outburst of a new life, not a resting on a clay pillow from the wearyful toil of this life. All things in him and around him are felt to be beginnings, and the curtains of the unseen world, as if lifted by the wind, wave ever and anon into his face,

and cling to it like a mask, and he sees through, or
thinks he sees. This is the last thing we have to note
of this man, as he sits upon the hill-top, in the sunshine,
part and parcel of the creatures round about him. He
finds himself in existence by the act of another. He
knows nothing of what has gone before him, nothing
of what is to happen to himself, and next to nothing of
what is to come, and that little only by revelation. He
was not consulted about his own birth, nor will he be
about his death. He has to die out, and has nothing to
do with the when or the how. He did not make the
world he finds around him, and therefore it is not his.
Neither can he resist the conviction that this world is
for him only the porch of another and more magnificent
temple of the Creator's majesty, wherein he will enter
still further into the Creator's power, and learn that to
be in the Creator's power is the creature's happiness.

It is not our present business to explain or comment
on all this, we are only concerned to state facts. This
is the position of each one of us as men and creatures,
the position wherein we find ourselves at any given
moment in which we may choose to advert to ourselves
and our circumstances : and the fact that such is our
position is no small help towards an answer to our question, What is it to be a creature? But let us now
advance a step further. Let us pass from the *position*
of this creature to what we know to be his *real history*.
Let us look at him on the hill-top, not merely in the
sunshine of nature, but in the light of the Gospel of
Jesus Christ. Now we shall gain fresh knowledge
about him and understand him better. We shall
know his meaning and his destiny, and can then infer from them his condition, his duties, and his responsibilities.

He may occupy a very private position in the world. He may not be known beyond the sanctuary of his own family, or the limits of a moderate circle of acquaintances. The great things of the world have no reference to him, and public men do not consult him. He has his little world of hopes and fears, of joys and sadnesses, and strangers intermeddle not with either. His light and his darkness are both his own. But he is a person of no consequence. The earth, the nation, the shire, the village, go on without his interference. He is a man like the crowd of men, and is not noticeable in any other way. Yet the beginning of his history is a long way off. Far in the eternal mind of God, further than you can look, he is there. He has had his place there from eternity; and before ever the world was, he lay there with the light of God's goodness around him, and the clearness of God's intentions upon him, and was the object of a distinct, transcending, and unfathomable love. There was more of power, of wisdom, and of goodness in the love which God bore through eternity to that insignificant man, than we can conceive of, though we raise our imaginations to the greatest height of which they are capable. May we say it? He was part of God's glory, of God's bliss, through all the unrevolving ages of a past eternity. The hanging up in heaven of those multitudes of brilliant worlds, the composition, the adornment, and the equipoise of their ponderous masses, all the marvels of inanimate material creation, all the inexplicable chemistry which is the world's life, were as nothing compared to the intense brooding of heavenly love, the compassionate fulness of divine predestination, over that single soul. Think of that, as he sits among the trees and shrubs, with the insects and the birds about him!

So long as there has been a God, so long has that soul
been the object of His knowledge and His love. Ever
since the uncreated abyss of almighty love has been
spread forth, there lay that soul gleaming on its bright
waters. O no wonder God is so patient with sinners,
no wonder Jesus died for souls !

But this is not the whole of his real history. There
is more about him still. We do not know what the
secrets of his conscience may be, nor whether he is
in a state of grace, nor what might be God's judgment
of him if He called him away at this moment. But
whatever comes of these questions, it is a simple matter
of fact that that man was part of the reason of the Incarnation of the Second Person of the Most Holy Trinity.
He belongs to Jesus and was created for Jesus. He
is part of his Saviour's property, and meant to adorn
His kingdom. His body and his soul are both of them
fashioned, in their degree, after the model of the Body
and the Soul of the Word made flesh. His predestination flowed out from, and is inclosed in, the predestination of Jesus. He is the brother of His God, and has
a divine right to call her mother who calls the Creator
Son. He was foreseen in the decree of the Incarnation.
The glory of his soul and the possibilities of his human
heart entered as items into that huge sum of attractions
which drew the Eternal Word to seek His delights
among the sons of men, by assuming their created
nature to His uncreated Person. His sins were partly
the cause why the Precious Blood was shed ; and Jesus
suffered, died, rose again, and ascended for him, as completely as if he were the only one of his race that ever
fell. There must be something very attractive in him
for our Lord to have loved him thus steadily and thus
ardently. You see that He counted that creature's sins

over long and long ago. He saw them, as we blind men can never see them, singly and separately in all their unutterable horror and surpassing malice. Then He viewed them as a whole, perhaps thousands in number, and aggravated by almost every variety of circumstance of which human actions are capable. And nevertheless there was something in that man which so drew upon the love of the unspeakably holy God, that He determined to die for him, to satisfy, and over-satisfy for all his sins, to merit for him a perfect sea of untold graces, and to beguile him by the most self-sacrificing generosity to the happiness of His divine embraces. All this was because that man was His creature. So you see what a history his has been, what a stir he has made in the world by having to do with the Incarnation, how he has been mixed up with eternal plans, and has helped to bring a seeming change over the ever-blessed and unchanging God! Alas! if it is hard to see good points in others, how much harder must it be for God to see good points in us, and yet how He loves us all!

But to return to our man, whoever he may be. It is of course true that God had a general purpose in the whole of creation, or to speak more truly, many general purposes. But it is also true that He had a special purpose in this man whom we are picturing to ourselves. The man came into the world to do something particular for God, to carry out some definite plan, to fulfil some one appointed end, which belongs to him in such a way that it does not belong to other men. There is a peculiar service, a distinct glory, which God desires to have from that man, different from the service and the glory of any other man in the world; and the man's dignity and happiness will result from his giving God that service and glory and no other. As he did not make himself, so neither can he give himself his own vocation. He does not know what special function it has fallen to him to perform in the immense scheme and gigantic world of his Creator; but it is not the less true that he has such a special function. Life as it unfolds will bring it to him. Years will lay his duty and his destiny at his door in parts successively. Perhaps on this side of the grave he may never see his work as an intelligible whole. It may be part of his work to be tried by this very obscurity. But with what a dignity it invests the man, to know of him that, as God chose his particular soul at the moment of its creation rather than countless other possible and nobler souls, so does He vouchsafe to be dependent on this single man for a glory and a love, which, if this man refuses it to Him, He will not get from any other man nor from all men put together! God has an interest at stake, which depends exclusively on that single man: and it is in the man's power to frustrate this end, and millions do so. When we consider who and how infinitely blessed, God is, is not this special destiny of each man a touching mystery? How close it seems to bring the Creator and the creature! And where is the dignity of the creature save in the love of the Creator?

Furthermore, this man, it would appear, might have been born at any hour of the day or night these last five thousand years and more. He might have been before Christ or after Him, and of any nation, rank or religion. His soul could have been called out of nothing at any moment as easily as when it pleased God in fact to call it. But it pleased God to call it when He did, because that time, and no other time, suited the special end for which that man was to live. He was born, just when he was, for the sake of that particular purpose. He would have been too soon, had he been born earlier; too late, if he had not been born as early. And in like manner will he die. An hour, a place, a manner of death are all fixed for him; yet so as not in the least to interfere with his freedom. Everything is arranged with such a superabundance of mercy and indulgence, that he will not only die just when it fits in with the special work he has to do for God, and the special glory God is to have from him, but he will most probably die at the one hour when it is safest and best for himself to die. The time, the place, the manner, and the pain of his death will in ordinary cases be better for that man than any other time, place, manner, or pain would be. The most cruel-seeming death, if we could only see it, is a mercy which saves us from something worse, a boon of such magnitude as befits the liberality even of the Most High God.

Once again: a particular eternity is laid out for that man, to be won by his own free correspondence to the exuberant grace of his Creator. There is a brightness which may be his for ever, a distinct splendour and characteristic loveliness by which he may be one day known, admired, and loved amid the populous throngs of the great heaven. His own place is ready for him in the unutterable rest of everlasting joys. That man, who is gazing on the landscape at his feet, has an inheritance before him, to which the united wealth of kings is poverty and vileness. A light, a beauty, a power, a wisdom, are laid up for him, to which all the wonders of the material creation are worse than tame, lower than uninteresting. He is earning them at this moment, by the acts of love which it seems as if the simple cheer of the sunshine were drawing out of his soul. They have a strange disproportionate proportion to his modest and obscure works on earth. God, and angels, and saints, are all busy with solicitous loving wisdom, to see that he does not miss his inheritance. His eternity is dependent on his answering the special end of his creation. Doubtless at this moment he has no clear idea of what his special work is; doubtless it is one of such unimportance, according to human measures, that it will never lay any weight on the prosperity, or the laws, or the police of his country. His light is probably too dim to be visible even to his neighbourhood. Yet with it and because of it, he is one day to shine like ten thousand suns, far withdrawn within the peace of his satisfied and delighted God !

Such is the man's real history, traced onward from the hour when it pleased God to create his particular soul. And how many things there are in it to wonder at ! How great is the dignity, how incalculable the destinies of man ! All these things belong to him, not certainly in right of his being a creature, but at least because he is a creature. Creation explains all other mysteries, or is a step towards explaining them. No wonder God should become man, in order to be with him, or should die for him, in order to save him. No wonder He should abide with him in mute reality in the tabernacle, to feed his soul, and to sustain him and keep alive His creature's love by His own silent company. No wonder the angels should cling about a man so fondly, nor that the one master-passion of the saints should be the love of souls. The wonder is that God should have created man ; not that having created him, He should love him so tenderly. Both are wonders ; but the first is the greater wonder. Redemption does not follow from creation as a matter of course : but creation has so surprised us, that we are less surprised at new disclosures of the Creator's love. In a series of surprises the first surprise is, in some sense, the greatest, because it is the first, while, in another sense, further surprises are greater, precisely because they are further ones. In truth, man's dignity, wonderful as it is, is less a wonder than the creating love of God. How He holds His creature in His hand for ever! How all things, dark as well as bright, are simply purposes of unutterable goodness and compassion! How difficulties and problems are only places where love is so much deeper than common, that the eye cannot pierce it, nor the lines of our wisdom fathom it! O of a truth God is indescribably good, and we feel that He is so whenever we remember that He made us! What a joy it is to be altogether His, to belong to Him, to feel our complete dependence upon Him, to lean our whole weight upon Him, not only for the delight of feeling that He is so strong, but also that we are so weak, and therefore so need Him always and everywhere! What liberty is like the sense of being encompassed with His sovereignty! What a gladness that He is immense, so that we cannot escape from Him, omniscient so that we are laid open and without a secret before Him, eternal so that we are in His sight but nothingness, nothingness that lives because He loves it!

Something more is still required in order to complete our picture of the creature. We have represented his *position*, and have traced his *real life;* but we have got to consider the *condition* in which he is as a creature. We shall have to plead guilty to a little repetition. The nature of our subject renders it unavoidable, and we must crave the reader's indulgence for it.

The first feature to be noticed in the condition of this
5 †

creature man is his want of power. Not only is his
health uncertain, but at his best estate his strength is
very small. Brute matter resists him passively. He
cannot lift great weights of it, nor dig deep into it
Even with the help of the most ingenious machinery
and the united labour of multitudes he can do little but
scratch the surface of the planet, without being able to
alter the expression of one of its lineaments. Fire and
water are both his masters. His prosperity is at the
mercy of the weather. Matter is baffling and ruining
him somewhere on the earth at all hours of day and
night. He has to struggle continually to maintain his
position, and then maintains it with exceeding difficulty.
Considering how many thousands of years the race of
man has inhabited the world, it is surprising how little
controul he has acquired over diseases, how little he
knows of them, how much less he can do to alleviate
them. Even in his arts and sciences there are strangely
few things which he can reduce to certainty. His
knowledge is extremely limited, and is liable to the
most humiliating errors and the most unexpected mis-
takes. He is in comparative ignorance of himself, of
his thinking principle, of the processes of his immaterial
soul, of the laws of its various faculties, or of the combinations of mind and matter. Metaphysics, which
should rank next to religion in the scale of sciences, are
a proverb for confusion and obscurity. Infinite longings
perpetually checked by a sense of feebleness, and circumscribed within the limits of a narrow prison,—this
is a description of the highest and most aspiring moods
of man.

Such is the condition of our man if we look at him
in his solitary dignity as lord of the creation. But
even this is too favourable a representation of him.

His solitary dignity is a mere imagination. On the contrary he is completely mixed up with the crowd of inferior creatures, and in numberless ways dependent upon them. If left to himself the ponderous earth is simply useless to him. Its maternal bosom contains supplies of minerals and gases, which are meant for the daily sustaining of human life. Without them this man would die in torture in a few days; and yet by no chemistry can he get hold of them himself and make them into food. He is simply dependent upon plants. They alone can make the earth nutritious to him, whether directly as food themselves, or indirectly by their support of animal life. And they do this by a multitude of hidden processes, many of which, perhaps the majority, are beyond the explanation of human chemistry. Thus he is at the mercy of the vegetable world. The grass that tops his grave, which fed him in his life, now feeds on him in turn.

In like manner is he dependent upon the inferior animals. Some give him strength to work with, some warm materials to clothe himself with, some their flesh to eat or their milk to drink. A vast proportion of mankind have to spend their time, their skill, their wealth, in waiting upon horses and cows and camels, as if they were their servants, building houses for them, supplying them with food, making their beds, washing and tending them as if they were children, and studying their comforts. More than half the men in the world are perhaps engrossed in this occupation at the present moment. Human families would break up, if the domestic animals ceased to be members of them. Then, as to the insect world, it gives us a sort of nervous trepidation to contemplate it. The numbers of insects, and their powers, are so terrific, so absolutely

irresistible, that they could sweep every living thing
from the earth and devour us all within a week, as if
they were the fiery breath of a destroying angel. We
can hardly tell what holds the lightning-like speed of
their prolific generations in check. Birds of prey,
intestine war, man's active hostility,—these, calculated
at their highest, seem inadequate to keep down the
insect population, whose numbers and powers of annoyance yearly threaten to thrust us off our own planet.
It is God Himself who puts an invisible bridle upon
these countless and irresistible legions, which otherwise
would lick us up like thirsty fire.

What should we do without the sea? Earth and
air would be useless, would be uninhabitable without
it. There is not a year but the great deep is giving
up to the investigations of our science unthought of
secrets of its utility, and of our dependence upon it.
Men are only beginning to learn the kind and gentle
and philanthropic nature of that monster that seems so
lawless and so wild. Our dependence on the air is no
less complete. It makes our blood, and is the warmth
of our human lives. Nay, would it be less bright or
beautiful, if it allowed to escape from it, let us say, one
gas, the carbonic acid, which forms but an infinitesi-
mally small proportion of it, the gas on which all
vegetation lives? It exists in the air in quantities so
trifling as to be with difficulty discernible, yet if it
were breathed away, or if the sea drank it all in, or
would not give back again what it drinks, in a few
short hours the flowers would be lying withered and
discoloured on the ground, the mighty forests would
curl up their myriad leaves, show their white sides,
and then let them wither and fall. There would not
be a blade of grass upon the earth. The animals

would moan and faint, and famished men would rise
upon each other, like the maddened victims of a
shipwreck, in the fury of their ungovernable hunger.
Within one short week the planet would roll on bright
in its glorious sunshine, and its mineral-coloured plains
speckled with the shadows of its beautiful clouds, but
all in the grim silence of universal death. On what
trembling balances of powers, on what delicate and
almost imperceptible chemistries, does man's tenure of
earth seem to rest ! Yes ! but beneath those gauzelike
veils is the strong arm of the compassionate Eternal !

It would require a whole volume to trace the various
ways in which man is dependent upon the inferior creatures. All the adaptations, of which different sciences
speak, turn out upon examination to be so many depen-
dencies of man on things which are beneath him. In
material respects man is often inferior to his inferiors,
But there is one feature in his dependency, which does
not concern his fellow-creatures, and on which it is of
consequence to dwell. There is a peculiar kind of
incompleteness about all he does, which disables him
from concluding anything of himself, or unassisted.
It is as if his arm was never quite long enough to reach
his object, and God came in between him and his end
to enable him to realize it. Man is ever falling, God
ever saving: the creature always on the point of being
defeated, the Creator always coming to the rescue
opportunely. Thus man plants the tree and waters it,
but he cannot make it grow. He prepares his ground
and enriches it, he sows his seeds and weeds it; but he
cannot govern the weather, or the insects, on which his
harvest depends. Between his labour and his labour's
reward God has to intervene. When he lays his plans,
he does nothing more than prepare favourable circum-

stances for the end which he desires. In war, in
government, in education, in commerce, when he has
done all, he has insured nothing. An element has to
come in and to be waited for, without which he can
have no results, and over which he has no controul.
Sometimes men call it fate, or fortune, sometimes
chance or accident. It is the final thing, it is what
completes the circle, or fires the train, or makes the
parts into a whole. It is the interference of God, the
action of His will. In every department of human
life we discover this peculiarity, that of himself, that is
with means left at his own disposal, man can approach
his end, but not attain it: he can get near it, but he
cannot reach it. He is always too short by a little;
and the supplement of that littleness is as invariably
the gratuitous Providence of God. Nothing throws
more light than this on the question, What is it to be a
creature?

All this is very common-place. Everybody knows
it, has always known it, and never doubted it. True:
yet see, if when all these things are strung together
and presented to your mind, there does not rise up an
almost unconscious feeling of exaggeration, nay, an
almost outspoken charge of it, against the statement of
the case. This will be a test to you, that you have
not realized the case, that you have not taken it in,
and consequently that you have something still to learn
from facts which seem so undignifiedly familiar. For
both the value of the lesson and its significance depend
upon its strength. We cannot exaggerate the abject-
ness of the creature in itself, looked at as if it were
apart from God, which happily it can never be, though
it will be something like it when it is reprobate; and
then, what more unspeakably abject than a lost soul?

What we are always to feel, and never to forget, is that we are finite, dependent, imperfect, that it is our nature to look up to some one higher, to lean on some one stronger, and that it is as unnatural for man to try to go alone and trust himself, as for a fish to live on the land, or a bird of the air in the flames of the fire. Dignity we have, and super-abundantly, and we ought never to forget it. But then we must remember also that the creature man has no dignity except in the love of Him who made him.

But our real history adds a great deal to our condition, which is full of important consequences. Man is not as he came forth at first from the hand of his Creator. He has fallen; and his fall is not merely an external disability, consequent on an historical fact so many thousand years old. He bears the marks of it in himself. He feels its effects in every moral act, in every intellectual process. He is the prey of an intestine warfare. Two conflicting laws alternate within him. He has lost his balance, and finds it hard to keep the road. Notwithstanding the magnificent spiritual renewal which the mercy of his Creator has worked within him by the supernatural grace of a sacrament, each man has added to the common fall a special revolt of his own. Nay, most men have repeated, imitated, aggravated the act of their first father. They have fallen themselves, and their sin has been accompanied with peculiarly disabling circumstances of guilt. Then the unwearied compassion of the Creator has come forth with another sacrament to repair this personal wilful revolt of the poor fallen creature. With its grace fresh upon him, he has revolted again, and then again. He has diversified his falls. He has multiplied his treasons by varying their kind. He has broken, not one, but numerous laws, as if to show that it was not the hardness of any particular precept, so much as the simple fact of being under God's yoke at all, which he found so unbearable. And again and again and again has the merciful sacrament repaired and absolved him, and grace goes on with a brave patient kindness of its own, fighting against seemingly incorrigible habits of sin; and even at the hour of death how reluctantly does mercy seem to capitulate to justice ! Now see how all this affects his condition as a creature. A man born under civil disabilities has no guilt in the eye of his country's laws, yet he does not take rank with a true citizen. A pardoned criminal to his last day will not cast the inferiority which he has brought upon himself. No pardon, no honours, can ever cover the fact either from others or himself. Nay, so far as he himself is concerned, they will only keep the fact bright and burnished in his mind. The man who has been tried and cast for nearly every crime in almost every court in the land, and who is at large by a simple and amazing act of royal clemency, must feel that he has made a condition for himself which he never can forget, and out of which he draws every hour peculiar motives of conduct and demeanour; and the better man he becomes, the less likely is he ever to forget his past. So surely it is with us men. If looked at without advertence to the original fall, or to our own fall, or to our renewed falls after grace given, what are we but finite, dependent, imperfect : but when those three additional facts of our real history are added to our condition, how much more narrow, and little, dependent, and inferior do we appear to become. The least word seems too big to express our littleness.

But we can go lower still. Pardon lowers us.

The abundance and frequency of mercy humbles us. The goodness of God gives a new life to the sense of our own misery and hatefulness. It quickens our knowledge of our own inferiority into a positive feeling of self-contempt. It is true that the first fall, and our own fall, and our repeated falls, all flow, voluntary though they be, out of our necessary imperfections as creatures; yet nevertheless they add something to the consciousness that we are creatures, just as all developments seem to add to their germ, even though, like sin, they are not inevitable but free developments. And then God's pardoning mercy adds again to our consciousness that we are creatures. It appears to sink us lower and lower in our own nothingness, to envelop us more and more in the sense of our *createdness*. For in our sin God has condescended to make a covenant with us, and He is hourly fulfilling His share of it. On His part the covenant seems an abandonment of His own rights, a waiving of His own dignity, a service gratuitously given, or for a nominal payment which makes it less dignified than if it were gratuitous, a lowering of Himself towards our level, a series of apparent changes in Him who in His essence and knowledge and will is gloriously and majestically immutable. All this makes us feel more and more intensely what it is to be a creature. The consciousness that clung to the beautiful soul of the unfallen Adam becomes a deeper consciousness to the fallen sinner, and that deeper becomes deepest in the chastened joy and humbled peace of the forgiven sinner.

Thus each of us finds himself in his place, his own allotted place, in nature and in grace, with this threefold consciousness upon him. Beneath the weight of this happy and salutary consciousness he has to work out his destiny. Criticism of his position is not only useless; so long as he remembers himself, it is impossible. Not only does he know in the abstract that all *must* be right; he knows by his feeling of being a creature that all *is* right. To him criticism is not only loss of time ; it is irreligion also. He does not know how to sit in judgment upon his Creator. He cannot comprehend even the mental process by which others do it, much less the moral temper. For, while he has this three fold consciousness that he is a creature, he cannot conceive of himself without it, nor what he would be like if he was without it, and therefore those who are without it are beyond his comprehension for the time both in what they say and do. There are not two sides to the question of life, God's side and man's side. God's side is all in all. Not only is there nothing to be said on the other, there is no other. To think that man has a side is to forget that he is a creature, or at least not realize what it is to be a creature. Encompass man's littleness with the grand irresponsible sovereignty of God, and then is he glorious indeed, his liberty large beyond compare, and his likeness to God more like an equality with Him than we can dare to put in words.

Now let us go back to the man we left sitting on the hill-top in the brightness of the summer sun. We have to draw some conclusions about him from what has been already said; and the first is this. As "crea-ture" is his name, his history, and his condition, he must obviously have the conduct and the virtues befitting a creature. He must behave as what he is. His propriety consists in his doing so. He must be made up of fear, of obedience, of submission, of humility, of prayer, of repentance, of responsibility, and above all, of love. As fire warms, and frost chills, as the moon

shines by night and the sun by day, as birds have wings
and trees have leaves, so must man, as a creature, conduct himself as such, and do those virtuous actions,
which are chiefly virtues because they are becoming to
him and adapted to his condition. The demeanour, the
behaviour, the excellences of a creature must bear upon
them the stamp of his created nature and condition.
This is too obvious to need enforcing; obvious when
stated, yet most strangely forgotten by most men during
the greater part of their lives.

Our second conclusion about this man is that, whatever may be his attainments or his inclinations, the
only knowledge worth much of his time and trouble,
the only science which will last with him and stand
him in good stead, consists in his study of the character
of God. He received everything from God. He belongs to Him. He is surrounded by Him. His fate
is in God's hands. His eternity is to be with God, in
a companionship of unspeakable delights. Or if it is to
be in exile from Him, it is the absence of God which
will be the intolerableness of his misery. His own
being implies God's being; and he exists, not for himself, but for God. Of what unspeakable importance
then is it for him to find out who God is, what sort of
Being He is, what He likes and what He dislikes, how
He deals with His creatures and how He expects His
creatures to deal with Him. Can his understanding
be employed upon anything more exalted? Is there
any novelty equal to his daily fresh discoveries in the
rich depths of the Divine perfections? Is there any
person in the world whose ways and works are of such
thrilling interest to him as those of the Three Uncreated
Persons, the Father, Son, and Holy Ghost? Is there
any existing or possible thing to be conceived or named

one half so curious, one half so attractive, one half so exciting, as the adorable self-subsisting Essence of the Most High God? O no! Obviously, whatever that man may be thinking of now, he ought to be thinking of God. As long as he sits beneath the fragrant shadow of that pious thought, that he is a creature, so long will he feel that his one wise and delightful task, while he is a lodger among the mutable homes of this swift-footed planet, must be the study of his Creator's character.

Our third conclusion is that, if God is to be the subject of the man's intellectual occupations, God must be equally the object of his moral conduct. God must have his whole heart as well as his whole mind. We have no doubt that that man's soul is a perfect mine of practical energies, which the longest and most active life will not half work out. The muscle of the heart acts seventy times a minute for perhaps seventy years, and is not tired; yet what is this to the activity of the soul? He has far more energy in him than his neighbours are aware of, more than he suspects himself. He can do wonders with these energies if he concentrates them on any object, whether it be pleasure, wealth, or power. Our conclusion implies that, while he may *use* his energies on any or all of those three things, he must *concentrate* them on God only, on the loving observance of his Creator's law. We do not see what being a creature means, if it does not mean this; though we know that there are creatures who have irrevocably determined not to do it, and their name is devil, a species they have created for themselves in order to escape as far as they can to the outskirts of the creation of eternal power and love. Why be like them? Why go after them? Why not leave them to themselves, at the dreadful, dismal pole of our Father's empire?

These three conclusions are inevitable results of that man's being a creature. If he does not intend to make them the law of his life, he has no business to be in the sunshine. If he wants to be a god, let him make a world for himself. Ours is meant for creatures. Why is he turning all our bright and beautiful things to curse and darkness, all our sweet gifts to gall and worm-wood? What right has he to be lighting the fires of hell in his own heart at the beams of that grand loving sun? A creature means "All for God." Holiness is an unselfing of ourselves. To be a creature is to have a special intensified sonship, whose life and breath and being are nothing but the fervours of his filial love taking fire on his Father's bosom in the pressure of his Father's arms. The Sacred Humanity of the Eternal Son, beaming in the very central heart of the Ever-blessed Trinity,—that is the type, the meaning, the accomplish-ment, of the creature.

If we take all the peculiarities of the creature and throw them into one, if we sum them all up and ex-press them in the ordinary language of Christian doc-trine, we should say that they came to this,—that as man was not his own beginning, so also he is not his own end. His end is God; and man belies his own position as a creature whenever he swerves from this his sole true end. Every one knows what it is to have an end and how much depends upon it. To change a man's end in life is to change his whole life, to revolu-tionize his entire conduct. When he sees his aim dis-tinctly before him, he uses his sagacity in planning to attain it, his courage in removing the obstacles which intervene, and his prudence in the selection of the means by which he is eventually to succeed. More or less consistently, and more or less incessantly, the man's mind and heart are occupied about his end. It forms his character, it possesses his imagination, it stimulates his intellect, it engrosses his affections, it absorbs his faults, it is his measure of failure and success, it is ever tending to be his very standard of right and wrong. A creature, in that it is a creature, is like a falling stone. It seeks a centre, it travels to an end, irresistibly, impetuously. This is its law of life. Hence it is that the end gives the colour to the creature's life, describes it, defines it, animates it, rules it. This is true of pleasure, of knowledge, of wealth, of power, of popularity, when they are sought as ends. They lay passionate hold upon a man, and make him their slave, and brand their mark all over him, and the whole world knows him to be theirs. But all this is still more true when man makes God, what God has already made Himself, his single and magnificent end. And how glorious are the results in his capacious soul! To make God always our end is always to remember that we are creatures; and to be a saint is always to make God our end. Hence to be a saint is always to remember, and to act on the remembrance, that we are creatures. Yet, horrible as it sounds when it is put into words, it is the common way of men to make God a means instead of an end, a purveyor instead of a judge, if they make any use of Him at all. He has to forecast for their comforts, to supply their necessities, to pay for their luxuries. All men seek their own, murmured the indignant apostle. To seek the things of Christ was his romance, which worldly disciples did not understand. How few can turn round upon themselves at any given moment of life, when they do not happen to be engaged in spiritual exercises, and can say, " God is my end! At this moment when I unexpectedly look in upon myself, while I was acting almost unconsciously, I find that I was doing, what a creature should always be doing,—seeking God. My worldly duties and social occupations were understood to be means only, and were treated accordingly. There was nothing in my mind and heart which partook of the dignity of an end, except God." Yet is it not our simple business? We expect even a dog to come when he is called, and a clock to go when it is wound up, and in like manner God, when He creates us, expects us to seek Him as our only end and sovereign good.

We are almost frightened at what we have written. We covenanted not to speak of high things, nor entangle you in discourses of spiritual perfection: and we honestly do not intend to wile you to commit yourselves to any-thing which is not common-place and necessary. Yet when we simply say what it is to be a creature, we seem to be demanding the highest sanctity. The creature seems to slip into the saint. The natural temper and disposition proper to us because of our created origin seems to put on the hue and likeness of supernatural grace and contemplation, and the common-place insen-sibly to glide into the heroic. There must be some mis-take. Where is it? Our conscience tells us that we have been honourably checking ourselves a score of times in the last score pages, from saying what was burning in our heart to come out. It is not we that have broken faith with you, gentle reader. Have we then overstated the case of the creature? Have we drawn any conclu-sion without a premiss to warrant it? Have we invented what does not exist, or falsely embellished what does? The more we consider the case, the less we seem to have done so. We may have wearied you with telling you what was so old and trite; we do not think we have told you anything new, or that there is any part of our statement from which you dissent. How then have we come to this pass? Is it true that every one is obliged to be what is technically called a saint, or what theology styles perfect, simply because he is a creature? We cannot say Yes, and yet we hardly dare say No. What if it be true that perfection is only the result of corresponding to grace as it is given, and thus that all good people are in the road to perfection always; so that perfection is not one thing, and common holiness another; but that common holiness is perfection in its childhood, and perfection is common holiness in its maturity? We will not say that this is so. But we will say thus much, that the simple statement of our position and condition as creatures brings us to this—that to serve God out of love is not the peculiar characteristic of what is termed high spirituality, but that, without reference to perfection, nay without reference to redemption, creation, of and by itself, does bind the creature to serve the Creator out of love; and we confess that this conclusion is as pregnant of consequences as it is inevitable in its truth.

In the last chapter we said that a heathen, who without revelation should act consistently (if he could) with the constant remembrance that he was a creature, would, bating certain gifts and graces, be a portrait of a catholic saint. Now that we have examined more in detail the characteristics proper to a creature, and so the duties which become him, the same truth comes out still more clearly. What on a superficial view seems the peculiar excellence of high spirituality, namely, that in it God is served out of love, turns out to be a universal obligation undeniably founded on the simple fact of creation. Thus all practical religion is based upon a man's behaving himself becomingly as a creature. It is the humility and modesty that come out of that thought which give to his actions all their gracefulness and beauty, and commute them into worship and adoration. When we seek for the first principles of holiness, we find them where the heathen finds the roots of his moral duties, and where asceticism and mysticism discover the axioms out of which they draw unerringly that vast series of amazing truths which theology records and classifies. These axioms are all implied in the fact of our creation. They are the religious intuitions proper to a creature. Bind yourself to no more than on reflection you will acknowledge yourself to be bound to by the simple fact that God created you, and then you will become holy. It needs no more than that.

If we examine the falls both of angels and men, we shall see that what lay at the root of them was a forgetfulness that they were creatures, or a perverse determination to be something more. Whether the angels contemplated their own beauty and rested with an unhallowed complacency in themselves as their end, or whether they would not bow to the divine counsel of the Incarnation and exaltation of Christ's human nature above their own, in both cases they forgot themselves as creatures, and demanded what it was not becoming in a creature to demand. You shall be as gods, was the very motive which the tempter urged in order to push man to his ruin. Man insisted upon sharing something which it had pleased God for the time to reserve to Himself. The knowledge of God was the object of Adam's envy; and so unsuitable was it for him as a creature, that, when he got it, it ceased to be science, and turned into guilty shame. In both cases,

6 †

it was not merely that the angels and man refused to
obey their Creator; they wanted themselves to be more
than creatures. They would not acquiesce in their
created position. Can anything show more plainly the
importance of keeping always before us the fact that we
are creatures?

Yes! we may go still higher. We say of our
Blessed Lord that He is our example as well as our
mediator. Yet He was God as well as man. What
is this then but saying that of such consequence was
it to the happiness of man that he should know how to
behave himself as a creature, that it was necessary the
Creator should take a created nature, and come Himself
to show him how to wear it? Thus one of the many
known reasons of the sublime mystery of the Incarnation was that the Creator Himself might show the creature how he should behave as a creature. What interest
does not this throw upon the minutest incidents and
most rapid graphic allusions of the Four Gospels! The
mysteries of Jesus are man's studies of the beauty of
holiness. His soul drinks beauty out of them, and so
is imperceptibly transformed into the likeness of God
made man. He takes the form and the hue of the
Incarnate Word.

If we turn from our Lord's example to His work for
us as our mediator, the same truth meets us in another
shape. Not only was His created nature necessary for
this office in the counsels of God, but special stress is
laid upon those things which are eminently characteristic of a created nature as created. Speaking of His
intercession the apostle says that " in the days of His flesh
He was heard because He feared," and again he speaks
of the crucifixion in the same way, " He was obedient
unto death, even the death of the Cross." It is as if

Jesus redeemed the world especially by acknowledging in an infinitely meritorious manner through His created nature the sovereignty and dominion of the Creator.

To sum up briefly the results of this chapter, it appears, that to be a creature is a very peculiar and cognizable thing, that it gives birth to a whole set of duties, obligations, responsibilities, virtues, and proprieties, that it implies a certain history past and future, and a certain present condition, that on it are founded all our relations to God, and therefore all our practical religion, and that it involves in its own self, without reference to any additional mercies, the precise obligation of loving our Creator supremely as our sole end, and of serving Him from the motive of love. Thus, as we may say to the misbeliever that he would be a catholic if he only had an intelligent apprehension of the mystery of creation, so we may say to the catholic that he would be more like a saint, if he only understood with his mind and felt in his heart, what it was to be a creature.

CHAPTER III.

WHAT IT IS TO HAVE A CREATOR.

Debemus intelligere ut amemus, non vero amare ut intelligamus.

S. Anscim.

As creatures we are ourselves surrounded with
creatures in the world. Above us and beneath us and
around us there are creatures, of manifold sorts and of
varying degrees of beauty. The earth beneath our feet,
and the vast sidereal spaces above us, are all teeming
with created things. When we come to reflect upon
them, we are almost bewildered with their number and
diversity, on the earth, in the water, and in the air,
visible and invisible, known to science or unknown.
Then theology teaches us that we are lying in the mighty
bosom of another world of spiritual creatures, whom we
do not see, and yet with whom we are in hourly relations of brotherhood and love. The realms of spirit
encompass us with their unimaginable distances, and
interpenetrate in all directions our material worlds.
Creation is populous with angels. They are the living
laws of the material world, the wise and potent movers
of the wheeling spheres. All night and day they bear
us company. They hold us by the hand and lead us
on our way. They hear our words, and witness our
most hidden acts. The secrets of our hearts are hardly
ours; for we let them transpire perpetually by external
signs before the keen vision of the angels. Nay, have
we not asked God to let our own angel see down into

our hearts and know us thoroughly, so that he may
guide us better with his affectionate and surpassing
skill? Because we are creatures, creatures exercise a
peculiar influence over us. Love is stronger than the
grave. Blood and family and country rule us with an
almost resistless sway. We can so attach ourselves to
an unreasoning animal as to love it beyond all bounds,
and to weep when its bright little life is taken from us.
The very trees and fields of our village, and the blue
dreamy outline of our native hills, can so possess our
souls as to sway them through a long life of travel or of
money-making or of ambition. Alas! we are so satu-
rated with creatures, that we think even of our Creator
under created symbols; and God's merciful condescensions seem to show that a material creature could hardly
worship with a spiritual worship, until the Creator had
kindly put on a created nature. Thus every report of
the senses, every process of the mind, every form and
figure in the soul's secret chambers of imagery, every
action that goes out from us, every pulse of our natural
life, the atoms of matter that circulate through us in
swift and endless streams, clothing the soul with its garment of marvellous texture which is being woven and
unwoven every hour, as swiftly as the changes on a
dove's bright neck,—all of them imply creatures, are
kindled by them, fed by them, lean upon them, and
cannot for one moment be disentangled from them, except by some most rare process of supernatural grace.
Our life seems inextricably mixed up with creatures,
and, to use a metaphysical term, is unthinkable without
them.

How difficult then is it to conceive of a Life without
creatures, a Life which was from everlasting without
them, which needs them not, which mixes them not up

with itself, to which they can add nothing, and from which they can take nothing! We have to banish from our minds, or to attempt it, the ideas of time and space, of body and of motion; and even then the unimaginable void, which is not space, or the colourless light which is not body, is still a created image built up of created notions. There is something unutterably appalling in a Life eternally by itself, self-sufficing, its own glory, its own knowledge, its own magnificence, its own intense blessedness, its own silent, vast, unthrilling love. Surely to think of such a Life is to worship it. But It —it is not It—there were no *things* then—it is *He*, our God and our Creator! Out of that Life we came, when the Life had spent an eternity without us. The Life needed us not, was none the happier because of us, ruled not over a wider empire through us, multiplied not in us the objects of omniscience. But the Life loved us, and therefore out of the Life we came, and from its glorious sun-bright fountains have we filled the tiny vases of our created lives. O how the sublimity of this faith at once nourishes our souls like food and re-creates the mind like rest! Of how many illusions ought it not in its magnificent simplicity to disabuse us! The very idea of the Life of God before ever the worlds were made must of necessity give a tone and a colour, impart a meaning, and impress a character upon our own lives, which they would not otherwise have had. It furnishes us with a measure of the true magnitudes of things which teaches us how and what to hate and despise, and how and what to love and esteem. To put the thought into easier words, we cannot fully know what it is to be a creature, until we know as fully as we can what it is to have a Creator.

It is the peculiar beauty of the Old Testament that

it brings out this truth to us in the most forcible and attractive manner. This is probably the secret of the hold which it lays of the minds of those who have become familiar with it in early youth, and of the deep basis of religious feeling which it seems to plant in them. Though it is made up of various books, differing in date, and scene, and style, though psalm and prophecy and moral strains mingle with history and biography, every one feels that it has, almost as completely as the New Testament, one spirit, one tone, one colour, one scope. Whether it is when Adam and Eve are doing penance in Asia, and Cain is wandering out on the great homeless earth, or whether it is in the patriarch's tent beneath the starry skies of Mesopotamia, or amid the brick fields of the Nile, or the silent glens of stern Sinai, or during the rough chivalric days of the Judges, or in the palaces of Jerusalem, or by the waters of the captivity, whether it be when Debbora is chanting beneath her palm, or the king of Israel is singing to his harp, or amid the allegorical actions of some wailing prophet, or the conversations of the wise men of the Stony Arabia, we are ever learning what it is to be a creature, and what it is to have a Creator.   We are being taught the character of the God of Abraham and of Isaac and of Jacob, the God that was not like the gods of the heathen.   We either see or hear what He desires of us, how He will treat us, the ways, so unlike human ways, in which He loves us and will show His love, His style of punishment, His manifold devices of mercy, what He meant human life to be, and how men were to use both each other and the earth which He had given them to farm.   We do not know why it is that a tale, the like of which in common history would barely interest us, should fascinate us in the words of inspiration, why ordinary things should

seem sacred because they are related there, and why
simple expressions should have a latent spell within
them enabling them to fix themselves deep in our souls
to be the germs of a strong and dutiful devotion through
a long life, and then be a helpful power to us in death.
It can only be because it is all so possessed with God.
The true humble pathetic genius of a creature comes
into our souls, and masters them. The knowledge of
God becomes almost a personal familiarity with Him,
and the thought of Him grows into the sight of Him.
Look at the fathers of the desert and the elder saints of
the catholic church, and see what giants of holiness they
were, whose daily food was in the mysterious simplicity
of the Sacred Scriptures! The Holy Book lies like a
bunch of myrrh in the bosom of the Church, a power
of sanctification like to which, in kind or in degree,
there is no other, except the sacraments of the Precious
Blood.

It would not be easy to throw into words the exact
result of the knowledge of God which the Bible infuses
into us. It is hard to fasten and confine in terms the
idea of a Creator. When we try to do so, something
seems to escape, to evaporate, to refuse to go into
words; and it is just that something, as we are conscious, wherein most of the power and beauty of the
idea reside. Just as we may find it hard to describe
the character of our earthly mother, to refine upon her
peculiarities, to select her prominent and distinguishing
traits, and yet we have an idea of her so distinct that
we see her more plainly, and know her more thoroughly
than any one else we love, so is it with our knowledge
and love of God. We cannot look at Him as simply
external to ourselves. Things have passed between us;
secret relationships are established: fond ties are knit-

ted; thrilling endearments have been exchanged; there
are memories of forgivenesses full of tenderness, and
memories of punishments even yet more full of sweetness and of love; there have been words said, which
could never mean to others what they meant to us;
there have been looks which needed not words and were
more than words; there have been pressures of the
hand years ago, but which tingle yet; there are countless silent covenants between us, and with it all, such a
conviction of His fidelity! So that it is true to each
one of us beyond our neighbours, as it was true to the
Israelites beyond other nations, Who is so great a God
as our God, and who hath God so near?

We can therefore but try to express in cold and
vague words the idea which a loving Christian heart
has of the Creator. It is plain that our Creator is one
who stands in a relation to us which has no parallel
whatever among the relations which exist between ourselves and other creatures. It is not a question of
degree; it is one of kind also. It stands by itself, and
we can compare it with nothing else. We cannot even
understand it in its fulness. Do we know what the act
of creating a soul out of nothing implies? Do we comprehend the difference between being nothing and possessing an immortal life? Do we fathom what it is to
be loved eternally? Do we quite take in what it is to
interest God in our happiness, and to have Him employed about us? Do we understand what it is that
there should be the infinite and everlasting God, and
also, beside Him, something which is not Himself?
Yet unless we know all these things, we could not know
what the relationship of creature and Creator involves.
But we can easily perceive so much as this. Not only
is the relationship between our Creator and ourselves

unlike anything else, without parallel and beyond comparison, but it is far closer than any other tie of love by which the human soul can possibly be bound. He is obviously nearer to us than father or mother. We come more directly from Him than from them. We are more bound up with Him, and owe Him more. We cannot come of age with God, nor alter our position with Him. We cannot grow out of our dependence upon Him, nor leave the home of His right hand. The act of our creation is not done once for all, and then ceases. Preservation is but the continuance of creation, the non-interruption of the first act of divine power and love. The strong spirit of the highest angel needs the active concurrence of God every moment, lest it should fall back into its original nothingness.

But not only is our relation to our Creator the closest of all relations, it is also the tenderest and the dearest. Nay its sweetness may almost be said to follow from its closeness; for the closer the union, the more perfect should be the love. It is not within the power of God's omnipotence, if we may speak so boldly, to make Himself otherwise than infinitely desirable to His creature. He is in Himself so surpassingly beautiful, so attractively good, so unspeakably compassionate, that He must of necessity draw us towards Him. Even those, who of their own will are lost, struggle towards Him, in spite of their reluctant aversion, with all the might of their nature and with the burning thirst of an incessant desire. Whatever then is sweet, whatever is delightful, whatever is satisfying, in human love, parental or filial, conjugal or fraternal, is but a poor shadow of the love which enters into the tie between the Creator and the creature. Hence we are not surprised to find that this tie is so durable that it can never be broken.

The child in heaven owes no allegiance to its earthly father, and like the saints, may be in glory far above him. In heaven there is no marrying nor giving in marriage. The resurrection has emancipated all from every earthly bond. Whatever of earthly ties may survive in heaven, it survives not as a bond. But it is not so with the relation between the creature and the Creator. Everywhere and always that remains the same. Nay, as the lapse of time is ever adding to the creature's debt, swelling the huge sum of his obligations for benefits received, opening out new reasons for dependence upon his Maker, and drawing him into still closer union with Him, we may even say that the tie is continually acquiring new strength, and is being drawn tighter instead of being relaxed. It is God's unbounded love, rather than His immense magnificence, which makes Him ever new to us, and His beauty always a fresh surprise and a fresh delight. It is not only, to use the distinction of the psalm, the greatness of His mercy, but it is the multitude of His mercies, which make our trust and confidence in Him so inexpressibly consoling, and our union with Him so far more intimate than any other tie of which we can conceive. We are one with Him, as our Lord prayed we might be, even us the Father and the Son and the Holy Ghost are One.

If we endeavour to take to pieces the idea of a Creator, it may seem as if we were raising idle questions, and satisfying a barren curiosity rather than ministering to solid edification. Yet it will not be found so in reality; and there is no other way by which we can get the idea clearly into our minds. If then we reflect attentively on the trains of pious thought excited in us, when we meditate on God's glorious and fatherly title

of Creator, we shall find that there are at least nine
different considerations involved in it, none of which we
could spare without injuring the idea.

When we meditate on our Blessed Lord's Passion,
there is something lying unexpressed and only implicitly perceived under all our thoughts, and which gives
to the different mysteries their peculiar attraction and
solemnity. It is our faith in His Divinity. However
exclusively we may seem to be occupied with His
Sacred Humanity, we never in reality for a moment
forget that He is God. So in like manner when we
think of God as a Father or a Spouse, however much
we appear to ourselves to be engrossed with the peculiar and special relationship in which He has been
pleased to reveal Himself to us, our whole mind is in
fact pervaded by the invisible thought that He is of a
different nature from ourselves, that He is in truth God,
and all that is implied in that blessed Name; and it is
just this which makes us thrill all over with joy and
surprise as we venture to call Him by names which we
could not have used without His permission, and which
are only applicable to Him in a certain transcendental
sense, which is rather to be felt than either spoken or
conceived. The difference of nature between Him and
us, which faith never loses sight of, is the first element
of the idea of a Creator, and one which pervades all the
others. The Divine nature is the grand thought which
is the fruitful mother of all our thoughts; and by the
memory of it are all our memories magnified.

But this leads us still further. For the difference
between His Nature and ours is not like that which
separates the angels from men, or men from the various
tribes of animals below them. It is an infinite difference. And thus when we call Him Father or King,

Shepherd or Friend, our language implies only a privilege which He allows to us, not any duties to which
He is bound or rights to which we are entitled. We
have no compact with God, except the unmerited enjoyment of His merciful indulgence. As our Creator His
rights are simply unfathomable. He has no duties to
us, nothing which can rigorously be called duties. He
has made promises to us, and because He is God, He is
faithful. But, as creatures we have no claims. We
are bound to Him, and bound by obligations of duty,
and under penalties of tremendous severity. He on
His part overwhelms us with the magnificent liberali-
ties of His unshackled love. Yet God is neither a
slavemaster nor a despot, not only because of His infinite goodness and unutterable sweetness, but because
His rights are not limited like theirs. No creature can
feel towards his fellow-creature as we feel towards Him,
in the grasp of whose omnipotence we are at once so
helpless and so contented. Though the blaze of St.
Michael's beauty and power were able to put us to
death, if we saw it in the flesh, we could never feel ourselves in his hands as we are in the hands of God.
Though we are unable to imagine the risk we would
not trust to Mary, our most dear and heavenly Mother,
or to conceive anything which should weaken our confidence in her one atom, yet it is not in our power, it
is not a possibility of our nature, provided we know what
we are about, to trust her as we trust God, simply
because His perfections in Himself, and therefore His
rights over us, are illimitable.

Hence also we never think of questioning the wisdom of God, or His power, or His love. Our confidence in the worth of men is in a great measure pro-
portioned to the degree in which we consider them

pledged to us, whether by duty, by gratitude, by relationship, by honour, or by necessity. Whereas it is just the reverse with our trust in God. Our confidence in Him is boundless, because His sovereignty over us is boundless also. We have our doubts about holy persons: we criticize the saints: we take views about the angels. There is nothing in creation which we do not seem to have some sort of right to question. But with God it is not so. Here we are simple belief, implicit reliance, unhesitating dependence. We should be mad to have any other thoughts where He is concerned.

Then, as we cannot question Him, we must take Him on faith. It does not perplex our dealings with Him, that we do not understand Him. His height above us does not obscure our perception of His sovereignty. We can trust Him without knowing Him. We listen and obey, even when He gives no reasons; for we know that we should possibly not appreciate His reasons if He gave them, and that no reasons could enhance our certainty that His orders are the perfection of what is just and holy, compassionate and good. Our fellow-men must be reasonable, if they would govern us and use us for their purposes. But God's will is to us above all reason, more convincing than all argument, more persuasive than any reward, because of the very infiniteness of His superiority over us. We take God on faith, because He is God; and we take nothing else on faith except so far as we account it to represent God, either as His instrument, or His representative, or His likeness in goodness, in justice, in fidelity, or in love.

Thus looking at our Creator as it were outside of ourselves, we form an idea of Him, and of our relations to Him, which can be accounted for only by His unspeakable eminence in power, in wisdom, and in goodness. The nothingness to which He has given life, and being, and His own image, has a secret bond to Him, which has more to do with its worship of Him than even His superlative excellence and unimaginable glory. But the idea of a Creator is yet more singular, more isolated, more special, and more intimate. For we are never really outside of God nor He outside of us.* He is more with us than we are with ourselves. The soul is less intimately in the body, than He is both in our bodies and our souls. He as it were flows into us, or we are in Him as the fish in the sea. We use God, if we may dare to say so, whenever we make an act of our will, and when we proceed to execute a purpose. He has not merely given us clearness of head, tenderness of heart, and strength of limb, as gifts which we may use independently of Him when once He has conferred them upon us. But He distinctly permits and actually concurs with every exercise of them in thinking, loving, or acting. This influx and concourse of God, as theologians style it, ought to give to us all our lives long the sensation of being in an awful sanctuary, where every sight and sound is one of worship. It gives a peculiar and terrific character to acts of sin. It is hard to see how levity even is not sacrilege. Everything is penetrated with God, while His inexpressible purity is all untainted, and His adorable simplicity unmingled with that which He so intimately pervades, enlightens, animates, and sustains. Our commonest actions, our lightest recreations, the freedoms in which we most unbend, —all these things take place and are transacted, not so much on the earth and in the air, as in the bosom of the omnipresent God.

* Some writers, in avoiding pantheism, seem to deny one-while omnipresence, and another-while providence.

Thus when we use the words "dependence," "submission," "helplessness," "confidence," about our relation to God, we are using words which, inasmuch as
they express also certain relations in which we may
possibly stand to our fellow-creatures, are really inadequate to express our position towards our Creator.
We have no one word which can fully convey to the
mind the utterness of that honourable abjection in which
we lie before Him who made us. But this is not all.
The liberality of God is not satisfied with pouring out
upon us in such profusion the wonderful gifts of a
reasonable nature, He enriches us still more nobly, He
unites Himself to us still more intimately, by the yet
more marvellous gifts of grace. Sanctifying grace is
nothing less than a participation of the Divine Nature.
If we try to think of this, we shall soon perceive that
even imagination cannot master the greatness and the
depth of this stupendous gift, any more than it can sensibly detect the manner of its intimate existence within
us, or the delicacy of its manifold and incessant operations when stirred by the impulses of actual grace
within our souls. "God," says Thauler,* "has created
us for so high a degree of honour, that no creature
could ever have dared to imagine that God would have
chosen it for so great a glory; and we ourselves are
now unable to conceive how He could raise us higher
than He has done. For, as He could not make us
Gods by nature, a prerogative which can belong to Him
alone, He has made us Gods by grace, in enabling us
to possess with Him, in the union of an eternal love,
one same beatitude, one same joy, one same kingdom."
The fact that God created angels and men at first in a
state of grace and not merely in a state of nature, and

* Institut. cap. viii.

then further that He heaps upon us now such an abundance of grace and makes us members of Himself by the Incarnation, causes us to feel that He did not create us to be simply His subjects and outside of Himself, but to be drawn up to Himself, to live with Him, to share His blessedness, nay, and His nature too. Moreover our continual dependence upon grace, upon gifts which are by no means due to us as creatures, but which are simply supernatural, compels us to acknowledge that we cannot even do the good we intensely desire to do, except by a sort of miraculous communion with Him; and this gives to our dependence upon God another of its peculiar characteristics.

But He is not only our first cause and fountain, not only our constant living preservation, not only the source of supernatural gifts and graces over and above the ornaments of our nature, not only Himself the original of which He vouchsafed to make us copies, but He is also our last end. And He is so in two senses. He is our last end, because He is the reason of our existing at all, because it is for Him, for His own glory, that we live, and not in any way for our own sakes: and He is also our last end, because we go to Him, and rest nowhere but in Himself, not in any gifts which He gives us, but simply in His own living and everblessed Self. Our eternity reposes on Him, and is in Him, and with Him, and is the sight of Him, and His embrace. This is something which no creature, nor all creation together, can share. It is the sole prerogative. of God, and one which gives out a whole class of affections proper to itself. Nothing in life has any meaning, except as it draws us further into God and presses us more closely to Him. The world is no better than a complication of awkward riddles, or a gloomy store-

7. †.

house of disquieting mysteries, unless we look at it by
the light of this simple truth, that the eternal God is
blessedly the last and only end of every soul of man.
Life as it runs out is daily letting us down into His
Bosom; and thus each day and hour is a step homeward, a danger over, a good secured.

Hence it is, because God alone is our last end, that
He alone never fails us. All else fails us but He.
Alas! how often is life but a succession of worn-out
friendships! Youth passes, with its romance, and
crowds whom we loved have drifted away from us.
They have not been unfaithful to us, nor we to them.
We have both but obeyed a law of life, and have
exemplified a world-wide experience. The pressure of
life has parted us. Then comes middle life, the grand
season of cruel misunderstandings, as if reason were
wantoning in its maturity, and by suspicions and cir-
cumventions and constructions were putting to death
our affections. All we love and lean upon fails us.
We pass through a succession of acquaintanceships;
we tire out numberless friendships; we use up the
kindness of kindred; we drain to the dregs the confidence of our fellow-labourers; there is a point beyond
which we must not trespass on the forbearance of our
neighbours. And so we drift on into the solitary
havens of old age, to weary by our numberless wants
the fidelity which deems it a religion to minister to
our decay. And there we see that God has outlived
and outlasted all : the Friend who was never doubtful,
the Partner who never suspected, the Acquaintance who
loved us better, at least it seemed so, the more evil
He knew of us, the Fellow-labourer who did our work
for us as well as His own, and the Neighbour who
thought He had never done enough for us, the sole

Superior who was neither rude nor inconsiderate, the one Love, that unlike all created loves, was never cruel, exacting, precipitate, or overbearing. He has had patience with us, has believed in us, and has stood by us. What should we have done if we had not had Him? All men have been liars; even those who seemed saints broke down, when our imperfections leaned on them, and they wounded us, and the wound was poisoned; but He has been faithful and true. On this account alone He is to us what neither kinsman, friend, or fellow-labourer can be.

The more deeply we enter into these plain truths and the more assiduously we meditate upon them, the more we find growing over us a certain humility, which consists not so much in prostrating ourselves before the majesty of God, as in a kind of hatred of ourselves which increases together with our increase in the love of God. It is not the contempt of our own vileness which follows after sin, and is a part of Christian repentance. It is not like that fresh burst of love to God, which follows when He has inflicted some just punishment upon us for our sins, and which turns our hearts with such exceeding tenderness towards Him. It is a sort of ignoring of our own claims and interest, a forgetting of ourselves because of the keenness of our remembrance of God, and an abandonment of our own cause for His: and all this with a sort of dislike of ourselves, of patient impatience with our own meanness, a pleasure in acknowledging our own unworthiness, like the pleasure of a contrite confession, a grateful wonder that God should treat us so differently from what we deserve, and ultimately a desire to remind Him of our own self-abasement, of that intolerable demerit of ours, which He seems in His mercy so entirely to forget.

In a word, self-abasement is the genius of a creature as a creature; it is his most reasonable frame of mind; it is that which is true about him when all else is false.

Yet in apparent contradiction to this self-hatred, the idea of our Creator is accompanied with a familiarity, for which it is difficult to account, but which seems an essential part of our filial piety towards our Heavenly Father. We can say to Him what we cannot say to our fellow-creatures. We can take liberties with Him, which in nowise impair our reverence. We are more at ease when only His eye is full upon us than when the gaze of men is fixed upon our actions. He mis-understands nothing. He takes no umbrage. He makes us at home with Him. Childlike simplicity is the only ceremonial of our most secret intercourse with Him. His presence does not oppress our privacy. His knowledge of our nature, or rather our knowledge that He created it, gives us a kind of familiarity with Him, for it is a question of kind rather than of degree, such as we can never have with the great ones of the earth, nor even with those nearest and dearest to us. We could not bear to let our fellow creatures always see us. But nothing makes us common to God. He never—may we say it?—loses His reverence for those whom He has deigned eternally to love.* There is no need of concealment with Him, who sees through us, who regards the acknowledgment of our manifold

---

* It has always seemed to me as if a whole revelation of God were in those words of the Book of Wisdom (xii. 18.) Cum magna reverentia disponis nos. Most of the modern Donays render it, With great *favour* Thou disposest of us, thereby missing both the beauty and the meaning. The old Douay, which has seldom been altered for the better by modern hands, translates the verse, But Thou, Dominatour of power, judgest with tranquilitie, and with great reverence disposest of us; for it is in Thy power, when Thou wilt, to be able. The Greek of the Septuagint is μετὰ πολλῆς φειδοῦς διοικεῖς ἡμᾶς. The passage is a perfect fountain of meditation.

weakness almost as acceptable worship of His Majesty, and to whom our infirmities are His own laws, and our indignities but the timely exhibition of our needs.

Such are the considerations which make up our idea of a Creator in our minds. They lie there implicitly. Sometimes we realize them, sometimes not. Now one of them starts to view, and for a while occupies our thoughts, and now another. But on the whole this is what the idea comes to when it is analyzed. We think of Him as one who is not like our parents, because He is not of the same nature with us, of one whose rights are illimitable and rest on no compact, of one whose wisdom, power, and love we may not question, and whom therefore we must take on faith, and trust, simply because of the infiniteness of His superiority ; of one who penetrates us with the influx of His omnipresence, and concurs with all our movements, who enlightens nature with grace, and as our last end recompenses grace with glory ; to trust in whose never-failing faith-fulness is as much a joy as it is a necessity, to love whom is to despise ourselves, and yet with whom we are on terms of mysterious intimacy far transcending the closest equalities and most unreproved freedoms of any human tie. This is our idea of a Creator ; all these things seem to follow from our knowledge of that eternal Love, who saw us from the first, and when the time came called us out of nothing.*

* Thus the delighted admission of the very absoluteness of God's sover-eignty over us seems to bring us to a more manifest equality, a more privi-leged intimacy with Him, than that view of God which represents the rela-tion of Creator and creature as a beautifully just discharge of mutual obligations, wherein He respects the charter He has given us, and we obey His laws as well as His knowledge of our weakness gives Him a right to expect. I have not a word to say of condemnation of that system of theology which endeavours to clear the relationship of Creator and creature of all difficulty, and justifies God to man by representing Him as exercising over us

To analyze our idea of a Creator is the first step towards answering the question we proposed to ourselves, What it is to have a Creator. We have now to take a further step. If our Creator is such as we have described, if the fact of His having condescended to create us puts Him in such a position towards us, what must the service of Him necessarily be to us His creatures? The service of the Creator must obviously be the end and purpose of the creature. God is His own end; and He is ours also. Everything short of God is to the creature a means, not an end, something transitory, and not permanent, something in which at

a sort of limited sovereignty which fully satisfies our ideas of perfect equity, such equity as subsists between a powerful monarch and his subjects. But I am quite unable to receive such a system of belief into myself. A controversialist who makes out that there are no difficulties in revelation seems to me to prove too much ; for to say that a disclosure from an Infinite Mind to finite minds is all easy and straightforward, is almost to say that there is no such disclosure, or that the one claiming to be so received is not divine. So in like manner, when we consider what it is to be a creature, and what it is to have a Creator, we cannot but suspect a theological system which represents our relations with our Creator as beset with no difficulties, and makes all our dealings with Him as smooth and intelligible as if they were between man and man. It makes me suspicious, because it proves so much, and this quite irrespectively of any of its arguments in detail. There must be at the least a *look* of overbearing power, and an exhibition of justice unlike the fairness of human justice, or I shall not easily be persuaded that the case between God and man has been stated candidly or even quite reverently. It is indeed an act of love of God, as well as of our neighbour, to make religious difficulties plain ; but he is a bold controversialist who in an age of general intelligence denies the existence of difficulties altogether, or even under-estimates their force ; and as the facts on man's side are too obvious to be glossed over, the temptation is almost irresistible to make free with God, and to strive to render Him more intelligible by lowering Him to human notions. In the long run this method of controversy must lead to unbelief. Most men are more satisfied by an honest admission of their difficulty than by an answer to it ; few answers are complete, and common sense will never receive a religion which is represented as having no difficulties. It forfeits its character of being divine, by making such a claim. Religion, as such, cannot be attractive, unless it is also true ; and when we are sure of the truth, we must not mind its looking unattractive, but trust it, as from God, and therefore, as His, possessed of a secret of success which will carry it securely to its end.

best we can have but a fitful joy, not a contented and blessed rest. The value of everything in life depends on its power to lead us to God by the shortest road. But as the service of God is the creature's real work, so also is it his true dignity. The rank and pageantry of the world cannot clothe us with real dignity. To serve God is the only honour, which it is worth our while to strive after. The order of holiness is to the eyes of the enlightened angels the only authentic precedence in the world. So what is man's true dignity is also his greatest happiness. We do not value as we ought our inestimable privilege of being allowed to worship God. We do not prize our heavenly prerogative of being permitted to keep His commandments. We look at that as a struggle which is in truth a crown. We look at that as an obligation which is more properly a boon. We call it duty when its lawful name is right, the right of best-beloved sons. Have not millions tried to be happy in something which was not the service of their Creator, and how many of them have succeeded? And did ever one creature seek his happiness in God, and not find unspeakably more than he had ventured to conceive? Why, the very austerity of the saint is more lighthearted than the gaiety of the worldling. So many men die in a minute the world over, and what is the last lesson of every one of them, but that the service of God is the highest happiness of man?

But we talk of interest. Interest leads the world. It is self-love's god. It is strong enough to warp the stoutest mind, and to beat down the most romantic affections. All things give way to interest. The days of chivalry are past; and perhaps when they were present, interest was as much the crowned king

of society as it is now. Yet if the best interest
is that which is first of all most secure, and then
most abundant, and after that most lasting, and
finally to be gained with the least outlay, what interest
can compare with our interest in serving God, and
speculating only on His favour and fidelity? We talk
of wisdom also. These are days- of wisdom. Knowledge covers the earth as the waters cover the sea.
Yet the prophecy is not fulfilled, for it is hardly the
knowledge of God which abounds amongst us. But
if that be the highest wisdom which sees furthest
and clearest, which embraces the greatest number of
truths, and the highest kind of truths, which contem-
plates them with the most complete and accurate
certainty, and which is of practical use to all eternity,
then what earthly wisdom will compare with the wisdom
of serving God? How is it that we are so fascinated
by the various sciences of mind and matter, and yet
find theology so tame and dull? Why is it that we
are so excited by a new book on geology or chemistry,
and turn away with weariness from the old-fashioned
traditions of the Christian Church? Surely it is because we have no love of God, because we do not keep
up our relations with Him as our Creator. Were it
not so, we should find our modern sciences uninteresting
in their details and sterile in results, unless we ourselves make a theological commentary upon them as we
read.

Liberty is another idol of the sons of men, and
one whose worship is of all false worships the least
blameworthy, although the greatest of crimes have been
perpetrated in its name. Yet what does our liberty
amount to? Freedom of action, of speech, and of pen,
are indeed noble achievements of civilization and

mighty missionaries of the Gospel too. Yet is a man really free who is not free from self? If he is a slave to base passions, or the tool of his own spite and malice, or the pander to his own criminal pursuits, or the victim of his own self-love, with what kind of liberty is he free? If he is chained down to earth, then he is disabled for the liberty of heaven. If he has practically sold himself to the evil angels, who is more a bondsman than he? From satan, world, and self there is no liberty, but in the service of our Creator: and His service is liberty indeed, not only the truest and the sweetest, but the widest also. O for the unconstrained spirit of the saints, who have cut off all ties and snapped all bonds asunder, that they might fly away and be with Christ!

The service of the Creator is also the creature's most enduring reality. The unreality of the world is an old story. It was told in Athens, before ever our Saviour preached in Palestine. It is a miserable thing to build on sand, or to give our money for that which is not bread. Yet it is what we are all of us doing all our lives long, except when we are loving God. Human love is a treachery and a delusion. It soon wears threadbare and we die of cold. Place and office slip from us, when our hands get old and numb, and cannot grasp them tight. Riches, says the Holy Ghost, make to themselves wings and fly away. Good health is certainly a boundless enjoyment; but it is always giving way beneath us, and our years of strength are after all but few, and our vigour seems to go when we need it most. There is a noiseless unriveting of our strength by the lapse of years, which comes before old age, and is more prostrating than any sickness. But the service of God improves upon acquaintance, gives more than it promises, and after a little effort is nothing but rewards, and rewards which endure for evermore.

But this is not all. Not only are all these things the truest, greatest, highest, wisest, best, widest, and most enduring dignity, happiness, interest, wisdom, liberty, and reality ; but the service of the Creator is the creature's *sole* end, dignity, happiness, interest, wisdom, liberty, and reality. He has no other, none that have a right to the name, none that are not pretenders ; and he who seeks any other will never find them. However deliberate his evil choice, he will not gain earth by forfeiting heaven. If he works for Here, he will lose Here as well as Hereafter. Whereas if he works for Hereafter, he will gain Here as well. Moreover the service of the Creator is not only the creature's solitary end, dignity, happiness, interest, wisdom, liberty, and reality ; but the opposite evils of all these things will flow from its neglect. In a word, unless we serve God, the world is a dismal, unmeaning heart-breaking wilderness, and life no more than an insoluble and unprofitable problem. Look how cruel life is to the wicked man! Take him at his best estate, reckon up the pains he takes, the efforts he makes, the activity he expends, how he is burnt up with the fever of insatiable desires, running a race after impossible ends, impoverishing heart and mind with excitements which are their own punishment; what a tyranny the slow lapse of time is to him, what a bitter stepmother the world he has so adored! The flood-tide of irritation and then the ebb of helpless languor, who would live a life of which those are the incessant alternations? The wilful sinner is but a man who, in order to get rid of God, explores, to his own cost, every species of disappointment, and nowhere finds contentment or repose.

What is it that we have said? The service of the
Creator is the creature's last end, his true dignity, his
greatest happiness, his best interest, his highest wisdom,
his widest liberty, and his most enduring reality: the
service of the Creator is, furthermore, the one solitary
thing which answers truly to any of the above names:
and lastly, from its neglect, the very opposites of dignity, happiness, interest, wisdom, liberty, and reality,
follow to the creature, and the end of all is everlasting
perdition. We are almost ashamed to write down such
simple things, and to take up your time with reading a
string of propositions which no one in his senses would
dream of controverting, It is like printing the merest
rudiments of Christian doctrine under a more preten-
tious title than that of a catechism. Yet, when we look
at our past lives, perhaps our present lives, in the light
of these elementary truths, it would seem as if they
could never be stated too often, and as if there was no
one, learned or simple, saint or sinner, to whom the
statement of them was ever an unseasonable admonition
or an unnecessary repetition. God has established His
right to our service by so many other titles than that of
creation, that self-love is able, almost unconsciously, to
think more of those titles, the acknowledgment of which
implies more faith and more generosity in us, and to
dwell less on that which is at once the most self-evident,
involves the completest submission, and will not admit
of more than one opinion. No one can exaggerate the
extent to which God is ignored in His own world. It
is a miserable fact which is always a discovery, and is
always new, because we see more of it every day of our
lives. To the friends of God it is a growing unhappiness, because as they advance in holiness and know Him
better, it seems to them less and less possible not to

love Him with the most ardent, enthusiastic, and exclusive love, and yet at the same time experience is forcing
upon them the unwelcome conviction that they know
not one-tenth part of the wickedness of bad men, or of
the criminal inadvertence of those who profess to acknowledge the sovereignty of God.   The world has many
trades and many tasks for its many sons; but there is
one daily labour which it seems to add to all of them,
the effort to put away from its children the remembrance that they are creatures, in order that they may
the more undoubtingly forget that they have a Creator.
Blessed be the goodness of God, for giving us the grace
to remember Him ; for out of that grace will all others
come; and thrice blessed be His infinite compassion for
the further grace of loving Him, and of yearning to
make others love Him more !

It follows from what has been said that there cannot
be much question as to the extent of our service of God,
or the degree in which we are to serve Him.   If He is
our last end, then His service is that one thing needful
of which our Lord spoke in the Gospel.   With all our
heart, with all our mind, with all our soul, and with all
our strength—it must be thus, and only thus, that we
should serve our Creator ; for any service short of this,
or short of a real effort to make it this, would be dis-
loyalty to His infinite majesty and goodness.   But in
what way, or in what spirit, are we to serve God?
This question also appears to be settled, without any
further argument or appeal, by our own idea of what it
is to have a Creator.   It is plain that the kind of worship which we pay to Him must be something of the
following description.   It must be an easy service, as
well because of His immense compassion as because of
our unhappy weakness.   It would be doing a dishonour

to His goodness to suppose He has made the way to His favour difficult, or that He does not efficaciously desire to save countless, countless multitudes of His fallen creatures. It would be an unfilial irreverence to our most dear and loving Creator to imagine that His service would not be easy and delightful.

But it must not only be the easiest of services, it must be the noblest also. We must not offer to God except of our best. It must be the noblest, as for Him who is noble beyond word or thought, and it must be the noblest as ennobling us who serve Him, and making us more like Himself. It must be the happiest of services. For what is God but infinite beatitude and eternal joy? His life is joy. All that is bright and happy comes from Him. Were it not for Him, there would be no gladness, either in heaven or on earth. There can be nothing melancholy, nothing gloomy, nothing harsh, nothing unwilling, in our service of such a Father and Creator. Our worship must be happy in itself, happy in look and in expression, happy in blitheness and in promptitude and in beautiful decorum ; and it must also be such a worship, as while it gladdens the tenderness of God and glorifies His paternal fondness, shall also fill our souls with that abounding happiness in Him, which is our main strength in all well-doing and in all holy suffering.

It must be a service also which calls out and occupies the whole of man. There must not be a sense of our bodies, nor a faculty of our minds, nor an affection of our hearts, not a thing that we can do, nor a thing that we can suffer, but this service must be able to absorb it and transform it into itself. We must not only worship God always, but the whole of us must worship God. Our very distractions must be worship, and we must have some kind of worship which will enable them so to be. Thus it must be an obvious service, one which at the very first sight shall strike a creature as reasonable and fitting; and in order to be so, it must be such a service as a creature would wish to have rendered to himself. It must have that in it which alone makes any service graceful or acceptable. But as our wants are many, our feelings manifold, and our duties multiplied, our service of the Creator must be one which includes all possible services, expresses all our numerous relations with Him, satisfies all His claims upon us, at least in some degree, and has power to impetrate for us the many and various supplies of our diversified necessities.

It must be a service also, which in a sense shall comprehend God, and embrace the Incomprehensible. It must honour all His perfections, and all of them at once, even while it sees God, rather as Himself universal perfection, than as having any distinct perfections. It must not worship His mercy to the detriment of His justice, or His simplicity to the injury of His beauty ; it must not lose sight of His jealousy in His liberality, nor lightly esteem His sanctity because of His facility in pardoning. And it must settle all these difficulties in a practical way, the wisdom of which will be acknowledged as soon as it is stated, and which will not perplex our simple communion with God by subtleties and distinctions. It must be a service whose direct effect must be union. It must have such a special power over the human soul, and at the same time so peculiarly prevail with God, as to join God and the soul together in the most mysterious and indissoluble union. For the creature tends to close union with the Creator, and union alone is the perfection of all true worship. Finally this

service or worship, as it is union, must last, and out-
live, and take up into itself, and develop, and magnify,
all other graces.   Moreover it must be something more
than they are, something besides, which words cannot
tell, but which will be an inconceivable and eternal
gladness, brightening in our souls for evermore.

Any service, either short of this or different from this,
would plainly be unsuitable as an offering from the
creature to the Creator.   It is implied in the very
notion of creation ; for we cannot understand creation
otherwise than as an act of eternal love.   Our own idea
of a Creator has already settled the question for us.
We do not anticipate the least objection to any of the
requirements specified above ; and numerous as they
are, and differing in so many ways, there is one spirit,
one worship, one temper, one act, one habit, one word,
which at once satisfies all of them in the completest way
possible to a finite creature.   That one word is love.
The creature cannot serve the Creator except with a
service of love.   Love is the soul of worship, the foundation of reverence, the life of good works, the remission
of sins, the increase of holiness, and the security of final
perseverance. Love meets the first of our requirements;
for of all services it is the easiest.   Its facility has
passed into a proverb.   It is also the noblest and the
happiest of services, the noblest because it is the least
mercenary, the happiest because it is the most voluntary.
It is the only one which calls out and occupies the
whole man ; and it is naturally a creature's obvious
service ; for it is the only service which he would care
to have rendered to himself.   Love alone fulfils all the
commandments at once, and is the perfection of all our
duties.   It is the only one which does not deny, or at
least pretermit, something in God.   Fear, when exclu-

sive, denies mercy, and familiarity weakens reverence,
when the familiarity is not profoundly based on love;
whereas love settles the equalities and rights of all the
attributes of God, enthrones them all, adores them all,
and is nourished in exceeding gladness by them all.
Love also, and alone, accomplishes union ; and while
faith dawns into sight, and hope ends in everlasting
contentment, love alone abides, as we said before, outliving, taking up into itself, developing, and magnifying
all other graces, consummating at least that mystical
oneness with God which the Saints have named Divine
Espousals.

Once more you must remember that we are not
speaking of perfection, nor describing the heroism of the
saints. We are saying nothing of voluntary austerities,
nor of the love of suffering, nor of the thirst for humilia-
tions, nor of martyrdoms of charity, nor of silence under
unjust accusations, nor of a positive distaste for worldly
things, nor of an impatience to be dissolved and be with
Christ, nor of the hidden life, nor of the surrender of
our own will by vows, nor of mortification of the judgment, nor of holy virginity, nor of evangelical poverty,
nor of the supernatural mysteries of the interior life,
of the arduous and perilous paths of mystical contemplation. We are speaking only of what God has a
right to, simply because He has created us, of what we
cannot with decency refuse, of what common sense alone
convinces us, and of what we must be practical atheists
if we venture to withhold. And yet it amounts to our
making the service of God our sole end, dignity, happiness, wisdom, interest, liberty and reality ; and to our
devoting ourselves to it out of love as the most obvious
as well as the only sufficient worship of our Creator.
Simple as the statement seems, and unanswerable as it

is in all its details, it comes to far more than men will ordinarily allow; and yet if it proves itself as soon as it is propounded, what can we conclude except that men will not think of God, and that they have so long neglected to think of Him, that they never for one moment suspect either how little they know of Him or how utterly they neglect Him?   Alas! who has not seen many men and many women, gliding quietly down the waters of life, full of noble sentiments and generous impulses, kind and self-forgetting, brave and chivalrous, without one flaw of meanness in their character, ardent, delicate, faithful, forgiving, and considerate, and yet— almost without God in the world; though we are sure they would be just the persons to adorn His faith and name, if only it occurred to them to advert to either of the two sides of that childish truth, that we are creatures, and that we have a Creator?

In concluding this chapter, even at the peril of repeating, we must once more allude to the evils which follow from not realizing what it is to have a Creator. In the first place it introduces wrong notions into practical religion.   It gives an erroneous view of the mutual relations between God and ourselves, and substitutes lower motives, where higher ones would be not only more religious, but more easy also.   It destroys the paternal character of God, and makes His sanctity obscure His tenderness instead of illustrating and adorning it.   It leads us to look upon God as an independent power who has, as it were, come down upon us from without, and stands aloof from us, even while He governs us, and not as if we were from Him, and through Him, and in Him.   It is as if He had conquered us rather than created us.   Hence our submission is the submission of the conquered.   We do not dispute His right of

8 †

conquest, for our subjection is evidently complete, but
we make the best terms we can with Him, and hold
Him to the conditions on which we surrendered. It is
as if His service were simply a sacrifice of ourselves to
Him, an immolation of ourselves to His surpassing glory,
and as if His interests were not really the same as ours,
His end, which is Himself, the same as ours, and our
happiness wrapped up in His beatitude. It would be
less unreasonable to look upon ourselves, if we could, as
external to ourselves, as a foreign power with whom we
were on a kind of armed neutrality, as an adverse interest to be suspected and watched, than to look upon
God, as we must inevitably look upon Him, if we put
out of view that He created us out of nothing. Dryness,
weariness, reluctance, instability, and scantiness, in
practical religion, are in a great measure the results of
this forgetfulness that we have a Creator.

Then again has real piety a greater or a deadlier
enemy than the popular ideas of enthusiasm? If a person loses his taste for worldly amusements and blameless dissipations, if he prefers the church to the theatre,
early mass to lying in bed, almsgiving to fine dress,
spiritual books to novels, visiting the poor to driving in
the park, prayer to parties, he is forthwith set down
as an enthusiast; and though people do not exactly
know what enthusiasm is, yet they know that it is
something inconceivably bad; for it is something young
people should be especially warned against, and above
all pious people, as most needing such admonition.
The mere word enthusiasm is a power in itself; for it
accuses, tries, condemns, and punishes a man all at once.
Nothing can be more complete. Yet, in the first place,
dear reader, look over your numerous acquaintance;
and tell us,—whatever may be your notion of religious

enthusiasm, did you ever know any one injured by it?
You have heard that it makes people mad: did you
ever have one of your own friends driven mad by it?
And while you condemned their enthusiasm, did you
ever yourself get quite rid of a feeling that, however
unfit it was for life, it would be far from an undesirable
state to die in? In the next place, what is enthusiasm?
Dr. Johnson tells us that it is a " vain belief of private
revelations :" did any of your devout friends dream that
they had had private revelations? It is " a heat of
imagination:" did not your friends seem to grow cold
rather than hot? Were they not often tempted to go
your way because it was pleasanter? Did they not
find it hard to persevere in spiritual practices, and did
they not embrace them, not at all from any imagination
hot or cold, but simply because they thought it right,
and because grace had begun to change their tastes?
It is " an exaltation of ideas:" now were not the ideas
of your friends, in any true sense of the word, rather
depressed than exalted? Were they not more humble,
more submissive, more obliging ; or, at least, whenever
they were not so, did you not distinctly feel that they
were acting inconsistently with their religious profession? Were any of their ideas in any sense exalted,
even of those which had most to do with their pious
practices? Were not even those ideas rather subdued
than exalted? These are Dr. Johnson's three defini-
tions. They will not suit you. Do you mean then by
enthusiasm, doing too much for God? You would not
like to say so. Do you mean doing it in the wrong
way? But is daily mass wrong, is almsgiving
wrong, are spiritual books wrong, is visiting the poor
wrong, is prayer wrong? Or will you say it is doing
them instead of other things, which are not sinful?

Well! but is not this tyranny?   A man might answer,
If an opera would be to me the most tiresome of penances, or a ball the most unendurable of wearinesses,
why am I obliged to go?.   Or if I simply prefer prayer
to the opera, or spiritual reading to the ball, why am
I to have less liberty in gratifying my tastes than you
in gratifying yours?   Do you mean that God spoils
everything He touches, and is a mar-pleasure wherever
He interferes?   The truth is that by enthusiasm men
mean the being more religious than themselves.   And
this is an unpardonable offence; for they are the standards of what is moderate, sober, rational, and reflective.
Enthusiasm, in common parlance, has no other meaning.
Whoever uses the word is simply making public confession of his own tepidity.   Thus the whole popular
standard of practical religion is wrong and unfair, because it is fixed with reference to a false calculation;
and it is this which leads to the popular fallacy about
enthusiasm.   If men realized more truly and more
habitually what it is to have a Creator, and how much
follows from that elementary truth as to the nature and
amount of the service we owe Him, there can be no
doubt they would assent to a far higher standard on the
unsuspicious evidence of natural reason and common
sense, than they will now concede to the arguments
of spiritual books which are founded on higher motives,
and appeal to a greater variety of considerations.   The
fact is that we only appreciate God's goodness, in proportion as by His grace we become good ourselves; and
His goodness is so great and high and deep and broad,
that it makes little impression upon the dulness of our
spiritual sense, until it is quickened and sharpened with
heavenly light.   And thus, when we are low in grace,
and unpractised in devotion, the simple truth that God

is our Creator, and that a Creator necessarily implies what we have seen it implies, will come home to us with greater force, and make a more decided impression, than the complex consideration of the further and higher mercies which God has so multiplied upon us that they almost seem to hide one another's brightness. No man would accuse his neighbour of enthusiasm, which is a practical endeavour to lower the standard of his religious practice, if he saw that his practice already fell short of what plain common sense and decency require from a creature.

But it is remarkable that it is not only the great multitude of men who would find their account, and in truth a thorough reform, in dwelling more habitually on what it is to be a creature and what it is to have a Creator. This is one of the points in which the extremes of holiness meet, its rawest beginnings with its highest perfection. The tendency of the spiritual life, especially in its more advanced stages, is to simplify the operations of the soul. The variety of considerations, the crowd of reasons, the number of heightening circumstances, the reduplicated motives, which characterize the arduous work of meditation, give place to a more austere unity, and a more simple method, and a more fixed sentiment in the loftier practice of divine contemplation. The multiplicity of lights, which filled us with a very trouble of sweetness at the first, grow pale before the one fixed ray of heavenly light which beams upon us as we approach the goal. Hence we find that one common-place truth, which would seem tame and trivial in our meditations, is enough to a saint for long hours of extatic contemplation. This is the reason why we are so often surprised at the apparently exaggerated esteem in which the saints have held certain spiritual treatises, that we in our lower and duller state have condemned as spiritless, or prosy, or uninteresting. The book is but one half the work. The interior spirit of the reader is the other and the better half. And it is this last in which we fail. Thus the very truths which we are considering in this treatise, what it is to be a creature and what it is to have a Creator, have no varied interest or exciting novelty, and yet it is just to these two elementary truths of Christian doctrine that the highest contemplatives return, with all the power of lifelong habits, and of intense prayer, with their intelligence purified by austerities which make us tremble, and with the seven gifts of the Holy Ghost, those mighty engines of spiritual enterprise. Look at St. Francis Borgia, the saint of humility. It seems a less wonderful thing to raise the dead, than to spend, as he did, three hours daily in the absorbing and undistracted contemplation of his own nothingness. Is it easy to conceive how the three times sixty minutes were spent in the embrace of this single and so homely a truth? One ascetical author tells us that it was when St. Francis of Assisi was at the very culminating point of his contemplation that he cried out, "Who art Thou, Lord! and who am I? Thou art an abyss of essence, truth and glory, and I am an abyss of nothingness, vanity and miseries!" Father Le Blanc tells us that chosen souls make much of this truth, and lay great stress on the meditation of it. The B. Angela of Foligno cried out in a loud voice, "O unknown Nothingness! O unknown Nothingness! I tell you with an entire certainty that the soul can have no better science than that of its own nothingness." Our Lord has Himself revealed His complacency in this practice of the saints. He said to St. Catherine of Siena, "Knowest thou, My daughter, who I am and who thou art? Thou wilt attain blessedness by this knowledge.   I am that I am, and thou art that which is not." St. Gertrude thought that of all God's miracles, the greatest was the fact that the earth continued to endure such undeserving nothingness as hers.

The common misapprehensions, which exist with regard to the doctrines of religious vocation, religious orders, and generally what is called priestcraft, may be enumerated also among the mischiefs resulting from the popular oblivion of what it is to have a Creator. It would be difficult to exaggerate the fearfulness of hindering a true vocation, especially when we consider how often, not the perfection only, but the actual salvation of the soul is compromised by its disobedience to the call.   The doctrine of vocation rests upon the fact that we are creatures.   God has an absolute right to us. It is our business to be where He wants us, and occupied in the work He specifies, and we have no right to be anywhere else, or otherwise engaged.   He has ways of making this special will and purpose known to us, which are examined and approved by His church.   Now relatives and others often talk and act as if the question were to be decided by their narrow views and individual tastes.   They say too many people are going into convents in these days, and that domestic circles are being drained of all their piety.   There are not enough secular priests; therefore for the present we must have no more monks.   Active orders are suited to the genius of the day; therefore contemplative vocations are to be discouraged.   They not only overlook the question of the person's own salvation, but they forget that the whole matter turns on a fact, Has God, or has He not, called that particular person to that particular order? If He has not, then we must come to that negative decision in the way the church indicates. If He has, then there is no more to be said. In either case, all those views about orders, and the wants of the present day, are very dangerously beside the purpose. They may at last come to this; nay, they often have come to this:—God wants your brother or your sister in one definite place: you want them in another; and, taking advantage of the natural indecision of their free will, you have got your way, and beaten God. A bitter victory! If forcing vocations is wanton work, and if touting for vocations is the malediction of religious orders, there is hardly any account a man had not better take to his Creator's judgment-seat, than one which is laden with the spoiling or the thwarting of a vocation. All this comes from not recognizing the Creator's absolute right to His creature, and from not clearly perceiving that His will is the one only thing to be considered. The same may be observed of the popular notions of priestcraft. It is enough to say of them, that they are never found apart from a dislike of the supernatural altogether, and an uneasiness and impatience of any interference on the part of God, or of any reference being made to Him.

To the same forgetfulness of what it is to have a Creator may be attributed the wrong principles now so much in vogue, by which we regulate our intercourse with misbelievers. We look at them rather than at God, at their side of the question rather than His; or it would be more true to say that we in reality do our best to betray their interests, because we do not look first at His. Those, who realize what it is to be a creature and what it is to have a Creator, will never make light of any disturbance or interruption in the relations between the Creator and the creature. Every fraction of divine truth is worth more than all the world besides, and every rightful exercise of spiritual jurisdiction is of nobler and more lasting import than all the physical sciences will be when they have pushed their discoveries to the uttermost limits of their material empire. The spurious charity of modern times has stolen more converts from the church than any other cause. While it has deadened the zeal of the missionary, it has fortified the misbeliever in his darkness and untruth, and stunted or retarded in the convert that lively appreciation of the value of the gift of faith, upon which it would appear that his spiritual advancement exclusively depends.

The ancient fathers of the Church seemed to have looked in different ways at the two bodies of men which then lay outside the fold, the heathen and the heretics. They regarded the heathen, with horror indeed, yet still rather with compassion than dislike. They contemplated them as their own future conquest, the raw material out of which by the preaching of the gospel they were to build up an empire for their Lord. They were to them monsters of ignorance rather than monsters of perversity; and with kindliness and yearning, they found no difficulty in detesting the falsehood while they clung tenderly to those who were astray. But they looked on heretics in a very different way. It was less easy to separate their errors from themselves. They had received the truth, and had corrupted it, and a direct, schismatical, and personal hostility to the church actuated them. They had mixed the doctrine of devils with the pure Gospel. They had been guilty of personal treason to Jesus. As Judas was more odious than Pilate, so were heretics more hateful than the heathen. Hence, amidst all their charity and patience and sweetness, the elder Christians looked on heresy with a sternness of spirit which did not actuate them towards the heathen. St. John would not enter the building where Cerinthus was: we find no such thing recorded of him in his intercourse with those who worshipped Diana of the Ephesians. We have no difficulty in recognizing the difference between the two cases, and in understanding the grave charity of the apostle of love. The whole truth, even when preached ungently and with frowardness, is a more converting thing than half the truth preached winningly, or an error condescended to out of the anxiety of mistaken love.

We trust it will not seem a paradox to say, that the great mass and multitude of the English people are to be regarded rather as heathen than as heretics, and are therefore entitled to the more kindly view which the ancient fathers took of those without the fold. So far they are in better case than the heathen, because they possess, at the least implicitly, a belief in so many of the principal doctrines of the Christian faith. The present generation, we speak of them in the mass, have no determinate choice of error rather than truth, no self-will, no obstinate, perverse adherence to the principles of a sect. They have no personal hostility to the church; and the national war-cry of No Popery is no real proof to the contrary. Their religious errors are the traditions of their forefathers, and they know no others. They know nothing of the catholic church. Their ideal church is very like it, though it falls below the reality. But the actual church they have been taught to believe is the enemy of God, and Jesus Christ, and the souls of men. They have no more notion that such a state of things exists on the surface of the earth

as we know the inside of the catholic church to be, than
they know how the angels spend their time, or what
the glory of the third heaven is like.   They look on us,
as an old heathen did, who believed that Christians met
early in the morning to slay infants and to eat their
flesh ; and of such sort is their honest conviction.
Furthermore the consequences of their misbelief has
been a total misconception of God, a misconception
really rather than an ignoring of Him.   They have the
word God, and an idea attached to the word, and a
sense which goes along with the idea; but, if we may
so speak, He is as much a different God from ours, as
the old Christian's Father of our Lord Jesus Christ was
from the Jupiter Tonans of the poor heathen, or the
Primal Cause of the proud philosopher.   Hence, while
we can neither compromise nor conceal the truth, we
may look with the kindest compassion on our fellow-
countrymen, as our future conquest, as the raw materials
for an ardent host of Christians, as poor wanderers in
darkness who want to be taught rather than controverted,
and who above all things desire to have their sins forgiven, if they only knew the way.   But one word, one
look, which goes to show that being in the Church and
being out of the Church are not as fearfully far asunder
as light from darkness, as Christ from Belial, will rob
God of more souls than a priest's life of preaching or a
saint's life of prayer has won.   It is an old proverb that
the worst of all corruptions and counterfeits is the corruption and counterfeit of that which is most excellent.
If charity then, both in heaven and on earth, both for
time and for eternity, is the most excellent of gifts, how
sad must be the desolation, how wide the ruin, how
incurable the wound, of spurious charity, which satisfies

its own worthless good-nature at the expense of God's truth and its neighbour's soul ?

By far the greater number of objections which are urged against the catholic doctrines have their root in this oblivion of the respective positions of creature and Creator. And this is equally true of difficulties which sometimes haunt and harass catholics themselves, and of difficulties which seem to prevent others from receiving the teaching of the church at all. If we remove from the objections urged against the Incarnation, or against the Blessed Sacrament, or against the doctrine of grace, all those which are founded in an inadequate view of God, or are derogatory to His perfections as reason represents them, or to His rights as implied in the very fact of His being our Creator, very little indeed will be left to answer. Neither would it be difficult to show that most of the misconceptions about catholic devotions and practices have their rise from the same copious fountain. All worldliness comes from it. Who would be worldly if he always remembered the world was God's world, not his? And as to sin, it must of necessity be either a forgetfulness of what it is to have a Creator or a revolt against Him.

But—we speak now to more loving souls,—there is another mischief which comes from the same error. In all ages of the world it has been a temptation to good and thoughtful men, and the speculations of modern philosophy have perhaps now increased the number, to take inadequate views of God's love. Nothing is more fatal to the soul, nor more dishonourable to God. The world, with the sun extinguished, and the hideous black moon whirling round our benighted planet, is but a feeble picture of what life becomes to a susceptible conscience which puts

God's love of man too low. Take what views we
will of grace, it must come to this, that the immensity of God's love is our only security.* Because
He is our Creator, He must love us; His love must
be immense; He must compassionately desire the salvation of every one of His rational creatures; He must
grudge every single soul that maliciously eludes the
embrace of His merciful longing, and escapes from Him
into outer darkness; He must do all but offer violence
to our free will in order to save us; His own glory
must, because of His magnificence, be in the multitude
who are saved, and, because of His liberality, it must
also be in the completeness of their salvation.† Nay,
on our view as Scotists, He was incarnate because He
was our Creator, and He is with us in the Blessed
Sacrament because He is our Creator. Even if we
take the Thomist view that the Incarnation and the
Blessed Sacrament were a second love, and because of
sin that second love came out of the first love wherewith He created us out of nothing. True it is, that we
have no name for the feeling with which one must
regard a being whom we have called out of nothing;
we may call it paternal love, or by the name of any
other angelic or human love; and yet we know that it
must be a feeling far transcending, in height, and depth,
and comprehensiveness, in kind, endurance, and degree,
all loving ties which we can conceive. Surely when
reason tells us all was meant in love, and that He who
meant that love was God, we may well trust Him for

* Dieu aime autant chaque homme que tout le genre humain. Le poids et
le nombre ne sont rien à ses yeux. Eternel, infini, il n'a que des amours
immenses.—*Joubert*, i. 103.

† Sicut enim gloria principis sæcularis dicitur consistere potissimum in
splendore et *multitudine* aulicorum, ita externa gloria Dei objectiva a consistit
potissimum in splendore et *multitudine* aulicorum cœlestium.—*Lessius*.

details which we cannot understand, or for apparent
contradictions which should not make a son's heart fail
or his head doubt. Oh uncertain and distrustful soul!
God be with you in those not disloyal misgivings, which
ailment of body or turn of mind seem to make in your
case inevitable! The mystery of Creation is the fountain
of your pains. As it has been your poison, so take it as
your remedy. Meditate long, meditate humbly, on
what it is to have a Creator, and comfort will come at
last. If broad daylight should never be yours on this
side the grave, He will hold your feet in the twilight
that they shall not stumble, and at last with all the
more love, and all the more speed as well, He will
fold you to His bosom who is Himself the light eternal.

BOOK II.

THE DIFFICULTIES OF CREATIVE LOVE.

THE CREATOR AND THE CREATURE

BOOK II.

THE DIFFICULTIES OF CREATIVE LOVE.

CHAPTER I.

WHY GOD WISHES US TO LOVE HIM.

Quid ergo tibi accessit ad bonum quod tu tibi es, etiamsi ista, vel omnino nulla essent, vel informia remanerent, quæ non ex indigentia fecisti, sed plenitudine bonitatis tuæ?—*St. Augustin.*

A CHILD'S first sight of the ocean is an era in his life. It is a new world without him, and it awakens a new world within him. There is no other novelty to be compared with it, and after-life will bring nothing at all like it. A rapid multitude of questions rush upon the mind; yet the child is silent, as if he needed not an answer to any of them. They are beyond answering; and he feels that the sight itself satisfies him better than any answer. Those great bright outspread waters! the idea of God is the only echo to them in his mind: and now henceforth he is a different child because he has seen the sea.

So is it with us when we sit by the ocean of creative love. Questions throng upon us; problems start up on all sides; mysteries intersect each other. Yet so long as we are children, are childlike in heart and spirit, the questions are not difficulties. Either they

9 7

answer themselves, or they do not need an answer, like
questions which are exclamations only, or we would
rather not have an answer, lest peradventure some high
thing should be lowered or some holy thing be made
common. To gaze—to gaze is all we desire. The fact,
that so much is mystery to us, is no trouble. It is
love. That is enough. We trust it. We would almost
rather it was not made plainer. It might be darker if
it were. Whereas now, though it is indistinct, it is
tranquillizing also, like the beauty of a summer night.
We have thoughts which cannot be put into words, but
it seems to us as if they more than answered all difficulties. How the broad waters flow and shine, and
now the many-headed waves leap up to the sun and
sparkle, and then sink down into the depths again, yet
not to rest; and placid as the azure expanse appears,
how evermore it thunders on the hard white sand, and
fringes the coast with a bewitching silver mist! Why
should we ever stir from where we are? To look on
the sea seems better than to learn the science of its
storms, the grandeur of its steadfastness, or the many
moods of its beautiful mutabilities. The heathen called
the sea-spirit father. There was much in the thought.
But when we cease to be children and to be childlike,
there is no more this simple enjoyment. We ask
questions, not because we doubt, but because when love
is not all in all to us, we must have knowledge or we
chafe and pine. Then a cloud comes between the sun
and the sea, and that expanse of love, which was an
undefined beauty, a confused magnificence, now becomes
black and ruffled, and breaks up into dark wheeling
currents of predestination, or mountainous waves of
divine anger and judicial vengeance, and the white surf
tells us of many a sunken reef, where we had seen

nothing but a smooth and glossy azure plain, rocking gently to and fro, as unruffled as a silken banner.

We shall be children once again, and on the same shore, and we shall then never leave it more, and we shall see down into the crystal depths of this creative love and its wide waters will be the breadth and measure of our joy, and its glancing splendour will be the light of our eternal life, and its soft thunder will be the endless, solemn, thrilling music of our beatitule. O happy we! but we must be changed first of all, and perchance by fire!

But we must not altogether cease to be childlike, when we begin to ask and answer questions. Pride can understand nothing about God. We may question then, but it must be in faith and trust and love, content with half an answer when more cannot be given, and to be left without answer at all, when the heights of God's goodness soar beyond all vision but that of faith, whose prerogative it is in some sense to equal and to comprehend its Giver and its Author.

We have endeavoured so far to get some idea of what it is to be a creature and of what it is to have a Creator; and it seems to have taken many words to explain those simple things. Our next step must be to ask and answer, as well as we can, five questions which concern so many wonders of Divine Love; and we shall then be in a condition to examine certain phenomena in the actual life of the world, which seem at variance with our doctrines. Thus, speaking generally, the present treatise may be said to have three parts. The first which stated the case, and which was concluded in the last chapter: the second, which is concerned with the five mysteries of the relation between the Creator and the creature, and which will occupy this and the next

four chapters : and the third, which deals with certain
objections from the state of things in the world, and
which will occupy the ninth, tenth, and eleventh chapters. After which nothing will be left but to close the
work and leave it to the blessing of God and St. Matthew, under whose invocation we have ventured to place
it, and to the judgment and reflection of the reader.
The five questions now to be asked are as follows: 1.
Why God should wish us to love Him; 2. Why He
Himself should love us; 3. What sort of love we have
for Him; 4. In what way we repay His love for us;
and 5. In what way He repays our love of Him. They
are all abysses of creative love, and wonders which
make us wiser even when they refuse to give up the
secrets which they contain.

We have therefore now to enquire why it is that God
wishes us to love Him. At first sight it seems one of
those facts which are so very obvious that we never
think of asking the reason of them. But on reflection
this old and common-place fact unfolds so much that is
strange and wonderful, that we almost unconsciously
ask ourselves if we are quite clear of the fact, if it is
really so completely beyond all doubt that God wishes
us to love Him.

The difficulties, which make us begin almost to doubt
the fact, are some such as these. That God should
wish us to love Him appears to imply some sort of want
in Him. A desire is a kind of confession of imperfection; and according to the strength of the desire so is
the appearance of imperfection and incompleteness.
Yet we know that to attribute any sort of want to the
Creator would be simple blasphemy. Thou art my
God, says the psalmist, *because* Thou desirest none of
my goods. But our love is our greatest good, the

affections of our heart are the noblest of our possessions, and God, we are told, earnestly desires to have them. Besides, if we once grant this fact, we are led into a further difficulty. For immediately this fact assumes such an importance that it becomes the interpretation of all God's doings. Almost all we know of Him has at once to be resolved into this desire. A hundred other difficulties come up and claim to be explained in the same way. We cannot conceive of God except as our Creator, nor of our Creator except as our Father, for creation is unintelligible unless it is defined to be a Free Act of Eternal love, and then everything He does is the act of a Father, and is to be understood by the fact of our being His sons. We see that God cannot, simply because He is God, be moderately good to us. If we grant that He cares for us at all, then forthwith we see that He must care for us so very much, that the vision of it tries our faith. So God cannot desire our love with a weak and indifferent desire. If He desires it at all, He must desire it with all the might of His ever-blessed perfections, and it requires strong faith and stronger love to look at this consequence, and not draw back before its seeming audacity.

If He reveals Himself to us at all, it is because He wants us to serve Him, and as we saw in the last chapter, He being what He is and we being what we are, the creature cannot serve the Creator with any other than a service of love. This is what the Church means when she tells us, that without some love in our repentance, we are incapable of absolution. If He gives us positive precepts or an acceptable ceremonial, it is as a way to Him, because He would fain secure our love. If He sends His Son to save sinners, it is because He vouchsafes to appear as if He cannot make

up His mind to lose the love of men. If He takes us
to Himself in heaven, it is that He may have us with
Him, and feed His glory on our love. For we creatures
cannot be His end: His end must be Himself, and
nothing can exist except for His glory. If He detains
us in purgatory, it is to multiply earth's harvest of
love, and to make a greater profit on imperfect souls.
If, dread thought! He lays us in the hopeless dismal
deep of fire, it is because we have frustrated His yearn-
ings, and refused Him the love He vouchsafed so incomprehensibly to covet.

But this is not all. He seems to forget that He is
God, because of the greatness of this desire. His ever-
blessed Majesty will forgive us words of this sort, by
which alone we can force upon our dull hearts the conviction of the immensity of His love. He appears to
deny His own nature and greatness in order to obtain
our love. Is the facility of pardon consistent with the
rigour of His vindictive justice, or with the spotlessness
of His overwhelming sanctity? Is it easy to see how
He should require the unspeakable sufferings of our
dearest Lord, and should take them as an expiation for
the sins of others, and for sins that were not to be committed till hundreds of years had come and gone? Is
it easy to see why baptized infants should be admitted
to enjoy the Beatific Vision, or to reconcile with our
notions of right that he who came to toil only at the
eleventh hour should receive the same wages with him
who had borne the burden and heat of the day? Does
God seem to legislate so much for His justice, or His
sanctity, or His dignity, as for procuring the greatest
number of souls to love Him, and for rendering the
harvest of redemption as enormous as the perversity of
our free-will allows?

There is a further difficulty in the unintelligible value
which He seems to set upon our love. Think of what
our love is like, and of what good it can possibly be to
God, and then conceive its being worth the price He
paid for it on Calvary! Yet if we do not suppose it
was worth it, we bring a charge against His wisdom,
as if the Incarnation and the Passion were gratuitous
and exaggerated. And it is no answer to say that it
was all for our sakes, and rather a proof of His love for
us, than of His desire for our love. For we must continually bear in mind what sound theology teaches us,
that God alone can be His own end, and not we creatures. He can only bless us for His own glory. It
is His perfection, that He must needs seek Himself
in all things. He would not be God, if it were not
so. We can hardly conceive of God creating, if He
did not set a value upon His own creation. Yet we
could not bring ourselves to believe that God set any
great value upon a few millions of round orbs, or on
their velocity, or on their fidelity to their orbits, or to
their eccentricities, or to the mere vastness of sidereal
space, or to the various structure of matter, or to the
threads of metal in the bowels of the mountains, or to
the vivifying force of the solar ray, or to the gigantic
play of the ubiquitous electricity, or to fine trees, or to
clear lakes, or to sylvan dells, or to the outlines of a sea
coast, or to the gorgeousness of sunsets, or to the pomp
of storms, or to anything whatever of that sort. Even
we creatures should feel that we were lowering Him
in our own estimation, if we thought that He set a
value upon, or took pains with, or had an interest in,
such things as these. Yet we are told that He does
distinctly set a value on the spirits of angels and the
hearts of men. Man is the end of the material world,

but God alone is the end of man. Physical philosophers can love strata of rock, or the distribution of
plants, or a peculiar fauna, or the habits of earthquakes,
or the occultations of stars, or the physical geography of
the sea, or the delicacies of chemistry, more than they
love the hearts of men, the slaves of the south, or the
inmates of a hospital. But God cannot do so. All His
own material creation is worthless to Him in comparison with one peasant's heart, or with one child's first
serious prayer. He has given away with the indifference of interminable wealth, all the rest of His creation;
but hearts He has kept for Himself, and will not even
share them, much less surrender them. Yet where
is their value? What is finite love to an Infinite
Beatitude? Really it is not easy to see. Yet can
we doubt that it is something, and something very
precious in His eyes to whom all things else are nothing
worth?

One difficulty more. What is the meaning of that
surpassing joy which human love causes in God?
Surely this is a profound mystery. The life of God
is joy, joy illimitable, joy ineffable, joy unimaginable,
joy eternal. The whole bewildering immensity of
angelical, and human joy is but a tiny drop out of
the boundless ocean of the joy of God. What a
variety of joys there are in each human heart! No
two of these joys are exactly the same. They differ
as one note differs from another note in music. They
make new joys by new combinations. Different scenes,
different phases of life, different ages, all diversify the
throng of joys which one human heart can experience.
Yet no two hearts are exactly alike; so that the multitudinous joys of the heart are to be multiplied by the
myriads and myriads of hearts, dead, alive, or yet

unborn. Now every one of these joys has its representative in the simple plenitude of the joy of God.
But what are human joys to joys angelical? Yet they
too are all but a manifold umbrage of the one joy of
God. The joys of the animal creation, their joy in
health and strength, in light and air, in cold and heat,
in wet and dry, in their sweet songs or their loud wars,
in their speed of flight or their spring of muscle, in
tending their young or tearing their prey, all are shadows, lowest, dimmest, faintest, poorest shadows of the
joy of God. And who is sufficient to compute these
things? And what if the joys of the Immaculate
Heart of the Divine Mother are to be reckoned also,
and those of that Sacred Heart which the Person of the
Word deluged with its oil of gladness, and yet left it
human still? Yet when we have got so far, we can
hardly be said to have begun. Who can tell the joy
of the Father in His Innascibility, or the joy of the Son
in His eternal and perpetual Generation, or the joy of
the Holy Ghost in His everlasting and incessant Procession from the Father and the Son? The Jubilee of
the Father and the Son is Himself, not a thing or a
perception, but an eternal Person, Himself the illimitable Limit of the illimitable God. Who will dare to
picture to himself the awful and majestic jubilation of
the August Trinity in the Threefoldness of Persons
and the Unity of Essence? God's joy in His own
Oneness,—who can look at it except either he be
stricken with an extasy of rapture, or be dissolved in
tears of believing love? And is all this not enough?
Is God seeking joy, more joy, joy elsewhere? And
is it joy in creatures, created joy? Can His own joy
hold more, can it grow, can it receive, can it want?
If not, why break the silence of eternity to create,

why this hunting after human love, why this ardent
patient pursuit after sinful hearts, why this joy over
returning sinners, why this preciousness in His sight
of the death of His saints? We may indeed ask, why:
but can we give an answer? O heaven and earth!
O angels and men! What a being God is! What a
joy it is to be a creature! What a glory to have a
Creator!

What is to be done with all these difficulties? One
thing is plain. We need not try to answer them. St.
Thomas himself, if he rose from the dead, could not
answer them. But there is one thing to be observed
about them, and it is this. While they are such
difficulties as make us doubt whether God really does
desire our love, they are at the same time irrefragable
proofs of the fact of His desiring it, and of His desiring
it with a most mysterious intensity. They prove the
fact, if they do not account for it; and they prove it in
such a way as that we need not have it accounted for,
in order to receive it. For we can have no doubt about
the fact. But can we approximate to a solution of the
problem? Can we throw any kind of light upon the
mystery? Can we diminish the difficulties which we
confessedly are unable to answer? This must be our
next endeavour; and whether we succeed or not, we
shall at least gain a great amount of additional evidence
to the fact that God does desire our love. We have our
misgivings whether we shall do more than this.

Let us look first of all at the kingdom of nature,
whether Divine, angelical, or human, and see if it does
not disclose to us reasons why God should so yearn
for the affection of human hearts. One reason why
it is impossible for us to comprehend the Divine
Nature, or even to make an imaginary picture of it, is

its extreme and adorable simplicity. Properly speaking, God has no perfections. He is Himself His
own one sole perfection, the perfection of perfections.
What we call the divine perfections are only our imperfect ways of approaching towards a true idea of Him.
Nevertheless we are capable of considering Him as not
our Creator, and then again as our Creator. We know
that although God is immutable, still there was a time
when He had not created us, and again a time when
He had created us. Or if we consider that He had
always created us in His own mind, still we can, from
what He has been pleased to tell us of Himself, conceive of Him as being without any creatures at all. As
a world is the largest thing we know of, a cosmos, an
order, a beauty, all on the vastest scale, so we may
dream of the great God as fourteen worlds in Himself,
of surpassing beauty and variety, yet all without limit
and circumscription, and one, absolutely one in their
own simplicity, although fourteen in our conceptions.

Four of these worlds seem—remember how utterly
short of the mark, and beside it, human words are in
the matter—to contain the inmost life of God. We
call them His Infinity, His Immensity, His Immutability, and His Eternity. They are at once conditions
of His Essence, and of all the perfections which we can
attribute to His Essence. Around them stand four
other worlds, of ravishing loveliness enough to separate
body and soul if we might see them uncloudedly.
They are Omnipotence, Wisdom, Perfection, which is
the natural goodness of God, and Sanctity, which we
may call His moral goodness. Now in these eight
worlds there is not necessarily any respect to creatures.
They belong to the eternal Self-sufficiency of God independent of any creation whatever. They furnish us

with no reason at all why God should desire our love. On the contrary they are so magnificently self-sufficing, so adorably complete, that they are rather so many arguments against the existence of any such unfathomable desire.

Around these eight worlds are six other worlds, to be mentioned only with the wondering humility of filial and more than filial love, worlds which concern ourselves and are coloured by our destinies, worlds in which we ourselves also dwell from eternity, and which are at this hour, and will be evermore, our only country and our only home. They are the Divine Benignity, Dominion, Providence, Mercy, Justice, and that perfection of God which we call His being the Last End of all things. If God were to be conceived without creatures, nothing can be added to the first eight worlds, and nothing taken from them, without His ceasing to be God. If He be conceived as with creatures, as He is actually, then the addition of anything to the whole fourteen worlds, or the subtraction of anything from them, would inevitably alter our idea of God. We may use many other great words of Him, but the meaning of them, the excellence intended by them, is already implied and included in one of these fourteen worlds.

Now the very existence of those six worlds in God of itself will furnish us with most overwhelming proofs of His desire that we should love Him. Yet it does not appear that it in any way accounts for the existence of that desire. And the fact that this desire is founded in the very nature of God, and the very immensity of His perfection, is the more overwhelming when we reflect that, although we can by an arbitrary act of our imagination, conceive God to be without creatures, yet in point of fact He never was so, as He had created the world in His own mind from the beginning : and thus the idea of Creator, and consequently of all that it implies, is inseparable from Him.

The eternity of God before creation is a collection of mysteries, which it is vain for us to sound. In what way His decrees, enclosed in His own mind, ministered to His glory, or gave exercise to His mercy or His justice or His providence, why the primal creation of the angels took place as soon as it did, or why it did not take place sooner, why He,—not broke, not interrupted, not disturbed, all that is impossible— but why He superadded to, the tranquil self-sufficiency of that eternity, not the effort, not the toil, but the fulfilling of His will, in the act of creation, whether the absence of a heaven full of rational and beatified worshippers could in any sense at all add anything to the uncreated solitude of the Three Divine Persons, whether their foreseen worship in His mind, to whom there is no past or future, but only one active unsuccessive present, was precisely the same to Him as its actual existence external to Himself, how it was that this worship did not in any way illustrate or beautify God's perfection in His own esteem,—what can we say of all these things than that they are beyond us: and yet also that they make us feel how astonishingly intimate to God is His desire of His creature's love? Surely in this wide field of colossal miracles, here is fresh proof of the desire, fresh example of its intensity, yet no solution of the enigma.

We have nothing to do here with theological disputes regarding the order of the Divine Decrees. We know that none could have any precedence or priority in respect of time. Their order could be only that

of dignity and eminence. But what a fountain of
affectionate thoughts, thoughts honourable to God in
the highest degree, is opened up in the dark depths of
His mysterious predestination. We know that God is
free, and that nothing can impair the spotlessness of
His transcendent liberty. Yet how can we conceive
otherwise of predestination than as God binding Himself, putting conditions, like fetters, on His own royal
and everlasting liberty ; and for our sakes, out of love
of us, in order to have our love ? Inconceivable
mystery! how can we believe it without a very miracle
of grace and infused faith? Men talk as if it was *their*
liberty which suffered in the act of predestination.
Nay, rather it is the liberty of God. Wayward men!
as if we were to be always suspecting God, always on
our guard against Him, as if He could be infringing
our liberty, who has already given us His glory to make
as free with almost as we please ! How can that act
injure our liberty, when without it, we should not even
have had life? We owe our liberty to our life, and
our life to God's predestination. We are free as air,
only too free, all things considered. But it has puzzled
the wisest understandings of mankind to see how the
magnificent liberty of God rests unimpaired by the
prodigal compassions of His eternal predestination.
But it was as if a necessity were upon Him. Give me
children or I die, said the impetuous Rachel, longing to
be a mother. So, at all costs, God must have creatures
to love Him, sons to honour and to serve Him and to
keep Him immortal company. At any cost He must
have created love, over which to outpour Himself with
a stupendous communication of uncreated love, complacency, and joy.

Hence who does not see that He created all men,

together with all angels, to be saved; and yet by that act He left their freedom unimpaired? Before—we are speaking as words compel us—before He had foreseen aught else, and moved only by the excess of His own unspeakable goodness, He decreed to create the natures of angels and men, simply that He might raise them to the vision of Himself and to participate in His beatitude. He chose no certain number, so as to exclude others. In the adorably real sincerity of His own will, He would have all men, and all angels, saved, and was ready to give, to each and all, the necessary graces. Hence also came that marvellous determination of superabundant love to create both angels and men in a state of grace, that they might the more readily attain to their supernatural end, by beginning with grace instead of having to wait for it. Creation in a state of grace is the wonder of creation doubled. Then when He foresaw the free and wilful demerits of some, and the free loyal correspondence to grace in others, there was no energy in that prevision to secure the condemnation of the first, while His mercy rejoiced already to adorn and set aside the crowns for the second. Nor was it, as we suppose, until after this prevision that there was any absolute election or reprobation. And thus man's liberty was secured throughout: and the result is, that of all the multitudes of those who are lost, not one can attribute his ruin to any predetermining act of God, but simply to their own efforts to free themselves from the solicitudes of His grace, while of all the countless souls and spirits of the blessed, there is not one who does not owe his joy to the eternal predestination of his Maker. And what is all this but another set of evidences to prove the greatness of God's

desire to have our love, while it still leaves deep down
in the abyss of His goodness the reason of this desire ?

If we consider the arrangements of creation and
natural preservation, we shall see that they in like
manner testify to the Creator's desire to excite our
love.   It is impossible to make too much of the fact
that both angels and men were created in a state of
grace. The more we think of it, the more we see that it
is a complete revelation in itself.   Then again there is a
sort of superabundance in our natural gifts. We have so
many more than seem absolutely necessary to our dis-
charging the duties for which we came into the world.
Life is itself an intense pleasure ; so much so that men
prize it above all other things.   The most miserable of
men will hardly part without reluctance with the simple
power of living.   All our natural gifts also are so con-
structed as to be avenues of enjoyment and delight.
There is not a sense, in whose exercise there is not a
keenness and a peculiarity of satisfaction, of which those
who lack that sense, can form no adequate conception.
It requires a soul, either in the strength of its first integrity or in the vigour of supernatural grace, to hold us
back from being swept away by the might of sensual
pleasure.   The exercise of the various faculties of the
mind also open out new sources of the strangest delight
and the most thrilling happiness.   We can think of
and count up a score of different pleasurable feelings
consequent on the use of our minds, not one of which
we can adequately describe in words.   What then shall
we say of the romance and nobility of the affections of
our hearts, those very hearts God so much covets?
Almost as many loves grow in the soil of the heart, as
there are wines in the vineyards of the earth : and has

not the whole world many a time gone wild with their intoxication?

So also in the adaptation of material nature to our dominion, everything is characterized by excessive profusion, by unnecessary beauty. Everything almost has a sweetness beyond and beside its own proper function. The heathen talked of Mother Earth; and truly God has filled her teeming bosom with the milk of more than a mother's kindness. Whether she feeds, or heals, or soothes, or inspires, or simply wins us by the lustre of her physical beauty, she is ever doing more than she promises, and enhances her gifts by the fondness of her ministrations. There is something to make us tremble to see with what fineness of balance, with what nicety of restraint, our Creator tames the huge elements in our behalf, and makes us live at ease amid the bewildering vastness of their operations, and close by the uneasy laboratories of their titanic power. Everywhere, and for our sakes, He governs, not through the catastrophes of violent power, but through the meekness of a patient and a pleasant uniformity. Here is fresh demonstration that He craves our love, and no reason given but the blessed one of His free benignant will.

Once more, before we leave the kingdom of nature, let us look at the way in which the Bible discloses Him to us in successive dispensations. He plants an Eden for His new-made creatures, and then comes to them Himself, and the evenings of the young world are consecrated by familiar colloquies between the creatures and their Creator. He tests their love by the lightest of precepts; and when they have broken it, clear above the accents of a strangely moderate anger are heard the merciful promises of a Saviour.

10. †

Then comes centuries of mysterious strife, like Jacob
wrestling with God by the tinkling waters of the midnight stream.   No sin seems to weary Him.   No waywardness is a match for the perseverance of His love.
Merciful and miraculous interventions are never want-
ing.   No gifts are thought too much or too good, if
the creatures will but condescend to take them.   On
the Mesopotamian sheep-walks, in the Egyptian brick-
fields, in the palm spotted wilderness, among the vineyards of Engaddi, by the headlong floods of harsh
Babylon, it is always the same.   God cannot do without us.   He cannot afford to lose our love.   He clings
to us; He pleads with us; He punishes only to get
love, and stays His hand in the midst; He melts
our hearts with beautiful complainings; He mourns
like a rejected lover or a suspected friend; He appeals
to us with a sort of humility which has no parallel
in human love.   What a character of God we should
draw from the Bible only! and what would it all
come to, but that to win the love of His creatures
was the ruling passion of the Creator?   Oh! horrible
beyond all horrors must the heart be that will not
love God, that particular God of the Bible, the God
of Abraham, Isaac, and Jacob, the Father of our Lord
Jesus Christ!   God desiring, and man withholding,
and then God getting, as it were by stealth or by
caress, less than a tithe of His due from less than a tithe
of His creation, and then as it were spreading Himself
out in a kind of joyous triumph at His success,—is not
this a truthful compendium of the Bible history?

If from nature we turn to grace, we shall find that
the whole resolves itself into a loving pursuit of souls
on the part of God.   We shall meet there the same
evidence of the fact with as little solution of the diffi-

culty. The kingdom of grace, if it is not founded on
the permission of evil, seems at least to imply it; and
the permission of evil is nothing less than the intense
desire of the Creator for the free love of His creatures.
Surely that is what lies at the bottom of this terrific
mystery.   At what a price must He estimate the love
of angels and of men, if He would run so fearful a risk
to gain it? Nay, it could be no risk to Him whose
foreknowledge made all things present to Him.   Every
possible, as well as every actual, consequence of that
permission was vividly before Him, and yet He persisted.   It was worth while.   It was for His glory, and
His glory is our inestimable good.   If evil was not permitted, angels and men would not, according to the
present dispensation, be free. If they were not free,
they could not serve Him with a service of love; for
freedom is necessary to love.   They, whom the sight of
Him now confirms in holiness for evermore, would not
have won their crowns; and therefore a heaven of saints
ready made from the beginning would not in fact have
been, in the same sense that it is now, a service of free
·allegiance and voluntary love.*   Yet what a fearful
venture, rather what an appalling certainty, was that
permission of evil!   The All-merciful saw before Him
the burning abyss, so sadly populous.   It was to Him
a vision of more unutterable horror than it could be
even to the capacious soul of Mary or the keen intelligence of Michael.   Yet onward He drove right through

* A world of reasonable beings, either with ungrowing merits, like those of
the Sacred Humanity, or confirmed in grace from the first, like our Blessed
Lady, is a thing of which we have no experience, and which is opposed to
the divine laws as exhibited in the two creations of which we know, and from
which alone we can argue, and not from the exceptional cases of the Sacred
Humanity or our Lady. We can hardly conceive the permission of evil to
have been simply gratuitous, without any moral reasons in the character of
God.

it, in the plenitude of that greater and more overwhelming goodness wherewith He yearned for His
creature's love. O what clearness of demonstration is
there here in the pitchy darkness of that intolerable
secret!

Then that grave permission came to His eldest sons,
to that primeval world of angels. For one moment they
looked at Him in all the beauty of His kind dominion,
and then they looked at self with its enticing liberty,
and forthwith one whole multitude, a third of that wide
empire, ten million times ten million spirits, a very
universe of loveliness and gifts and graces, made their
irremediable choice, and in the madness of their liberty
leaped into the stunning war of the fiery whirlpool,
far away from the meek paternal majesty of God.
Their irremediable choice! what a thought is that for
us! The angels could not complain. They had had
a marvellous abundance of love. The gifts of their
nature were something beyond our power of imagining.
They were so bright and vast and sure as to be almost
a security in themselves against a fall. They had also
been created in a state of grace, and doubtless of the
most exquisite and resplendent grace. Moreover they
had all perhaps merited immensely by the first act of
love with which they greeted their Creator in the exulting moment when at His dear will their grand spirits
sprung from nothingness. Yet one chance, one only!
Our different experience of God makes us tremble at
the thought. When we broke our light precept, and
forfeited our original integrity, He would not lose us
so. He only redoubled His mercies, and multiplied
our means of salvation; so that it has become almost a
doubt in theology whether we are not better off now
that we have fallen, than we should have been had we

preserved the innocence and rectitude of paradise.
When we consider the various dispensations which
followed the fall, the antediluvian times, the patriarchal
dispensation, the levitical, the Christian, as if God
would still leave us free, yet for all that, and in spite
of fearful losses, would not be baffled in His yearning
for our love, we might almost venture to compare His
infinite Majesty to one of His own insignificant creatures, to the spider who with the same quiet assiduity
of toil is ever repairing its often broken web, still
trusting the same treacherous site, still braving the
same almost inevitable calamities. Can we give any
reason for this, or say more, than that there is a reason
which God has hidden in the greatness of His own
goodness?

The Incarnation, that mystery of the divine magnificence, in which all the intelligible perfections of God
pass in array before us as in beautiful procession,
teaches us the same lesson. If God would have come
to His unfallen creatures, and been borne within the
womb of a human Mother, and have shared our nature,
and have lived among us, and for three-and-thirty
years have unfolded countless mysteries of glory, surpassing even those of the paschal forty days, what can
we say but that it would have been a proof of His
desire for His creature's love, which we could only have
adored in silent thankfulness? A creature the Creator
cannot be; but He will have a created Nature, and
make it unspeakably one with His Divine Person, so
that He may be more like one of us, and heighten our
reverence by the trembling freedoms of our familiarity,
if only He may so enjoy vast augmentations of human
love. If because we fell, He changed the manner of
His coming, if rather than abandon His coming He

plunged His Mother and Himself in a very ocean of
sorrows, if, without humbling us by telling us of the
change, He contentedly took shame for glory, suffering
for joy, slavery for a kingdom, the cross instead of the
crown, what did it all show but that He would still
have our love, and that with ingenious compassion,
which could only be divine, He would take the advantage of our miseries to exalt us all the more, and so win
more abundant love ? If He came only because we had
fallen, if He condescended to be but a remedy for an
evil, if He stooped to fight our battle in person, and in
human flesh, with our triumphant enemy, if the Incarnation was an interference to prevent His own world
from being stolen from Him, if it was a fresh invention
out of the boundless resources of the divine pity, then
still what does it mean but that He would not let us
go, He would not let us lose ourselves, because in His
strangely persevering goodness He would not lose our
love ?

So again what is the Church but His way of rendering the blessings of His Incarnation omnipresent
and everlasting ?   What is the Baptism of infants but
a securing prematurely, and as it were against all
reason, the eternal love of their unconscious souls?
What is Confession, but mercy made common, justice
almost eluded, the most made out of the least?   These
are human words, but they express something true.
What is the sacrament of Confirmation but an act of
jealousy, lest the world should steal from God what He
had already got? What is the sacrament of Matrimony,
but a taking of the stuff and substance of human life,
its common sorrows and joys, its daily smiles and tears,
the wear and tear of its rough and smooth, and elevating
it all by a sort of heavenly transfiguration into a ceaseless

fountain of supernatural and meritorious love? What
is Extreme Unction, but an expression of affectionate
nervousness, if we may so speak, of our dearest Lord,
lest we should fail Him just at the last, when so many
risks are run? What is the sacrament of Order, but
systematising and ensuring a succession of daily miracles, such as consecrations, absolutions, exorcisms, and
benedictions, each one of which is to create, and then
to fertilize, and then to beautify, a little world of
love for Him? Ask the Divine Solitary of the tabernacle why He lives His hermit life amongst us, and
what could His answer be but this—I wait, to show
love and to receive it? But wide as He has made the
ample bosom of His Church, and though He has
multiplied with a commonness, which almost injures
reverence, the potent sacraments, this is not enough.
None must slip through, if He can but help it. None
must be lost except in His despite. There must be
something still left, which needs no priest, something
as wide as air and as free, which men may have when
they cannot have, or at the needful moment cannot
find, the sacraments of His own loving institution.
One thing there is, and one only, and we are not surely
now surprised to find that one thing,—love. If need
be, love can baptize without water, can confirm without
chrism, can absolve without ordination, can almost
communicate without a Host. For, great as are the
sacraments, love is a higher emanation of that priesthood which is for ever according to the order of Mel-
chisedech. How shall we read these riddles, if they
may not mean that God so desires our love, that He
almost tires our attention and outstrips our imagination
by the novelty and profusion of His merciful desires to

secure this marvellously priceless treasure, the puny
love of finite hearts?

There are many difficulties in the doctrine of grace,
as well as in those of predestination and the permission
of evil, which seem to interfere with our perception of
God's love, with its impartiality as well as its completeness. But if we, each of us, remove the cause
from the theological schools to the court in our own
hearts, these difficulties will be greatly diminished, if
not entirely dispelled. Let our own hearts therefore
be the last part of the kingdom of grace which we shall
examine. Can any one of us say that we have not
received numberless graces to which we have not cor-
responded? Have we ever sinned, not only without
its being wilfully done, but also without a distinct resistance to conscience, grace, or contrary inspirations?
If we were to die and be lost at this moment, is it not as
clear as the sun at noon that we have no one to blame
for it but ourselves? Has not our whole life been one
series of merciful interferences on the part of God?
Have there not been many times when our petulance
and waywardness have reached such a point, that we in
like case should have given up our dearest friends, our
closest kindred, as past the possibility of amendment, or
not worth the trouble of reproof? And yet God has
not given us up. His tenderness, His liberality, His
assiduity, His patience, His hopefulness, and if we may
use the word, His extraordinary unprovokedness, have
been beyond all words. And how do we stand at this
hour? We have merited hell. Perhaps we have
merited it a thousand times over. We ought to be
there now, if justice had all its rights. But it is an
unjust world, and God is the grand victim of its injustice. He alone has not His rights. He lets His mercy

do strange things with His liberty. We have merited hell purely of our own free will : nay, we have had to stifle inward reproaches and to make considerable efforts in order to accomplish our own perdition. That we are not yet in hell, that we have actually a good chance of heaven, is simply because God cannot find in His heart to abandon the possibility of our love. In a word, look at yourself, for self is the only thing which concerns you in these difficulties of grace and predestination. Has God ever done you anything but good? Has He not done you an overwhelming amount of good? Has He not simply been so good to you, that you yourself cannot conceive of anything, except the Divine Nature, being so good? Either in kind, or in degree, in manner, or in matter, can you so much as conceive of any created goodness being anything like so good? O merciful God! Thou art too good to us. Thou standest in Thine own light. Thy mercies hide in one another; they go out of sight because they are so tall: they pass unnoticed because they are so deep: they weary our thankfulness because they are so numerous: they make us disbelieve because they are so gratuitous, so common, so enduring. We should more readily have acknowledged what Thou hast done for us, if Thou hadst only done much less!

Are we tired of this evidence, especially when it leaves still unexplained the mystery it so amply proves? This is not the place to discuss the joys of the Beatific Vision, although there is hardly a more tempting province of theology. Nevertheless we can hardly close our case without some consideration of the kingdom of glory, considered in reference to our present enquiry. In the case of a parent or a teacher we judge of the value set upon a particular line of conduct, by the

greatness of the reward promised and actually conferred. Now, if we love God, the reward promised us
is nothing less than the sight of God Himself, face to
Face, not transiently, not as a glorious flash of light
renewed once in ten thousand years to feed our immortality with contentment and delight, but an abiding
Vision, a glory and a gladness, a marvellous rapture of
the will, and an extasy of vast intelligence, for evermore. Think how such a reward transcends all the
expectations, all the possibilities even, of our nature!
How God must love us, and how too He must love our
love, to have prepared for us such joys as these, which
eye has not seen, nor ear heard, nor man's heart
conceived !

We must consider also that although our beatitude,
quite rigorously speaking, does not consist so much or
so directly in love, as in the actual vision of God by
our understandings, nevertheless love is that which immediately follows from it, and which is directly connatural to it. So that it comes to this: our reward is
for having loved God; it is no less a reward than God
Himself, not any of His gifts ; and it is an ability to
love Him infinitely better than we have ever done
before, and also eternally. He takes us to Himself. He
makes us His own companions for evermore. He multiplies Himself in us, and reflects Himself in our beatified
souls, as if it were in so many images of Himself. "In
other created things," says Lessius, "as in the fabric of
the world, and the various degrees of things, certain
thin rays of His divinity shine forth, from which we
can, as it were by a conjecture, learn His power, His
wisdom, and His goodness. But in our minds elevated
by the light of glory and united to Him in the Beatific
Vision, the whole plenitude of the divinity shines

forth, the whole of His beauty softly glows ; so that, although the divinity is one in itself, it is in a marvellous manner multiplied, so that there seem to be as many divinities as there are beatified minds." Love is the reason of the reward, love is the consequence of the reward, love is the conduct rewarded, and the reward itself is love. If we knew nothing more of God than this, need more be known ?

We must not forget also the huge price which this reward has cost our Creator. When we had forfeited it, it required as it were an effort of all His conjoined perfections to recover it for us once again. A God made Man, the shame of a God, the sufferings of a God, the Blood of a God, the death of a God ! Such was the price of what we shall one day enjoy in heaven. What can we do but weep silently ? How do all complaints about the permission of evil and the mystery of election die away, when we think of things like these ! How ungraceful, ungraceful rather than ungrateful, do they seem ! The Incarnation of a God, the shame of a God, the sufferings of a God, the Blood of a God, the death of a God ! That was what I cost ! It is now my daily bread, my daily light, my daily life. I confess that faith is almost overwhelmed with these considerations. O for some corner, the least, the lowest, and the last in the world to come, where we may spend an untired eternity in giving silent thanks to Jesus Crucified !

But, if what God paid was so great, the littleness of what earns it on our part is a mystery almost as wonderful. A Magdalen's love was but a paltry price to pay for a reward so vast. But think of the dying thief ! One act of love, one act of contrition, the brief tardy graces of a death-bed,—what must be the might of our Saviour's Blood when it can concentrate the whole merit of eternal life in such little momentary things as these? If we died at this moment, it is our firm hope that we should be saved; and yet can our hope rest on what we ourselves have done? Is there not something painful in confronting the magnitude of our recompense, with the trifling service we have given God but grudgingly, out of hearts only half weaned from the world, and scarcely weaned at all from self? Surely God must desire our love with an amazing fervour of desire, when He gives so much to have so little in return!

There is one thing more to remark about the Beatific Vision, before we close our case. It is a very obvious reflection, yet perhaps we do not dwell upon it sufficiently, that now, in our fallen state, it is not innocence which earns the sight of God, but love, humble, repentant, penance-doing love. Nay, even in an unfallen or angelic world, it would only be innocence in the shape of love, which could earn the heavenly recompense. Thus also in our journey heavenwards, it is love which takes every step, and love alone. It is not the sharpness of the austerity which merits, but the love. It is not the patience in sickness, or the silence under calumny, or the perseverance in prayer, or the zeal of apostolic labour, which win the crown, but just the love, and the love only that is in the patience and the silence and the prayer and the zeal. Martyrdom without love is unprofitable before God. He has no longing for anything but love. He puts no price on other things. His taste is exclusive. His covetousness is confined to that one thing. O if we could be as simple and as single in our desires as God! He only wants our love, and more of it, and more, and more. Why should not we also want one thing only, to love Him, and to love Him more, and more, and more? Surely if we prayed only for that after which He longs so earnestly, our prayer would not wait for its answer long; and then in His eyes, and who would wish to be so in other eyes? we should soon be like the saints.

We conclude from all these considerations, that of the fact that God condescends intensely to desire our love, there can be no possible doubt; and we think it is more true to say that this fact, that He desires our love, is the foundation of all practical religion, than the equally certain fact that He loves us. We mean that our duties and our love flow more obviously from the one than from the other. The one comes nearer to us than the other. But as to the reason which we are to assign for this desire on the part of our beneficent Creator, we can only say that often in religion the answer to one mystery is another mystery greater than the first. We can find no better answer than this, He wishes us to love Him, because He so loves us. Upon which we are obliged forthwith to ask ourselves the further question, Why does God love us? And this must be the enquiry for the next chapter.

Meanwhile we are not at all disconcerted with the vagueness of our answer, nor with the apparently small result of our enquiry. The fact is, that religious truth is always fruitful and enchanting; and God is our truest enjoyment even already upon earth; and as we shall enjoy Him in heaven, yet never comprehend Him, so it is life's greatest joy on earth to watch the operations of God and to muse upon His wonders, though their meaning is either only partially disclosed to us, or perhaps even hidden from us altogether. Oh is any one so dead in heart, so blighted in mind and aspira-

tion, as to be able to look all this divine love in the
face, and not be won by it to better things ?   Blessed,
blessed God !   Wonderful Father !   Compassionate
Creator !   This mystery of His desiring our poor love
should of itself be a lifelong joy to us in our time of
pilgrimage.   It puts a new face upon the world.   All
things glow with another light.   A feeling of security
comes upon us, like a gift from heaven, and wraps us
round ; and the cold chill goes from our heart, and its
dark spots are illuminated ; and we want nothing more
now, nothing.   Earth has nothing to give, which would
not be a mere impertinence after this desire of God.
Our hearts are full.   We have no room for more.   This
desire of God solves all the problems of our inner life ;
for it at once calms us in our present lowness, and spurs
us on to higher things, and the name of that double
state, the calm and the spur,—what is it but perfection ?
God loves me—God desires my love.   He has asked for
it ; He covets it, He prizes it more than I do myself !
I would fain tell the poor trees, and the little birds that
are roosting, and the patient beasts slumbering in the
dewy grass, and the bright waters, and the wanton
winds, and the clouds as they sail above me, and that
white moon, and those flickering far-off stars, that God
desires my love, mine, even mine !   And it is true,
infallibly true.   O God, Thou art my God because my
goods are nothing unto Thee !   What shall I do ?   If I
may not doubt this mystery, what can I do but die of
love ?   Oh Thou, who in the world above givest us the
light of glory that we may bear to see Thy beauty, give
us now the strength of faith to endure these revelations
of Thy love.

CHAPTER II.

WHY GOD LOVES US.

Nemo amatorum carnalium, etiamsi sit in hoc ultra modum insaniens, sit exardescere potest in amorem dilectæ suæ, sicut Deus effunditur in amorem animarum nostrarum.—*S. Chrysostom.*

If the answer to our first question, why God wishes us to love Him, only resulted in a mystery, we may be sure the answer to this second question, why God loves us, will only bring out a still greater mystery. Nevertheless we must proceed to the discussion of it. Enquiry is more solid and more fruitful in divine things, than the most complete and satisfactory results in human sciences.

The whole creation floats, as it were, in the ocean of God's almighty love. His love is the cause of all things and of all the conditions of all things, and it is their end and rest as well. Had it not been for His love, they never would have existed, and were it not for His love now they would not be one hour preserved. Love is the reading of all the riddles of nature, grace, and glory; and reprobation is practically the positive refusal on the part of the free creature to partake of the Creator's love. Love is the light of all dark mysteries, the sublime consummation of all hopes, desires, and wisdoms, and the marvellous interpretation of God. Light is not so universal as love, for love is in darkness as well as light. Life is less strong than love; for love is the victory over death, and is itself an immortal life. If it pleased God at this moment to destroy the air, the planet would have wheeled but a few leagues eastward before it would have become the home of universal death and desolation. Myriad myriads of warm and joyous lives would have been extinguished in one inarticulate gasp of choking agony. Not only would the streets and fields have been strewn with the suffocated dead, but the birds on the wing would have fallen lifeless to the ground. The deep blue waters of the sea would not have screened their multitudinous tribes from the energy of the destroying edict. The subterranean creatures would have been found out and stifled in the crevices of the rocks, the black waters, or the winding ways beneath the ground. Swift death would have penetrated through the breathing-holes of the earth to the strange fish of Egypt's Artesian wells, and to the fishing-birds of the caverns of Laybach and Carniola. Earth's green vesture would be unrolled, and the fair orb would revolve in space an ugly mass of dull, discoloured matter. Yet this picture of ruin is but a faint image of what would happen if God withdrew into His own self-sufficient glory, and called off that immensity of gratuitous love with which He covers all creation. For the destruction of the air would be but a material desolation. It would not invade the vast kingdoms of moral beauty, of spiritual life, of natural goodness, of infused holiness, of angelical intelligence, or of the beatitude of human souls. As far as creation is concerned, God, as it were, concentrates all His attributes into one, becomes only one perfection, and that one perfection is to us the whole of God: and it is love. God is love, says St. John briefly; and after that, nothing more was needed to be said. He has infinite power, boundless wisdom, indescribable holiness, but to us the power, the wisdom, and the holiness come simply in the shape of love. His justice is one of His most ravishing beauties, but it ravishes us by being such a glorious illumination of His love. What looks like justice far off is but a higher kind of love when we come near. To us creatures His infinity, His immensity, His immutability, His eternity are simply love, infinite, immense, immutable, eternal love.

When we proved God's desire of our love, we at the same time proved undoubtedly His love of us. Reason and revelation, science and theology, nature, grace, and glory, alike establish the infallible truth that God loves His own creatures, and loves them as only God can love. The question is, why He loves us; and our first step towards an answer must be to examine the character and degree of this love. The nature of a thing is often the best explanation both of its existence and its end. Let us see what God's love of us is like.

In the first place, it passes all example. We have nothing to measure it by, nothing to compare it with. The creatures, which God has created, furnish us with ideas by which we can imagine creatures which He has not created. We could not have conceived of a tree, if God had not made one. But now we can imagine a tree which shall be different from any actual tree, either in size, or in foliage, or in flower, or in fruit, or in the character of its growth and outline. So also of an animal, or even of a possible world. Whether we are unable to imagine any possible thing, which shall be more than a combination of certain actual things, or a variety of them, or an excess of them, is a question which we do not touch. God gives us something to build our imaginary creatures upon, because He has

11 †

surrounded us with a countless variety of creatures; and we can judge of imaginary things in poetry, painting, or sculpture, according to the standard of nature. But we have no such help in understanding God's love of His creatures. It is without parallel, without similitude. It is based upon His own eternal goodness which we do not understand.

This leads us to its next feature, that it does not resemble human love, either in kind or in degree. It does not answer to the description of a creature's love. It manifests itself in different ways. It cannot be judged by the same principles. We cannot rise to the idea of it by successive steps of greater or less human love. The ties of paternal, fraternal, conjugal affection all express truths about the divine love; but they not only express them in a very imperfect way; they also fall infinitely short of the real truth, of the whole truth. If we throw together all the mutual love of the angels, of which doubtless among the various choirs there are many nameless varieties, if we cast into one heap all the passionate fidelity and heroic loyalty and burning sentiment of all the husbands and wives, parents and children, brothers and sisters, friends and neighbours, that ever were, ever will be, or in the vast expanse of omnipotence ever can be, our total will be something inconceivably more short of the reality of God's love for us, than the drop is short of the ocean, and the minute of eternity. If we multiply the same total by all the figures we can think of without losing our heads in the labyrinths of millions and billions, we shall not mend matters. When we have come to an end we have not got the shadow of an idea of the degree of fervour with which God loves us. And then if we contrived to comprehend the degree, where should we be in our reckon-

ing? There remains the fact that God's love of us is a
different kind of love from any for which we have got
a name. O how it gladdens our souls to think that
when we shall have been a million of years in the Bosom
of our Heavenly Father, we shall still be sinking down,
deeper and deeper, in that unknown sea of love, and be
no nearer the bottom of its unfathomable truth and
inexhaustible delights!

This is our third feature of it, that not even a glorified soul can ever understand it. The immaculate
Mother of God at this hour is almost as ignorant of it
as we are. Almost as ignorant, for there can scarcely
be degrees in a matter which is infinite. The gigantic
intelligence of St. Michael has been fathoming the depths
of divine love through countless cycles of revolving ages,
longer far than even those seemingly interminable geolo-
gical epochs which men of science claim, and he has
reported no soundings yet. And still these endless
calculations are the happy science of the Blest. Still
the saints on earth, in ardent contemplation, work this
problem which they know beforehand they shall never
solve. And we, who creep upon the ground, what
better can we do than bewilder ourselves in these mazes
of celestial love? For we shall still be learning to love
God more, still learning to wonder more at what He has
done for us, and to wonder most of all at the nothing
which we do for Him. If even they who see God, cannot comprehend His love, what manner of love must it
necessarily be? And yet it is ours, our own possession; and God's one desire is, by hourly influxes of
grace, to increase that which is already incalculable, to
enrich us with an apparently unspeakable abundance of
that whose least degree is beyond the science of arch-.

angels, beyond the glory-strengthened eye of the Mother of God herself!

It is another feature of this love, that it seems so to possess God as to make Him insensible to reduplicated wrongs, and to set one attribute against another. At all costs love must be satisfied. There is nothing like God's love except God's unity. It is the whole of God. Mercy, the most exquisite, tender, delicate, susceptible mercy, must be risked by the permission of evil; and the very risk is but a more beautiful manifestation of it. That choice perfection of the Most High, His intolerably shining, unspotted, simple sanctity, must be exposed to inevitable outrage by the freedom of created wills. Only, love must be satisfied. The most stupendous schemes of redemption shall seem to tax the infinity of wisdom, so as to satisfy justice, provided only that the satisfaction be not made at the expense of love. Love is the favourite. Love appears—Oh these poor human words!—to stand out from the equality of the divine perfections. Yet even love, for love's own sake, will come down from the eminence of its dignity. It will take man's love as a return for itself. It will consider itself paid, by a kind of affectionate fiction. It will count that for a return, which bears no resemblance to the thing to be returned, either in kind or in degree. The mutual love of God and man is truly a friendship, of which the reciprocity is all on one side. Compared to the least fraction of God's enormous love of us, what is all the collective love He receives from angels and from men, but as less than the least drop to the boundless sea? And yet, in the divine exaggerations of His creative goodness, the whole magnificent machinery of a thousand worlds was a cheap price to pay for this.

Hence we may well reckon as a fifth feature of this love, that its grandeur is a trial even to the faith which finds no difficulty in the Blessed Sacrament, nor even in the mystery of the Undivided Trinity. If we have had to work for God as priests, have we not found more men puzzled and tempted by the love of God than by any other article of the faith? Indeed most of the temptations against the faith, when properly analyzed, resolve themselves into temptations arising from the seeming excesses of divine love. We might dare to say that God Himself, in spite of our daily prayer, leads us into temptation by His incredible goodness. It is the excessive love of the Incarnation and the Passion, which makes men find it hard to believe those mysteries. It is the very inundation of love with which Mary is covered, which really makes her a stumbling-block to proud or ill-established faith, or to enquiry which has not yet reached the strength of faith. The Blessed Sacrament is a difficulty, only because it is such an exceedingly beautiful romance of love. If God's love had not as it were constrained Him to tell us so many of His incomprehensible secrets, the doctrine of the Holy Trinity would have been less fertile of objections. We confess it seems to us that he who, on reflection, can receive and embrace those two propositions, that God loves us, and that God desires our love, can find nothing difficult hereafter in the wonders of theology. They exhaust and absorb all the possible objections a finite intellect can make to the incomprehensible dealings of its infinite Creator. O how often in the fluent course of prayer does not this simple fact that God is loving us, turn round and face us, and scatter all our thoughts, and strike us into a deep silence, and repeat itself out loud to us, and the soul answers,

not, and is not asleep and yet is not awake, and then
the truth passes on, and we are left weak in every limb,
and sweetly weary, as if we had been hard at work for
hours upon some deep study or toilsome deed of charity!
We saw no vision : only God touched us, and we shrank,
and now are marvellously fatigued.

Another feature of this love is that it is eternal,
which is in itself an inexplicable mystery. As there
never was a moment when God was not, in all the
plenitude of His self-sufficient majesty, so there was
never a moment when He did not love us. He loved
us not only in the gross, as His creatures, not only as
atoms in a mass, as units in a multitude, all grouped
together and not taken singly. But He loved us individually. He loved us with all those distinctions and
individualities which make us ourselves, and prevent
our being any but ourselves. As the Eternal Generation of the Son and the Eternal Procession of the Holy
Ghost were in God what are called in theology necessary acts ; because without them God would not be One
God in Three Persons; so His eternal love of us was
God's first free act. It was the glorious liberty of
God spreading beyond Himself in the form of creative
love. What is predestination but the determining of
this sweet liberty by almighty love? What is our
election but the eternal embrace of our Creator's unbe-
ginning love? Ever since He was God, and He was
always God, He has been caressing us in the complacency of His delighted foresight. We were with Him
before ever the planets or the stars were made, before
angelic spirit had yet streamed out of nothing, or the
hollow void been bidden to build up millions of round
worlds of ponderous material substance. What must
a love be like which has been eternal and immutable?

And is it simply to be believed that I, a speck in the world, a point in time, a breath of being, fainting back into my original nothingness every moment, only that an act of God's will and influx keeps me in life by force,—that I, most intellectually conscious to myself that I have never of myself done or said one worthy, one unselfish thing, one thing that was not vile and mean ever since I was born,—that I, such as I am, or even such as I may hope to be, have really been loved by God with an everlasting love? Why what mean all those controversies about the counsels of perfection? Is it possible that God's children can be talking together, to see how much they are obliged to do for God, and how little is enough to save them? Yes! yes! eternal love allows even this, brooks even this, and to all appearance is content! If we will not give, God will bargain with us, and buy. O inexplicable love! Thy doings are almost a scandal to be put into words!

Once more. The seventh feature of this love which God bears us, is that it is in every way worthy of Himself, and the result of His combined perfections. It would be of course an intolerable impiety to suppose the contrary. Nay rather, it is the most perfect of His perfections, His attribute of predilection, if we might dare so to speak. If it be a finite love, where is its limit? If it went to the Crucifixion, if it comes daily to the Tabernacle, who can say where it will not go, if need should be? Jesus has more than once told His saints that He would willingly be crucified over again for each separate soul of man. Where can such love stop? If it be a love short of immense, who has ever exhausted it? Who ever will exhaust it? Look at it in heaven at this moment—oh that we too were

there!—it is rolling like boundless silver oceans into
countless spirits and unnumbered souls. How Mary's
sinless heart drinks in the shining and abounding
waters! How the Sacred Heart of Jesus seems to embrace and appropriate the whole gracious inundation in
itself! A few years, and you will be there yourself,
and still the same vast flood of love. Ages will pass
uncounted, and still the fresh tides will roll. Is not this
an immensity of love? O beautiful gateway of death!
thou art a very triumphal arch for the souls whom Jesus
has redeemed.

If His love be mutable, when did it change? Is a
whole past eternity no warrant for its perseverance?
Is not fidelity its badge and token, a fidelity which is
like no created thing, although we call it by a human
name?. If it be not eternal, when did it begin, and
when will it end? The day of judgment, which will
be the end of so many things, will only be the beginning of a fresh abundance of this love. If it were a
love less than omnipotent, could it have created worlds,
could it have assumed a created nature to an uncreated
Person, could it have accomplished that series of marvels required in the consecration of the Blessed Sacrament? Could it have been unhurt by the coldness of
men, or unimpaired by their rebellion? Is it not a
wise love? Shall we dare to say, even of its excesses,
that they are inconsistent with faultless wisdom? Had
its wisdom been at all less than inexhaustible, could it
have accomplished the redemption of mankind as it has
done, could it have distributed grace with such profound and unerring decision, could it have made the
complicated arrangements of a vast universe testify so
uniformly of itself, could it judge the world when the
time shall come? Is it in any way an imperfect love?

Where does it fail? What purpose does it not fulfil?
To whom does it not extend? For what need is it not
sufficient? Is it an unholy love? The very thought
were blasphemy. On the contrary it is the very
highest expression of God's ineffable holiness. Is it
not also a benignant love? a merciful love? a just
love? Is it not a love which directs the whole providence of God, and makes His absolute dominion over
us our most perfect freedom? And finally, is it not
its very characteristic that it should be itself our end,
our reward, our consummate joy in God? Thus it is
the result of His combined perfections, a sort of beautiful external parable of His incommunicable unity.

But not only is love the preacher of God's unity; it
expounds the Trinity as well. Let us confine ourselves
to the single act of Creation. The Eternal Generation
of the Son is produced by God's knowledge of Himself.
The Eternal Procession of the Holy Spirit is produced
by His love of Himself. The Father's knowledge of
Himself produces a divine Person, coequal, coeternal,
consubstantial with Himself. The love of the Father
and the Son produces also a divine Person, coequal,
coeternal, consubstantial with the Other Two, from
whom, as from a single principle, He everlastingly
proceeds. Now see how, with awful distinctness, creation shadows forth and adumbrates this adorable and
surpassing mystery, how the free acts of God outside
Himself are shadows cast by the necessary acts within
Himself! Creation is in a sort a son of God, a mighty
family of sons, expressing more or less partially His
image, representing His various perfections, and all with
sufficient clearness to enable the apostle to say that we
are without excuse if we do not perceive the Invisible by
the things that are seen. Creation is a knowledge of

God, a manifestation of Him given forth by Himself,
and which, when complete, He viewed with divine complacency. But creation is especially a knowledge and
manifestation of God's love; it is His love to us, and
our love to Him. He created us because He loved us,
and He created us in order that we might love Him.
Creation was itself the external jubilee of that immense
perfection, of which the inward jubilee was the everlastingly proceeding Spirit. As the image of God's
perfections, Creation was the faint shadow of that most
gladdening mystery, the eternal Generation of the Son:
and Scripture lays stress on the fact that God produced
the worlds by His Son. As the communication of His
love, and the love of His own glory, Creation also dimly
pictured that unspeakable necessity of the divine life,
the Eternal Procession of the Spirit. We have already
seen that Creation was only and altogether love. As
the Son is produced by the inward uncreated knowledge
which God has of Himself, so is creation the outward
and created knowledge of Himself; and as the Holy
Spirit is produced by the inward uncreated love of God,
so is Creation His outward and created love. Creation
is a mirror of His perfections to Himself, as well as to
His creatures; this must be always borne in mind; and
as He is His own end, and seeks necessarily His own
glory, Creation is His love of Himself strongly and
sweetly attaining its end through His love of His creatures and their love of Him. Perhaps all the works of
God have this mark of His Triune Majesty upon them,
this perpetual forthshadowing of the Generation of the
Son and the Procession of the Spirit, which have been,
and are, the life of God from all eternity. Nature,
grace, and glory, the Incarnation, the Blessed Sacrament, and the Beatific Vision, may thus perhaps all be

imprinted with this mark of God, the emblem, the de-
vice, the monogram, of the Trinity in Unity. And
thus, when the Word has enlightened every man that
comes into the world, and the Spirit has brought all
willing hearts to loving obedience and accepted sanctity,
through the grace of the Sacred Humanity of Jesus, it
is mysteriously written by the apostle, that our Lord
shall deliver up the kingdom to God and the Father,
and the Son also Himself shall be subject in His human
nature unto Him that put all things under Him, that
God may be all in all. The Father has created us, the
Son redeemed us, and the Holy Ghost sanctified us; and
when the Son and the Holy Spirit have brought us from
our wanderings, the Father shall give Himself to us, and
then, as the apostle said to Jesus, It suffices us. Then
will His love be perfected, His most dear will accomplished, and His Creation crowned.

The likeness of Creation to the Generation of the Son
and the Procession of the Holy Ghost is still more
striking, when we come to consider the real nature of
that perpetual and intimate conservation by which God
sustains and preserves all things. Creation and preservation are not two different actions. They can be
separated only in idea. The one is the going on of the
other. It is an opinion which has found favour in the
schools, and which is peculiarly in harmony with the
language of the ancient fathers, that no less an influx
of God is required to preserve a thing in being than to
call it at first out of its original nothingness. In treating of this question theologians necessarily came to
examine the real character of the act of Creation.
Durandus expressly says, "As it is always true in
divine things to say that the Son is ever being begotten
of the Father, so is it true to say of the creature, as

long as it exists, that it has been created and is being
created by God; for the creation of things is the same
act as the preservation of them." Scotus says, " A
thing may be always said to be being created, as long
as it abides, because it is always receiving its being from
God," and he quotes S. Augustine as saying that "with
respect to God a creature is never ultimately made, but
is always being made." Vasquez declares that " the
continuous preservation of things by God is a true creation out of nothing." Molina says, "By the same
influx of an *indivisible* action by which God first conferred being upon an angel, He also now preserves him,
and confers the same being upon him throughout the
whole course of time." Suarez in his metaphysics
teaches the same doctrine. Lessius says, " A created
thing is nothing else than an assiduous creation and
actual production of its being:" and Scotus again marvellously says, " Created essence of any kind is nothing
else than a dependence upon God." It is needless to
point out how this indivisible continuity of Creation
adumbrates the perpetual Generation of the Son, and
the incessant Procession of the Holy Ghost.*

---

* This very interesting question of preservation is discussed by Lessius in
his third book De Summo Bono; and then at greater length in his tenth
book De Perfectionibus Divinis. In the opinion given in the text that creatures bear on them the mark, not only of a Creator, but of a Triune Creator,
I have ventured to differ from De Lugo. The whole subject is one of great
interest; but I cannot do more than advert to it here. It is common with
theologians to regard our Blessed Lady as a world by herself, a sort of exemplar and epitome of creation; and the following passage from F. Binet's
Chef-d'-Œuvre de Dieu illustrates the view I have put forward in the text.
Speaking of our Lady's soul, he says, N'est-elle pas veritablement le miroir de
la Majesté de Dieu, représentant naivement ce qui se passe dans les splendeurs
de l'éternité, où par une generation éternelle est engendré le Fils dans le
sein de son Père, où, par une émanation ineffable, le Saint-Esprit procéde,
du Père et du Fils? *Partie* 1ere. *cap.* 5. *sect.* 11.—See also the conclusion
of S. Thomas in the 45th question, vii. article of the P. Prima. In ratio-
nalibus creaturis est imago Trinitatis; in cacteris vero creaturis est vesti-

Such is the love of God; such its character and its degree. This is the love He is loving us with at this very moment : a love passing all example, a love rising above all created loves, a love which even a glorified spirit cannot understand, a love which seems to govern God, a love that tries our faith from its sheer immensity, a love which is eternal, and a love which is in every way worthy of God Himself, and the result of His combined perfections. Let us pause to think. At this very moment God is loving me with all that love. Lord! I believe; help Thou mine unbelief. O what then are all things else to me? Pain or ease, sorrow or joy, failure or success, the wrongs of my fellow-creatures or their praise,—what should they all be to me but matters of indifference? God loves me: now is the time to die.

But we have next to seek for the reasons of this love. They must be either on our side, or on God's side, or on both. Let us examine our own side first.

The first thing which strikes us is that man is in himself nothingness. His body has been formed of the dust of the earth, and his soul has been directly created out of nothing by God Himself. Consequently we can have nothing original in us to attract this love of our Creator. Nay, the very act of our creation showed that His love for us existed before we did ourselves. Our very being was because of His love. This consideration alone would seem to settle the question of man's independent possession of any title to the love of God. We have simply nothing of our own, nothing but the

gium Trinitatis; in quantum in eis inveniuntur aliqua, quæ reducuntur in Personas Divinas. Since writing the passage in the text I have found the same view in some hitherto unedited works of Ruysbrok, published by Arnswaldt at Hanover, 1848. The treatise is entitled *Spiegel du Seligkeit*.

disgrace of our origin.   There is not a gift of our nature
but, if God loves it, He is only loving what is His own,
and which in the first instance came to us from His
love.   There can be nothing therefore in our own being
to love us for, when that very being is nothing more
than the effect of a pre-existing love.

Moreover, when God had once called us into life, our
extreme littleness seems a bar against any claim to His
love, founded on what we are in ourselves.   We are
only a speck even amidst rational creatures.   What are
we individually?   What is our importance in our
country, or even our neighbourhood?   What is our
moral or our intellectual greatness?   We are almost lost
in the number of men who are now living on the earth.
Our leaving it, which must happen one day, will hardly
be perceived.   We shall leave no gap behind us.   We
shall hardly want a successor ; for what will there be to
succeed to ?   And if we are mere atoms in the huge
mass of men now living, what are we compared to all
the multitudes of men who have ever lived, or the enormous hosts who are yet to live before the judgment-
day?   And after the judgment-day, if God goes on
filling the immensity of space, and the numberless orbs
of the nightly heavens, with new rational creations,
new subjects of the Sacred Humanity of Jesus, more,
angels, or more men, or beings that shall be neither
angels nor men, we shall become imperceptible motes
in the great beams of creative love.*   And even now

---

* The hypothesis hazarded here, and at page 333 of the Blessed Sacrament,
that the creations of angels and of men were possibly the beginnings of creations, and that other planets and fixed stars may be hereafter the seats of
new creations of reasonable beings, eludes some difficulties arising to the
doctrine of Christ's Grace of Headship from previous or contemporary worlds
of such beings.   Yet such an hypothesis is in nowise necessary to the
coexistence of that doctrine with any such actual worlds.   I have since

there are the angels, and who shall tell their number?
For we know that multitudinousness is one peculiar
magnificence of their glorious choirs.   It is even said,
by some, that the lowest choir, which is the least in
number, far outnumbers all the men that shall have
been born from Adam to the day of doom.   What have
we to present to the eye of our Creator but an almost
indescribable insignificance?

If there is anything positive about us at all, it is our
badness.   To our nothingness we have contrived to add
rebellion.   That really is something of our own.   We
have thoroughly mastered with our understandings the
difference between right and wrong, and have deliberately chosen the last and rejected the first.   We have
looked God's commandments in the face, and then broken
them.   Grace has come to us with quite a sensible heat
and force, and we have summoned up our power of will,
and resisted it.   The Holy Ghost has spoken, and we
have listened, and then returned an answer in the negative.   Conscience has proclaimed the rights of duty, and
without so much as taking the trouble to deny the assertion, we have refused obedience to the mandate.   We
have looked calmly at eternal punishment, we have
clearly perceived that nothing short of an omnipotence

learned that in Germany H. Steffern has suggested the same idea in his
Christl. Religions-Philosophie, and Hegel seems to say something very like
it. The reader will understand at once, how intimately this hypothesis is
connected with the Scotist view of the Incarnation. Hence that view has
also come up again among German protestants. Kurz maintained it in the
earlier editions of his Exposition of the Biblical Cosmology, but rejected it in
his third edition, evidently from a total misconception of it. It is upheld
by Liebner, Dorner, Martensen, and Lange, and denied by Thomasius, and
Julius Muller. I venture to think that the more philosophical a man's idea
of creation becomes, the more he will incline to the Scotist view. It is
remarkable that the revival of this view in German protestant theology
should be contemporary with a more enlarged and systematic study of
nature.

of anger has been required for the creation of those
unutterable tortures, and then for an hour of sin we
have braved it all. Time after time we have put God
in one scale, and some creature in the other, and then
of our own will have pressed down the scale, and
made the creature outweigh the Creator. We have
neglected God and outraged Him also. We have at
once disobeyed Him and forgotten Him. We have
both ignored Him and yet have insulted Him as well.
All this is our own. There is no one to share it with
us. Truly we are wonderful creatures, to have done so
much in so short a time, to be able indeed to do such
things at all. Yet are we making out a very promising
case for a title to eternal love ?

We have said, there was no one to share these miserable prerogatives with us. It is true, and yet it is not
true either. For think awhile. Has not Jesus at least
offered to share them ? There have been times when
their real nature, their awful wretchedness, came home
to us, and a world would have been a cheap payment to
get rid of the guilty past. To be a door-keeper in the
house of God seemed then an infinitely better lot than a
thousand years amid the splendours of ungodliness. And
Jesus came to us in one of those times. He offered to take
all this horrible accumulation of rebellion and self-will,
and to make it His own, and to give His sufferings for
it, and to pay His blood to ransom us from the intolerable debt of fire, which we had wilfully and scornfully
incurred. And we were too glad to accept an offer of
such almost fabulous love. And then in a little while,
leaving all that old debt on Him, we left His service
also. We took back our rights; we re-entered upon
the exercise of our unhappy prerogatives; and trampling
mercy underfoot now, in addition to the other divine

perfections we had outraged before, we once more earned for ourselves an endless death, and preferred to the holy love of God the blackness of everlasting fire. And perhaps this process has been repeated a score of times, in our short lives, or a score of scores of times. And certainly such conduct is all our own. An angel never had the opportunity given him of such new choice of evil. Here is the first time in which we come in sight of anything which belongs undoubtedly to ourselves as men ; and it were strange indeed if such excess of guilt should be the blissful cause of such exceeding love.

But if, instead of being such quite incredible sinners, we were equal both in our faculties and our innocence to the highest angels, should we be much better able to establish our right and title to the inestimable love of God? What can we do for God? What can we add to Him? What can we give Him, which He does not possess already, and possess to an infinite extent and with an infinite enjoyment? Is there one of His perfections to which we could put a heightening touch, an additional beauty ? Could we by any possible contribution of ours swell the overflowing ocean of His essential glory? Is there a little joy, however little, which we can give Him, and which is not His already? We could not even be of any real help to Him in the government of the world. If He condescended to make use of our ministrations we should only add to the weight on the shoulder of His omnipotence, not take anything from it. For He would have to concur to every act we did, to every movement we made. He would have actively to fill our nothingness with life, to fortify our feebleness with strength, to illuminate our darkness with His light. The most magnificent of the angels is no help to God. On the contrary, if we may use the word. he is rather a

12   †

drain upon Him.   For the creature thirsts for the influx
of the Creator, and the more capacious his nature the
more vast are his needs, to be supplied from the undi-
minished plenitude of God.   When God lets His creatures work for Him, it is rather that they make more
work for Him to do, as children do when they pretend
to help their father.   It is a condescension, an honour-
ing of the creature, the clearest proof of God's exceeding
love for us.   Thus though St. Michael's brightness daz-
zles us, while we look at it, until we gaze upon it
through the many-coloured veil of a creature's necessary
imperfections, we can see even in him no right or title
to his Creator's love, except the gifts which that love
placed there first of all.   But we are not St. Michael.
We are not magnificent angels.   We are but the most
miserable of men, relapsed sinners, even now perhaps
only half repentant, with a most cowardly repentance.

   If then we must judge of ourselves by human rather
than angelic principles, let us apply these human
measures to our actual service of our Maker.   What is
our service of God like?   What is its worth, what its
true character?   Let us for a moment put aside from
God the consideration that He is God.   He is our
Father, our Master, our Benefactor, our fondly loving
Friend.   In His immense longevity He has been busy
doing us good.   It seems to have been His one occupation.   He lived for us.   We were His end.   Words
cannot tell the amount of self-sacrifice He has made for
us.   He slew an only Son to keep us out of harm.
Figures could not put down the number of graces He
has given and is hourly giving to us.   His life will be
prolonged, not for His own sake, but for ours, some
more centuries, in order that He may go on and complete the sum of His prodigious benefactions.   It is not

easy to tell what He has been to us. We feel that we do not half know it ourselves. Suffice it to say that this ancient earth has never seen a Father like this Father, or a master half so kind or half so like an equal, or a Benefactor more prodigal or more self-forgetting, or a Friend more ardently romantic in his attachment. And we have all this love to return. And how do we return it? A certain amount of pious feeling, a scant obedience of a few easy commandments, a respect for His expressed wishes when they do not too much clash with our own interests, a fluctuating quantity of prayer and of thanksgiving, but which engrosses us so little that we are generally thinking of something else all the time. This is what we do for Him in a very irregular and perfunctory kind of way. And if we ourselves were goodnatured human fathers, should we be satisfied if our sons did as much for us as we do for God, and no more? If a friend of seven years standing repaid thus our love and loyalty, should we not think his friendship and his service almost insulting? Should we not think it so cold, so fitful, so self-seeking, so unjust, that, although charity hopes all things and believes all things, we should consider ourselves justified in saying that it would be utterly impossible, however disposed we might be to waive our rights and to stretch a point, to put a favourable construction upon the conduct of our friend?

But all the while it is God, not merely a friend and benefactor, but God whom we are thus treating, with His ten thousand other ties upon us, and His incomparably greater tenderness, and His absolutely eternal love! O is it not humiliating to think of these things? But we have not yet drunk our vileness to its dregs. While we are thus abusing the long-suffering of God by

our ungraceful slackness, by our injurious coldness, and
by our insulting scantiness of service, we have the
effrontery to persuade ourselves that we are doing some
great thing for Him, that we are almost laying Him
under an obligation to us, and that any one who urges
upon us a higher perfection is a troublesome dreamer, who
is far from doing justice to the reasonable and moderate
profession of piety on which we pride ourselves. And
all this to God, remembering who God is! And all
this after all He has done for us, and is doing now!
And all this, when we have so much of the criminal
past to undo, so much lost time to make up, so much
of actual rebellion to repair and expiate! Surely it
was not too much to say that even on human principles our very service of God is almost insulting, our
very reparations a new affront. If they be not so, to
what is it owing but to the unlimited forbearance of
Him upon whose paternal love experience teaches us we
can with so much security presume?

But if God is His own end, and by a sort of necessity
cannot but seek His own glory in all things, it would
seem as if to be like God would be a legitimate title to
His love. He will look with complacency upon that
which reflects Himself. Still if even on this account
God loved men, it would be a reason rather on His
side than on our own. Nevertheless let us see what
the real truth of the matter is. We are the contradictory of God in almost every respect. To say nothing
of the finiteness and feebleness belonging to us as
creatures, our moral qualities present a more fearful
dissimilarity from His holiness and perfection. We are
deficient in the very virtues which we are able to
acquire, and for the acquisition of which He has given
us special aids of grace. Nay, when He has summed

up all that shall entitle us to the forgiveness of our sins, all that shall win for us the very kindness and favour which we seek from Him, into one simple precept, and told us to forgive if we would be forgiven, and to do to others as we would He, as well as they, should do to us, our corrupt nature finds the simple lesson an infinite hardship in practice. Times have been, alas! who will say those times are not now? when the world's sins have so sickened God that He has repented, immutable though He be, that He ever created man. And now what in all the world does He behold like Himself? Nothing but the grace He has planted there, like an ailing exotic in an uncongenial soil, stunted in growth, with a few pale leaves scarcely hanging on to its boughs, flowering hardly ever, and only under great forcing heat, and bearing fruit in this climate never. Is that the heavenly tree? Who would know it in such woful plight? Of a truth God has much to bear not to be downright offended with the grace He sees on earth, to say little of the nature there, and still less of the prolific sin. We know our own hearts far too well: and can we believe that God can look down from heaven, and see Himself reflected there? Earth has but one consolation. Truly there is something on man's side, something which is man's own, on which God's eye can rest, and love not only what it sees, but be so ravished thereby, that it will pour itself out in floods, and run over, and deluge the universe with light and loveliness; and that sight which is man's own, though it is not in man, is the Blessed Sacrament, where the patience of God securely rests its foot, and the divine anger reposes, and sleeps sweetly, and wakes not to remember its errand of vindictive purity.

There is one characteristic of man which especially

precludes our finding in him the reasons of God's amazing love. It is not exactly sin. It is not precisely any
one of the imperfections to which as a finite being he is
subject. It is rather the combined result of all his
imperfections. He is characterized by meanness.
When we do really great things, we fail in some little
point of them. There is a flaw of meanness running
across our generosity, and debasing every one of its
products. Our love and hatred, our praise and blame,
our anger and our good humour, have all got the same
crack in them, this flaw of meanness. With ourselves,
what is self-deceit but meanness, what is slavery to
bodily comforts, what greediness at meals, what rude-
ness in manners, what personal vanity, what a hundred
idle extravagances of self-praise in which we daily
indulge, what the inexhaustible pettiness of wounded
feeling, but meanness, downright meanness? In our
intercourse with others, what is lying but meanness,
what are pretence, selfishness, irritability, and more
than half the world's conventions, but meanness, syste-
matized meanness? In our relations with God, what
are lukewarmness, and hypocrisy, and self-righteousness, but meanness; what is venial sin but miserable
meanness? Many a man, who has found it hard to
hate himself, when he looked only at his sins, has found
the task much easier when he had the courage to hold
close to his eyes for a good long while the faithful
picture of his incredible meanness. What a piercing,
penetrating vision it is, running all through us with a
cold sharpness, when grace lets us see how low and vile,
how base and loathsome, how little and how sneaking—
forgive the word, we cannot find another—we are in
everything. Everybody seems so good, except ourselves; and we, O so intolerably hateful, so ugly, so

repulsive, such a burden to ourselves! And if this can be made plain to our dull, gross sight, what must it be to the clear penetration of the All-holy Majesty of God?

But surely it is useless going on. We have doubtless by this time lost sight of all claims to love, which we might have fancied we had when we started. It is plain that the reasons for God's love of man are not at all to be found on our side, and therefore they must be on the side of God. If any truth in the world is established, this is. Certainly the extremity of our lowness may be the measure of the height of God's love, but it cannot furnish us with the reason of it. We are often tempted, when reflecting on these matters, to say shortly that God loves us because we are so peculiarly unloveable. This may do well enough for a paradox in the pulpit to strike sleepy auditors; but we must go deeper down than this when we read or meditate.

Now every one of the reasons for God's loving us being on His side, not on ours, is it not remarkable that in our service of God we should feel as if it were a bargain between two more or less equal parties, and that, if we did our share, the other would be held to do his? We do not at all realize the spiritual life as an intercourse where all the duty is on one side, and all the liberality on the other. Yet surely it must be so. If certain things are due to us as creatures, when once we have been created, so that God would not be God, if He did not give them, yet that we were created at all was an immense gratuitous love. If He condescends to make a covenant with us, yet it is of His own free love that He stoops to bind Himself; and again love, eternal love, must first have created us, before we could exist to be parties to a covenant. So that all is love. The analysis of creation resolves itself simply into love. Moreover what would become of us, if God gave us nothing but our due, or if He kept His munificence within the limits of His strict covenant? Is not His love breathing out everywhere, and breaking down our pride into humility, as the summer rain beats down the fragile flower, while we are weighing with minutest scales each ounce, and drachm, and scruple, of the miserable alloy with which we are paying Him under the sweet-sounding name of love?

So far then is clear, that all the reasons for God's love of us are to be found exclusively on His side. No reasons whatever exist on ours. It is still a further enquiry what these reasons are; and one to which we must now betake ourselves. Alas! with our puny minds it is a hopeless inquisition to search through the vast recesses of the Divine Nature to find the reasons of God's love. God Himself is love, simple love; and we may well suppose that if we might question each one of His perfections, the answer from them all would still be love. We are so sure of this that we do not anticipate any difficulty. Yet when we come to make the trial, the results are not altogether according to our expectations.

There are few of God's attributes more beautiful or more adorable than His justice. There is no justice like His, for it is founded on His own divine nature, not on any obligations by which He is bound. Some of the saints have had a special devotion to His justice, and have made it in a peculiar manner the subject of their contemplations. An intelligent creature would rather be in the hands of God's justice, than at the mercy of the most loving of his fellow-creatures. The apostle tells us that the acceptance of our contrition and

the forgiveness of our sins depends upon God's justice.
His distribution of the gifts of nature, grace, and glory,
is the masterpiece of His justice, which alone and of
itself could fill us with gladness and wonder for a whole
eternity. His promises are the children of His justice,
and His fidelity to them is His exercise of that most
royal attribute. It is because His love is so great a
love, that His justice is so perfect and so pure. His
punishments even are at once magnificent to look at, yet
most dreadful to endure, because of the extremity of
their unalterable and comprehensive and truthful justice.
Even the vengeance of our God is a subject which love
trembles to contemplate, but from which it will not turn
away. His justice moreover, even in the acceptance of
our works, is a justice due to His own perfections rather
than to the efforts of our misery; for what He receives
from us is much more His own than ours. And is
there a sight more exalting or more affecting amid all
the wonders of theology, than to see the beautiful, the
faultless rigour of divine justice satisfied to its utmost
demand, its enormous and most holy requirements paid
in full, and its dread loveliness and majestic sternness
worshipped with an equal worship, by the Precious
Blood and the mysterious Passion of our Blessed Lord
and Saviour Jesus Christ, God and Man? He has
hardly begun to know God who has not addicted himself, with humility and fear, his mind hushed and
his heart in his hand, to the study of God's tremendous
justice. But is it there that we can look for the reason
of His love? Was our creation a debt of justice due
to our original justice? Has our use of the gifts of
nature, or our correspondence to the calls of grace, been
such, that we dare to call on God to come and note it
with all His justice, and pay it according to the rigour

of its merits? Listen to the sweet lamentation that
issues evermore from the souls of purgatory through the
breathing-places of the Church on earth—is it not more
true? O Lord, if Thou shalt be extreme to mark what
is done amiss, Lord! who shall abide it? Of a truth
we must be well clothed with the grace and justice of
Jesus, before we shall dare to say with Job of old, Let
Him weigh me in the balance of His justice. Surely if
justice alone were to be concerned, we should look for
punishment rather than for love.

In the seventeenth century a succession of holy men
were raised up in France, who were drawn by the Holy
Spirit to honour with a peculiar intensity and devotion
the sanctity of God, and by the same unerring instincts
of grace they were led to couple with this devotion a
special attraction to the spirit of the priesthood of Jesus.
Let us approach this attribute of sanctity, and see if
we can find there the reason for God's exceeding love
of creatures. God is infinite holiness, because He is
essential purity. Who can stand before the blaze of
such a blinding light? He is holy, because the Divine
Essence is the root and fountain of all holiness. He is
holy because He is the rule, the model, the exemplar of
all holiness. He is holy, because He is the object of all
holiness, which can be nothing else than love of God
and union with Him. He is holy, because He is the
principle of all holiness, inasmuch as He infuses it into
angels and men, and as He is the last end to which all
their holiness is inevitably directed. He is infinitely
holy, because He is infinitely loveable; and as all
holiness consists in the love of God, so God's holiness
consists in the love of Himself. Thus, and what an
adorable mystery it is! the infinite purity of God is
simply His self-love. We know not if a creature can

gain a higher idea of God than is given out by this stupendous truth.

But let us suppose that we are ever so holy, how
will this created holiness stand by the side of that of
God ? He is holy in Himself, and of Himself, holy in
essence, which it is impossible for a creature to be. To
no creature, says theology, can it be natural to be the
Son of God, to be impeccable, to have the Holy Ghost,
and to see the Divine Nature. Our holiness consists in
gifts gratuitously superadded to the feebleness and impossibilities of our finite nature. The holiness of God
is substantial, His own very substance ; ours is but a
quality and an accessary, an illumination of mind and
impulse of will imparted to us by Himself. God is
holy infinitely, both in intensity and in extent. Whereas
we have alas! no words low enough to express the
extreme littleness, the deplorable languor, the soon
exhausted capacity, of our brightest and most burning
holiness. The holiness of God can neither grow nor
be diminished. It cannot grow, because it is already
infinite. It cannot be diminished, because it is His
Essence. Ours is but a speck, whose very nature, hope,
and effort it is to grow. The holiness of Mary might
grow for centuries, with tenfold the rapidity that her
vast merits grew on earth, and at the end she would be
as little near the holiness of God as she is now. God's
sanctity is eternal, ours but of a year or two ; perhaps
it began quite late in life. God's sanctity is unintelligible from its excess of purity and its depths of unspotted
light ; ours alas! a fellow-creature could see through
and appreciate in less than half an hour. The holiness
of God is ineffably fruitful ; for it is the cause which
originates, preserves, sets the example, and gives the
aim, to all created holiness whatsoever. Ours is fruitful

too; for holiness, as such, must be fruitful: but how little have we done, how many souls have we taught to know God and to love Him? If the scandal and edification we have given were put into the scales, which would weigh down the other?

All this is on the supposition that we are as holy as we might be. But we are not so. We are hardly holy at all. And knowing ourselves to be what we are, is it possible for us to conceive that infinite sanctity bade love create us out of nothing, because it was so enamoured of what it foresaw we should become? The holiness of God has no necessary respect to creatures, as His mercy has; and yet, strange to say! it is this seemingly most inimitable of all His attributes, which is expressly put before us as the object of our imitation. We are to be holy because God is holy, and perfect even as our heavenly Father is perfect. Do we then so represent and reflect this sanctity of God, as to become the object of such exuberant affection? If it were only to God's holiness that we might appeal, should we expect to find there the reason of His love? Nay, if we had not truer views of God's equality, could we not more easily fancy omnipotent love required to hinder infinite holiness from turning away from us in displeasure and aversion? What did David mean when he said in the eighty-fifth psalm, first of all, Incline Thine ear, O Lord, and hear me, for I am needy and poor, and then, Preserve my soul for I am holy? He was a man after God's heart: but what manner of men are we? Yet, while he was pleading his own holiness,* it was not to the holiness of God he was appealing; for he adds,

---

* Many commentators suppose him to allude to his consecration as king,

For Thou, O Lord, art sweet and mild, and plenteous in mercy to all that call upon Thee.

Is it the divine beauty which is so in love with us miserable creatures? Yet how shall we search the unsearchable loveliness of God? One momentary flash of His beauty would separate body and soul by the vehemence of the extasy which it would cause. We shall need to be fortified with the mysterious strength of the light of glory, before in the robust freshness of our immortality we can lie and look upon that beauty, tranquil and unscathed. We shall see before us in living radiance, in the light of its own incomprehensibility, in the shapeliness of its own immensity, infinite light and infinite power, infinite wisdom with infinite sweetness, infinite joy and infinite glory, infinite majesty with infinite holiness, infinite riches with an infinite sea of being; we shall behold it not only containing all real and all imaginary and all possible goods, but containing them in the most eminent and unutterable manner, and not only so, but containing them, O breathless exhibition of most ravishing supernal beauty! in the unity of most transcending and majestic simplicity; and this illimitable vision is in its totality the beauty of the Divine Nature; and what we see, though we say *it*, is not a thing, but Him, a Being, Him our Creator, Three Persons, One God. This Beauty is God, the beautiful God! O how we ourselves turn to dust and ashes, nay to loathsome death and corruption, when we think thereon! We are going to say that God has His beauty from Himself, we ours from Him, that His was illimitable, ours almost imperceptible, that His was within, ours borrowed from without, that His could neither grow nor fade, while ours is a vague, uncertain, fluctuating shadow: but is it not more

true to say that we have no beauty whatsoever? O my
heart! my heart! how loudly art thou telling me to
stop; for, as for infinite beauty, unless it might be
infinitely deceived, it could only be repelled by thy
guilt and wretchedness!

Infinite wisdom must strangely have forgotten itself,
if it can be in love with us for our own sakes. The
most fearful thing about the divine wisdom, and that
which makes it so adorable, is that it is God's knowledge of us in Himself. He does not look out upon us,
and contemplate us, like an infinitely intelligent spectator, from without. But He looks into Himself, and
sees us there, and knows us, as He knows all things,
in the highest, deepest, and most ultimate causes, and
judges of us with a truth, the light and infallibility
of which are overwhelming and irresistible. St. Mary
Magdalen of Pazzi examined her conscience out loud
in an extasy, and we look upon it as a supernatural
monument of delicate self-knowledge. But what is the
self-knowledge of an examination of conscience, by the
side of God's instantaneous, penetrating, and exhausting knowledge of us in Himself? That wisdom also
is the capacious abyss in which all the manifold beauties
of possible creatures, and the magnificent worship of
possible worlds, revolve in order, light and number
amidst the divine ideas. And what are we by the side
of visions such as these? As the flood of the noontide
sun poured cruelly upon wounded eyes, so is the regard
of God's knowledge fixed sternly on the sinner's soul.
Oh the excruciating agony it must be, added to the torments of the lost, to feel how nakedly and transparently
they lie in the light of God's intolerable wisdom! Must
not we too have some faint shadow of that feeling? If
the Sacred Humanity of Jesus did not cover our cold

and nakedness and shivering poverty, as with a sacred
mantle, or if we fell out from beneath it into the broad
day of God's unsparing wisdom, we should surely faint
away with fear and terror in the sense of our abject
created vileness. Can we dream then that God loves us
so well, because He knows us so thoroughly? O no!
like little children must we hide our faces in the lap of
our dearest Lord, and cry with half-stifled voice, Turn
away Thy face from my sins, and blot out all my
iniquities! Infinite wisdom has almost taxed itself
with ingenious desires to save our souls and to win
our love; and what, in spite of all its curious array of
graces and inventions, have we become: and how can
that wisdom look upon us and be otherwise than disappointed? And what must disappointment be like,
in God?

That which is most like a limit to omnipotence is
the free will of man: and that which looks most like a
failure in unfailing power is the scantiness of the love
which God obtains from man. We have no words to
tell the power of God. We have no ideas by the help
of which we can so much as approach to an honourable
conception of it. What a boundless field of wild speculation possible creatures and possible worlds open out
to view! Yet all this does not aid us to imagine God's
unimaginable power. Possibility seems to us almost
infinite, so widely does it reach, so much does it imply,
so stupendous is the variety of operations within its
grasp. But a Being who is not bound by impossibility,
to whom the impossible is no limit whatever, to whom
nothing is impossible, what can He be like? We may
heap up words for years, and we get no nearer to realizing what we mean. We have no picture of it in our
minds. Now, if to such terrific power, there could

be great or small, should not we be so small as to be contemptible in its sight, and so it would pass us over? But if we have restrained this grand omnipotence, if we have dared to brave its might, if we have ventured to try our strength with its strength, if we have dared to throw our wills as an obstacle beneath the rushing of its impetuous wheels, should we not expect, if God were only and simply power, that it would tread us out of life, trample us back into our darksome nothingness, and then onward, onward, onward still, upon its swift resplendent way through exhaustless miracles, uncounted worlds, and nameless fields of unimaginable glory?

God is truth, all truth, the only truth. Truth is the beauty of God, and His beauty is the plenitude of truth. Everything is what it is in the sight of God, and it is nothing else. Truth is the character of God's mind, and the perfection of His goodness. All truth in creatures is a derivation from the truth of God. Everything in the divine ideas has a peculiar fitness and congruity which makes it worthy of Him, because it makes it truthful. God is truth, not only in Himself, absolute unapproachable truth, but He is especially truth as He is the exemplar of creatures. Whatever is true in them is so, because it is in accordance with Him as their rule and pattern, or, as philosophers call it, their exemplary cause. The whole truth of creation is therefore in its conformity to God; and whatever is not conformed to Him is a distortion, a horror, and a lie. Yet there is perhaps none of the divine excellencies which more broadly distinguish the Creator from the creature than this of truth, none with which it is more important for us to communicate, and none whose communication is more thoroughly supernatural, or in

which perseverance is more difficult. Moreover so
necessary to creation is this divine perfection in the
Creator, that all creatures might say, by instinct as well
as by inspiration, Let God be true and every man a
liar. But now if truth, the only created truth, is likeness to God, conformity to God, a direct aiming at God,
how far is there any truth in us? How far do we differ
from our original, how do we vary from our pattern,
how do we swerve from the straight line, and are
awkward in the hands of Him who builds the heavenly
Jerusalem after the model of His truth? Must not
truth abhor that which is so untrue, as we know ourselves to be? Is it not the case that many a time in
life the Holy Ghost has wakened us up to a sense of
our exceeding untruthfulness, so that we see our whole
reality fading away in the darkness of hypocrisy, con-
ceit, pretence, vainglory, intentional falsehood, half
deliberate diplomacy, circuitous insincerity, and unin-
tended unavoidable concealments, which yet make us
be all the while acting a part, and seeming to be what
we are not? O we feel all miserable and shameful
with the uncleanness of untruth, and love to think, in
the agony of our self-hatred, that at least the eye of
God sees through and through our dishonourable dis-
guises, and pierces with His rays of light abysses we
ourselves only suspect and do not know, of the most
undignified and monstrous self-deceit! Does God love
us then because we are so truthful?

　　Let us ask our question of one more attribute, and
then we will conclude our search. But how shall we
speak of thee, O beautiful mercy of God? It is mercy
which seems above all things to make us understand
God. While the practice of it in reality makes the
creature like the Creator, it seems to us as if when He
　13　✝

practised it, it made the Creator like the creature. For
it has about it an appearance of sadness and of sympathy, a pity, a self-sacrifice, a pathos, which belong
to the nobility of a created nature. It makes God to
be so fatherly, as if truly He sorrowed for His sons,
and spoke kind words, and did gentle things out of the
exuberant affection of the pain He feels for our distresses and our needs. How shall we define this golden
attribute of mercy? Is it not the one perfection which
we creatures give, or seem to give, to our Creator?
How could He have mercy, were it not for us? He
has no sorrows that want soothing, no necessities that
need supplying; for He is the ocean of interminable
being. Mercy is the tranquillity of His omnipotence
and the sweetness of His omnipresence, the fruit of
His eternity and the companion of His immensity, the
chief satisfaction of His justice, the triumph of His
wisdom, and the patient perseverance of His love.
Wherever we go there is mercy, the peaceful, active,
broad, deep, endless mercy of our heavenly Father. If
we work by day, we work in mercy's light; and we
sleep at night in the lap of our Father's mercy. The
courts of heaven gleam with its outpoured prolific
beauty. Earth is covered with it, as the waters cover
the bed of the stormy sea. Purgatory is as it were its
own separate creation, and is lighted by its gentle moonlight, gleaming there soft and silvery through night and
day. Even the realm of hopeless exile is less palpably
dark than it would be, did not some excesses of mercy's
light enter even there.

What but mercy could have divined the misery of
non-existence, and then have called in omnipotence and
love to build a universe, and fill it full of life? This
was its first essay. Yet, as if in the very instant of

peopling nothingness with angelic and with human life it outstripped itself, and was not content with its mighty work, it raised its creation to a state of grace simultaneously with its state of nature. Then when the human race perversely fell from this supernatural order, and drifted away from God, to deluge the world with grace was not enough for mercy. It brought down from heaven the Person of the Eternal Word and united it to human nature, that so it might redeem the world with the marvels, almost incredible marvels, of a truly divine redemption. Anything therefore might be asked of mercy. It might be asked to furnish the reasons of the Creator's love. Yet, if we may say so, mercy seems to be but one method of His love. His love is somehow wider than His mercy, although His mercy is simply infinite. Mercy is one of His perfections, while love is the harmony of all. Mercy does not tire of us, does not despair of us, does not give over its pursuit of us, takes no offence, repays evil with good, and is the ubiquitous minister of the Precious Blood of Jesus. But love seems more than this. Love fixes upon each of us, individualizes us, is something personal. Love is just and equitable no less than kind, is wise as well as powerful. Love is tantamount to the whole of God, and is co-extensive with Him. Mercy is something by itself. Love is the perfection of the uncreated in Himself. Mercy is the character of the Creator. Mercy pities, spares, makes allowances, condescends. But love rewards, honours, elevates, equalizes with itself. The idea of predilection does not enter into mercy, whereas it is the secret life of love. We do not know; but it does not seem as if mercy quite answered the question we are asking. And yet if mercy is not the reason of God's love, where else shall we find it in His infinity ?

But it is time to close. We have seen with what a love it is that God loves us, and we have asked why it is He loves us. It must be for reasons to be found either on man's side, or on God's side. Not on man's side; for he in himself is nothingness; he is but a speck even amid rational creations. To his nothingness he has added rebellion, and in no way can he add anything to God. Even on human principles his very service of God is almost insulting. He is the contradictory of God in all things, and if he is characterized by any one thing rather than another, it is by pusillanimity and meanness. We have therefore had to look for the reason on God's side; and looking at His chief perfections, one after another, we have hardly found what we were seeking. Infinite justice would lead Him to punish us. Infinite sanctity would turn away from us in displeasure. Infinite beauty would be repelled, and infinite wisdom be disappointed. Infinite power would regard us as contemptible and pass us over. Infinite truth would contemplate us as an hypocrisy and a lie. Finally, mercy all but infinite would tire of us, and it is just the infinity of mercy which does not tire. But love is something more than not being tired.

Why then does God love us? We must answer, Because He created us. This then would make mercy the reason of His love. But why did He create us? Because He loved us. We are entangled in this circle, and do not see how to escape from it. But it is a fair prison. We can rest in it, while we are on earth; and if we are never to know anything more, then we will make our home in it for eternity. Who would tire of such captivity?

God loves us because He has created us. What sort of a feeling is it which the peculiarity of having created some one out of nothing would give us? Who can tell? We suppose it to be a feeling which contains in itself all the grounds of all earthly loves, such as paternal, fraternal, conjugal, and filial; and of all angelic loves besides, of which we know nothing. We suppose it to contain them all, not only in an infinite degree, but also in the most inconceivably eminent manner, and further than that, with an adorable simplicity which belongs only to the Divine Nature. But when we have imagined all this, we see that something remains over and above in a Creator's love, which we cannot explain; but which we must suppose to be a feeling arising out of His having created us out of nothing, and which is what it is, because He is what He is, the infinitely blessed God. This then is our answer: He loves us because He has created us. Certainly the mystery does not fill our minds with light; at least not with such light as we can communicate; but, which is far more, it sets our hearts on fire.

CHAPTER III.

OUR MEANS OF LOVING GOD.

Magna res amor. Nam cum amat Deus, non aliud vult quam amari:
quippe qui ob aliud non amat, nisi ut ametur, sciens ipsos amore beatos
qui se amaverint. O suavitatem! O gratiam! O amoris vim!

S. Bernard.

It has often been the benevolent amusement of sages
and philanthropists to draw pictures of imaginary re-
publics. Sometimes they have placed their ideal citizens in positions unusually favourable for the exercise
of the highest virtues; at other times they have represented the whole duty and happiness of men to consist
in some one virtue, as patriotism or simplicity; or again
these legislators have delivered their imaginary people
from all the restraints and conventions of civilization, in
order that the development of their liberty might take
its own direction and have the fullest play. So we also
might amuse ourselves by conceiving some possible
imaginary world. We might suppose that, when the
day of doom is over, God's creative love will move to
some other planet of our system, and people it with
rational creatures, to serve Him and to glorify His
Name. We might picture to ourselves these creatures
as neither angels nor men; but of some different species,
such as God knows how to fashion. They might preserve their original integrity, and neither fall partially,
as the angels did, nor the whole race, as was the unhappy fortune of man. They would of course be the

subjects of Jesus, because He is the head and first-born
of all creatures.   But their way of worshipping Him
might be quite different from ours.   They might also
be under different material laws ; and different powers
of mind and will might involve varieties of moral obligation very different from those which belong to us·
They might thus be another variety in the magnificence
of Christ's Church.   They might be higher than angels,
or lower than men, or between the two.   They would
be least likely to be lower than men, because then our
Blessed Lord would not have carried His condescension
to the uttermost.   When we have fully pictured to ourselves this possible world, we might curiously descend
into every conceivable ramification of that new planetary
life, and see what the behaviour of these creatures would
be like.   We might watch them in the arrangements of
their social system, in the complications of their public
life, or in the minute habits of their domestic privacy.
We might picture to ourselves their trades and professions, their standards of the beautiful, their arts and
sciences, their philosophy and literature, their rules of
criticism, their measures of praise or blame.   We might
imagine war to be an impossibility of their nature, their
political revolutions to be without sin, their sufferings
not to be penalties of a past fault, or solitude to be to
them the same sort of normal state which society is to
us.   When we had completed our picture, this possible
world would have some kind of likeness to our own,
although it would be so very different, partly because
God would be its Creator, and partly because we could
not paint the picture without copying in some degree
from ourselves.

    This imaginary world would probably however differ
less from ours, than ours would differ from itself, if the

precept of the love of God were fully kept by all the
inhabitants of the world.   Let us try now to put a
picture of this before ourselves.   It need not be altogether imaginary, and it may actually help to realize
itself.   Every man and woman in the world, and every
child as soon as it comes to the use of reason, is bound
by the golden chains of that delightful precept.   Christian or Jew, Mahometan or idolator, all souls in all
their degrees of darkness and of light, are under the
bright shadow of that universal commandment.   Nothing
can be more reasonable.   Every creature was created
by God for God's own sake.   Hence he has nothing to
do but God's work, nothing to seek but God's glory;
and that work and that glory God has been pleased to
repose in love, in the easy service of a rational and yet
supernatural love.   Neither has He left us in uncer-
tainty with respect to the extent of the precept.   Hear,
O Israel, the Lord our God is one Lord.   Thou shalt
love the Lord thy God with thy whole heart, and with
thy whole soul, and with thy whole strength.   St.
Matthew tells us that a doctor of the law said to Jesus,
Master, which is the great commandment in the law?
Jesus said to him, Thou shalt love the Lord thy God
with thy whole heart, and with thy whole soul, and
with thy whole mind.   This is the greatest and the first
commandment.   Where Moses says, with thy whole
strength, St. Matthew says, with thy whole mind.
Thus God is solemnly declared to be the object of our
love, which love is to be distinguished by two characteristics.   It is to be universal: heart, soul, mind, and
strength are to go to it.   It is to be undivided: for it
claims the whole heart, the whole soul, the whole mind,
the whole strength.

Putting it then at the lowest, and setting aside such

heroic manifestations of love as are either the ornaments of a devout piety or the counsels of a high perfection, what is every one bound to by this precept, as
soon as he attains the use of reason? He is bound to
love God better than anything else: he is bound to put
a higher value upon God than anything else: he is
bound to obey all the will of God about him as far as
he knows it : and he is bound, at least in general intention, to direct all his actions to the glory of God. In
his heart nothing can be allowed to come into competition with God. His soul must be engrossed by nothing
short of God. His mind must esteem nothing at all in
comparison with God ; and all his strength must be at
God's service in a way in which it is not at the service
of anything else. Whatever he falls short of all this
from the first day of reason's dawn to the closing hour
of life, he must repair with a loving sorrow based on
God's eternal goodness. This is of simple obligation to
the whole world, through the populous breadth of Asia,
in the crowded coasts and vast cities of Europe, across
Africa from one ocean to the other, from the northern-
most dwelling of America to where its extreme head-
lands face the antarctic ice, and in every island of the
sea and palm-crowned coral reef, both great and small.
It is as much of obligation, more so if it could be more,
as to do no murder. Not a creature of God ever has
entered or ever will enter into His eternal joy, who has
not kept this precept, or by sorrow won his forgiveness
for the breach, except the baptized infants of the catholic
church.

Many considerations may be more startling than this :
but we know of none which are more profoundly serious.
For we must bear in mind that we are speaking, not of
counsel but of commandment, not of perfection but of

obligation, not of possibilities but of necessities. It is
the very alphabet of our religion, the starting point of
our catechism, the first principle of salvation; and
reason claims to join with revelation in imposing this
universal precept on the souls of men.

Does the world keep it? Let us see what it would
be like if it did keep it. We are to suppose that all
the men, women, and children over seven, throughout
the earth loved God always, God supremely, and God
with an undivided heart. The earth might then be
called a world of undivided hearts. It would be the
peculiarity of this planet, of this portion of God's creation, of this fair moonlit garden third in order from the
sun : it would be its peculiarity that it was a living
world of loving human hearts, over which God reigned
supreme with an empire of undivided love. This, we
must use human words, is what God intended, what
God expected, the paradise and court He had prepared
for His Incarnate Son. And if it were so, would it be
less unlike the real world than that imaginary possible
world which we were picturing to ourselves just now?

If all classes in their places, and all minds in their
measure and degree, were loving God according to the
precept, wonderful results would follow. To realize
them we should have to penetrate into every corner of
the world, into every secret sanctuary of life, and watch
the revolution which divine love would bring about.
No one thing would be the same. The world would not
be like a world of saints, because we are not supposing
heroic, austere, self-sacrificing love, but only the love of
the common precept. Voluntary suffering is part of the
idea of the Incarnation, or flows from it: for Christian
austerity is a form of love, which has little in common
with the proud expiating penance of the Hindoo, except

the look. It would not be like an immense monastery;
for all men would be in the world, not leaving the
world; and the world would be a means of loving God,
not a hindrance which our courage must vanquish, or a
snare from which our prudence is fain to fly. There
would be no wickedness to make a hell on earth : yet
earth could not be heaven, because there would be no
vision of God. It would be more like purgatory than
anything else. For the love of God would not hinder
suffering, though it would almost abolish sorrow. But
it would make all men pine very eagerly and very
patiently to love God more, and to see Him whom they
already love so much. The whole earth would be one
scene of religion, not of religious enthusiasm or the
romance of sanctity, but of active, practical, exclusive
business-like religion. Common sense would be engrossed with religious duties. Each man would be
unimpassionately possessed with religion, as if it were
his ruling passion, working powerfully under control.
Yet all this would be within the bounds of the common
precept, not like the sublime preternatural lives of the
canonized saints. Remember—we are not speaking of
what is possible, so much as of what is conceivable.

What a change would come over the political world!
The love of God would be the honest and obvious and
exclusive end of all states and nations. Diplomacy
would fade away into mutual counsel for God's glory,
and having lost all its mystery, it would lose all its
falsehood too. Commercial treaties, questions of boundaries, the rights of intervention—what a new character the love of God would infuse into as many of these
things as it still allowed to live! The mercantile world
how calm and indifferent it would become ! No one
would make haste to be rich. Except food and raiment

and ordinary comforts, we say comforts because, on the hypothesis, men would not be saints, all else of life would be prayer and praise and works of mercy, with confession perhaps for venial sins. The literature of these men would give forth nothing but what was chaste and true, ennobling and full of faith. A daily newspaper, such as we are acquainted with, would be a blissful impossibility. We fear that antiquarian questions might be pursued with somewhat less of zest than now, and possibly fewer sacrifices of life be made to advance the interests of science. A most vigorous reality would enter into and animate everything. Many professions would change their characters: many more would cease to exist. Systems of education would be greatly modified; and prisons and police would disappear from the land. Sessions of parliament would be very short, and little would be said, and very much be done. The tone of conversation would be changed, and a sort of strange tranquillity would come over the race of men, with which energy would not be necessarily incompatible, but under which our energy would be so different from what it is now, that we cannot at all adequately represent it to ourselves.

But in return for this apparent dulness, which might affect some of the things on which our activity at present fastens by morbid predilection, the world would gain much in other ways. How magnificent would be the controversies of such a world! The peace and light of the love of God would elevate the intellect a thousand fold. The products of the human mind would be incalculably more profound and beautiful than now, and the amount of intellectual activity would be immeasurably increased, while a larger proportion of it also would be employed on the higher branches of mental philosophy.

What elevation too, and gigantic progress, would the physical sciences probably receive, as well from the greater cultivation of mental philosophy, as from the reach and grasp of intelligence which more abundant grace would restore to us! Who can believe we should not know much more of nature, and of its mysterious properties, if we knew more of Him who originated them all, and love would teach us more of Him? The sciences of beauty too, how much more beautiful and abundant would they come, when they were called to minister to the sanctuary of God, and not to the mere material indulgences of men! The amount of private happiness would be likewise augmented beyond all calculation. All other loves would be as it were glorified by the love of God, and would be poured out of each human heart with an intensity and an abundance to which sin is now a complete impediment. The moral perfections of our nature would bring forth exquisite and generous fruits, of which we have at present but rare instances at distant intervals. But above and beyond all this, there would be a world of supernatural actions, flowing in incessant streams from every heart, uniting us to God, purifying our commonest intentions, and transforming us day by day into an excellence far beyond ourselves. What must the precept be whose common observance would do so much as this? And yet this precept actually lies upon each one of us at this moment with the most inevitable universality and the most stringent obligation! Surely we must see to this.

Hitherto we have been engaged in two very elementary enquiries: Why does God wish us to love Him, and why does He love us. If God desires us to love Him, there must be some sort of love with which it is

possible and right to love Him. This is obvious. Yet
in the course of our investigations we have come across
so much in ourselves that is little and vile and mean,
that we may be tempted to think that we cannot love
God with any real or acceptable love. It is just here
that God meets our self-abjection, guards it from excess,
and hinders its doing us any injury, by laying upon us
the absolute and essential precept of loving Him with
our whole heart and soul and mind and strength. He
enables us to fulfil this commandment by disclosing to
us a beautiful variety of grounds or motives for our
love, and He makes the fulfilment easy by the many
kinds of love, of which He has made our souls capable,
and which suit the different temperaments of men. So
what we have to do now is to examine our grounds for
loving God, and then the various kinds of love with
which it is happily in our power to love our most merciful Creator.

We must observe, first of all, that the love which is
required of us by the precept is a personal love. None
else will satisfy. It is not the love of the approbation
of conscience, or of the self-rewarding sense of duty, or
of the loveliness of virtue, or of the immensity of our
recompense, or of the attraction which a well ordered
mind has to rectitude and propriety. It is a personal
love, and must be characterized by the warmth, the
generosity, the intimacy, the dominion, and all the
peculiar life which belongs to a personal love, as distinguished from the love of a thing or of a place. It is
the love of a Being, of Three Divine Persons, of God.
He reveals Himself to us in various affectionate relationships, so as to make our love more intensely personal,
more like a loyalty and a devotion, and at the same time
to adapt it better to our human nature.

But when we return the love of another, it very much concerns us to know what kind and amount of love it is which we have to return. At the risk of repetition we must therefore briefly sum up the love of God to man, as theology puts it before us. God's love of His creatures is not the fruit of His mercy, or of any of the Divine Perfections by themselves. His love of us is part of His Natural Goodness ; and His natural goodness is simply the excellence of His Divine Nature considered in itself. God's goodness, we are taught in the catholic schools, is threefold. He is good by reason of the perfection of His nature, and this is His natural goodness. He is good also by reason of His sanctity, and this is His moral goodness. He is good also by reason of His beneficence, which is called His benignity. But in reality this last goodness is simply a part of the first, a necessary consequence of the perfection of His Nature, of His natural goodness; so that love of creatures, or the Divine benignity, is part of the perfection of the Divine Nature. How unspeakable therefore is the value of the love of God, how transcending the dignity with which it invests the poor helpless creature, and how completely does the origin of His love of us, deep down in the primal fountains of the Godhead, simplify Him, and all His condescensions, and His gifts, and His justice, and His anger, to pure and simple love !

Let us follow the teaching of theology a little further. The Divine Nature is a plenitude of perfection, a fulness and a " super-fulness," as St. Denys calls it. Not that God is too full, or can ever cease being filled, but He is eternally filled to overflowing with the true, the beautiful, the magnificent, and the good. Fulness leads to communicativeness. Communicativeness is the

consequence of abundance. It is the necessity of an
overflowing abundance. It seems a law even among
creatures, a shadow of a higher law, that in proportion
as a thing is perfect, it is full of perfection in its own
kind, and longs to communicate itself, and at last breaks
its bound and does communicate itself. This is the case
with human love, human kindness, human knowledge.
Exuberance is an inseparable accompaniment of perfection. So this "super-fulness" of God, this exceeding
plenitude of the Divine Nature, must needs communicate itself, and be eternally communicating itself. This
communication may be of two kinds, the one natural or
necessary, which must be and which must always be;
the other free, which God may withhold, which is a gift,
which is not necessary, but which, when God has once
been pleased to make it, cannot easily be separated from
Him even in idea. We can conceive that there could
have been such a Being as an Uncreating God. But
we cannot conceive what He would have been like.
He would not have resembled our own present God.
He would not have been our Heavenly Father merely
short of Benignity, Dominion, Providence, Mercy, Justice, and of that perfection which makes Him the End
of all things. His natural goodness would have been
different, not less infinitely perfect, but inconceivably
otherwise than it is now.*

As the perfection of the Divine Nature is infinite, so
the communication of it which is natural and necessary
must be infinite as well; and it must have this mysterious and adorable characteristic, that it must communicate itself without multiplying itself; for how can that
which is infinite be multiplied? Hence comes the fecun-

---

* Lessius de Perfect Divin. lib. ix.   Also S. Thomas i. q. xiii. art. 7.

dity of the Divine Nature, considering that Nature in Three Persons, the Father as the Fountain of the Godhead, the Son as the Eternal Knowledge of itself, and the Holy Ghost as its eternal Love of self, as one Essence in Three Equal Divine Persons. From the communicativeness, or fecundity of the Divine Nature, it must necessarily be that the Father ever generates, the Son is ever generated, the Father and the Son ever breathe forth their love as one, and the Holy Spirit is ever being breathed forth. And because of the infinite plenitude of the Divine Nature there can, in this necessary and natural communication of itself, be no sort of inequality, no precedence, no priority, no diminution, no inferiority, no subordination.* These are not mere words. They are God's eternal life. They will be our eternal life as well.

Besides this necessary communication of the Divine Nature, which is natural to it, and inevitable, there is also a free communication of it, an overflow which is a gift, a magnificence deeply appertaining to God's natural goodness, and yet which He could withhold, and still be God. As we call the necessary communication of the Divine Nature its fecundity, so we call the free communication of it, its benignity, both being in fact consequences of God's natural goodness, only the one necessary, the other free. There is no limit to the number of ways in which the Divine Nature may freely communicate itself to intelligent beings ; and each of these ways will represent a different and peculiar rational creation. We only know of two such ways, which have resulted, one in the creation of angels, the other in the creation of men. But there might be as

---

* The reader must distinguish between the Divine Essence communicating itself, and the Divine Essence generating itself, which last is forbidden by the Lateran Council to be said.

14   †

many divers rational creations as there are millions of
starry worlds, or all the stars multiplied a million times.
We cannot venture to suppose that the creations of
angels and men have exhausted the possible modes by
which the Divine Nature may freely communicate itself
to created intellects and to created wills. Creation, if
we may say so, is perhaps only in its infancy; and as God
seems to have an inconceivable love of order, and He, to
whom there is no succession, appears to delight in doing
things successively in realms of time and space, so
when the doom has closed the probation of the family
of man, other creatures may succeed, other natures
people material worlds, or immaterial homes of spiritual
beauty; and so God may go on in His fertile benignity
for evermore. I cannot look at the starry skies, but
this thought comes to my mind like a belief. There
may be rational creatures lower than man, though it
certainly is very difficult to conceive of them. But
even our limited capacities can imagine a perpetual
efflux of rational creations higher than man in almost
numberless degrees. Thus creation is God doing freely,
what in the Generation of the Son and the Procession
of the Holy Ghost He does necessarily. The natural
goodness of God, which is defined to be the excellence
of the Divine Nature, is the single explanation of all
His operations, whether within Himself or without.
So that the same love which evermore " produces" in
God, as theologians speak, the Holy Trinity, made of
its own free will both men and angels, and cherishes
them with an eternal compassion. What a view of creation does not this open out before us ! How is it we can
ever think of anything but God? O how more than
royal is the origin of our immortal souls, and in what
vast destinies does Divine love intend that they should

expatiate for evermore! Earth grows more and more
like a speck as our thoughts ascend: our affections
detach themselves from it more and more. As life
goes on, and life and grace together draws us nearer to
God, earth, in spite of all its affectionate memorials,
becomes only a peopled planet, and nothing more : but
alas! why is it we let slow time do the work which
swift grace would so much better do?

But this account of God's love of creatures does by
no means include all that is to be said of His love of
man. The creation of angels is incomparably more
magnificent than the creation of men. Men are all of
one species. The diversities of the angels are no doubt
specific. Some have thought that as angels do not produce each other, like the fruitful generations of men,
each angel must be a species himself. Others consider,
for reasons this is not the place to enter into, that each
choir consists of three species, which in the nine choirs
of the three hierarchies would make twenty-seven
species. None would doubt but that the hierarchies
and even the choirs must differ from each other speci-
fically. Nay, to us we confess it seems unlikely that
earth with its infinite variety of beasts and birds, of
insects and fishes, should outdo the great angelic world
in this peculiar kind of magnificence, namely, the
multitude of species; and if the specific differences
of the angels are more simple than those of earth, they
would be all the more striking because of their simplicity. Yet in spite of the superiority of the angelic
world, and because perhaps we are less acquainted with
its peculiar prerogatives, men seem to have many indubitable pre-eminences above the angels. The angels
imitate the virginity of the Most Holy Trinity without
its fruitfulness. Man shares in the fruitfulness of God ;

and Mary, a pure daughter of man and whose nature is
merely human, shares at once the fruitfulness and the
virginity of God, and, as His Mother, rules the angels
with queenly supremacy in heaven. This chosen planet
was the scene of the Incarnation and the Crucifixion of
the Son of God. He took man's nature upon Him, not
that of angels. He had a human Mother, a human
Soul, a human Body. He spoke human language, and
had human thoughts. He had human ways about Him,
human habits, gestures, peculiarities, and even infirmities. Furthermore, when the angels fell, He held out
no hand to check them as they went down the frightful
abyss. Man He forgives, not once, or twice, or seventy
times seven times, but many times a day, and all day
long. He stands in a different relation to man, and man
to Him. His love of man comes out of the same
natural goodness, which gives forth His love of the
angels. But His love of us is a different sort of love.
His love of us seems to contain more than His love of
them. At least it has certain peculiarities proper to
itself, a fondness, a clinging to us, a patience with us, a
pursuit of us, an attraction to us, which the pardon of
the Fall and the mystery of the Incarnation do nothing
but exemplify. Whence this predilection for the human
race? Whence this preference, on the part of the
Divine Nature, of human nature over the angelic? Is
it because we are so little and so low? Is it because
the Divine Nature in yearning to communicate itself,
yearned to do so to the uttermost, was not content short of the lowest point of the rational creation,
and that the depth of its abasement was the measure
of its gladness and its love? If so, new creations will
be higher than man, not lower: lower than the angels,
God's eldest born, but higher than that lowest step in

the scale of intellectual creations, whereon the Incarnate
Word has taken His stand that He may embrace all
creations beneath His Headship, and cement all of them
together, the highest with the lowest, as one dominion
pertaining to the Unity of God.

Such is the only picture that we, after trial, have
been able theologically to make to ourselves of the love
of God for man. It is this enormous love which it is
our duty to return. It is not a matter of choice, or of
perfection. It is a question of precept and obligation.
It is a commandment, which we shall be lost eternally
if we do not endeavour to fulfil. Our next step therefore must be to inquire upon what feelings of our human
nature God has engrafted the possibility of our loving
Him, in what channels He has bidden that love to run,
what motives are to actuate it, on what relationships to
Him it is to establish itself. For it will be found
that God is so essentially good that whatever position He
takes up with regard to us is a new right and title to
our love. We do not say that those who are lost will
love Him, but even in their case His mercy has a right
to love, both because punishment was so long delayed,
and because it is now inflicted with so much less severity
than they have both merited and could be supernaturally
strengthened to endure. But in our case, whose
account is mercifully not yet closed, it is simply true
that every relation in which God stands to us furnishes
us with new and constraining motives to love Him with
a fresh and daily beginning love.

First of all, we are God's subjects. There are none
of us who desire to question His dominion. We should
be simply ruined, annihilated, if we were not in His care
and keeping. Obedience to Him is safer and happier
for us than any liberty of which we could dream. He

is our king, and never monarch had so many claims to
enthusiastic popularity as He. His rule over us is the
gentlest we can conceive. It hardly makes itself felt at
all. His omnipresence is like the pressure of the air,
needful to health and life, yet imperceptible. His
government is one of love. His very penalties we have
to wring from Him by repeated treasons, and when they
come they are so disguised in mercy, that on this side
the grave it is hard to discern between chastisement and
love. His facility in pardoning is something beyond
compare. He seems to compromise His own regal
dignity by the profuse liberality with which He uses
His prerogative of mercy. He pardons not only after
the nervousness of trial and the ignominy of conviction,
but He pardons us without mentioning it, without
boasting of it, without warning us, without getting the
credit of pardoning, often as in baptism, and with forgotten sins, without even our acknowledgment of guilt.
Often He seems to forgive before the offence is complete. We sin, half knowing we shall be forgiven. As
to the consequences of our sins to others, it is comparatively seldom that He lays on us the responsibility of
attending to them. He charges His own administration
with that burthen, which of a truth requires a love, a
wisdom, and a power which He alone possesses. No
earthly king was ever like Him in His providence over
His subjects. No angelic monarch could come near
Him in this beautiful perfection. Every want is foreseen. The vast complications both of nature and of
grace fit close to the individual life, shield it from every
danger, penetrate it with a balm and sweetness which
give vigour and delight, and make each man feel as if
the world were made for him alone, and as if he were
rather the last end of God, than God the last end to

him. In the exercise of His royalty, all is equable,
timely, harmonious, pliant; nothing harsh, sudden,
abrupt, disconcerting, or domineering. Surely then,
simply as His subjects, we are bound to a loyalty and
love as warm, and generous, and faithful, as it is easy,
ennobling, and delightful.

But we are His servants also. He is our master as
well as our king. All servitude is full of motives of
humility. Servants, when they forget that they are
servants, cease that moment to be good servants. Yet,
if we thought and felt aright, presumption would be
more likely than abjection to grow upon the thought
that we are in the service of our Maker. The annals
of history give us many beautiful examples of the
attachment, which a noble-minded servant can have for
his earthly master; and the memorials of private life
are full of them all the year round. But what is it
which makes a master so justly dear to a good servant?
It is his considerateness. And who is so considerate as
God? Oh wonderful mystery! see how God always
shows by His manner to us His remembrance of our
little services, a forgetfulness of our slovenly short-
comings, an affectionate exaggerated satisfaction with
what we do, and at the worst a look only of wondering
wounded feeling, when disgrace, reproof, or chastisement would better have fitted our misdeeds! He never
lets us be oppressed with work. He never disregards
our fatigue. He cheers us under failure. It is, if we
must say it, almost the fault of His easy kindness that
we are apt to forget ourselves, to play the master, and
to wonder when He does not wait on us and serve,
though of a truth He seldom fails to change places with
us when we want it. His forbearance is one incessant
miracle. We should not keep a servant a month who

treated us as we treat Him. Awkward, ungracious,
reluctant, it is thus we always meet the courtesies of
His abundant love, which vouchsafes to treat us on equal
terms, lest even the look of condescension should wound
the silly susceptibilities of our childish pride. As to
wages, both those He has bound Himself to give, and
those which come in the shape of frequent gifts, and
perquisites unspecified, the bounty of an earthly master
is to His munificence as the poverty of the creature is
to the wealth of the Creator. Who would not rather
be the servant of such a Master, than to have a whole
world left to himself and to the liberty of his disposal?
Who would care to have creation for his property, when
he may have the Creator for his own?

God is our Friend. It requires an act of faith, and
not a little act, to say so. But so it is; the Infinite,
the Omnipotent, the All-holy is our bosom friend. We
doubt if any human friendship, ever really lasted the
whole of two mutual lives. Few men are habitually
sincere, even with the few whom they love extremely.
Fewer still trust their friends with a perfectly confiding
trust. Nay, friendship shows itself in a morbid readiness to take offence, in petty diplomacies to find out if
injurious suspicions are true, in proud silences which
will not ask for explanations, or in childish breaches
made for the childish excitement of reconciliations.
The truth is, friendship is a romance, that has been
written and spoken a thousand times among men, but
seldom acted, unless in a dramatic way. Thus we pray
proverbially to be saved from our friends, and we say
that a man who has many acquaintances, and few
friends, is at once the happiest and the safest of mankind. There have hardly been a dozen friendships since
the time of Jonathan and David, which could bear the

weight of an awkward-looking circumstance, or a
decently attested report. And friendship at its height,
in the fervour of its fever-fit, what is it but a tyranny?
Our friends think themselves gods, not men, and us their
instruments, the profitable implements of their pleasure,
their ambition, and their will. Friendship is not consecrated by a sacrament as marriage is. Nevertheless
we must have a friend. We shrink from unbefriended
solitude. Yet there is no real friend but God. He is
in His own world almost the solitary example of the
beauty of fidelity. See what a friend He is! He acts
as if He thinks better of us than we think even of
ourselves. He can suspect nothing; for He is God.
He forgives offences as fast as we commit them, and
appears to forget as soon as He has forgiven. His love
is always as fresh to us as it was at the beginning. He
keeps plighting His friendship with us by presents,
whose exuberant variety never tires, while their magnificence and exceeding price outstrip the fondest expectation, and the grace with which they are conferred
removes from the sense of obligation all the feeling of
oppression, and conduces rather to the equal familiarity
of love. Whenever we will we can be friends with God,
and He gives Himself up to His friends with such a
romantic exclusiveness, that we feel as if He belonged
to us alone, and that all of Him was ours.

God is our Father also, and we are the children of
His predilection. Truants and prodigals, no longer
worthy to be called His sons, and yet still His heirs,
still the objects of His most lavish paternal tenderness.
Did ever mother yearn over the cradle of her first-born,
as He has yearned over us? Did ever father make his
children's sorrows more his own than God has done, or
yet leave to them so generously untaxed, and untythed,

the treasures that were theirs? Did ever parental love
remain true love, and yet punish so infrequently as He,
or when it punished, did it with so light a hand or with
a sorrow more reluctant? Can Divine Love quite ex-
culpate itself from the charge of having spoiled us by
its indulgence? Did ever father so consistently or with
such grave affection win his children to repentance by
the sorrow that he showed and by the increased kindness of his manner, as God has melted our hard hearts
and drawn us, humbled yet doubly loving, to His knees
for pardon? Does not each chastisement seem worth
far more than the pain it gives, by the increase of love
and the new inventions of His favour with which He
follows it? O who is such a Father as God is! The
Eternal Father, the Father of our Lord Jesus Christ,
Father of His creatures, the Father from whom all
fatherhood is named in heaven and on earth! When
we think of Him we forget the love of our earthly
fathers; for they hardly look like fathers by the side of
Him.

He is our Creator also, and we are His creatures,
the least and lowest of those who can glorify Him with
a reasonable worship, and yet whom He has loved
above the angels, and chosen to be nigher to Himself.
Here we have no earthly term of comparison whereby
to judge of His surpassing love. He has chosen us;
and choice is the highest act of love. He chose us
when as yet we lay in the bosom of the great void,
distinguishable only to the piercing eye of His preference
and love. He chose us rather than others. He had a
special love for something we by grace might be, and
which others could not be or would not be. It was His
first choice of us. It was eternal. Our likeness lived
in the Divine Mind from everlasting, and was cherished

there with infinite complacency. He prepared a fortune for us, marked out a life, measured our sorrows to us with wise love, and tempered our joys so that they might not be an injury. He gave us a work, clothed us with a vocation, and destined for us a particular crown and place in heaven. We cannot name the thing which is bright and good within us, nor the thing which is attractive and delectable without us, but it comes from our creation. We have to do with it, as being the creatures of the infinitely benignant God. All we are or have is His, together with all we are capable of being and having. That we are not imprisoned in perdition at this moment is simply an interference of His goodness. Our creation is our share of the infinite goodness of God. What should we be without it? Can any love of ours be otherwise than a poor return for such a love as His?

But we are not only God's creatures; we are His elect as well. He made as it were a second choice of us in Jesus Christ. He foresaw our fall. He beheld not only what Adam's fall entailed upon us, but He saw our own actual sins and guilt. He did not exaggerate our shame, but He knew it as not all men and angels together could have known it. He penetrated its unbearable corruption. He laid its loathsomeness all bare before His eyes. It was incredible. Such graces slighted, such inspirations neglected, such sacraments profaned, and with a perversity, a frequency, an ingenuity of aggravating circumstances, so great that perhaps, if we saw the hideous vision all in one, we should fall back and die. Nevertheless it was not enough to repel His electing love. He chose us to be bathed in the Precious Blood of His Incarnate Son. He elected us to a magnificent inheritance of grace, and to the royalties of His Holy Church. By virtue of this election He gave us the gift of faith, and threw open to us the golden gates of the overflowing and joyous sacraments. By His first election He chose us out of nothing to have life : by His second out of darkness to have light. Here again His benignity outstrips all the comparisons of earthly love. When we think who it is that elected us, who we are that He elected, what He gives us through this election, the way in which He gives it, and the end for which He has elected us, we shall acknowledge that His election of us is a tie to be repaid, (and even then what payment is it?) with all the fervour and fidelity of life-long love. For wherefore was it that He chose us? He chose us in Christ before the foundation of the world, that we should be holy and unspotted in His sight, in love !

Can more be said? Yes! there is still another tie which binds us fast to God. It is the end of that whereof creation was the beginning; it is the consummation of God's eternal choice. It is the marriage of our souls with Him. We are His spouses, as well as His creatures and His elect. Indeed we are His spouses, because we are His creatures and His elect. But how can we tell wherein the peculiarity of that intimate union consists? When the saints are betrothed to God, it is by operations of grace so magnificent, by supernatural mysteries so transcendent, that the language in which they are related seems unreal and inflated ; and if such be the Espousals on earth, what will the Marriage be in heaven ? O who shall dare to picture the interior caresses which the soul receives from Him who loved it eternally, and chose it out of nothing in a rapture of creative love ? Who shall dare to fasten in ungainly human words the sort of inex-

pressible equality with God which the soul enjoys, or
her unspeakable community of goods with Him? And
wherefore does He use the word spouse, but to express
this glorious unity? Marriage was made a figure of
the unity of God, and a shadow of Christ's union with
His Church. Its love was to supersede all other ties.
It was to obliterate the father's and the mother's home
from the young wife's heart. It was to ride conqueror
over the fond mother's idolatry for her first-born. Yet
all this is the faintest of shadows, tho feeblest of figures,
to set forth the union of the soul with God! How
shall we love Him as we ought? Rather the question
should be, Can we love Him at all with anything worthy of the name of love? May we even try to love
Him who has loved us with such an overwhelming love?
Must not our only love be speechless fear? No! for it
is the law of all creation, the beautiful, benignant law,
the unexpected, the incredible commandment,—Thou
shalt love the Lord thy God with thy whole soul, with
thy whole heart, with thy whole mind, and with thy
whole strength!

Man's imagination can fly far, and picture the wildest
pictures to itself. But now let it loose to ride upon
the winds of heaven, to search the heights and the
depths, to dream the most marvellous dreams, and to
conceive the most impossible combinations. Can it
picture to itself, can it however dimly and remotely
divine a greater, a more wonderful, a more various, a
more perfect love, consistent with the liberty of the
creature, than the love which God has shown and is
daily showing to the sons of men? Short of His laying
violent hands upon our freedom, and carrying us off to
heaven by force, and then doing fresh violence to our
nature and making it endure and rejoice in the Vision

of God, which without holiness would be intolerable to
us,—short of this, which would be power rather than
love, can we imagine any salvation more complete or
more abundant than that with which God has rescued
man? Count up all that God has done for yourself.
There is your eternal predestination and the creative
love which called you out of nothing; there is your
rational and immortal soul with its beautiful dower of
gifts; there is your marvellous body with its senses,
which is one day to be transformed into surpassing
loveliness, while every sense with its glorified capacities
will pour into the soul such floods of thrilling and
exquisite delights, as it will require the strength of
immortality to bear: there is the whole material world
made for your intellectual or physical enjoyment and
support, so vast and glorious that a little knowledge of
one of its least departments, its minerals, for example,
or its plants, makes a man famous among his fellows:
there is the guardianship of bright and holy angels:
there is your election in Christ by which you now enjoy
the faith and sacraments: there is the giving up by
God of His only Son to take your nature upon Him,
to suffer, and to die, to redeem you from your sins:
there is the gift of His Precious Blood and of His
renewed forgiveness conferred upon you ten thousand
times ten thousand times, since you were seven years
old, nay from the very first hour of your regeneration:
there is His preservation of you, which is simply the
unbroken continuity of your creation, requiring every
moment of day and night, of time and of an eternity
to follow, as much influx from the Most High, as was
needed to call your soul out of nothing at the first:
there are all the special helps, the wisely adapted graces,
and the fresh arrangements of divine tenderness, which

are waiting ready for the hour when you shall come to
die: there is the indwelling of the Third Person of the
Holy Trinity by grace within your soul: and, finally,
there is your immeasurable reward, which is no gift
of God, no immense collection of created pleasures, no
multiplication by millions of the highest human and
angelic joys, but God, the living God Himself. So that,
strictly speaking, as a theologian says, it is not simply
God who is the end of man, but God Possessed, God by
an ineffable communication of Himself become our own
our property, and our enjoyment.

In this catalogue of the demonstrations of love there
are many things so great and so utterly divine that the
unassisted intelligence of the highest angel would never
have suspected them. Yet when once the Incarnation
was revealed, many imaginations might have been based
thereon. We do not know if we could have ventured to
dream of an Incarnation in humility and shame, in
poverty and hiddenness, unless we had been told it.
But if our dearest Lord had lived on earth His three and
thirty years, and then gone away, we think we might
have conceived some possible extensions of His love.
We might have thought it would have been an additional tenderness if He had remained on earth personally
until the day of judgment, that we might minister to
Him, and share the privileges of Mary and Joseph, the
apostles and the devout women in Judea, and have Him
near us sensibly, and thus worship Him as it were at
His own feet. But could we ever have dreamed of the
superabundant way in which He has effected this by
the astounding mystery of the Blessed Sacrament?

We might also have conceived that it would be a
great consolation to have Him still on earth that we
might ask Him for dispensations when we needed them,

that we might have intricate cases of conscience solved
by His unquestionable authority, that we might have
formal permission from Him to carry out our favourite
schemes for His greater glory, that we might receive
absolution from our most heinous sins, that we might
ask Him what difficult passages in Scripture meant,
and that we might hear from His infallible lips the
truth or falsehood of uncertain doctrines.   All this
would have been an immense consolation to us, as it
were a fresh dispensation of His love growing out of
the exuberant mystery of the Incarnation.   But it is
just this, which He has provided for us in the Papacy.
He has given out of His dominion, the plenitude of His
valid jurisdiction to the Holy Father, that we might
have it in our necessities, dispensed with a wisdom which
He guides, with a liberality like His own, and a valid
jurisdiction no whit inferior to His, because it is in fact
His own.   These two congenial mysteries of the Blessed
Sacrament and the Papacy seem to extend the loving-
ness of the Incarnation, as far as our imaginations can
conceive.

But there is a negative which is almost as inconceivable, a consequence which we should have expected to
follow from the Incarnation, which has not followed.
Surely, if, when the Incarnation had been first told us,
with all its prodigal tenderness, its unnecessary sufferings, its fierce deluge of intolerable ignominies, the
various atrocity of its pains, the pleading eloquence of its
spendthrift bloodshedding, we had measured its length
and breadth, its height and depth, to the best of our
ability, we should have expected that henceforth, under
the Christian law, perfection would be an obligation,
that a precept would have been laid upon us all to love
like the saints, and to live lives like theirs.   It would

not have seemed at all a stretch of jurisdiction, if our Lord had commanded very long fasts, frequent self-flag-ellations, voluntary austerities, sleeping on the ground, or painful vigils. We could neither have been sur-prised nor discontented, if in return for what He had done for us, and in likeness and honour of His suffering life, He had forbidden under pain of mortal sin all or most of the amusements and recreations of the world. But we think it is most surprising, in fact it would be incredible to us if the faith did not assure us of it, that the Incarnation and Crucifixion have not added one jot or tittle to the original precept of the love of God, that they have actually diminished instead of multiplied our obligations, that the more incalculably beyond our power of repayment divine love has become, it should in fact be easier to repay it, and that less on our parts will save us, now that so much more has been done on His part for our salvation. We are never weary of wondering at this result of the Incarnation, which is to us at once so unexpected, and at the same time so full of overwhelming love.

The conclusion we draw is this. Theology, with all its numberless and marvellous deductions, enables us to imagine possible things with an almost unlimited power of imagination. Now we have combined all the extremes we could, and conceived the most impossible conjunctures; and we cannot, do what we will, leave man his liberty, and conceive one additional instance of His love which God could give to the human race. We cannot heighten or embellish what is actual, nor can we dream of anything possible to add. The love of God for man exhausts the possibilities of our imagination. Did God mean more than this, did He mean that it had exhausted the possibilities of His wisdom and His

15 †

power, when He says so pathetically in Isaias, O ye
inhabitants of Jerusalem, and ye men of Juda, judge
between Me and My vineyard. What is there that
I ought to do more to My vineyard, that I have not
done to it?

It is this love outstripping all imagination, which
we have to return: and how? There are doubtless
numberless ways in which God can communicate
Himself to created intellects and wills, and each way
will produce a different rational creation, and each
rational creation be capable of loving God in a great
variety of ways. Thus among the angels there may
be thousands of different loves of God, for which we
have neither name nor idea; and all of them are
doubtless extremely beautiful, and highly spiritual.
We are so entangled with matter and material ties
that our love is debased in kind, as well as kept down
in degree. Whereas the angels, having no connection
with matter during their probation, doubtless loved
God in their lowest degree with a purity and a fixity of
contemplation which the highest saints hardly attain
amongst ourselves; though the merits of many saints
may have exceeded those of many angels. Leaving
then the capacious spirits of angels as an unknown land,
we come to the souls of men; and as far as we can
divide one sort of love from another, where in reality
each more or less involves the other, it seems we can
love God with seven different kinds of love, the loves,
namely, of benevolence, of complacence, of preference,
of condolence, of gratitude, of desire, and of simple
adoration. These are as it were so many capabilities of
the human soul; and if the fulfilment of the precept of
love is what concerns us most, both in this world and
in the world to come, the knowledge of these seven

varieties of love must be of the greatest importance to our happiness.

The love of benevolence is one which has been commonly practised by the saints, and often has seemed childish, or at best mere poetry, to those who love God less fervently. There is a strange pleasure in it, from our putting ourselves in an impossible position towards God, in order to confer it on Him. We make ourselves as it were His benefactors, instead of His being ours. We put ourselves on an equality with Him, or even above Him. So it seems. Yet in reality this love of benevolence is the fruit of a holy humility too deep for words, almost too deep for tears. By the love of benevolence we, first of all, wish God to be more perfect, if it were possible, than He really is. Yet what a wild impossibility! But if God's love of His creatures is itself so exaggerated, He must let us love Him with the simplicity of these fervid exaggerations. Moreover this habit of wishing God impossible perfections, is not only the result of a more worthy and true appreciation of His perfection and His majesty, but it tends also to produce it, to sustain it, and to increase it. It is at once the cause and the effect of honourable thoughts of God. Another while the love of benevolence takes the form of venturesome congratulations. We wish God all the immense joy of His unimaginable perfections. We know that He possesses it without our wishing it. We know that our wishes cannot swell by one drop the mighty sea of His interior jubilation. But it is an expression of our love, not in words only but in inward sentiment, which in His sight is an act, and a meritorious act. We bid Him rejoice. We wish Him countless happy returns of that eternal festival, which He has in His own blissful self. Or, another while, by the same love of benevolence, we wish Him all increase of His accidental glory; and our wish is efficacious prayer, and obtains for Him a real augmentation of that particular glory. The very wish of itself adds to it, and adds immensely when it comes out of a pure heart and a fervent spirit. It also obtains grace for others, and makes the cause of God to prosper in the world. Sometimes we earnestly desire that He may have accidental glory which He does not receive. We wish that purgatory were emptied into heaven, or that there were no hell, or that all the heathen were converted, or that all wanderers might return to the fold, or that some one day or night there might be no mortal sin in all our huge metropolis. All this, which the saints have reduced to as many practices as there have been saints to practise it, is the love of benevolence.

The love of complacence is of a different disposition. It is content with God. It not only wants nothing more, but it only wants Him as He is. It is adapted to different moods of mind, suits other characters, or meets the changeful dispositions of the soul, which now needs one class of sentiments and now another. Complacence fixes its eye upon what it knows of God, with intense delight and with intense tranquillity. It rejoices that He is what He is. It tells Him so. It tells it Him over and over again. Whole hours of prayer pass, and it has done nothing else but tell Him this. O sublime childishness of love! O most dear repetition, how far unlike the vain repetitions of the heathen, which our Lord reproved! Then it broods over its own joy. It slumbers over its own heart, a sweet and mystical repose, and wakes to renew its oft-told tale. Then a change comes over its spirit. A new strain of

music steals out from its inmost soul. It rejoices that
none else is like to God. It rejoices with Him in His
unity, one of His own deepest and most secret joys.
It exults that none can come near it. It asks all the
hierarchies of creation with a boastful certainty, vaunt-
ing in its triumph, Who is like unto the Lord our God?
There is none other God but He. But its eloquence
has so touched its own heart, that it becomes silent
once again. It leans on God, and at last seems lost in
Him, absorbed in quiet gladness and a rapture of holy
thought. Thence once more it wakes, and seeing there
is none like unto God, simply because He is God, and
for no other cause, it bursts forth into passionate re-
joicings, that He is not only what He is, but always
has been, always will be what He is, that He is of a
truth, and shall be, and must be, and alone can be,
eternally and victoriously God. These are the delightful occupations of complacent love.

The love of preference, or of esteem, hardly aims so
high. It is more mixed up with thoughts of creatures.
But it thinks of them only to despise them, and to
insult them with its intelligent contempt. It compares
God with all other things, as if it had tried them,
convicted them of falsehood, and grown weary of their
vanity. It tramples them underfoot, and makes steps
of their ruins whereby it may rise to God. Their
nothingness grows upon it. It becomes disabused.
Earthly ties no longer hold it down from heaven.
Detachment is its characteristic grace. It passes un-
resistingly over the world, as a swallow skims the green
meadow, and seems to have no need of resting. Hence
it comes to appreciate God rightly, because it appre-
ciates Him incomparably above all other things. It
began by terms of comparison, and ends by seeing that

nothing can compare with Him, and that all comparison is foolish, because He is infinite, eternal, and all-
holy.   It gives God His right place in the world, which
the multitude of men do not give Him.   What is
practical religion but giving God His right place in
our heart and in our life?   The misery of the world
is that God's rights are disallowed.   This it is which
makes it such a desolate and weary land.   It is the
confusion of the world which tires a loving heart and
a quiet spirit.   It is all a kind of base anarchy.   Words
and things not passing current for their right values
and their true acceptations; importance attaching to
the wrong things; darkness unaccountably held to be
light; everything just sufficiently out of its right place
to make a tumult all around it, and yet so nearly right
that we chafe because we cannot right it:—it is all
this which the love of preference remedies, by esteeming God, not as He deserves to be esteemed in Himself,
but as He deserves to be esteemed in competition with
creatures.   This love expresses itself by the energetic
abundance of its good works, by its active zeal, by a
most intense hatred of sin, by a neglect of comforts,
by sacrifice, and by austerity.   These are its natural
vents, and they at once depict its character.   It is
a love, which, while it worships all the attributes of
God, delights above all things to extol His sovereignty.

The love of condolence differs widely again from this.
It looks upon God as wronged, and outraged, and in
sorrow, as if He needed help, and were asking for an
ally.   Its tendency is to wed His interests, and to
become strangely susceptible about His honour.   Its
eyes are opened to see what common men cannot see.
It beholds God concerned and implicated, where others
cannot perceive so much as a vestige of religion being

in question. It sees God everywhere, as if His omnipresence had been made visible to it, like the whiteness
of the light or the blueness of the sky. It is a jealous
love, and considerately inconsiderate, so that men are
apt to take umbrage at it. It is very discreet but not
with a discretion which the world approves. Its discretion leads it to keep awake itself, and to awaken
others, lest God should pass by unseen, and men should
not uncover as He passed. It mingles its own cause
with God's, and speaks of the two in the same breath
and in the same way, as David does in the psalms. It
seeks God rather than looks at Him, and follows Him,
delighted with the humblest servitudes. It has one
life-long grief, like Mary's dolours; and that grief is in
the abundance and effrontery of sin. Sin is a sharp
pain to it. It does not make it angry, but it makes
it weep. Its heart sickens with the goings on of men,
and it tries to shroud God in the light of its own
affectionate compassion. It has no anger with sinners.
On the contrary it has quite a devotion to them. Our
Lord's passionate, piteous, complaining love of sinners,
as it is depicted in the divine Dialogue of S. Catherine
of Siena, is the food of its soul. The Sacred Heart is
the object of its predilection. It is ever telling God
how sorry it is for sin. It has a grand gift of abiding
contrition for its own sins, and takes a holy pleasure in
self-revenge. It lends God its eyes to weep rivers day
and night for sins that are not its own. The seven
dolours of Mary are as seven lives of sweet sorrow
which by grace it may lead, to soothe God for the
transgressions of His children. The gift of piety, that
peculiar gift of the Holy Ghost, moulds its spiritual
life, and its attitude towards God is eminently filial.
The atmosphere of its heart is a spirit of reparation;

and it lets its life, secretly yet usefully and beautifully, waste away, like sweetest aromatic gums, in sighs and tears before the offended Majesty of God. O happy they who love with such a love! for they have reached that height of virtue which the philosopher saw only as an ideal before him, to feel pleasure and pain, when and where we ought! O sweetest of all noviciates for heaven! to have their hearts on fire on earth, burning the sweet perfumes of human love before the throne of the Incarnate Word! To them, true dovelike souls, especially belongs that tender benediction, Blessed are they that mourn; for they shall be comforted.

It is to be observed of the four kinds of love already described, that their characteristic is disinterestedness. It is not that self is expressly excluded, as a false spirituality would teach, but that it is undeveloped. It is not rejected, but it is passed over. In the next two kinds of love it occupies, and without reproof, a much more prominent position.

If the quiet eye and the profound heart of the contemplative Mary delights in that love of condolence, which is such a favourite love with cloistered souls, the love of gratitude better suits the external diligence of the active Martha. The love of gratitude is preeminently a mindful love. It ponders things and lays them up in its heart, as our Blessed Lady did. It meditates fondly on the past, as Jacob did. It sings of old mercies, and makes much of them, like David in the psalms. It enters largely into the composition of the Missal and Breviary of the Church. Where another has the memory of his sins continually before him, a soul possessed with the love of gratitude is perpetually haunted by a remembrance of past benefits; and his abiding sorrow for sin is a sort of affectionate and self-reproachful reaction from his wonder at the abundant loving-kindness of God. The hideousness of sin is all the more brought out, when the light of God's love is thrown so strongly on it. Hence it comes to pass that a very grateful man is also a deeply penitent man; and as the excess of benefits tends to lower us in our own esteem, so we are humble in proportion to our gratitude. But this love does not rest in the luxurious sentiment of gratitude. It breaks out into actual and ardent thanksgiving; and its thankfulness is not confined to words. Promptitude of obedience, heroic effort, and gay perseverance, these are all tokens of the love of gratitude. It is loyal to God. Loyalty is the distinguishing feature of its service. It is constantly on the look out for opportunities, and makes them when it cannot find them, to testify its allegiance to God; not as if it was doing any great thing, or as if it was laying God under any obligation, but as if it was making payment, part payment and tardy payment, by little instalments, for the immensity of His love. It is an exuberant, active, bright-faced love, very attractive and therefore apostolic, winning souls, preaching God unconsciously, and though certainly busied about many things, yet all of them the things of God. Happy the man, whose life is one long Te Deum! He will save his soul, but he will not save it alone, but many others also. Joy is not a solitary thing, and he will come at last to his Master's feet, bringing many others rejoicing with him, the resplendent trophies of his grateful love.

But the love which has most to do with self is the love of desire. It is this desire which gives its value to what theologians call the love of concupiscence. Saints and sinners. the perfect and the imperfect, the young

and old, the penitent and the innocent, the cloistered
and the uncloistered, all must meet in the sanctuary of
this love, and draw waters with gladness from its celestial fountains.   What rational creature but must desire
God, and desire Him with an infinite and irresistible
desire ?   What created understanding but longs to be
flooded with His sweet light ?   What created will but
languishes to be set on fire by the ardour of His extatic
love ?   Daniel is called in Scripture the man of desires.
Most beautiful of appellations! as if he yearned so
eagerly for God, that he should pass into an honourable
proverb to the end of time !   How beautiful the sight if
we could see with the eyes of some sublime intelligence,
how this desire of God is the whole beauty and the
whole order of His vast creation, drawing onwards to
Himself across the spiritual realms of angelic holiness,
or over the land and sea, the mountains and the vales,
of earth, numberless created intellects and wills, and by
as many various paths as there are intellects and wills
to draw !   The tide of all creation sets in with resistless
currents to the throne of the Creator.   It is this desire
which saves and justifies, which crowns and glorifies.
It is in the sacraments, and out of them, in various degrees of intensity and purity.   It is this love which is
heightened and made more exquisite by the tremulous-
ness of holy fear.*   O glorious constraints of this

---

* Beatus vir qui timet Dominum.   Qua ratione beatus?   Quia in mandatis
ejus cupit nimis. S. Ambrose. A similar statement, made by the author
some years ago in All for Jesus, was animadverted on as inaccurate. It had
not however been made without both thought and reading. The expression
of St. Paul, desiderium habens dissolvi et esse cum Christo, is an act of the
love of desire, 1 from the force of terms, 2 on the ancient authority of St. Basil
de reg. fus. disput. cap. 2, 3 on the modern authority of Bolgeni. Amor di
Dio, p. i. c. ii, iii, and that such a love so expressed is an heroic love is
asserted on the authority of S. Thomas, 2. 2. qu. xxiv. art. 8. 9. This was
the authority on which the statement in All for Jesus was made, and in con

heavenly concupiscence! It is a love which makes us
not only desire God, but desire Him supremely above
all things. It makes us desire Him only, Him always,
and Him intensely ; and it allures us with untyrannical
exclusiveness to seek Him in all things here, and to long
for Him as being Himself our sole, sufficient, and magnificent Hereafter. By this love both high and low are
saved; and without some element of it was none ever
saved that was saved. A saint, if such an one could be,
fit to be canonized for all things else, for the want of
this love would be lost eternally ; and the death-bed
penitent who has never known a higher love will be
saved by this alone. And do we really desire aught
else but God? Or at least can we desire aught but
subordinately to Him, and far below our longing for His
unspeakable recompense, which is Himself? There is
nothing to satisfy us but God alone. All things weary
us, and fade. He alone is ever fresh, and His love is
daily like a new discovery to our souls. O sweet thirst
for God! Fair love of supernatural desire! Thou
canst wean us better far from earth, and teach us better
the nothingness of human things, than the cold, slow
experience of wise old age, or the swift sharp science of
suffering, loss, and pain!

There is still another love. We hardly know whether
to call it a child of heaven or of earth. It is the love
of adoration. It is a love too quiet for benevolence, too
deep for complacency, too passive for condolence, too
contemplative for gratitude ; but which has grown up
out of the loves of preference and desire, and is, besides,
the perfection of all the other loves. It is too much

sequence of the criticism on that passage, the references have been verified,
the statement reconsidered, and the doctrine of it here re-asserted in its
natural place.

possessed with God to be accurately conscious of the
nature of its own operations. It finds no satisfaction
except in worship. It comes so near to the vastness of
God that it beholds Him only obscurely, and instead of
definite perfections in God, sees only a bright darkness,
which floods its whole being and transforms it into itself.
It is passive ; God gives it when He wills. We cannot
earn it. Efforts would rather backen it, if it was near,
than bring it on or win it into the soul. It waits rather
than seeks. God is as if He were all Will to it. His
power, His wisdom, His sanctity, they all melt into
His Will; and all that comes to this love is His Will,
and except of that Will, it can take no distinct cogni-
zance of anything either in heaven or on earth. Self
goes out of it, and enters into that Will, and is only
contemplated in it, although it is eternally separate and
essentially distinct. It is oblivious of itself, as being
one with God. Its life is wonder, silence, extasy. The
operations of grace are simplified into one, and the
power of grace which is concentrated in that one is
above words : and that single action is the production of
an unspeakable self-abasement. It cannot be told. But
such was the humility of the Sacred Heart, and such the
strange loveliness of the sinless Mother, who so mightily
attracted God and drew Him down into her bosom.
As the morning sky is all suffused with pearly hues from
the unrisen sun, so is the mind, though still on earth, in
this love of adoration, all silently suffused, and flushed,
and mastered by a most exquisite repose, which can
come alone from that Beatific Vision which has not risen
yet upon the soul.

These are the seven loves whereby the creature man
can love his beneficent Creator. These are the seven
liturgies, ancient, authentic, universal liturgies of the

human heart. Truly it is little we can do for God, and yet how immeasurably more than we have done for Him as yet. A treatise might be written to reduce these loves to practice,* and to illustrate them copiously with the examples of the saints. But that is not our object now. Has earth any pleasure, of an intellectual, moral, or material sort, to compare with the fruition of a repentant life passed in the occupations of these various loves? The penitent seeks peace, and the end of all love is peace, peace and languishing desire, peace in the assured hope of the soul, and pining for the ever-coming, still delaying Face of Jesus in the eastern clouds: that east from which He will one day come. Before the dawn of day, a huge toppling mass of unwieldly clouds came up from the west horizon. With incredible swiftness and the loud roaring of sudden wind, it covered like a pall the brilliant moonlit heavens, and deluged the earth with slanting columns of whirling rain. It passed on. A star came out, and then another, and at last the moon; and then the storm drove onward to the east, towards the sea, murky and purple, and all at once a lunar rainbow spanned the black arch of heaven; and it seemed as if Jesus should have come, beneath that bow, and through that purple cloud that was barring the gates of the sunrise; but the wind was lulled, and all was still, by the time the moon had built that bow upon the clouds. And what is all this but a figure of our lives, one of nature's daily parables, of which we might make so much? Ours is a pilgrimage, a pilgrimage by night, beneath the gentle moon, from west to east, from the sunset to the sunrise; it is not like our natural life from east to west, from

* The reader must not confound these different *kinds* of love, with the different *states* of love expounded in mystical theology.

youth to age, from our rising to our setting; and we
shall best beguile the way, and let the storms go un-
heeded over, if we make God's "justifications our songs
in the house of our pilgrimage," and relieve our weariness by the various magnificence of these seven canonical
services of our supernatural love.

These are the loves we were made for. They are
our means of loving God. If we think too much of
their magnificence, we may forget the exceeding loveliness of God. Look at a saint who has loved heroically
with these seven loves, for even the love of desire may
be heroic, and see how little with all of them he has
done for God. He has not paid one of the least among
the commonest of God's countless benefits. This is a
sad thought, and for us, who are not saints, a grave
consideration. For remember how few saints there are,
and also how far off from their love is ours! Oh the
majesty of God! how it is left desolate, and unrequited!
Yet think again of the mysteriously huge price which
God puts upon even our little love, and upon the least
of our little love! How can it be? What can it mean?
When once we go deep into this subject of Divine Love,
mysteries thicken more and more. God alone can give
an account of His own love, and of how His unerring
wisdom comes to mistake the real price of ours. O
beautiful Goodness of God! why are we not really
beside ourselves with love of Thee?

CHAPTER IV.

OUR ACTUAL LOVE OF GOD.

Causa diligendi Deum, Deus est: modus, sine modo diligere. Est ne hoc satis? Fortassis utique, sed sapienti. *S. Bernard.*

A voluntary thought and a deliberate desire are not less actions in the sight of God than the words of our mouths or the operations of our hands. How wonderful therefore, is it to reflect on the countless multitudes of strong and vigorous acts which are rising up before the majesty of God from the unsleeping world of angels! Their active intellects with incredible swiftness vary their love and praise, their wonder and admiration, almost incessantly. They sweep all regions of creation with instantaneous flight, and bring back on their wings the odour of God's glory and His goodness, to present as worship before His face: though in their boldest flights they have come nigh no limits of His all-embracing presence. Another while, they plunge deep down and out of sight in some one of His mysterious and profound perfections, and rise again and scatter gladness round them, while their thoughts are as showers of light falling beautifully before His throne. Or again they return through the gates of the heavenly Jerusalem, like labourers wending homeward in the evening, bringing with them troops of human souls, dug out of the fires of purgatory, or disentangled from the briars of earth. In every one of their bright actions there flashes forth, as an additional beauty, their joyous dependence

on the Sacred Humanity of Jesus, and their placid obedience to His Human Mother.   There is harmony too
in the immense diversities of their unnumbered acts, and
they all make one vast unutterable concord of spiritual
music in the ear of God.   And all is sinless there.   No
taint, no spot, no venial fault, in all that universe of
abundant energy and of lightning-like activity.   Its
exuberance of sanctity is unflagging and everlasting.
God be praised for His goodness in securing at least
thus much worship for Himself!

A heart that loves God is often fain, for very weariness and sorrow, to rest upon the thought of that angelic
world and to talk of it in secret colloquies with its own
affectionate and faithful guardian angel.   Yet the heart
cannot rest there long ; it cannot rest there finally.   For
in truth no one act of that angelic worship is altogether
worthy of the Most High.   The whole concourse of
marvellous adoration, taken as one grand act, falls short
of the exceeding majesty of God, and simply falls short
infinitely.   God is very good to rejoice in it with that
abounding complacency.   But it is only another of His
condescensions.   It is only another proof that He is in
some mysterious manner wisely beside Himself with
love of His finite and imperfect creatures.   If they
have been proclaiming His praise in their transcendent
hymns for millions and millions of ages, they have not
yet paid Him, they never will have paid Him, for the
single creation of any one, the humblest, of their countless hosts.   And what they give Him, is it not all His
own already ?   Did He not evoke them out of nothing,
beautiful and radiant as they are ?   Is He not pouring
bright streams of being, into their deep, wide natures,
with assiduous munificence, each moment of a never-
ending immortality ?   Yet man, poor man, may well

rest awhile his tired and shamefaced heart upon this
angelic world of beautiful obedience, and the ravishing
tranquillity of its energetic love.

The world of human actions is much more limited;
especially if we regard only the inhabitants of earth.
Nevertheless to our apprehension it possesses immense
capabilities for the worship and the love of God. Each
one of those seven loves which we considered in the
last chapter, is capable of almost as many changes and
as many distinct peculiarities, as there are souls on earth.
Take away the hours spent in sleep, the years before
the use of reason, the dotage of extreme old age, and
the amount of insanity in the world, and still what a
vast number of human actions call for God's concurrence, and are performed in His sight in the four-and-
twenty hours! Yet none of these actions need be
indifferent in the individual case. All of them can
glorify God, and the least of them attain successfully
a supernatural end. There are the hundreds of thousands collected in the great manufacturing cities of the
European nations, with all the sleepless activity of mind
and heart which characterize them. There are the
wandering hordes of the desert and the steppe. The
crowded cities of the east, the masses of Africa, the
swiftly growing populations of the new world, the well-
peopled islands of the broad ocean, and those who dwell
near the arctic snows. If we bring before ourselves hill
and vale, the river side and wood, the sea shore and the
pastoral plain, and remember how vast and various are
the experiences of human joy and sorrow which are
going on in almost every one of the numberless inequalities of the earth's surface, we shall be overwhelmed by
the calculation of the human actions which are ever
being performed.

16   r

Now each one of these actions belongs to God by four different titles, and may be referred to Him by as many different sentiments of gratitude and love. His dominion over us is founded on His having created us, on His continuing to preserve us, on His redeeming us, and on His being our last end, our final cause. These are not so much four separate actions, four distinct mercies, the one separable from the other, as the prolongation and perfection of one divine action, namely, our creation out of nothing. Preservation, as we have already seen, is indivisibly one act with creation. Redemption is the preservation of our supernatural life, without which the preservation of our being would seem, not imperfect only, but hardly a benefit. While the tie, which binds us to God as being our Last End, is at once the cause of creation and its effect, the crown and consummation of the whole work of God. We may be almost said to belong more entirely to God by this last relationship than by any other. But all the four ought to enter more or less into every human action. We have no right to eat, or drink, or recreate ourselves without seeking with more or less determinate intention the fourfold glory of God as our Creator, Preserver, Redeemer, and Last End : and a mere mental reference to Him by a loving heart is sufficient thus to ennoble our most trivial doings, and to fasten it firmly to the throne of God.

Perhaps we have not as much devotion as we ought to have to that relation in which God stands to us as our Last End. We think of Him as our Creator and our Father, and these titles so abound in sweetness that they flood our souls with delight, and we cannot tear ourselves away from such heavenly contemplations. Or when our spirits are all freshly bathed in the cold foun-

tains of holy fear, we look up to God with child-like
and well-pleased awe, as our all-holy judge and omnipotent irresponsible king. It is less common with us to
meditate upon Him and to worship Him as our Last
End, and it seems as if our spiritual life sometimes
suffered from the omission. For this relation of Last
End brings God before us in a manner peculiarly divine,
and to which no earthly or heavenly relationship can
furnish either parallel or similitude. It puts the whole
of practical religion in a clear and undoubted light. It
explains all difficulties and answers all objections.
There is no satisfaction short of God, no completeness
out of God, no support but in God, no rest but upon
God, no breathing-time or halting-place except on the
Bosom of our Heavenly Father. He is the end to
which we are travelling. Like a stone falling on the
earth, so are we evermore falling upon God. Creation
is not solid ground. It lets us through, and we do not
stop until we come to God. He is not one of our
ends, but the end of ends, our only end. There is none
other end but He. All things else are means. It is
this truth which simplifies our lives, and which simplified the lives of the saints until they were pictures and
reflections of His own simplicity. So also if God be our
Last End, He is our only home. We are strangers
everywhere else but in God. All things are foreign to
us except God; and thus all our love of home and
country, of kith and kin, melts away into the single
love of God. He is the home where our welcome is
certain, and surpasses all our expectations. He is our
rest where alone we can lie down without fear and sleep
sweetly. He in His inaccessible splendour is the beautiful night wherein no man works, but when the weary
labourer reposes from his toil in everlasting bliss. He

is the cool and fragrant evening, in whose endless sunset
creation clothes itself with its final beauty, and reposes
in its golden beams, and all sounds of work and all sighs
of care are suspended, and all cravings satisfied, and all
created spirits filled with an extatic life, so full, so
glorious, so far-reaching, that the most untiring energies
of earth are but as dreary indolence compared with its
magnificent tranquillity.

But we must return to the world of human actions.
Who could number, at any one given moment, the multitude of such actions on the earth, the pains endured,
the sorrows borne, the anxieties combated, the temptations resisted, the words spoken, the thoughts thought,
the actions done, all of which the heart of man can
multiply and vary and complicate well nigh a hundred
times a minute?   All these things are the raw material
of our love of God, and all can enter into those seven
kinds of loving worship which we considered in the last
chapter, and all can have a different character of supernatural holiness impressed upon them, according to the
four different titles under which we may refer them to
God as our Creator, Preserver, Redeemer, and Last End.
But alas! is not this beautiful human worship like a fair
dream of some possible creation, which may be, but has
not been yet?   How much of these treasures of our
hearts does our Heavenly Father actually receive?
Truly the tribes of men are like a wilderness, capable
of cultivation, where corn and wine and oil might come
abundantly from the bosom of the earth, and flowers
bloom, and tall forests grow, and cattle feed, but which
now is little else than sand, and stony plain, and low
bushes, wearying the eye by the very expanse of its
cheerless monotony.

Yet when in our love of God, and fretted with the

feebleness of our own worthless endeavours, we turn to the world of angelic actions, and feed ourselves upon its fragrant and refreshing fulness, we not only soon come to feel how far below the majesty of God is even that transcendent worship, but we rest at last on human acts as after all the sole exclusive adequate worship of the Adorable Trinity. Our eye lingers on the fertile heart of the Virgin Mother, but there is no rest for it even there ; and what we seek for God, in our sympathy and affection for His slighted goodness, we find only in the human actions of the Incarnate Word, in the countless known and unknown momentary mysteries of the Three-and-Thirty Years, and in the multiplied lives, the daily births, and daily crucifixions, of the altar and the tabernacle. There we behold the Incomprehensible Majesty of the Most High compassed with a worship equal to Himself, as deep and broad and lofty and bountiful as His own blessed Self. There we see His infinity worshipped infinitely, with an infinite worship almost infinitely multiplied, and infinitely repeated, in the Sacred Heart of Jesus. We would almost rather be men than angels, because these are human actions, and that is a human Heart. Jesus is man, and not an angel. But then He is God Himself; and so it is after all to Himself, and not to His creation, that He owes this beautiful sufficient worship. Shall we sorrow then, and cry Alas! because nowhere is God rightly loved and adequately worshipped, and because the service of the Sacred Heart turns out to be in fact His own ? O no! rather let us bless Him again and again that He is such a God that none can worship Him as He deserves, that all which is good is at last discovered to be either Himself or at least His own, that all beautiful things come out of His goodness, and go into it again, and are inseparably mixed up with it, and that we only lose ourselves more and more inextricably in the labyrinth of His Sovereign goodness the deeper we penetrate into that dear and awful sanctuary.

But we must strive to enter more minutely into the labyrinth of our own manifold unworthiness. We have seen in the last chapter in what ways and to what extent it is in our power, with the aid of His grace, to love Almighty God. That enquiry was but a preface to this further one. As a matter of fact, how do we actually love Him? What is the positive amount of our love of God? From all this world of human actions what sort of proportion does He receive, and with what dispositions is the tax paid? Let us try to make ourselves masters of the statistics of the kingdom of God. Even if it be little in amount which we pay to God, yet much depends on the spirit in which it is paid. Little things are enhanced by the manner in which they are done, and the intention out of which they spring. Let us see then how our generosity ennobles the meanness and enriches the poverty of our love.

If we look at mankind with reference to their service of God we may divide them into three classes, comprising two extremes and a mean. The one extreme is occupied by the saints, the second by the great mass of men, and the mean by ordinary believers, such as we ourselves may be. By studying each of these three divisions, we shall obtain something like a clear view of the actual love of creatures for their Creator.

The first thing which strikes us about the saints is the extraordinary fewness of them. Those who are canonized bear no sort of proportion in any one generation to the numbers of the baptized; and if we multiply their number a hundred times, so as to include the hidden saints whom it is not God's will that the Church should raise upon her altars, still the grievous disproportion will scarcely be perceptibly diminished. Let us grant the largest probable allowance for extraordinary sanctity hidden in the silent cells of the Carthusians, or in other lives, cloistered or not, of singular abasement and abjection, nevertheless we may suppose the number of saints in any age to fall far below the number of baptized infants who die before the use of reason, and perhaps not to equal the number of death-bed conversions. If we love God really and truly, surely this consideration cannot be otherwise than a painful one. And yet it seems so easy to be a saint!   Graces are so overwhelmingly abundant, and God Himself so unspeakably attractive, that it appears harder to be ungenerous with Him than to be generous; and where perfection is made to consist simply in the fervour and the purity of our love, there is almost an intellectual difficulty in comprehending why it is that the saints should be so few.

But it is not only the fewness of their number which we must consider. We must think also of the immensity of the graces which they receive. We often get a sight in times of recollection and prayer of the fearful way in which our own practice falls short of the graces we receive. Nothing makes us feel our own baseness more keenly or more lastingly than this. Perhaps the disproportion between the practice of the saints and the graces which they actually receive may be almost as large as it is in our own case. At any rate we cannot read their lives without being struck with the unused and unemployed profusion of grace by which their souls

are deluged. Now all this is God's own outlay. It is
what He spends in order to obtain saints; and if we
measure extraordinary heights of sanctity by the greatness and variety of the graces given, we shall see that
even the holiness of an apostle will seem to be but a
poor return for so prodigal an expenditure of grace.
Our Lord once spoke of virtue going out of Him, when
a poor woman touched Him that she might be miraculously healed. So we may almost define a saint to be
one who drains God's abundance more than others do,
and costs God more. He is but crowning His own
gifts, when He vouchsafes to crown His saints. So is
it always when we come to look into the interests and
affairs of God's glory. It is at His own expense that
He is served. He furnishes the banquet to which He
is invited. Like earthly fathers, He must give to His
children the riches out of which they may make their
offerings to Him. His liberality supplies the means,
while His condescension stoops graciously to receive
back again what was His own in its first fulness, but
which has wasted and faded not a little in the transfer
through our hands.

But even at the best, if we make the most of the
generous and heroic love of the saints, it is absolutely
vile as compared either with *its* object or with *their*
grace. It is not enough that the little which they give
is already rather His than theirs; but it is also in itself
unworthy of His transcending greatness and surpassing
goodness. Even the saints are unprofitable servants.
The chosen apostles of the Incarnate Word were taught
so to look upon themselves. Yet these saints are the
good extreme among men. From them, if from any,
may God look for a plentiful harvest of glory. Their
purity of intention, their intensity of love, their gener-

osity of selfsacrifice, are the pastures in which His glory
is to feed. Yet even here how poor, how scanty, how
irregular is the return of the creature to the All-merciful
Creator! He has all the work to do Himself which He
pays them for doing; and when they have somewhat
marred the beauty of His design, He accepts their work
as if on the one hand He did not perceive its imperfection, and on the other did not recognize that all the
goodness and the beauty of it were His own. How
then must our Heavenly Father condescend to value the
worship and the loyalty of a free created will! And
how true it is that even the magnificence of the saints
is after all but meanness, in respect of the boundless
majesty and overwhelming holiness of Him upon whose
grace they live, and by whose Blood they are redeemed!

If we turn from the saints to the other extreme, the
mass of men, the vision which we are constrained to
look upon is truly of the darkest and most disheartening
description. By the side of the multitude, the heroism
of the saints does indeed appear falsely magnified into
the most gigantic dimensions. Can anything be said of
men's ignorance of God, but that it is boundless, universal, incredible? Could the lives of men be what they
are, if they had so much as the commonest elements of
the knowledge of God? Do not millions act and speak
and think, as if God was of a lower nature than themselves? Do they not attribute to Him an indifference
to right and wrong, which they would consider revolting
in a fellow-creature? Or again, do they not so completely overlook Him as to forget His existence, and to
live as if there were no one to consult but themselves, no
will to satisfy except their own? With many it would
almost be doing God too great an honour to be at the

pains to deny His existence; and others only advert to
His perfections to dishonour them by their unmanly
superstitions. Indeed in such complete ignorance of
God do crowds of men live, that we could not have
credited the possibility of it, if our own observation had
not presented it to us as a fact which no reasonable man
could doubt.

Moreover it by no means appears that, with the
appalling corruption of our nature, the knowledge of
God is sufficient to secure for Him even our esteem.
Horrible to relate, aversion to God is far from being
uncommon among His creatures. There are many bold
and impenitent sinners who are devils before their time,
to whom the Name of God or His perfections are not
so much terrible as they are odious. When they come
in sight of His commandments, or of some manifestation of His sovereignty, or even some beautiful disclosure of His tenderness, they are like possessed persons. They are so exasperated as to forget themselves,
until their passion hurries them on to transgress, not
only the proprieties of language, but even the decorum
of outward behaviour. There seems to be something
preternaturally irritating to them in the very mention
of God, quite irrespective of the absolute dominion
which He claims over them as their Creator. There
are others, whose habitual state of mind, when they
approach religious subjects, is to be on their guard
against God, as if there were some dangerous subtlety
in the greatness of His wisdom, or some artful overbearing tyranny in the condescensions of His majesty,
or some dishonest concealed purpose in the invitations
of His mercy. With these men the probabilities are
against God. He is not likely to mean well. It is
safest to distrust Him. Discretion must be aware of

Him. Moderation must not be excited by Him. We must not let Him throw us out of our wise sobriety. He has come to bargain with us, and we must be vigilant, or we do not know to what we may be induced to commit ourselves. With such men their first thought of God is to dishonour Him; for how shall a son doubt his father without doing him dishonour?

There are others who are not by any means to be reckoned among the mass of men, and who serve Him truly with a holy fear, but who seem not to have escaped altogether the contagion of this aversion to God. With them it shows itself in the shape of uneasiness, perplexity, and doubt. They entertain suspicions against the perfections of God's justice or the universality of His compassion. When they hear of certain things, jealousy of God starts up as it were unbidden in their hearts. It is not so much that they have definite intellectual difficulties in matters of faith. But they have not that instantaneous and unclouded certainty, that all is right, and best, and exquisitely tender, where God is concerned, which is the pure sunshine and invigorating air of the atmosphere of faith. Nay, have we not all of us moods, in which an allusion to God makes us impatient; and is not this fact alone the nearest of any fact to a deep-sea sounding of our corruption?

It is hard to see what God has done to deserve all this. It seems most unkind, most cruelly disloyal to the immensity of His goodness, and to the unalterable bounty of His compassionate dominion. Truly He is our King as well as our Father, our Master as well as our Friend. But are the relations incompatible? It is the very necessity of our case as creatures, that we must be under a law; and could we be under laws less

numerous, less onerous, than those under which we
are laid by the unchangeable perfections of God? Easy
laws, few laws, and laws which it is our own interest
to keep—these are the characteristics of the dominion
of God. Why then are we restless and uneasy, and not
the rather happily lost in amazement at the goodness
of our great Creator? It seems wonderful that He
who is so great should also be so good; and it is the
joyous lesson which the sands of life teach us as they
run yearly out, that His very greatness is the only
blessed measure of His goodness.

But ignorance of God and aversion to God are not of
themselves a sufficient description of the religious condition of the great mass of men. There are multitudes
also who are simply indifferent to God. It sounds
incredible. The mere knowledge that there is a God
should be enough to shape, control, revolutionize, and
govern the whole world. And this, quite independent
of the minute, infallible, and touching knowledge of
Him which revelation gives us. But when that is
added, surely it should be enough to strike indifference
out of the list of possible things. Surely every human
heart should be awake, and alert, to hear the sound of
God's voice, or discern His footprints on the earth.
Our Creator, our Last End, our Saviour, our Judge,
upon whom we depend for everything, whose will is
the only one important thing to us, whose Bosom is the
one only possible home for us, and He to be regarded as
simply the most uninteresting object in His own world!
Is this really credible? Alas! we have only to look
around and see. Does a day pass which does not prove
it to us? Nay very often, to our shame be it spoken,
is it not a considerable exertion, even to us to interest
ourselves in God? And this indifference, can we be

quite sure that it is less dishonourable to God than positive aversion?

These are melancholy results. Yet somehow they spur us on to try to do more for God ourselves, and to love Him with a purer and more disinterested love. Alas! if the saints are few in number, those who are either ignorant of God, or indifferent to Him, or have an aversion to Him, are countless multitudes. Many fair regions of this beautiful world are peopled by idolaters. The sacred places of scriptural Asia are tenanted by the followers of Mahomet. Heresy and schism usurp whole countries, which boast of the name of Christian; and even in Catholic lands, it is depressing to think how many thousands there are, who must be classed with those who are not on the side of God. These are very practical considerations; for if there is the least honesty in our professions of loving God, they must greatly influence both the fervour of our devotion and the amount of our mortification. They bring home to us that suffering and expiatory character, which, by a law of the Incarnation, belongs to all Christian holiness.

But we shall find considerations even yet more practical, if we turn from these two extremes to the mean, that is, to ordinary pious Catholics, such as we humbly hope we either are ourselves, or are endeavouring to become. We distinctly aim at making religion the great object of our lives. We are conscious to ourselves of a real and strong desire to love God, and as we grow older the desire grows stronger, and, to say the least of it, it bids fair to swallow up all our other desires, and become the one single object of our lives. The four last things, Death and Judgment, Hell and Heaven, are often before us, and fill us with a holy terror. We fear sin greatly, and we sometimes think we almost hate it for its own sake, because it is an offence against so good a God. We have times and methods of prayer. We examine our consciences. Wo hear mass often. We visit the Blessed Sacrament. We are devout to our Lady. We frequent the Sacraments. Who can doubt but that all this is the way of salvation? We are happy in the grace which enables us to do all this. We shall be happy indeed in the grace which will enable us to persevere. We are happy also in the thought that there are thousands and thousands in the Church who are thus serving God. But let us look a little more closely into this, and examine our lives first as to the *amount* of love of God which they exhibit, and secondly as to the *manner* in which we show our love.

There are twenty-four hours in the day, so many days in the week, and so many weeks in the year. We have various occupations, and manifold ways of spending our time; and the most careless amongst us must have some confused and general notion of the way in which his time is distributed. Now we know that the service of God is the grand thing, or rather that it is the only thing about us which is great at all. What amount of our time then is spent upon it? How many hours of the day are passed in prayer, and spiritual reading, in hearing mass, or visiting the Blessed Sacrament, or in other direct spiritual exercises? Of the time necessarily expended upon our worldly avocations, or the claims of society, how much is spent with any recollection of Him, or with any actual intention to do our common actions for His glory? Can we return a satisfactory answer to these questions? Furthermore, we know that it is essential to our love of God,

that we should appreciate Him above all things. Does
our practice show that this is anything but a form ot
words with us? Would strangers, who looked critically
at our daily lives, be obliged to say that, whatever faults
we had, it was plain that we put no such price on anything
as on God? When we ourselves look into the interests
and affections of our busy, crowded hearts, is it plain
that, if the love of God does not reign there in solitary,
unmingled splendour, at least it takes easy, obvious,
and acknowledged precedence of all our other loves?
This is not asking much: but can we answer as we
should wish? Again, our actions are perfectly multitudinous. If we reckon both the outward and the
inward ones, they are almost as numerous as the beat-
ings of our pulse. How many of them are for God?
I do not say how many are directly religious, but how
many are at all and in any sense for God? How many
in the hundred? Even if we are quite clear that a
virtual intention has really got vigour and vitality
enough to carry us over the breadth of a whole day, and
to push its way through the crowd of things we have to
think, to say, to do, and to suffer,—and this is a very
large assumption—is this virtual intention in the morning to absolve us from the necessity of any further
advertence to God, and must it not also have been
made in the morning with a very considerable degree of
intensity, in order to propel it for so long as twenty-
four hours through such a resisting medium as we know
our daily lives to be? To use our national word, are
we quite comfortable about this? Are we sure of our
view about virtual intention, and without misgivings,
and have we found our theory work well in times gone
by?

God does not have His own way in the world. What

He gets He has to fight for. What is true of the world
at large, is true also of our own hearts and lives.
Though we love God, and most sincerely, He has to
struggle for our love. He has to contend for the mas-
tery over our affections. The preferences of our corrupt
nature are not for Him, or for His concerns. Thus it
happens almost daily that His claims clash with those
of self or of the world. We have to choose between
the two, and give the preference to the one over the
other. We are for ever having Christ and Barabbas
offered to the freedom of our election. Now do we
always give the preference to God? Or if not always,
because of surprises, impulses, impetuosities, or sudden
weaknesses, at least do we never wilfully, deliberately,
and with advertence, prefer anything else to God, and
give Him the second place? And of the innumerable
times in which this conflict occurs, in what proportion
of times does God carry off the victory? And when
He does, is it an easy victory? Or has He to lay
long siege to our hearts, and bring up reinforcement
after reinforcement of fresh and untired grace, until
at last it looks as if He were almost going to throw
Himself on His omnipotence, and overwhelm the freedom of our will? Or again, let us look at the degree
of application which we bestow on what we really do
for God. Let us confront the carefulness, and forethought, and energy, and perseverance, which we
bestow upon our temporal interests or the earthly
objects of our love, with those which characterize our
spiritual exercises. And will the result of the examination be altogether what we should desire?

All these are childish and elementary questions to
ask ourselves. Yet the results are far more melancholy than when we contemplated the ignorance, aver-

sion, and indifference of the great mass of men. More
melancholy, because we profess to be God's champions;
it is as it were our place to be on His side. We live
encircled by His grace, which flows around us like
the plentiful bright air. Our minds are illuminated by
the splendours of heavenly truth, and our hearts led
sweetly captive by the winning mysteries of the Incarnation. Our lives are charmed by great sacraments, and we are each of us the centre of a very
world of invisible grandeurs and spiritual miracles.
And in spite of all this, I will not say it is sad, it is
really hardly credible, that our love of God should
amount to so little as it does, whether we regard it as
to the time spent upon it, or as to the appreciation of
Him above all things, or as to the proportion of our
numberless actions which is for Him, or as to our preference of Him when His claims clash with others,
or as to the degree of application which we bestow on
what we really do for Him. O look at all this by the
moonlight of Gethsemane, or measure it with the Way
of the Cross, or confront it with the abandonment of
Calvary! Turn upon it the light of the great love
of Creation, whose prodigal munificence and incomparable tenderness, and seemingly exaggerated compassions we have already contemplated! Can it be that
this is the creature's return to his Creator, when the
creature is holy and faithful and good, and that such
is to be God's strong point in the world, the paradise
of His delights, the portion of His empire where allegiance still is paid Him? Merciful Heaven! can we
be safe, if we go on thus? Are we really in a state of
grace? Is not the whole spiritual life a cruel delusion?
And are we not after all the enemies, and not the friends,
of God? O no! faith comes to our rescue. All is
17 T

right, though truly all is wrong. We are certainly in
the way of salvation. Then we say once more, as we
find ourselves saying many times a day, what a God is
ours, what incredible patience, what unbounded forbearance, what unintelligible contentment! Why is it
that very shame does not sting us to do more for God,
and to love Him with a love a little less infinitely unlike
the love, with which, do what we can, we cannot hinder
Him from loving us?

So much for the amount of our love of God. It is
little; so little that it would be disheartening were it
not always in our own power, through the abundance
of His grace to make that little more. Let us now
at any rate console ourselves by looking at the manner
and spirit in which we pay to God this little love.
Love, like other things, has certain rules and measures
of its own. It has certain habits and characteristics.
It proceeds upon known principles which belong to
its nature. It acts differently from justice, because
it is love and not justice. It does not obey the same
laws as fear, simply because it is not fear but love.
Everyone knows the marks of true love. They are
readiness, eagerness, generosity, swiftness, unselfishness,
vigilance, exclusiveness, perseverance, exaggeration.
In all these respects, except the last, our divine love
must at once resemble and surpass our human love. In
the last respect it cannot do so, because God is so infinitely beautiful and good that anything like exaggeration or excess in the love of Him is impossible. The
Sacred Heart of Jesus is the model of Divine Love.
The Immaculate Heart of Mary ascertains for us the
amazing heights of love at which a simple creature can
arrive by correspondence to the grace of God. The
Saints are all so many samples of divine love in some

one or more of its special characteristics and departments. We know then precisely the manner and spirit in which we are to love God. Let us see how far our practice squares with our theory.

Is the following an unkind picture of ourselves? We serve God grudgingly, as if He were exacting. We are slow to do what we know He most desires, because it is an effort to ourselves. We cling to our own liberty, and we feel the service of God more or less of a captivity. Our whole demeanour and posture in religion is not as if we felt God was asking too little, or as if we were most anxious to do more than He required. We serve Him intermittingly, though perseverance is what He so especially desires. We have fits and starts; pious weeks or devout months, and then times of remissness, of effort, of coldness: then a fresh awakening, a new start; and then a slackening again. It is as if loving God went against the grain, as if we had to constrain ourselves to love Him, as if it was an exertion which could not be kept up continuously, as if human holiness could never be anything better than endless beginnings, and trials which are always falling short of the mark. Thus we also love God rarely, under pressure, on great occasions, at startling times, or when we have sensible need of Him. All this looks as if we did not love Him for His own sake, but for ourselves, or for fear, or because it is prudent and our duty. There is unmistakeably a want of heart in the whole matter.

Have we ever done any one action which we are quite confident was done solely and purely for the love of God? If we have, it has not been often repeated. We are conscious to ourselves that there is a great admixture of earthly motives in our service of God. It is astonishing what an amount of vain-glory and self-

seeking there is in our love of Him. We are also
perfectly and habitually aware of this; and yet, which
is even more astonishing, we are quiet and unmoved.
It breeds in us no holy desperation, nor does it inspire
us to any vehement and determined struggles to get
rid of the desecrating presence of this unholy enemy.
Nay, it almost appears as if we should never have
dreamed of loving God, if He Himself had not been
pleased to command us to do so; and therefore we do
it just in the way in which men always do a thing
because they are told, and which they would not have
done if they had not been told. Many of us perhaps
have already given the best of our lives to the world,
and now it is the leavings only which go to God.
Alas! how often is He asked to drink the dregs of a
cup which not the world only, but the devil also,
have well-nigh drained before Him; and with what
adorable condescension does He put His lips to it,
and dwell with complacency upon the draught, as if
it were the new wine of some archangel's first unblem-
ished love!

Then again we exaggerate our own services, in
thought if not in words; and this shows itself in our
demeanour. True love never thinks it has done
enough. Its restlessness comes from the very uneasiness of this impression. Now this is not at all our
feeling about God. We do not look at things from
His point of view. It is only by a painfully acquired
habit of mind that we come to do so. Half the temptations against the faith, from which men suffer, arise
from the want of this habit, from not discerning that
really the creature has no side, no right to a point of
view, but that God's side is the only side, and the
Creator's point of view the creature's only point of

view, and that he would not be a creature were it otherwise. Another unsatisfactory sign is, that, ordinarily speaking, we have so little missionary feeling about us, and are so unconcerned whether sinners are converted, or whether men love God or not. Surely it is hard for true love to coexist with an un-missionary spirit.*

But we all of us have times when we love God more than usual, times of fervour, of closer union with Him, of momentary love of suffering, transitory flashes of things which are like the phenomena of the saints. They neither last long enough nor come often enough to form our normal state. They are simply our best times. Now we need not dwell either upon their rarity or their brevity; but we would fain ask if even then we love God altogether without reserves. Is nothing kept back from Him? Is our renunciation of self ample and faultless? Have we no secret corner of our hearts where some favourite weakness lurks in the shade, and which the strong light of heavenly love has not blinded to its own interests? I am afraid to go on with the picture, lest I should have to ask myself at last, what is left of the Christian life? But we have seen enough to confess of our love of God, that not only is what we give very little, but that even that little is given in the most ungraceful and unlover-like of ways. Surely this is a confession not to be made by words, which are not equal to the task, but only by silent tears, while we lie prostrate before the Throne of Him, whom, strange to say! we really do love most tenderly even while we slight Him!

On all sides of us there are mysteries. Our rela-

* Yet see the doctrine of Richard of St. Victor and Da Ponte quoted in Growth in Holiness, chap. vi. p. 94, Second Edition.

tions to God are full of them. Our coldness and His
love, His forbearance and our petulance,—we hardly
know which is the most strange, the most inexplicable.
If we consider attentively how little we love God, and
in what way we show it, honesty will compel us to
acknowledge that we men should not accept such
service at each other's hands. We should reject it
with scorn. We should regard it as an injury rather
than as a service. A father would disinherit his son;
a friend would put away from him the friend of his
bosom, if his love were requited as we requite the love
of our heavenly Father. Yet it is the ever-blessed
God, who is what He is, to whom we, being what we
are, dare to offer this mockery of worship. Will He
open heaven, and cast His fiery bolts upon us, and
annihilate us for ever, that we may be no longer a
dishonour to His beautiful creation? Or will He turn
from our proffered service with anger, or at least with
a contemptuous indifference? We cannot easily understand how it is that He does not. Yet on the
contrary He vouchsafes to accept and reward our
pitiful affection. But His very rewards and blessings
lead us astray; for we begin to put a price upon our
merits according to the greatness of His recompense,
not according to the reality of their lowness; and we
think we have treated Him with great generosity, and
that His reward is to us only the proof of our generosity; while on the contrary we consider Him to be
asking very much of us; and our minds do not see His
rights, and our hearts do not feel them. God sees all
this, and He makes no sign. It is not so much as if He
seemed insensible to our ingratitude; it is rather as if
He did not say that it was ingratitude at all. No love
can be conceived more sensitive than that of Him who

has eternally predestinated, and then called out of nothing, the objects of His choice and predilection. Yet God does not seem to feel our coldness and perversity. Rather He appears to prize what we give Him, and to rejoice in its possession. He wished it otherwise. He made very different terms at the outset. He asked for far more than He has got. But He makes no complaint; and not being able to have His terms allowed, He takes us on our own.

Is it possible that it can be God of whom we are daring thus to speak? Why do not all we, His children, league together to make it up to Him? Angels of heaven! why is your worship of that Blessed Majesty aught else but tears?

CHAPTER V.

IN WHAT WAY GOD REPAYS OUR LOVE.

Signore, volete dare per quello, che facciamo per voi, piu di quello che potete fare; e non potendo voi fare voi medesimo, restate solamente soddisfatto con dare voi medesimo: stupendo caso! che il Creatore non ritrovi in tutta la sua onnipotenza, cosa, che possa fare in aggradimento di qualsivoglia cosa, che fa un giusto per suo amore. Nieremberg.

WHEN angels offer the prayers of men with incense in their golden thuribles, there are none which rise up before the throne of God with a sweeter or more acceptable fragrance than the murmurs and complaints of loving souls, because God is not loved sufficiently. Everywhere on earth, where the true love of God is to be found, there also is this peaceful and blessed unhappiness along with it. In many a cloister, by the sea shore, or on the mountain top, in the still forest or the crowded city, there are many who in the retirement of their cell, or before the Blessed Sacrament, are sighing with the sweet grief of love, because men love God so coldly and so unworthily. There are many amid the distractions of the world, and who appear to be walking only in its ways, who have no heavier weight upon their hearts than the neglect, abandonment, and unrequited love of God. Through the long cold night, or during the noisy day, incessantly as from a tranquil holy purgatory, the sounds of this plaintive sorrow, this blessedly unhappy love, rise up into the ear of God. Some tremble with horror of the sins which are daily committed against His holy law. Some are saddened because those who by their faith know God so well, love Him with such carelessness and pusillanimity. Some, who are wont to make His resplendent attributes the objects of their daily contemplation, murmur because they see nowhere on the earth, not even among the saints, anything worthy to be called love of so great and infinite a goodness. Others with meek petulance expostulate with God, because He hides Himself, and does not constrain souls to love Him by open manifestations of His surpassing beauty: while others mourn over their own cold hearts, and pine to love God better than they do. There are even innocent children who weep because they feel, what as yet they can hardly know, that men are leaving so cruelly unrequited the burning love of God. All these sighs and tears, all these complaints and expostulations, all this heavy-hearted silence and wounded bleeding love,—all is rising up hourly to the Majesty on high, not unmingled with the sharper sounds of active penance and expiatory mortifications. It is at once intercession and thanksgiving and petition and satisfaction, and our Heavenly Father loves the sweet violence which this beautiful sorrow is doing to Him.

Meanwhile God Himself vouchsafes to appear contented, and even more than contented with the poverty of our love. He seems to be satisfied with that in us, which is very far from satisfying ourselves. Whether it is that His clear view of our exceeding nothingness stimulates His compassion to make allowances for us which we have no right to make for ourselves, or whether to the incomprehensible affection of a Creator there is some inestimable value in the least and lowest offering of the creature's love, so it is, that His magnificence repays our love with rewards of the most over-

whelming grandeur, while at the same time His justice
and wisdom contrive that these immense rewards should
be in exact and varying proportion with our merits.
He alone seems to be above the feeling of that which
His servants feel so deeply, their own coldness and ingratitude to Him. Yet we know that none can measure
so unerringly the hatefulness of our iniquity; none can
estimate so truly the glorious abundance of strong
celestial grace which is hourly conferred upon us; none
can know Him as He knows Himself, and therefore
none can abhor sin as He abhors it, or comprehend, as
He comprehends it, the insult of our lukewarm love.
Does it not even come to ourselves sometimes in prayer,
when we have been dwelling long upon some one beautiful attribute of the Divine Nature, to ask ourselves in
amazement, how it is that God can possibly forgive sin,
and forgiving it, can look so completely as if He had forgotten it as well, and even seem to esteem us more when
we rise from a shameful fall, than if we had stood
upright in His grace and our integrity all the while?

Yet our best notions of God are unspeakably unworthy of Him. When we get views of His perfections
which thrill through us like a new life, and throw open
to our minds grand vast worlds of truth and wonder,
these rays of light are full of dust and dimness, and do
not approach to the real beauty of the Creator. Thus
it is that we cannot take a step in this land of divine
love, but mysteries start up around us far more hard to
solve than the deepest difficulties of scholastic theology.
We are getting new graces every day, crowning our correspondence to the grace we had before. We are continually drinking fresh draughts of immortal life in
the Sacraments, which we are allowed to repeat and
renew day after day. But we are so accustomed to all

this, that we can scarcely realize the miracles of compassion and love, of which we are incessantly the objects.
All this continuance of grace is a manifestation to us of
God's contentment with us.   Not that He would not
have us better than we are, and is not always stimulat-
ing us to higher things.   But He takes gladly what we
let Him have; and, with loving eagerness, not only
furnishes us with instant means to serve Him better,
but almost anticipates with His rewards our little services.   For the recompense full often comes before the
deed, and as our good works are not sufficiently numerous to gratify His liberality, He is crowning all day
long a thousand good intentions which He knows will
never issue in results.   And why?   Because it is not
so much works, as love, for which He craves.   O the
mystery of the Divine Recompenses! how is it to be
unriddled except by the satisfaction of the Precious
Blood of Jesus?   And then how is that adorable Bloodshedding itself to be unriddled?   If the mystery of a
Contented God, with His blessed wrath appeased and
His all-holy justice satisfied, can only be explained by
the Cross of the Incarnate Word, it is only removing
the difficulty one step backward; for then by what is
the Cross itself to be explained?   Are we not for ever
obliged to take refuge in Creation as the grand primal
act of love, the fountain-head of all the divine compassions, and to acknowledge that the classes of mysteries,
which of all others are the most unfathomable, are those
which concern the nature, the degree, and the perfections of Creative Love?   O beautiful Abysses, in which
it is so sweet to lose ourselves, so blissful to go on
sounding them to all eternity and never learn the depths,
and in musing upon whose precipitous shores a loving
heart finds heaven even while on earth!   It is a day to

date from, when we first come to see, that the very fact of God having created us is in itself a whole magnificent revelation of eternal love, more safe to lean upon than what we behold, more worthy of our trust than what we know, more utterly our own than any other possession we can have.

But let us study in detail the way in which God repays that poor and fitful and ungenerous love of which we ourselves are more than half ashamed. Let us enquire when He repays us, with what He repays us, and in what manner He repays us. We shall find fresh motives of love at every step in the enquiry.

First of all, when does He repay us? He does not keep us waiting for our recompenses. We know well that one additional degree of sanctifying grace is of more price than all the magnificence of the universe. The objects upon which we often fasten our affections or employ our ambition, during long years of concentrated vigilance and persevering toil, are less worthy of our endeavours and less precious in the possession, than one single particle of sanctifying grace. Yet, let us suppose that a momentary temptation has assailed us, and we have resisted it, or that we have lifted up our hearts for an instant in faith and love to God, or that for the sake of Christ we have done some trifling unselfish thing, scarcely has the action escaped us before then and instantly the heavens have opened invisibly, and the force of heaven, the participation of the Divine Nature, the beauty, power, and marvel of sanctifying grace, has passed in viewless flight and with insensible ingress into our soul. There is not the delay of one instant. Moreover these ingresses of grace are beyond number, and yet, if we correspond and persevere, the influence and result of each one of them is simply eternal. Each

additional degree of sanctifying grace, represents and
secures an additional degree of glory in heaven, if only
we correspond thereto, and persevere unto the end.   At
the moment in which we receive each additional degree
of sanctifying grace our soul is clothed before God in a
new and glorious beauty which a moment ago it did not
possess.

The communication of sanctifying grace to the soul
is itself a marvellous and mysterious disclosure of the
divine magnificence and liberality.   It is assuredly
most probable, if it is not certain,* that each additional degree of sanctifying grace is given the very
instant it is merited by our actions, and is not
reserved as an accumulated reward to be bestowed
upon us when we enter into glory.   But each additional degree of sanctifying grace is not a mere enrich-
ing of us with the created gifts of God, but it is a
real and new mission to our souls of the Second and
Third Persons of the Most Holy Trinity, together with
the unsent coming to us and dwelling with us of the
Father Himself.   It is not only that the Three Divine
Persons are always in us by essence, presence, and
power; but by sanctifying grace They are in us in a
new and special and most real, though deeply mysterious way, and in the case of the particular graces of
the sacraments, They are with us for particular ends,
effects and purposes.   By an invisible mission this
real indwelling of the Divine Persons assumes a new
mode of existence at every one of the multitudinous
additions and degrees of sanctifying grace, a new

* Cf Suarez de Beatitudine, Disp. vi. Sect. l. n. 13.   Also De Gratia. lib. ix.
cap iii. 23.   Dico ergo gradus omnes gratiæ, quos justus per actus remissos
charitatis meretur, statim sine ulla dilatione, nullave spectata dispositione,
illi conferri, ac provide justum non solum per omnes hos actus mereri, sed
etiam statim consequi suæ gratiæ augmentum.   But it is a question.

mode of existence which it is hardly possible to explain
in words, as on the one hand it implies no manner of
change or motion in Them, while on the other there
is from Them some contact with the soul more personal, more intimate, more real, than that which existed but a moment before. If we are to allow some
theologians to say that where the gifts of grace more
concern the intellect, there is a mission of the Son,
and, where they more concern the will, a mission of
the Holy Ghost, yet we cannot hold any mission
of the Son which is not also a mission of the
Holy Ghost, nor any mission of the Holy Ghost
which is not also a mission of the Son, nor any
mission of the Two, apart and separate from the
coming and indwelling of the Father. If it is hard to
understand this, it is also extremely beautiful, and
ought to fill us with fresh love of God, and a more
loving wonder at His bounty towards His creatures.
This doctrine of divine mission with each degree of
sanctifying grace shows us how sanctifying grace is a
substantial and real anticipation of heaven, that even
now it is Himself, and not His created gifts only, that
God gives to us, and that He is our own God, our own
possession, from the very first moment of our justification. Moreover there is something to overawe us with
the sense of the divine intimacy with us, and to make
us glow with love even in our awe, to reflect that this
inexplicable operation, this celestial mansion in our
souls, this new and ever new mission of the Divine
Persons, which we cannot explain and can only dimly
apprehend, is actually being reflected in us, many, many
times a day, while we are in a state of grace, and seeking in our actions the glory and the will of God.* Nay,

* *Billuart de Trinitat,* vi. 4.

so substantially are the Divine Persons present to the soul by Their invisible mission, that if by impossibility They were not present to us by Their immensity, They would be so by reason of sanctifying grace. *

Moreover all through life our mere preservation of the gift of faith entitles us always to have the grace of God at hand when it is wanted, preventing and anticipating the rapid and subtle movements of our spiritual enemies; and even when it is not especially wanted, because we are not under the pressure of circumstances or in critical occasions, it is most likely that we are always insensibly receiving grace, except when we sleep; so that we live in a world of grace, and breathe its atmosphere unconsciously, thinking as little of it as of the air we breathe in order to support our natural life. The Creator is as it were bound to assist His puny creatures: but He is not bound, unless by the excess of His own goodness, to be always near us, in the

---

* There is no province of theology where language proves itself less adequate to the task of expressing doctrine, than that which concerns the relation of the Divine *Persons* to created things. For on the one hand theology is clear as to the reality of such relations, and on the other hand it is equally clear as to the axiom that the external works of the Holy Trinity are indivisible. There is a beauty, which we can only half see, about these relations, which, to judge from the explanations of theologians, baffles words, or as soon as it is put into words seems dangerous to dogma. See Schwetz. Theol. Dogmat. i. 361. The following passage from S. Cyril of Alexandria, is the more remarkable as coming from a post-nicene father:

Καί ἐστι μὲν καθ᾽ ὑπόστασιν ἰδικὴν πολυτέλειος ὁ πατὴρ, ὁμοίως δὲ καὶ ὁ υἱὸς· καὶ τὸ πνεῦμα· ἀλλ᾽ ἡ ἑνὸς τῶν ὠνομασμένων δημιουργικὴ θέλησις, ἐφ᾽ ὅτῳ περ ἂν λέγοιτο γενέσθαι τυχὸν ἐνέργημα μὲν αὐτοῦ, πλὴν διὰ πάσης ἥξεται τῆς Θεότητος, καὶ τῆς ὑπὲρ κτίσιν ἐστὶν οὐσίας ἀποτέλεσμα, κοινὸν μὲν ὥσπέρ τι, πλὴν καὶ ἰδικῶι ἑκάστῳ προσώπῳ πρέπον, ὡς διὰ τριῶν ὑποστασίων πρέποι ἂν καὶ ἰδικῶς ἑκάστη, πολυτελείως ἐχούσηκαθ᾽ ἑαυτήν. ἐνεργεῖ τοιγαροῦν ὁ πατὴρ, ἀλλὰ δι᾽ υἱοῦ ἐν πνεύματι, ἐνεργεῖ καὶ ὁ υἱὸς. ἀλλ᾽ ὡς δύναμις τοῦ πατρὸς, ἐξ αὐτοῦ τι καὶ ἐν αὐτῷ νοούμενος καθ᾽ ὕπαρξιν ἰδικὴν ἐνεργεῖ καὶ τὸ πνεῦμα, πνεῦμα γάρ ἐστι τοῦ πατρὸς, κὶ τοῦ υἱοῦ, τὸ πολυτουργικόν.—*S. Cyrilli Alexandr. de S. Trinit. dialog. vi.*

Christian sense of His being nigh unto all them who
call upon Him.   This nearness is His present and
instantaneous reward for our unworthy service of
Him.   Joy and sorrow have, each of them, their own
wants and trials and peculiar laws; and who has not
experienced the ready goodness of God in both of
them?   Life and earth and the world abound with
joy, even to running over.   Happiness sweeps the
whole earth with its gay illuminations, just as the
strong swift sunshine throws its unimpeded mantle over
hill and dale, and land and sea.   We are too happy.
Our happiness runs away with us.   Its superabundance
will hardly let us sober ourselves, or steady our views
of this transitory world.   Joys are thousandfold; we
cannot count them; their name is legion: we can
hardly class them by their kinds.   They run out from
beneath the throne of God, and electrify millions of souls
the world over at the same moment.   Our very life is
joy, if we will only be honest enough to acknowledge
it to God and to ourselves.   The unhappiest man on
earth has from sunrise to sunset more satisfaction than
unhappiness.   It is seldom he would even give up his
own self and take another, still less forfeit the pleasure
of living altogether.   What a Creator must ours be, in
whose world merely to live is a stronger joy than any
temporal misery, however unparalleled, which can befall
us!   And how marvellously God multiplies His graces
upon us in our joy, opening our hearts to love Him more
generously, enlightening our minds to see Him more
clearly, quickening our gratitude, giving us a surprising elasticity in our spiritual exercises, and taking
away the dangerous alluring beauty of earth's idols by
the very strength of the gladsome, disenchanting light
which He throws upon them.   But, above all, in joy we

full often receive a double portion of that dear grace, which is well-nigh all our salvation; the grace of true contrition; for there is no contrition, which, for strength, vividness, and endurance, is like the contrition of a joyous man.

Sorrow, too, when borne even with ordinary patience, has its own rewards from God at once, rewards both of nature and of grace. What can be more beautiful than the way in which He calculates our weakness, and then measures out our sorrows, and then rains vehement storms of grace upon our fainting wills! But we only see this now and then, and in dusky indistinct perspective. In eternity we shall behold our past life in God, and what a thrilling revelation it will be ! But is not this undeniably true of ourselves, so far as we have gone in life, that we have had far less sorrow and pain than we are quite conscious we could bear, that our powers of bearing have been sensibly augmented while the cross was on us, that we can look back upon chapters of our past life about which we distinctly feel that with our present grace we could not live them over again, that the fruits of sorrow have always been tenfold brighter in the issue than the darkness was ever deepened in the process, and finally that in the retrospect the very sorrows themselves have been full of joys, exotic joys whose large leaves and waxen blossoms and long-lasting perfumes show that they were grown in heaven and not on earth? Yet these are only the present rewards of grief, the earthly blessings of those who mourn ! But look into the wonderful faces of those rings of saints who encompass the throne on high; feed your soul on the grave intellectual beauty which is depicted there, the winning look of blameless purity, the impassioned intensity of their celestial love. With

most of them it was sorrow that chastened them into
that transcendent loveliness, sorrow that piloted them
to that happy shore, sorrow that put those jewelled
crowns upon their heads, sorrow, keen and deep and
long, that unveiled for them the ever-beaming countenance of God! O magnificent Creator! where hast Thou
left room for our disinterested love, when everywhere
it seems as though Thou hadst made our interests take
precedence of Thine own?

Look at death, which is a simple punishment! Can
a created intelligence conceive of anything more terrible than to fall into the hands of God for the single
solitary purpose of being punished? And we might
have thought that death would be like this, being the
firstborn child of sin, from which not even the Immaculate Mother might be exempt. Yet how should we
have miscalculated the love of God! The deaths of
His servants are among the most valued jewels of His
crown. They are among the best possessions which
He holds in right of His creative love. We know but
little of the sights and sounds, the tastes and touches,
of that last dark passage. There is a shroud of seeming dishonour as well as mystery thrown around that
dread event. But we know that in it men live whole
lives in one short hour, and accumulate experiences
which pass our understanding both for number, rapidity,
and truth. We know that grand act has peculiar needs,
peculiar distresses, and that the invisible and visible
world forget their boundaries at the deathbed, and
war together in dread conflict, of which for the most
part the dying eye is the sole spectator. If we think
long on death, we shall come to wonder how it is that
any one can die calmly; the interests at stake are so
terrific the moment so decisive, the horrors so thickly

strewn, the natural helplessness so complete. A whole
world is sensibly sinking and giving way under us, and
there is nothing but blackness, space, and the arms of
God. Who can dare to fall through without a shudder?
Yet when are God's graces and indulgences more
numerous, more triumphant, more accessible, than in
that dreadful hour? Grace makes a very sunset of
what to nature is the most impenetrable darkness, and
the plaintive strains of the Miserere merge in spite of
our humility into songs of triumph; for the walls
between the dying soul and the heavenly Jerusalem
are so nearly fretted through, that the loud alleluias
surprise and distract the contrite love whose eyes are
closing on the Crucifix. The creature's change is very
dear to the Creator. Precious in the sight of the
Lord are the deaths of His Saints. Listen to this
beautiful story from the revelations of St. Gertrude.
She heard the preacher in a sermon urge most strongly
the absolute obligation of dying persons to love God
supremely, and to repent of their sins with true contrition founded on the motive of love. She thought
it a hard saying, and exaggeratedly stated, and she
murmured within herself that if so pure a love were
needed, few indeed died well; and a cloud came over
her mind as she thought of this. But God Himself
vouchsafed to speak to her, and dispel her trouble.
He said that in that last conflict, if the dying were
persons who had ever tried to please Him and to live
good lives, He disclosed Himself to them as so infinitely
beautiful and desirable, that love of Him penetrated
into the innermost recesses of their souls, so that they
made acts of true contrition from the very force of their
love of Him: which propension of Mine, He vouchsafed
to add, thus to visit them in that moment of death,

I wish My elect to know, and I desire it to be preached and proclaimed, that among My other mercies this also may have a special place in men's remembrance.* Let us then tell each other this sweet doctrine, that our hearts may burn more and more with love of so compassionate a God.

Now all these are present rewards, ways in which God repays on earth our love of Him. They are but samples of what is incessant, abundant, superfluous, all through life. Every one's mercies are so great that they are, to him at least, rightly viewed, strange, wonderful, and unexpected. God tries our faith, and seems to delight in trying it, by the very reduplication of His benefits. But after all, this life is not the time of His recompenses. He does not profess to give us our wages here. He warns us not to expect them. Is it then that His love is so great, that He cannot help Himself, and that His Nature is under the blessed necessity of loving and of giving? Or is it that these mercies are only the casual drops which are spilled from the overflowing cup prepared for us in heaven? Oh even the most desolate of men may be so sure of His paternal love, that they may remember that eternity can be no long way off, and will repay the waiting!

But if the promptitude of His payment is in itself a proof of the greatness of God's love, still more strongly is that consoling fact brought out when we consider with what He pays us. The blessings of nature, the gifts of grace, the rewards of glory,—who is sufficient to declare the number, the beauty, the greatness, and the wonder of these things? There are three vast kingdoms, three magnificent creations, for so they might be called, which are simple expressions of the vastness of the Creator's

* Ap. Pennequin. Isagoge ad Amorem Divinum, p. 43.

love. They cannot enrich Him. They are not needed
to His bliss. They add nothing to what He possesses
already. His mercy contrives to reap some little harvest of accidental glory from them, but it is at the
expense of endless outrage, not only of His justice, but
even of His compassion. They are the product of His
love of the creature, our property rather than His,
almost more our dominion than His own.

In the kingdom of nature there are three vast pro-
vinces or separate worlds, which are full of the most
exquisite enjoyment to the creature; and we speak only
of enjoyments, which, if through our frailty they are
dangerous as stealing our hearts from God, are yet altogether without reproach of sin. The physical world is
full of God's rewards. Life is itself a joy. But what
shall we say of the abounding sense of health and
vigour, which they who enjoy it the most abundantly
can hardly value at its legitimate price? Yet to one,
whose head is always aching, whose limbs have always
in them some lurking pain, and whose languor and
feebleness is all day long playing the traitor to the
activity of his mind or the energy of his will, the sense
of health, when it comes, is almost like a miracle. There
is the surpassing beauty of scenery, the grandeur of the
mountains, the sublimity of the sea, the variety of fertile landscape, the rain, the wind, the sunshine, and the
storm. Every sense is an avenue of perpetual pleasure,
which, if we will, can raise the mind to God, and in-
flame our hearts with love. If we except the irregularities which sin has introduced into the physical world, and
which manifestly form no part of the system, the whole of
it is simple pleasure and enjoyment, an emanation from the
everlasting and inexhaustible gladness of the Most High.

But the pleasures of the intellectual world are yet

more wonderful. Can any pleasure be more exquisite than the sensible exercise of our mental faculties? The variety, the multitude, the depth, the rapidity, the interweaving of our thoughts, are full of boundless enjoyment, leading us through realms and realms of truth and beauty, and charming us at every turn with some enchanting discovery. Through some minds the pure delight of poetry thrills with feelings of the most indescribable nature. With others the sweet skilful strains of music wind into the uttermost recesses of their souls, with a beauty which is sometimes so gifted as almost to win back the reason that has already deserted its throne. To others form and colour, painting, statuary, and architecture, are like copious fountains of power and enjoyment streaming into them abundantly for ever. With many the labour of composition is only a pain because of the very excess of the pleasure, which is more than they can bear. The investigation of truth is only at times weary and irksome, because our tyrant minds are demanding of the body what it cannot give. No more can be said of the pleasures of the intellectual world than that they are marvellous shadows of the incomprehensible joys of God Himself.

If the moral world seems to afford a less variety of enjoyment than the intellectual, it far transcends it in the vividness and power of its enjoyments. The will is an inexhaustible mine of joys, which our nature seems to prize beyond all others. Our affections are complicated instruments of the most amazing and unexpected and diversified pleasures, which possess our whole nature and fulfil it with satisfaction in a way which no other pleasures do. Human love sits upon a throne above all other human joys, and there is no one who ever dreams of questioning its rights or of abating its prerogatives.

Indeed the joy of love is too great for life.   It breaks its bounds, runs riot, and makes wild work even with the strong framework of society and the destiny of kingdoms.   It fills every depth in our nature and then runs over, deluging mind and will, duty and even passion.   There is no abyss sufficiently capacious to hold the torrents of love, which one heart is able to outpour, except that sea without horizon, bed, or shore, the ever-blessed Being of God Himself. The Holy Ghost, the eternally proceeding Spirit, is the jubilee of the Father and the Son ; and His shadow lies for evermore upon the moral world, the vast reflecting waters of the human will.   As the physical world with its joys of substance and being appears to be a transcript of the Person of the Eternal Father, and the intellectual world with its light and laws to be an illuminated shadow of the Person of the Word, so does the moral world, the fiery thrilling world of love and will, represent Him who is the coequal limit of the Godhead, the third Person of the Ever-blessed Trinity.

Yet these three worlds, the physical, the intellectual, and the moral, are one world ; and in their unions, blendings, borrowings, comparisons, and intersections, we have so many fresh sources of the most delightful enjoyment, above and beyond those which these worlds furnish in their separate capacities.   Why then do we not worship more constantly and more intelligently in common daily things the wisdom of God, thus lending itself to the strong will of His goodness in every department of creation?   Every orb in the immeasurable fields of indistinguishable star-dust lies in the light of God's outpoured and everflowing joy.   Every created intelligence drinks its fill of the fountains of His gladness.   Every instinct of animals beats with a pulsation

of divine enjoyment. Every tree uplifts its head and
flings out its branches, every flower blooms and sheds
sweet odour, every mineral glances and sparkles, just as
the clouds sail, and the waters flow, and the planet
turns, in the excess of the happiness of God. His blessedness lies over the whole world, serenely shining, like
the waters of a spiritual sea beneath whose transparent
depths all creation with beautiful distinctness lies. Thus
in God's wide world there is no room for sin, no provi-
sion for sorrow, not a corner for unhappiness. Sin is a
stranger, an intruder, an enemy, as little at home on
earth as it would be in heaven. It is we who have introduced it into the bright and happy world, we, who
by the freedom of our wills, which were left at large
that we might love God the more magnificently, have
broken down the cloister of His paradise.

It is not altogether man's ingratitude which makes
him forgetful of the benefits of God. He Himself,
blessed be His Holy Name! throws His own mercies
into the shade, as well by multiplying them beyond our
powers of counting, as by surpassing and excelling them
by others. Thus it is with the kingdom of nature. It
is lost in the splendour of the kingdom of grace. Awhile
ago it looked so bright and beautiful, with all its features
so smiling and its outlines so soft and ethereal, and now,
like a mountain-side which the sunbeams have deserted,
it looks cold and bare, rugged and uninviting. We
have already seen how, in the kingdom of grace, God
rewards our efforts instantaneously by fresh supplies of
greater grace. Let us look for a moment at grace itself.
The gulf between God and ourselves seems infinite and
impassable; yet grace bridges it over, and passes it with
a rapidity to which the speed of the electric spark is
weary slowness. By sanctifying grace He is incessantly,

habitually, powerfully, superabundantly, pouring into us marvellous communications of His Divine Nature. Each undulation of it, as it reaches and informs our souls, is a greater miracle than the creation of the universe. One touch, and we pass from darkness to light; one touch, and all our eternity is changed. He endows our souls, even before reason dawns, with mysterious infused habits which make such utterly new creatures of us that the process can only be described as a being positively born again. Besides this, He plants even in the unconscious infant at the font seven wonderful gifts of the Holy Ghost, seven distinct heavens of the most beautiful splendours and unearthly powers, in which lie hid the possibilities of the very highest sanctity. Thus our souls are made as it were a musical instrument, worthy that the hands of God should play upon it, and out of which He can evoke such melodies of holiness, such strains of the exquisite music of perfection, as could ravish the angels of heaven, even as the Human Soul of Jesus is ravishing them this hour. Neither is this instrument to remain unused. The impulses of the Divine Will, the pressure of actual grace, is ever varying the music which they draw forth, as the rapid touch of the Creator's hand flies over the many keys of the complex heart of man; and all the while one grace is leading to another in wonderful progression, one the prophecy of what is yet to come, and another the crown of what has gone before, with such a vista of graces in the prospect that no man ever reaches to the term. The day will never dawn when he must not aspire to more and more; there is no term which is the limit of the grace which God intended him to reach; and, however long it may be delayed, death will find him full of beginnings, laying the foundations of a new and better, a more lofty and

spacious, fabric than he had built before. Most wonderful too is it to behold how all this grace elicits and
magnifies the freedom of the will, and, while it sup-
ports and strengthens and almost constrains it, makes it
all the while more undeniably, because more spiritually,
free.

The abundance of grace, again, is almost as wonderful as its nature. We live in an ocean of grace, as fishes
live in the deep sea. It is above, beneath, around us,
everywhere and overwhelmingly. It comes in floods,
which though they have sudden rises at times, are
always floods, and know no ebb or intermission. Its
continuity is another marvel which we must add to its
abundance. The want of duly reflecting upon this is
one cause of the pusillanimity which is so common in
the spiritual life. Men too often think practically that
grace is like the theatrical god of the heathen poet, and
does not interfere until it is wanted, and wanted with
such obvious urgency as to justify even to an unsupernatural apprehension some heavenly interference. This
inadequate conception of the incessant action of grace
at once diminishes their confidence in God, unnerves
them in temptations, deters them from attempting
generous enterprises, and makes them estimate far too
cheaply their responsibilities, privileges, and possibilities. It cannot be too often repeated that the wakeful
reason breathes grace, and lives in its light, and leans
on its support, as much as we breathe the air and see
by the daylight and have the hard safe crust of the
planet beneath our feet. The extent and universality
of grace, in the sacraments and out of them, in the
Church and in order to the Church, the way in which
it can combine with so much that is false and evil, and
its godlike importunity, the very thought of which is a

kind of prevision of our final perseverance,—all these characteristics of grace would fill volumes, were they treated of at length. Its variety too must not be forgotten. If the saints have graces which we hardly know how to name and classify, if no one man's grace is like another's, what must we think of the widespreading realms of angelical existence, and the seemingly fabulous arithmetic of graces which we must believe there is among those clear far-reaching spirits? Surely if it is not hard for a man to live in the pure bright air of heaven, and some shock of disease or outward accident must supervene, to cut short the thread of his existence, so it cannot be hard in this fresh, buoyant, bracing atmosphere of grace for a man to save his soul, and it must be some danger which he himself has sought, or some poison which he has wilfully imbibed, and after that pertinaciously refused the antidote, which can destroy his soul, and even then with difficulty. A man must struggle to be out of grace, when grace is so around him. We believe that in all things man's will is free, but that in nothing is he less free than to be lost eternally.

But all these blessings of nature and of grace are only in an imperfect and improper sense the rewards of the Creator. The kingdom of glory is the theatre of His recompense. It is in order to extend that kingdom, that the grace given us is so ineffably beyond what is due to our nature. But how shall we hope to measure the kingdom of glory, when it is to be measured only by the Divine Magnificence ? Both a prophet and an apostle join in teaching us that eye has not seen, nor ear heard, nor man's heart conceived, what God has prepared for them that love Him. When the bodies of the just rise at the general resurrection, with their senses

spiritualized and rendered capable of pleasures which
do not fall within their province now, and with perhaps
many new senses developed in the immortal body which
were unknown in its mortal days, the pure pleasures of
these glorified senses must be something quite beyond
the power of our imagination to picture to itself. He
who knows the blameless exultation of his soul when
the eye has conveyed to it a landscape of surpassing
beauty, or whose ear has thrilled with some inspiriting
or subduing strain of music, or who, when he heard a
passage of magnificent poetry, felt as if an immediate
and extraordinary accession of bold intellectual power
was given to him as he listened, may at least indistinctly guess the exquisite delights of the glorified senses of
the risen body, or which is perhaps more true, understand how their delicacy and charm must be beyond our
power of guessing.

Yet the heavenly joys of the illuminated understanding far transcend the thrills of the glorified senses.
The contemplation of heavenly beauty and of heavenly
truth must indeed be beyond all our earthly standards
of comparison. The clearness and instantaneousness of
all the mental processes, the complete exclusion of
error, the unbroken serenity of the vision, the facility
of embracing whole worlds and systems in one calm,
searching, exhausting glance, the divine character and
utter holiness of all the truths presented to the view,—
these are broken words which serve at least to show
what we may even now indistinctly covet in that bright
abode of everlasting bliss. Intelligent intercourse with
the angelic choirs, and the incessant transmission of
the divine splendours through them to our minds,
cannot be thought of without our perceiving that the
keen pleasures and deep sensibilities of the intellectual

world on earth are but poor, thin, unsubstantial shadows of the exulting immortal life of our glorified minds above.

The very expansion of the faculties of the soul, and the probable disclosure in it of many new faculties which have no object of exercise in this land of exile, are in themselves pleasures which we can hardly picture to ourselves. To be rescued from all narrowness, and for ever; to possess at all times a perfect consciousness of our whole undying selves, and to possess and retain that self-consciousness in the bright light of God; to feel the supernatural corroborations of the light of glory, securing to us powers of contemplation such as the highest mystical theology can only faintly and feebly imitate; to expatiate in God, delivered from the monotony of human things; to be securely poised in the highest flights of our immense capacities, without any sense of weariness, or any chance of a reaction; who can think out for himself the realities of a life like this?

Yet what is all this compared with one hour, one of earth's short hours, of the magnificences of celestial love? O to turn our whole souls upon God, and souls thus expanded and thus glorified; to have our affections multiplied and magnified a thousand fold, and then girded up and strengthened by immortality to bear the beauty of God to be unveiled before us; and even so strengthened, to be rapt by it into a sublime amazement which has no similitude on earth; to be carried away by the inebriating torrents of love, and yet be firm in the most steadfast adoration; to have passionate desire, yet without tumult or disturbance; to have the most bewildering intensity along with an unearthly calmness; to lose ourselves in God, and then find ourselves there more our own than ever; to love rapturously and to be loved again still more rapturously, and then for our love to grow more rapturous still, and again the return of our love to be still outstripping what we gave, and then for us to love even yet more and more and more rapturously, and again, and again, and again to have it so returned, and still the great waters of God's love to flow over us and overwhelm us until the vehemence of our impassioned peace and the daring vigour of our yearning adoration reach beyond the sight of our most venturous imagining;—what is all this but for our souls to live a life of the most intelligent entrancing extasy, and yet not be shivered by the fiery heat? There have been times on earth when we have caught our own hearts loving Go.l, and there was a flash of light, and then a tear, and after that we lay down to rest. O happy that we were! Worlds could not purchase from us even the memory of those moments. And yet when we think of heaven, we may own that we know not yet what manner of thing it is to love the Lord our God.

Meanwhile it is difficult to conceive how the pure pleasures of the glorified senses, or the delights of our illuminated understandings, or the expansion of our souls dilated with immortality, or the magnificences of celestial love, can be of any price at all in our eyes, seeing that they are but the outside fringes of heaven, the merest accessories of our true beatitude. To see God face to face, as He is ; to gaze undazzled on the Three Divine Persons, cognizable and distinct in the burning fires of their inaccessible splendours ; to behold that long coveted sight, the endless Generation of the All-holy Son, and our hearts to hold the joy, and not die ; to watch with spirits all outstretched in adoration the ever-radiant and ineffably beautiful Procession of the Holy Ghost from the Father and the

Son, and to participate ourselves in that jubilee of jubilees, and drink in with greedy minds the wonders of that procession, and the marvellous distinctness of its beauty from the Generation of the Son; to feel ourselves with extatic awe and yet with seraphic intimacy overshadowed by the Person of the Unbegotten Father, the Father to whom and of whom we have said so much on earth, the Fountain of Godhead, who is truly our Father while He is also the Father of the Eternal Son; to explore, with exulting license and with unutterable glad fear, Attribute after Attribute, oceans opening into oceans of divinest beauty; to lie astonished in unspeakable contentment before the vision of God's surpassing Unity, so long the joyous mystery of our predilection, while the Vision through all eternity seems to grow more fresh and bright and new:—O my poor soul! what canst thou know of this, or of these beautiful necessities, of thy exceeding love, which shall only satisfy itself in endless alternations, now of silence and now of song.

These are the rewards of God, these the ways in which He repays our love. To hear them or to read of them is not enough. Years of continual meditation will not even give us an adequate conception of them. To estimate them rightly we must have a true and profound knowledge of God, and be able to think worthily of His greatness. Without this we can never know the abyss of condescension to which He stoops in order to confer a grace upon the loftiest of His saints. He has as it were to humble Himself even to receive the burning worship of the purest seraphim. To what a lowness does He bend Himself in order to accept the love of the Immaculate heart of Mary! Without repeated meditation on the Divine Perfections

we cannot fathom the depth of our own nothingness,
the horror of our own baseness, the inconceivable per-
tinacity of our sin; neither can we realize, not only
the littleness of our love which is so little that the
poorest words give an exaggerated impression of it,
but also to what extent God is free from obligation
to us, and to how little, little at least compared with
the immensity of His actual mercies, our nature can
lay claim as its due because it is a creature. Yet an
accurate spiritual apprehension of all these things is
needful before we can appreciate the mysterious magnificence of the rewards of God. Only let us remember, for life is short and there is much to do, that right
down through the abyss of our own nothingness lies
the shortest road to the contemplation of the Divine
Beauty.

While I stand in the presence of these mighty recompenses of our Creator, I am abashed by their exceeding magnitude, and all things else which I otherwise
should love become insignificant and go almost out of
sight. I feel that I have no words to tell these great
things, no thoughts to think them; and yet it seems
to me as if the *way* in which God repays our love was
something even more wonderful than the rewards He
gives. To see God face to face is the crowning joy of
heaven; to be sensibly near Him is the greatest joy
of earth; and He never seems so near as in the way
in which He deals with us, His demeanour towards us,
His manner, His address, His courtesy, if I may for
the moment use such words. At first sight it is altogether so unlike what we should have expected; and
yet on second thoughts so right, so suitable, both to
His greatness and to our littleness, while at the same
time its being right and suitable does not in the least

detract from its gratuitous condescension. Nay, it rather enhances it. In truth God's goodness is unlike any other subject of human contemplation; for the more reasonable it appears to us, the more surprising does it grow, as if, even now and here, it partook somewhat of the eternal freshness of the Beatific Vision.

When the Creator of the world entered it in order to redeem it, in the obscure midnight, in a gloomy cavern, as the Babe of Bethlehem, it was an advent such as took the natural speculations of men by surprise, and was even a hindrance to their belief. So is it with God's demeanour towards us in the world. He is not like a great king. He is unlike one both in the frequency of His visits, or rather in His abiding presence, and also in the absence of pomp and notice when He comes. There is no attitude of command, no obvious graciousness of condescension. Blessed be His Majesty! His manner is not that of a master, nor even of an equal; it is rather that of an inferior mingled with the sweetness and fidelity of an earthly mother. When He blesses us, assists us, gives us graces, soothes our sorrows, or dries our tears, He does it all with an amazing tenderness, almost with a sort of bashful humility, like one whom we are laying under an obligation by accepting his services at all. The attentions of His love are also so minute, that no service, or half-service, or transitory intentions of ours, escape His divine yet just exaggerations. In our past life there are thousands of forgotten prayers, thousands of resisted temptations; but God has forgotten none of them. He repays them with a mindfulness which, unless it also awakens love, can hardly fail to try our faith. He must indeed desire our love, who tempts us with an eternal reward for a cup of cold water given

19   †

in His Name. He repays us also variously and with
a view to our tastes and desires, so as to enhance to
each of us the value of our own particular reward.
He repays us superabundantly. At first sight it seems
as if there was an absence of all similitude between the
service and the reward, both in degree and kind.
Nevertheless there is to His wisdom an exact and
unerring proportion in His recompense, which, while
the manner of it is a mystery to us, is at the same
time an encouragement to us to love Him more, as if
He had affectionately and condescendingly put it in
our own power to have as much of heaven and of Him
as we please. Last of all, throughout the whole proceeding, it is in reality love, and not services, which
He repays, not the acts we do, so much as the spirit
in which we do them. Can we conceive of a manner
more attractive, of an affection more winning, of a
solicitude more delightful, of a gratitude more touching, of an unselfishness more sweetly reproachful, of a
generosity more overwhelming, of a magnificence more
delicate, than this demeanour of the Creator towards
His creatures? And it is none other than the Creator,
the Boundless Ocean of Being, the abyss of unfathomable perfections, who to the gigantic stretch of His
omnipotence can wed these ineffable delicacies of
minutest love! And it is to us that all this is done,
to us who had no rights to begin with, and who have
again and again forfeited all rights we could imagine
might be ours, to us who in our secret hearts know
ourselves to be what we are, more unspeakably wicked
than any one of our fellow creatures suspects that we
can be! And the love which is thus repaid, alas!
what a mockery of love it is!

Let us think once more of heaven. How cheerfully

the thought of that bright home can humble us! What can be more wonderful than the contrast between man paying God on earth, and God paying man in heaven? We have looked at man's side in the last chapter. We have seen the misery and unworthiness, the scantiness and the meanness, the coldness, the reluctance, the distraction, and the ungracious delays of the creature with the Creator. And then comes death! A good death is one in which we feel that hither· to we have never done any good at all, but in which we seriously, though with alarming self-distrust, intend, if we survive, to begin to do good. And considering the greatness of God and the vastness of our obliga- tions to Him, this is by no means a fiction even to the Saints. We die, and in dying we fall into the hands of His justice, and there, fresh wonder of creative love! we find far more than mercy. Our guardian angel could scarcely let us into heaven if he wished, were he the judge. The Mother of mercy would have to borrow the Sacred Heart of Jesus, before she could see things as He sees them, and award a crown to us. If there could be shame in heaven, how should we be overwhelmed with confusion appearing there with the miserable tribute of our interested love and of our wisely selfish fear! But how does the Creator, the King of kings, receive His tribute? He bursts forth all divinely into triumph, because a half-converted sin- ner has condescended to accept His grace. He bids the angels rejoice, and holds high feast through all the empyrean heaven, not because He has evolved some new and wonder-stirring system out of nothing, not because He has called into being some million-worlded nebula, and cast upon it such an effulgence of His beauty as throws all the rest of His creation into the shade,—but because one wretched, unworthy, offensive man has, after an immense amount of divine eloquence and pleading, consented to take the first step towards not being damned,—because one outcast of human society, who has drunk his fill of every vice, has graciously condescended for fear of hell to accept heaven ! These are the Creator's triumphs, these the ovations of everlasting and of all-wise mercy. And God can do nought unworthy of Himself. He cannot demean Himself. Abasement is impossible to Him. Nothing can sully His incomparable purity. Nothing can He do which is not infinitely worthy of Him, worthy of His power, His wisdom, and His goodness. And therefore this triumph, this feast of angels, over one sinner that does penance, is altogether worthy of the adorable majesty of the eternally blessed God ! O who would not weep over the wonders of creative love, mystery after mystery, at every turn giving out fresh treasures of tenderness, compassion, and magnificence ?

Watch that soul which is now just entering heaven. Can any thing be more amazing than the caresses which God is lavishing upon it? Heaven itself has almost grown brighter by its entrance, and the anthems of the redeemed have sounded forth with a more full sonorous melody. Mary on her throne has been filled with joy, while an exulting thrill of sympathy ran through all the angelic multitudes. And why do they rejoice? Because there is a new joy for God, another glory for His complacency to rest on. It is the salvation of that soul which has just entered heaven. Some fifty years of the full use of reason it lived on earth. The world was its delight, wealth almost its idol. It drank its full of various pleasures, and thought not of His goodness out of which they come. Many times the divine law

came across that man's path, and when it did, he
straightway, and with little reflection, transgressed it.
He loved luxury, denied himself nothing, and was not
over-bountiful to the poor. He was surrounded by
comforts, as a city is compassed by its walls. He had
sorrows and troubles, who has not? But they were
light and infrequent. The world smiled upon its votary.
He was popular with his fellows. He had all that his
indolent ambition cared to have; and best of all,
he was blessed with almost unbroken health. There
was at last almost the weariness of satiety about his
undeviatingly prosperous fortune. Disease came, and his
old joys ceased to be joys at all. He had nothing then
to tempt him from God, but everything to draw him
nearer to Him. Fear also, with the belief of hell,
wrought strongly upon him; and by the help of priest
and sacrament, together with the grace of a sorrow easily
within reach of his faith and fear, he put together in
some ten days the dregs of half a century spent in the
service of the devil and the world; and he has now gone
through a very circuitous path in purgatory to heaven
to offer God this refuse of his probation. And heaven
keeps feast for this! And the great Creator takes
almost with avidity the leavings of the world, counting for chivalry the querulous helplessness of a sin-
enfeebled soul. There is not one word of reproach, one
look of discontent. Coupled with His extraordinary
mindfulness of minutest services, God is seemingly forgetful how all good is but His own grace. Moreover
He is as it were blind to the fact that the man was
after all doing what was best for himself, and when he
could hardly help himself, and even then with amazingly
little of self-indignation or of righteous zeal. See! His
arms are round that deathbed penitent. He is telling

him the secrets of His love. He is sealing for him
with a Father's kiss the eternity of his beatitude. That
man will lie for ever bathed in the beautiful light of the
Godhead !*

Is this credible? Should we dare to believe it, if it
were not of faith? O wonderful, wonderful God! of
whom each hour is telling us something new, making
premature perpetual heaven in our hearts! It is an old
history, that love makes the Creator seem to put Himself below His own creatures: it is an old history, yet
it surprises us almost to tears each morning as we wake.
So here we come to a Servant-God, like the Incarnate
Servant-Saviour, Jesus Christ. And yet there are men
to whom God is a difficulty! There are men who
think hard thoughts of Him, whose only trial of us is in
the prodigious excesses of His love, which wearies and
outstrips at times the slowness of our faith. O Heavenly

---

* This imaginary case, put forward here as a mere theological possibility, is given as actual fact in some of the revelations of the saints. I
will cite two, one a case of contrition and the other of attrition, which are
exact parallels, and easy of access. The first is the case of Lord Stourton, given
in Rosignoli's Maraviglie di Dio nell' Anime del Purgatorio, parte i. Maraviglia
v. The second is the famous revelation of the "Least in Heaven" made to
St. Mechtildis. Libro della Spiritual Grazia, lib. i. cap. 51. This last has before
now played its part in controversy. See Siurl. Theologia Positiva-Dogmatica
de Novissimis. Tractatus v. cap. 4. Sect. 55, where however the reference to
St. Mechtildis is given wrongly. From certain observations I *incline* to
believe that *contrition* is a commoner deathbed grace than *attrition*. If this
be so, it is another example of the way in which the excesses of God's mercy
further the interests of His exceeding sanctity. When attrition is given as a
deathbed grace it is most likely the result of an earnest endeavour after
contrition. I cannot fancy a dying sinner, roused to a sense of sin, trying
only for attrition. Still less can I believe that he would succeed in obtaining
it. The very idea seems to me incongruous with real earnestness, almost
an evidence of an unchanged heart with no honest wish to be changed. A
large proportion of deathbed conversions are cases of men who from un-
toward outward circumstances and inadequate instruction have their souls
for the first time really roused to a sense of sin and a right view of God, when
lying on their bed of death, with the priest by their sides.

Father! it is the greatness of Thy goodness which bewilders our humility by mocking our knowledge of ourselves; and that is the only difficulty we find in Thee. May it grow still more difficult, still more beyond our grasp, for therein is our eternal life!

What then is the conclusion to which we come about this repaying of our love by God? It is simply this. In the first place, He has made His glory coincide with our interests. Secondly, from a privilege He lowers love into a precept, and this one act is a complete revelation of Himself. Thirdly, He so puts our interests into His, that it is hard to look at His interests only, without falling into heresy. Do these conclusions solve the five questions we have been asking? No! but they lead to the one answer of all the five; only that, ending as we began, the answer is itself a mystery. St. John states it; no one can explain it; earth would be hell without it; purgatory is paradise because of it; we shall live upon it in heaven, yet never learn all that is in it;—God is love!

.

BOOK III.

OBJECTIONS CONSIDERED.

THE CREATOR AND THE CREATURE.

BOOK III.

OBJECTIONS CONSIDERED.

CHAPTER I.

THE EASINESS OF SALVATION.

L'estat de la redemption vaut cent fois mieux que celuy de l'innocence.
S. Francis of Sales.

THE result of the preceding enquiry has been at the
very least to satisfy us as to the fact that God loves us,
and as to the nature and character of His love. We
have seen that Divine love is at once creative, redeeming, sanctifying, uncreated, and without respect of persons. As creative it was not content to call angels and
men out of nothing, but it constituted them at the outset
in a state of grace, which was not connatural to them, and
was in no way due to their nature. As redeeming, it
pursued men when they fell; and at no less an expense
than the Incarnation of One of the Divine Persons, and
with every circumstance of attraction and prodigality,
it bought them back again when they had sold themselves as slaves to evil. As sanctifying, it is incessant
in its visitations of grace, and marvellous in the heights
of sanctity to which it can raise those whom sin had
sunk so low. As uncreated, it is especially astonishing

and adorable, and naturally includes, and while it includes surpasses, all created ties and all diversities of
human love.   As without respect of persons, it enables
us to repose our trust, not only on the all-efficacious
power of God, but upon that beautiful justice and
exquisite fidelity which are the true foundations of our
love.

In this love of God we have already passed an eternity.   In this love we have lived without beginning.
He has never seen His glorious Word, but He has seen
us in Him, and the mutual love of Father and of Son
from the first has scattered its brightness on our foreseen
lives.   There is something awful in such enduring love,
something which overshadows the spirits of creatures so
capricious and inconstant as ourselves.   It frightens us
that we should have been loved eternally.   At the same
time what must be the necessary efficacy of an eternal
love?   Here is a very mine of golden consolation.   He
who has not ceased to love us from for ever, will not
lightly withdraw His love.   He will not easily surrender to His enemies a creature whom He has borne
in His bosom like a nurse from the beginning.   Into
the least of His blessings He pours an endless love.
There are no infirmities which He disdains, no prayers
which He disregards.   He cannot love otherwise than
with an overflowing love, rewarding the most trivial
actions, canonizing the most transitory wishes, and
placing around every step of life such a retinue of graces,
such an attendance of angels, such an apparatus of sacraments, that the self-will must be strong indeed which
can break away from God and lose itself.

He apparently consults our interests rather than His
own, by making in reality the last identical with the
first.   His first thought for sinners is to make repen-

tance easy and light, and strange indeed are the things to which His wisdom can persuade His justice, or His goodness bend His sanctity. By His own order our liberty seems to take precedence of His law, while the whole of creation is apparently disposed for the convenience of our salvation. The increase of this love depends upon ourselves. On this side the grave we can have it when we will, and there is always grace to enable us to ask it and to will it. The more we ask the more He will give, and reckon the obligation to be on His side rather than on ours. All that is wanted of us is, to take God's side, to love what He loves, to hate what He hates, and, to sum up all in one word, to belong to Jesus Christ.

This is a summary of the results at which we have arrived, and it brings us to the conclusion of the second division of our treatise. In the first we enquired what it was to be a creature and what it was to have a Creator, and we saw that creation meant and only could mean love. Full of the knowledge we had thus acquired, we proceeded to ask five questions, concerning the principal mysteries of this Divine Love, which from its eternal hiding-place in God came into sight at creation, and we saw that our position as creatures made it important to us to have these questions answered. But it may be objected, All this is so much special pleading for God. It does not state man's case fairly, because it does not state it completely. There are certain phenomena which are practical objections to this view, and they have hardly been considered. This is what may be said. I do not own the justice of it, because, as I have said before, if I understand rightly what it is to be a creature, and what it is to have a Creator, I do not see how the creature can have any side at all. It appears that God's side is also the creature's side, and that he can have no other. If we imagine for ourselves an immensely benevolent despot, in possession of the most legitimate claims upon our obedience, but bound by the rectitude of his own character, as well as by our rights, to the exercise of commutative justice, and call him the Creator, under such a being we should obviously have a side of our own, and a point of view belonging to us. But that is no adequate description of God. It is only an uneasy intellectual creation of our own. But, if there be a chance of gaining any more love for God from the hearts of His creatures, most willingly should we engage in the task of meeting these objections, the more willingly because the soil to be turned up is so rich, concerning, as it does, the Creator's love of His creatures, that it will bloom with fresh and fresh blossoms almost before the plough has furrowed up the surface.

Our object however is strictly a practical one. Hence we are not going to enter into any of the abstruse questions about the origin of evil, or the existence of hell, or the permission of idolatry, or the eternal destiny of those outside the Church. We are speaking to the children of the Church, and however dark such questions may be to them, or however worthy of their most vigorous intellectual research, they have no right to be practical difficulties to a Catholic in the pursuit of holiness. Strictly speaking we have no right to have any difficulties at all; for a speculative difficulty can hardly become a practical one to men who take the teaching of the Church on faith; and men who do not, —how shall they dream of attaining holiness at all? Nevertheless there are some questions which, if not without fault of ours, at least without grievous fault, tease and molest us, and become, not unfrequently, sometimes the sources and at other times the hotbeds of temptation. Of these we may select three especially, because in handling them we shall implicitly and indirectly answer many more. The first is the difficulty of salvation; the second, the ultimate fate of the great multitude of the faithful; and the third, the perplexing question of worldliness; and these will occupy this and the two following chapters.

It is objected that all that has been said of the creative love of God would lead to the conclusion that it is easy to be saved, or that if it is not easy, the case has not been stated in its entireness. To this objection it does not seem a sufficient answer to say, that God is not less good, but that the awful malice and corruption of man's will are too strong even for His will to save us. For, though it is true that God cannot both leave us free and constrain us to be saved, yet His redeeming love might be expected to make such allowances for the unhappy degradation of man by sin, as to make his salvation not a work of more than ordinary difficulty. Surely these allowances are implied in the very notion of redemption. If heaven be not easy of access, neither its beauty nor the generosity with which it is offered are such motives of love as they would be on the contrary supposition. The most perfectly satisfactory answer to the objection, if it be true, is, that salvation is easy. We are speaking only to and of believers, and are not concerning ourselves with a secret which God has reserved for Himself, and into which we do not attempt to penetrate even by guesses, because it has no practical bearing upon our own service of God. To a believer salvation is easy, so easy in fact that to each individual soul in the Church the chances are greatly in

favour of his salvation. This may not be true of him
at any given moment, as when he has just relapsed into
sin, or when he is enfeebled by a long wilful captivity to
sinful habits ; but looking at his life as a whole, and
considering things in the long run, it is true that the
chances are greatly in favour of his salvation ; and I
have my misgivings that I am even thus understating
his prospects of success. His life must be a life of
efforts ; but the efforts are easy, easy in themselves, easy
in their auxiliaries, easy in both the prospect of a future
and the enjoyment of a present reward. What else is
the meaning of our Lord's words: Come to Me, all you
that labour, and are burdened, and I will refresh you.
Take up My yoke upon you, and learn of Me, because I
am meek, and humble of heart ; and you shall find rest
to your souls. For My yoke is sweet, and My burden
light.* Or again what can be more distinct than the
words of St. John : For this is the charity of God, that
we keep His commandments ; and His commandments
are not heavy. For whatsoever is born of God overcometh the world ; and this is the victory which overcometh the world, our faith ?†

The first point then for us to consider is the easiness
of salvation in itself. Let no one be afraid, that if the
affirmative of this proposition be proved, it will make
any of us sluggish and indifferent in the pursuit of
Christian perfection. Divine truth is continually exert-
ing an influence and putting forth an attraction, which
baffle and deride the guesses and predictions of our
human criticism. If the view be true, it will lead men
to love God who do not love Him now, and it will lead
those who love Him already to love Him more. It
is not the fear of hell which draws men to aim at per-

* St. Matt. xi.   † I. St. John v.

fection, nor is it the ambition to be saints which buoys
them up, through mortification, weariness and prayer.
It is the beauty of God, which has touched them and
taken them captive; and whatever discloses more of
that beauty, will be but a stronger attraction enabling
them to scale higher summits. So while our enquiry
will give us sweet and hopeful views of sinners, it will
also humble, edify, and stimulate ourselves, if we are
trying to advance in the ways of God.

Let us then trace from the first the process by which
God vouchsafes to save a soul. Not many days elapse
after a child of catholic parents is born, before he is
carried to the baptismal font. There by the almost
momentary action of pouring water in the name of the
Most Holy and Undivided Trinity, the child is regen-
erated. Nothing can be more easy, or more instantaneous. Yet let us consider all that is involved in an
infant's baptism. Not only are the eternal consequences
of the fall to his particular soul in one instant destroyed,
but the child becomes entitled to the most stupendous
privileges and inheritance, which would not have been
due to him naturally, even if Adam had not fallen. He
is at once raised to a far higher state than one of pure
nature. He is the child of God. The Divine Nature
has been communicated to him by sanctifying grace.
Extraordinary possibilities of spiritual developments
and earnests of everlasting life have been implanted in
him by certain mysteriously infused habits of the theological virtues, faith, hope, and charity, perhaps of the
other virtues also.* Seven other supernatural habits,

* Benedict XIV. (de Canonizat. iii. 21) says it is as yet a disputed point
whether there is at baptism an infusion of the moral virtues together with
the theological. St. Thomas (1. 2. qu. 63. art. 3) discusses the question
whether any moral virtues are given to us by infusion, and he answers it
affirmatively, because it is necessary that effects should correspond propor-

20 †

standing in the same relation to the actual impulses of
the Holy Ghost as the other infused habits stand to
actual grace, and which bear the name of the Gifts of
the Holy Ghost, are also infused into him, containing
in themselves spiritual provisions for the greater occasions of his life, for his more intimate intercourse with
God, and, if so be, for the magnificent operations of
heroic sanctity. Meanwhile, if he dies before the use of
reason, there is secured to him the eternal vision of God,
with all the intellectual glories of an immortal spirit,
whose intelligence had never been developed upon earth
at all. Now all this haste, if we may so speak, with
which the divine mercy seizes the infant's soul, refusing
to wait for his consent or till he can accept God's great
gift by a rational act of his own, implies such a determined and exuberant love on the part of the Creator,
that it is not easily to be conceived, that the rest of the
process of salvation shall not partake of the same character of divine impatience and facility.

The baptized child, when he comes to the use of
reason, finds himself under a code of laws, the object of
which is to secure his salvation by prescribing the conditions on which it is to be obtained. These are the ten
commandments of God and the six precepts of the
Church. They are few in number and easy of observance, at least easy under ordinary circumstances; and
on the occasions when they are difficult, quite marvellous assistances of supernatural grace are prepared and

tionately to their causes and principles. (Cf. Salmanticenses in cursu iii. tr.
ii. disp. 3.) Scotus on the other hand denies the infusion of the moral virtues.
(In iii. sent. dist. xxxvi. qu. unic. art. 3.) A gloss on the decree of Clement
V. in the council of Vienne, gives these opposite opinions, and the question
of the connection between the habits of the theological and moral virtues is
left open, because of the authority of those doctors who do not admit the
infusion of the moral virtues in infant baptism. See also the author's Essay
on Canonization, pp. 48, 49.

heaped upon the soul. The man finds himself in a world of many pleasures, and, of these, comparatively few are sinful; and if the world is full of dangers too, it is always to be remembered that the fatal enemy of the soul, mortal sin, cannot lie in ambush for it or take it by surprise. Full deliberation and advertence are necessary to the commission of a mortal sin. When we think who God is and ponder His eternal truth and ineffable sanctity, it must be a wonder to us that any sin is venial, that no number of venial sins can make a mortal sin, and that no habits of venial sin, however inveterate, unworthy, deliberate, or against special lights, can of themselves destroy the soul. It is wonderful that a man can be graciously visited by the inspirations of the Holy Spirit, can feel assured in his own mind that such and such practices or self-denials are really the desire of God in his case, and yet be also sure that those inspirations are not intended as a law, and the resistance of them therefore not a sin, though all want of generosity with God will ultimately and indirectly work its way to sin. Furthermore the condition of the creature seems to be untruthfulness. Every thing is false around us, full of excuse, pretence, and insincerity. Yet falsehood is the very opposite of God, who is eternal truth, and it is equally the characteristic of the evil one whom our Lord Himself has named the father of lies. Nevertheless lying is a venial sin. No number of lies however wilful, so long as they are not sins against justice also, can of themselves destroy the soul. Surely this doctrine is full of difficulty.

The whole subject of sin abounds with truths of this description, which are more trying to the faith than the mysteries either of the Holy Trinity or the Eucharist. Thus the remission of venial sin, one of the most inte-

resting questions in the whole range of theology, appears
to be so easy as to be almost unconscious, and to be
quite as incessant as its commission. Blessings, holy
water, other sacramentals, the sign of the cross, the
Name of Jesus, passing acts of sorrow, nay, some have
said, any lifting up of the mind to God, and behold!
the guilt of these sins falls from us like a withered leaf
from an autumnal tree. And what hosts of venial sins,
forgotten and unrepented of, may not a man possibly
take with him into the next world, as matter for the
fires of purgatory, and which can only delay, and not
prohibit, his entrance into glory! All this does not
look as if God were a taskmaster, or as if heaven were
only for the few. Indeed the way in which He can
show all this leniency and make these singular allowances for our infirmity, and at the same time secure
purity of heart and real love of Himself, is the most
astonishing phenomenon which falls under the observation of those who have to minister to the consciences of
men. How men can be so very good at the same time
that they are so very bad, it is not easy to explain,
while experience leaves us in no doubt whatever of the
fact.

What is said of the doctrine of venial sin may be said
also of the doctrine of intention. What duty could
seem more simple on the part of a creature than a perpetual application of mind and heart to his Creator?
We are not our own, and we are not left to ourselves.
We are working under our Father's eye, and it is for
Him that we are working, and at His appointed work.
Hence the road to sanctity is by the way of actual
intentions for the glory of God. It should be every
one's prime occupation to make his intentions actual.
All other virtues will come along with this. Surprising

treasures of grace will be unlocked to us if we attempt
it. This one practice will turn darkness into light all
over our souls, and no sinful habit, however inveterate,
can exist in the atmosphere of this most glorious of all
spiritual exercises. Yet does any one believe that an
actual intention is absolutely necessary to the goodness
of an action? Does God get no glory from man's free
will, except when man there and then intends it? It
may be a question how long a virtual intention lasts, to
what extent it can inform and invigorate our actions,
and insinuate a supernatural character into them, or
what amount of original intensity is required in the
morning's intention to give it momentum enough to
push its way through the crowded actions of an entire
solar day. All these may be questions. But no one
maintains that any such assiduous application to God as
is a notable difficulty to our infirm and easily distracted
nature is at all necessary to salvation.

Such are the strange relations in which our baptized
child finds himself to his Creator as he grows up, and
life broadens out before him. But there are graver
matters still than venial sins, together with apparently
countless untruths, neglect of inspirations, or the paucity
of actual intentions for God's glory. There is the question of mortal sin. It is a fearful thing for the creature to turn away wholly from the Creator, and we can
well understand how it should at once destroy the life
of grace in the soul. Grace can live with any quantity
of venial sin. So long as the eclipse of God in the soul
is not total, so long with amazing condescension and
as it were a blind love of souls does He continue
to dwell within us. But when the eclipse is total,
what can follow but total darkness also? This seems
inevitable, and yet it is not so. Notwithstanding the

horrible malice of mortal sin, as being fully perceived
and deliberately admitted, the grand gift of faith, that
almost unfailing power of coming right again, survives
the commission of a mortal sin.   The life of hope does
not become extinct; nay, it requires a fresh, distinct,
and most difficult mortal sin to destroy that supernatural habit, which gives the soul the buoyancy and
elasticity requisite to its conversion.   Now is it quite
easy to see how two supernatural habits, two heavenly
powers, two divine elements, not natural to man, but
gratuitously infused into him at baptism, are not forfeited and expelled by the extinction of the life of grace
in the soul by mortal sin?   God is eclipsed in the soul;
hell has begun in it, hell's worst punishment, the loss
of God; and there are two celestial virtues preaching
in the darkness still, conspiring against the reign of
evil, holding their fortresses with magnanimous patience,
it may be for long, long years of siege, and attracting
to themselves incessant crowds of volunteers in the
shape of actual graces.   Is not all this wonderful?   Is
it compatible with the theory that salvation is difficult?
Is not mortal sin itself, against its will, a new revelation
of the pertinacious love of God?

But more still.   Of the thousands of souls in the
world to-day, unhappily immersed in the gulfs of mortal
sin, is there one whom a whole multitude of beautiful
actual graces is not soliciting to return to God?   O
such pathetic invitations to come back to Him, such
fair lights of God's tender compassion riding over the
dark soul like the white sunbeams over a stormy landscape, such sweet remorses, sharp, but very, very sweet,
such cold sobering thoughts of future punishment, such
wise artful alternations of crosses and consolations, such
lifelike speakings of dead books, such barbed words

of preachers, such solemn eloquence of the deaths of
those we love, such a nameless sensible thraldom of
God and grace and heavenly presences, which we never
can shake off:—all these, now with a very clamour of
assaulting armies, now with low, soft, and songlike
pleadings, are the forces of actual grace, which have
never been drawn off from before the gates of the heart,
however long they may have been obstinately barred
against God by a countless garrison of mortal sins.

But the most remarkable feature of the baptized
soul's position with regard to mortal sin is the perpetual, unlimited iteration of the sacrament of penance. That there should be such a sacrament at all,
after the completeness and magnificence of Baptism,
is a miracle of divine love. But that the Precious
Blood of the Incarnate Word should be always at hand,
like a public fountain at a road-side, open, gratuitous,
and everflowing, for the convenience of all passers by,
could not be believed, if the Church did not assure us
of it. Our sheer inability to comprehend a love so
great as God's would make simple Novatians of us, if
we had not the Church to inform the littleness of our
own conceptions by the magnificence of her dogmas.
Is it easy to imagine the mercy which will absolve from
different mortal sins the same soul perhaps five hundred
times in ten or twenty years, and some thousands of times
in the course of a long life? Yet this is not an extravagant or fabulous case. Then again think of the completeness of the absolution. Each time it destroys the
guilt of the sin completely, so that it can never rise
again, never bring back, even to the relapsed sinner,
its consequences of everlasting punishment, while at
the same time it wakens to vigorous life again merits
that have been killed a hundred times by sin. How

special, how ingenious, how peculiar, how unlike any thing human is this process; and yet on reflection how naturally outflowing from the Divine Perfections!

No kind, no number, no duration of sins impede the facility of absolution. Its efficacy is always instantaneous. The word is spoken, and the work is done. But what is still more marvellous is the little which is required for absolution, the ordinary fidelity of the confession, the positive imperfection of the sorrow, the moderate resoluteness of the purpose of amendment! Supernatural as all these must be, the confession, the sorrow, and the purpose, and depending for their validity on certain theological requirements, yet are they not among the commonest graces in the Church ? Is attrition a romantic flight of generosity, or the purpose of amendment akin to the heroism of martyrdom? Surely these requisites for absolution seem completely within the compass of our infirmity. And after all it is God Himself who is supplying more than half of them Himself by grace. In truth this enquiry into the easiness of salvation is beginning to fill us with fear, because it is carrying us so far. But might it not have been expected that as Penance is more troublesome than Baptism, so each time that the Sacrament of Penance is repeated, the requisites for absolution might have been increased, that the sinner should have bidden higher for pardon after every fall, and that there should have been at least so much punishment for his relapses as consists in an increase of his difficulties in winning God back to him again. Yet we know that this is not at all the case. The habitual sinner and he who has once fallen, the sinner of a day and the sinner of half a century,—to all, the simple requisites for absolution remain the same. Nay even where the confessor exacts from the penitent more convincing evidence of his repentance, it is only the confessor's inevitable infirmity as a creature, and as such unable to read the heart; God leaves the light conditions of absolution just what they were before. If all this were not among God's daily mercies, how inscrutable would it not seem to us; but we are obliged without fault of ours to tread God's common mercies underfoot, because He has so profusely strewn the whole earth with them, that there is not room to move.

There still remains a debt due to God from remitted sin, a debt of temporal punishment. This men may be content to bear, seeing that salvation has been made so easy to them, and the malice of their sins has been so great. But God will not suffer this. Straight from the confessional the Church leads her son into the fertile and exuberant region of Indulgences. There the Precious Blood is made to flow even over the temporal consequences of forgiven sin. God would not stop at mere salvation. It is His way to overflow and to exceed. There shall not be a disability in the sinner's path, not a relic of his own foolish covenants with sin, which shall be left to molest him. Nay the relics of sin shall have a strange sacrament to themselves in the Extreme Unction of the dying. But even this is not enough. Souls must be saved, and the saved multiplied, and the heavenly banquet crowded, even if the constraints of fire be needed to anneal the hastier works of grace. Therefore is it that the vast realms of purgatory are lighted up with the flames of vindictive love. Thus a huge amount of imperfect charity shall bring forth its thousands and its tens of thousands for heaven. Redemption shall cover the whole earth, and be plenti-

ful indeed, and the very unworthinesses and short-com-
ings of the creature shall only still more provoke the
prodigality of the Blood of the Creator. O the mercy
of those cleansing fires! What could have devised them
but a love that was almost beside itself for expedients?
Yet even these fires the sinner can avoid, if he
please, and without the difficulties of heroic charity.
For they shall be made to cast their light even upon
earth before their time, and the Precious Blood shall
be turned upon them by Indulgences, and they shall
be quenched before their blistering tongues have
touched the sinner's soul. O talk of the difficulty of
salvation after this! And what was Divine Love
doing, when we last caught a glimpse of it at work?
As at first, so at last, there is the divine impatience,
the divine facility, of a Creator who seems as if He
could not do without His creature. We saw love, and
it was bending over purgatory, over the net which was
almost breaking with the portentous draught of unlikely
souls which it had taken. Mary was moving on her
throne; the saints were filling heaven with their intercessions; angels were ascending and descending every
moment: mass bells were ringing all over the earth,
and beads being told, and numberless indulgences
sealed in thousands of communions, and alms flowing
in to the poor, and penances and pilgrimages being
performed; for Divine Love called loudly on angels,
saints, and souls of mortal men, to do violence to it,
while Jesus supplied the means in His daily adorable
Sacrifice and the plentiful treasury of His Precious
Blood. Our last sight of love showed it to us impa-
tiently shortening the appointed time of those suffering
souls, and heaven and earth astir, as if some great
catastrophe had happened, because God Himself seemed

as if He wished to cut short by swifter mercies that last grand consummate invention of His creative love, the quiet, unreluctant, beautifying pains of that cleansing fire!

When God came to His creatures visibly, He scandalized them. His Three-and-Thirty Years were almost a series of scandals, taken by cold hearts at what appeared the very extravagances of His condescension. What wonder then that a scheme of salvation so easy, so pliant, so accommodating, so full of arrangement, and so exuberant, should be a scandal both to heretics and unbelievers? It is the same Jesus who ate with publicans and sinners, who pleaded with the Samaritan woman, who rewarded the humble petulance of the Syro-Phœnician, who acquitted the woman taken in adultery, who absolved the Magdalen, and who carried off with Him as His first trophy to an instantaneous paradise the thief who hung upon the Cross. And shall we call that process hard, while our Mother the Church is maligned all day long for representing it as so easy and so large?

Look at God's side of the question, and what can fall upon us but utter confusion, perhaps, if it were not for His grace, utter unbelief? Let us narrow our view to the mystery of our dearest Saviour's Passion. Count it all up, measure it in its length and breadth, fathom its depth, handle it and see what it weighs: then pray and suffer for a while, and count and measure and fathom and handle it all again, and see how it all has grown; then pray and suffer more, and then repeat the process; and at the end of a saintly life you will have but a superficial estimation of that astonishing life-giving mystery. From the sacrilegious communion and treachery of Judas to the little garden of

Gethsemane, through the brook up the rugged steep to Jerusalem, through the halls of Annas, Caiphas and Pilate, and the court-yard of Herod, at the pillar of the scourging, in the guard room of the thorny crowning, along the way of the Cross, up Calvary, at the nailing and the elevation, to the last cry about the ninth hour —follow the Eternal through this appalling drama, which was all for you, all one excess of His uncontrollable creative love to save your soul : and then put by the side of it the requirements which are of obligation, our necessary amount of love and worship of Him, the prescribed frequentation of the sacraments, the extent of manly effort entailed upon us, and who can say that salvation is not easy, easy indeed to us, however hard it was upon the shoulders of the Incarnate Word. And then at last, the Beatific Vision ! Was there ever such a history ? And yet, simple in her faith, and confiding in the inborn beauty and celestial charm of truth to protect itself, this is the Gospel which the unwearied Church is now boldly proclaiming to the corrupt populations of the nineteenth century, as if it were a Concordat between the Creator and the Creature.

Can we say more ? Or if there is more to be said, do we need to have it said ? Yes ! New love, more love, unexpected love of God—we always need to know it, because we always need to love Him more and more. We thought of salvation as easy in itself, let us now look at it as easy because of its assistances. It appears already as if the utmost allowance had been made by God for the weakness and corruption of our nature, so as to put salvation within easy reach of us. But to secure it still more, He has formed alliances for us with Himself and the invisible world, and prepared a system of auxiliaries, both outward and inward, so ingenious

and wonderful, as to be a stumblingblock to those who
are not of the fold.

First and foremost among these, and entering more
or less into all of them, is Grace, a various, supernatural, potent, and unintermitting gift, about which
enough has been said for the present purpose in the
last chapter. There is not a characteristic either of it
or of God's way of giving it, which does not bear upon
the question of the easiness of salvation. Let us then
keep this in mind, as well as what has just been said
of the easiness of salvation in itself, while we enumerate
some of those incredible aids and consolations which
God has devised to make still easier what was already
so easy in itself. What Catholic is there who does
not know how the four great wants, and duties, and
worships which the creature owes to the Creator, the
petition of His infirmity, the intercession of his bro-
therly affection, the thanksgiving of his startled speechless gratitude, the intelligent joyous acknowledgment
of God's absolute dominion, are supplied to him, with
an infinite worthiness equivalent to the worth of the
Creator Himself, in the Adorable Sacrifice of the Mass?
The perpetual Real Presence of Jesus with His faithful,
His perseverance in the obscure tabernacle, and His
frequent benedictions, which preside over the evenings
of our toilsome days, just as Mass so beautifully fills
the morning with its light and love, so that it is Jesus
all day long, courting our society, and mingling with
us with an intimacy we get to understand less, and to
prize more, the longer it is vouchsafed,—surely this is
enough to supernaturalize the whole world, to make
hard things easy, and dark things bright, and throw
an invisible armour round us which will charm our
lives against the weapons and the wiles of hell. But

what shall we say of Communion? All ideas of familiarity with God, of intimacy with the invisible world,
of the spiritual union of heavenly love, fail us here.
The creature, trembling, bashful, eager, backward,
frightened, delighted, is bidden to kneel down, and feed,
not figuratively or by faith, but with an awful bodily
reality, upon his Incarnate Creator. And this eating
of the Creator by the creature is the highest act of worship which he can perform! We need not stay to
follow out the many-fountained grace of a good Communion, nor to see how it branches out into every
faculty of the soul, every power of the mind, every
affection of the will, every delicate sensibility of the
conscience, carrying with it secret blessings multiform
and manifold, and insinuating even into flesh and blood
and bone the seeds of a glorious resurrection. And this
miraculous feast on our very Creator may be, and He
loves it to be, our daily bread! And this to us, who,
if we rightly appreciate our vileness, should be astonished
every morning that our common food and clothing were
continued to us still!

All helps must seem little after this ; yet as they are
all so many fresh disclosures of creative love, we must
not pass them over. Loneliness is one of the dangers
which we have to fear, because of the inability of our
mortal nature to cope with the adverse forces of the
invisible world ; and, to meet this danger, the provident
love of God has given us our Guardian Angel. Ever
at our sides there is a golden life being lived. A princely
spirit is there, who sees God and enjoys the bewildering splendours of His Face even there, where he is,
nearer to us than the limits of our outstretched arms.
An unseen warfare is raging round our steps: but that
beautiful bright spirit lets not so much as the sound

of it vex our ears. He fights for us, and asks no thanks, but hides his silent victories, and continues to gaze on God. His tenderness for us is above all words. His office will last beyond the grave, until at length it merges into a still sweeter tie of something like heavenly equality, when on the morning of the resurrection we pledge each other, in those first moments, to an endless blessed love. Till then we shall never know from how many dangers he has delivered us, nor how much of our salvation is actually due to him. Meanwhile he merits nothing by the solicitudes of his office. He is beyond the power of meriting, for he has attained the sight of God. His work is simply a work of love, because his sweet presence at our side he knows to be a part of God's eternal and creative love towards our particular soul.

How great a joy and how real a support it is in sorrow, to have the prayers of a saintly man! We can hardly exaggerate the value of the blessing. To seek it is a sign of predestination. But look up to heaven! What are good men on earth to the giant spirits there, and how many thousands and thousands are praying to our good Creator that we may not miss of the happy end of our creation. There are our patron saints whose names we bear, the saints whom we especially love, the saints of our order, our vocation, or our country, the saints that were patrons of the holy souls whom we have liberated from purgatory, those holy souls now saints as well: all these are like so many beadsmen for us before the throne of the Most High. Glassed in Him, as in a pellucid mirror, they see the threads of our lives weaving their variously patterned web. They understand the purposes of God upon us. They are amazed at the diversity

and suitableness of His loving artifices and delicately
suited vocations. They see the dangers which threaten
us, the temptations which penetrate furthest into us,
the graces which are weakest in us, the critical moments
of life which peril us; and as they see, so do they pray.
If we could but remember in our struggles with sin,
how we are being backed before the throne of God, we
should surely spurn the tempter from us in the exulting
force of our Christian joy and the superhuman energy
of the communion of saints.

The Mother of God! In what surpassing heights
is she sublimely throned! Yet not a day passes in
which she does not interest herself for us. A thousand
times and more has she mentioned our names to God
in such a sweet persuasive way, that the Heart of Jesus
sought not to resist it, though the things she asked were
very great for such as we are. She has been in the
secret of all the good things which have ever happened
to us in life. She has our predestination at heart far
more than we have ourselves. She is ever mindful of
that second maternity which dates from Calvary, and
how we cost her in the travail of her dolours a price
which has no fellow except the sacrifice of her Son, our
Brother and our God. What a light does it not shed
on life, to think that the same love, the nameless love,
the inexhaustible love, wherewith the heart of Mary
loved her Blessed Son, is for His sake and by His own
command being poured out over us this very hour!
We are living now on earth, dear to heaven, because we
are suffused with its pathetic splendours. Angels envy
us a love which in their case cannot be, as ours is, identical in kind with that which the sinless Mother had for
her adorable Son. But it is not the poetry of this
thought on which we need to dwell, bright revelation as

it is once more of God's creative love, but on the real help, the substantial support, the immense solid advantages, the positive efficacy, of this love of Mary in the matter of our salvation.

Then we have the power of prayer ourselves. We dare not dwell much on this. But of how many theological controversies is the grace of prayer the secret and the key! The universal grace of prayer is one of the sweetest, as well as the fullest, expressions of the doctrine of the easiness of salvation. But can prayer mean that God will give up His own will, and accommodate it to ours? Ask, and you shall have; seek, and you shall find; knock, and it shall be opened unto you. The fervent prayer of a just man is of great avail. Intellectually speaking, it is very hard to believe in prayer; but let us spend but one week in the real earnest service of God and the exercise of a spiritual life, and the fact, and far more than we ever surmised to be the fact, will lie before us bright beyond the brilliance of any human demonstrations. All experience concurs with God's written word to tell us that the immutable is changed by prayer. The saints turn aside the great universal laws of nature by the blow of an ejaculation. Even the unexpressed will of a soul in union with God is a power with the omnipotent Creator, and looks like what it cannot be, a limit to His liberty. And this is always in our reach, instant, lightning-like, peremptory, and efficacious; and on its way to heaven it unites itself with the prayer of Jesus upon earth, with the intercessions of Mary, with the appeals of all the saints, and the earnest outcries and entreaties of the wide militant Church on earth, and thus like a beautiful storm of supplication, like a loud-voiced litany of all creation, it breaks round the throne of God with majestic

power, and the echo is heard in our hearts almost before
the inward prayer is breathed, and the sounds of bluster-
ing temptation are hushed within, and the big drops of
the impetuous rain of grace are falling thick and fast
upon us.   It will be one of the joys of heaven to learn
the secret of the power of prayer.   But now it is a great
abyss to the rocky edge of which we climb and look
over, and all is sonorous darkness, and turn giddy,
and recover not our senses until we kneel down and
adore the one only supreme, infinitely lovely, and unspeakably adorable will of God.

Even dead things have a wizard life put into them,
and help us on our road to heaven.   Dumb things have
a voice, and inanimate things lay strong hands on us,
and turn us round to God.   The Spirit of God is
hiding everywhere, so that the world is an enchanted
place, and all the enchantment is for God.   Books,
sermons, services, scenery, and the examples of those
around us, sorrows, joys, hopes, fears, winds and waves,
heat and cold, animals and plants—strange powers
are touching them at unexpected moments, and they
electrify us with thoughts of God, nay often with keen
contacts of His presence.   All these things teach us one
truth, and that one truth is in itself an amazing help,
that it is the will of God to each one of us that we
should be saved eternally.   And are not all the chances
blessedly in favour of the accomplishment of that dear
Will ?

We have already considered the sacraments of baptism, penance, and the eucharist.   But there are other
sacraments which deserve special notice as auxiliaries
to us in the work of our salvation.   Just when boy-
hood is taking us out into the world, and when the
first-fruits of our young independence are at once so

dangerous and so dear, the sacrament of confirmation steps in, seals up the grace of our baptism, fills us with the one grace which at that season we need above all others, the gift of fortitude, tries to be beforehand with the world, and enrolls us in the actual militia of God, so that, in addition to our former character of His sons, we have now the further character of being His soldiers, and are placed in a peculiar way under the light, the guidance, and the love of the Third Person of the Most Holy Trinity. Nothing can be more opportune or more complete than this sacrament of force.

There are few sources of grace in life more plentiful than marriage, both because of the abundance of its joys, and also because of its innumerable retinue of trials. It makes or mars the happiness of the majority of men, and it is one of the most active powers on earth in fostering or in frustrating the work of God within the soul. Now that we are used to the thought, it seems most natural and fitting that our Lord should have exalted this domestic contract to the exceeding dignity of a Christian sacrament. Yet, beforehand, who would have dreamed of such a thing? Possibly the souls are countless whom this very sacrament has saved, and whom that state of life would have been more likely to ruin than to save, had it not been for its sacramental grace. In no respect does religion so boldly encroach upon the world as in making marriage a sacrament; it is almost the longest reach and the most determined grasp of our sweet Saviour's arm, when He was bent to rescue His dear souls from the fiery ordeal of the world.

Death too with its unknown necessities, must have a sacrament which it can call its own, as well to finish the demolition of sin, as to anoint the failing warrior with a

heavenly unguent for his last dire combat, and enable
him in defiance of earthly calculations to elude the hold
which the unseen powers of evil lay upon him in that
hour.   If we ever need help, will it not be in that
dreadful agony; for neither earthly love nor earthly
power can help us then? With many, doubtless, the
battle has gone hard, though they who stood around
neither heard nor saw the mortal wrestle, and with
many it was the secret strength of that holy oil, the
hidden operation of that sacramental grace, which turned the scale, and consigned to the Good Shepherd's
arm that sheep which is now His own for ever.   Must
not God mean us to be saved, when there is not a con-
juncture in our fortune, not a winding in the road of
life, but at the turn we find Him waiting with some
strange beautiful invention of love, the very mechanism
of which none but an all-wise artist could have contrived?

The supernatural power, which God confers upon
virtuous actions, is also a remarkable assistance to us in
the work of our salvation.   It is like adding power a
hundred-fold to the machines and tools of the mechanic.
Here again God does not look to the importance or
solemnity of the action, but to the purity of intention
with which it is performed.   Each pious act, however
trivial, has three supernatural forces bestowed upon it.
There is, first of all, the force of impetration by which,
even while we are unconscious and forgetful of it, our
prayers acquire a new vigour and exercise a greater influence over the adorable will of God.   When we consider how much we want from Him, and how almost
our whole life must needs be spent in the attitude of
petition, even when we are not formally and directly
praying, when we reflect how our very vileness is an

incessant supplication to the greatness of our Creator, we shall see how this mysterious power of impetration, hung upon our lives, must aid us in attaining heaven. Of ourselves it would seem as if we were the most unlikely creatures to be heard, relapsed rebels against the majesty of God, and even when we return to our duty, surrendering only on jealous conditions, and with a hundred mean reserves. But this power of impetration makes us really worthy to be heard, and is a sort of invisible beauty glowing in our lives on earth, anticipating that consummate loveliness which gives the interceding saints such power in heaven.

Not less wonderful is the power of meriting which grace communicates to our good works, as though the Heart of Jesus were supposed to animate each one of them, and the infinite worth of His Precious Blood were secretly folded up within them. We have seen how magnificent the rewards of heaven are, and yet one obscure and momentary good work, full of the love of God, and fair to look at because of the purity of its intention, has only to settle but for one instant upon the cross of Christ and thence wing its way to heaven, where its merit has such transcending power as to pass the guards and open the gates of the citadel of the King of kings. See then in what a condition this places us as regards our salvation. Earth is strewn so thickly with the materials of meriting, that all day long we have nothing to do but to gather them up in armfuls, as the poor gather firewood in the forest, and even with less toil than theirs. Grace is superabundant and incessant and universal. We can hardly get out of the way of it, if we are perverse enough to try. The process of touching our materials with this heavenly grace is so easy and simple, that by use it becomes almost

natural to us, and except for the warm feeling of love
in our hearts, we should in the great multitude of our
actions, be almost unconscious of the process.   So that
from our waking in the morning till our falling asleep
at night, we are throwing up the merest dust and ashes
of earth to heaven, and it is stronger than the laws of
its own material vileness, and rises thither, and is put
into the divine treasury as the purest gold of Christian
merit.

But there is yet another mysterious power infused by
grace into our actions, the power of satisfaction.   Alas!
our sins are both tall and broad, and their malice deep
and fearful, while the justice of God is sparkling intolerably and flashing with angry splendour in the light of
His jealous and exacting sanctity.   We have need to be
calling every hour on the atoning Blood of Jesus; for
nothing short of that can satisfy for the guilt of sins to
which eternal death is due.   But through the merits of
that same dear Saviour our own humblest actions can
appease the wrath of God, can give Him real substantial
satisfaction, can atone for the temporal punishments in
store for our sinful past, and constrain, O with such
beautiful constraint! even His justice to give us orders
on the treasury of His compassion.   It would have been
indeed a huge mercy, and to our unillumined sense a
perfectly inexplicable one, had our Creator been pleased
to let our works of penance, our aching fasts, our cold
vigils, our burning disciplines, satisfy in some degree
the claims of His high justice.   But that we should be
allowed to steep the slightest of our ordinary inconveniences, the trouble of getting up in the morning, the
coldness of the east wind, the heat of the summer sun,
or the insignificant self-denial of a kind action,—that
we should be allowed to steep these things in the Blood

of the Incarnate Word, and make them strong, vigorous, and heaven-reaching satisfactions for our sins, is
marvellous indeed. What then shall we say to the love
which has made all our Christian actions, even those in
which there is no inconvenience at all, nay, still more,
even those which are pleasures and privileges, such as
mass, and benediction, and giving alms, and making the
sign of the Cross, and reading the lives of saints, into
solemn, serious, and efficacious satisfactions for our sins?
Surely such a love as this, busy, inventive, ubiquitous,
must be bent on saving us, and on saving us as nearly
against our wills, as can be with our wills still free!

But He does more. The power of impetration gives
us influence over Him for others as well as for ourselves. We can thus obtain gifts for them, which we
could not give ourselves. The power of meriting is a
personal privilege. Our merits are our own; they
cannot belong to another. The glory of heaven is inexhaustible, so that we may go on multiplying our
merits, like our Blessed Lady, and yet we shall not
drain the rewards of heaven. But strange to say! we
may do more than satisfy the justice of God for the
temporal punishment of our own sins, whether that
punishment consist of the withdrawal of the graces of
repentance, or of the sorrows and calamities of life, or
of the active fires of purgatory. We may have satisfactions to spare, satisfactions which may go into the
treasury of the Church and supply materials for future
indulgences, satisfactions which we may at once transfer
to others, and God at once accepts the transfer, and
bestows the grace, withholds the punishment, or alle-
viates the suffering, as the case may be. Nay, if Ho
will, He allows us to alienate the satisfactions which wo
really need ourselves, and bestow them upon others, as

an exercise of heroic charity towards our fellows, or of disinterested generosity towards His glory; so that we may not only save ourselves, but help Him also in His grand labour of saving the world which He created without any labour at all. He multiplies saviours, by making us saviours ourselves, at the very moment when He is also multiplying for us the means by which we are the more easily to save ourselves.

But there is still a finishing stroke left to perfect this work of divinest art. There is what theologians call satispassion. In other words, for Christ's sake,* and because nothing about men can escape the universal contagion of His redeeming grace, there is in mere suffering, in the simple pressure of pain, in the sheer tortures of mental anguish, in the very weight of labour and weariness of endurance, a secret underground virtue which is not without its own peculiar acceptableness to the justice of God. It is not that He loves to see His creatures suffer, it is not that His glory can feed itself on mere torments, which are but irregularities we have brought into His glad creation, and formed no part in the primeval plan of Him who is Himself an uncreated ocean of joy, a glorious abyss of unutterable beatitudes. His love gives an inward dignity even to the most inevitable suffering of the creature. Who can doubt that it is because of Christ, and the luminous shadow of His redeeming Passion which falls with a soft light on every human woe and mortal pain, and so mellows them into that beautiful landscape of earth which God once looked at and blessed for its exceeding loveliness? Thus He, who made Mary merit even

---

* It is not meant here that there is not satispassion in the sufferings of those who are not in a state of grace, or indeed of the heathen. Yet even this may be in some way for Christ's sake, and because of the Incarnation.

while she slept, communicates to us wretched sinners some faint similitude of that astonishing privilege. Even while we are concentrated in our sufferings, while pain absorbs us in itself or else distracts us by its vehemence, some sort of dumb sacrifice to the justice of our Creator is rising up from our clouded minds, as if our bed of pain were an altar to His purity, or our broken heart gave out a faint odour of Christ, or our aching limb were as cinnamon burning in the fire.

Thus it is that divine love follows us everywhere with helps to our salvation. Thus it is that God's blessed will that we should all be saved bears down upon us with almost a tyranny of goodness, in order that we may not escape His eternal company in heaven. Down to teaching us how to make virtues of our necessities, down to the acceptance of the almost unreasonable sacrifice of satispassion, this will of God for our salvation persecutes us with the prodigality of its gifts. Why is it then that so many Christians go wrong and fail, so many more at least than ought to fail, even granting that all who fail are but comparatively few? Is the difficulty of salvation the only answer to this melancholy fact? Have we not seen with our own eyes that it is not difficult? Does not experience teach us with children, and we are as children before God, nay does it not teach us with wise grown-up men, that there are easy things in which disobedience will not obey? The facility of a thing is sometimes a temptation to disobedience. So it will occasionally come across us in our meditations that God does Himself an injury by all this prodigality of His love, that He makes Himself too common, that He does not sufficiently stand upon His dignity, that He may miss of His end by the mere eagerness with which He pursues it, that He may hamper and embarrass generous souls who would run more freely if they were less encumbered with help, that His exuberance may be on the one hand a temptation to unbelief, and on the other an allurement to presumption. We know such thoughts are sins, if we deliberately entertain them; and when we do not entertain them, then they are the broken foolish incoherent speech of men intoxicated with the wine of God's love, whose very babblings tell what is working in their souls, and how the excesses of His goodness are perplexing them. He knows best; and we know Him sufficiently well to be assured that not one artifice of His compassion could be spared without the sacrifice of a multitude of souls, who are saved just by that one thing, that single special contrivance of creative love.

If there are Christians who will not meditate upon eternal things, nor use the same rules of patience and discretion in the matter of salvation, which they use in temporal affairs, or if there are any who let evil habits master them, or if by a special wile of Satan they will not let themselves be brought within the influence of a priest, it is not because salvation is not easy, but because they will not comply with its indulgent requisitions. Some men speak as if salvation could not be easy, unless it actually destroyed free will, and carried them off to heaven by force. Yet in reality the love of God goes as near to this as it can do consistently with free will, so near that none but He could have gone so near, and yet avoided the destruction of it. What is it we would have? Our benignant Creator has bewildered us with the rapid, intricate, enormous machinery of His love. He has not only outstripped our imagination, He has tried our faith. What more could we desire?

But salvation is not only easy in itself and because of its helps; it is easy also because it is our interest. What interests us is by a law of our nature easy, and nothing interests us so much as a thing in which our own welfare is manifestly and deeply involved. This will become evident to us if we compare the pleasures of sin with the pleasures of a state of grace. The pleasures of sin are not lasting. The fires go out for want of fuel. They only burnt brightly and swiftly at first because it was but dry weeds, thorns, and thistles, which supplied them. There is also a want of continuity in sinful pleasures. Sin is not pleasant to look back upon, as a good action is. It lives in excitement and moral intoxication. Its very vehemence makes it subject to relapses. Somehow also the pleasure of sin wastes and devastates the spirit; it blights our human affections; it scorches places in our hearts where green things were wont to grow, and unlike Christian suffering, it does not fertilize hereafter what it is burning now. It leaves behind it remorse which makes our whole life ache, and weariness which turns the very sunshine into a burden. It causes us to be peevish both with ourselves and others; and to a peevish man his own company is more tedious than words can tell. At last bodily health fails, and our spirits give way beneath us; for sin is the twin brother of sickness. Worldly misfortune not seldom supervenes; and the loss of the respect of others is one of those losses which are almost inevitable to the sinful man. Most sinners also are ambitious in their own line, and they are cramped even in their means of sinning; they cannot fulfil their own dreams of profligacy, nor sin upon the grand scale which they intended. Pain and sickness, which are always hard to bear, are desperately intolerable to a

man who is not in a state of grace. They involve loss
of time, waste of life, diminution of pleasures, when all
is so fleeting, and sin so longs to catch each moment
as it flies. Moreover they are so unmeaning, or what
is worse, so purely penal to the wicked man. Then
there is the slavish dread of death, or what is hardly
a less sickening misery, the wild forced unbelief of the
eternity which is beyond. In a word, a downright
habitual sinner is in the long run neither loved nor
loving; and if he does not lose the present world altogether, as well as the world which is to come, it i
because the justice of his Creator pays him here for
such natural kindliness and moral respectability as he
may have shown.

Now contrast all this with the delight of being in a
state of grace. Is there any earthly joy like the sense
of pardon? How deep it goes down into our nature,
unlocking such secret fountains of tears as were far
beyond the reach of ordinary hopes and fears! There
is also a satisfyingness about it, which seldom accom-
panies other joys. A void is filled up in our hearts,
which had ached before. Peace comes where before
there was a trouble of uncertain fears, and love awakens
with a keener, fresher appetite for its obedient work
for God. In prosperity, in adversity, in the love of
others, in the enmity of others, in hard work, in old
age, in sickness, and in death, the state of grace seems
just to add what was needed, to supply that very thing
the absence of which was regretted, to throw light upon
the darkness, or to subdue the glare, to level the rocks
or fill in the sunken places, to drain what was marshy
or irrigate what was dry. It has shed upon the whole
of life repose, plenitude, satisfaction, contentment. It
has positively given us this world, while it was in the

act of transferring to us the other. And is not salvation easy, when it is our own present interest, our
immediate reward, and downright earthly happiness to
boot?

I do not think that if we kept in view the perfections of God, we should venture to believe, unless the
Church taught us, that there was in creation such a
place as hell. When it has been revealed to us we can
perceive, not only its reasonableness, but also how
admirably it is in keeping with the various attributes
of God, and, not least of all, with the exquisiteness of
His mercy. There is an awful beauty about that
kingdom of eternal chastisement; there is a shadow
cast upon its fires, which we admire even while we
tremble, the shadow of the gigantic proportions of a
justice which is omnipotent; there is an austere grandeur about the equity of God's vindictive wrath, which
makes us nestle closer to Him in love, even while we
shudder at the vision. But to us who live and strive,
who have grace given us and yet have the power of
resisting it, who have room for penance but are liable
to relapse, who are right now but can at any time go
wrong,—who can doubt that hell is a pure mercy, a
thrilling admonition, a solemn passage in God's pathetic
eloquence, pleading with us to save our souls and to
go to Him in heaven? There is no class of Christians
to whom hell is not an assistance. The conversion of
a sinner is never complete without the fear of hell.
Otherwise the work cannot be depended on. It has a
flaw in its origin, a seed of decay in its very root. It
is unstable and insecure. It is shortlived and unper-
severing, like the seed in our Saviour's parable which
fell upon a rock, sprung up for a season, and then
withered away. Hell teaches us God, when we are

too gross to learn Him otherwise. It lights up the
depths of sin's malignity, that we may look down,
and tremble, and grow wise. Its fires turn to water,
and quench the fiery darts of the tempter. They rage
around us, so that we dare not rise up from prayer.
They follow us, like the many-tongued pursuing flames
of a burning prairie, and drive us swiftly on, and out of
breath, along the path of God's commandments. O
Hell! thou desolate creation of eternal justice! who
ever thought of finding a friend in thee?

Even to those aiming at perfection the thought of
hell is an immense assistance. The common things of
the faith are in reality far above all the high lights
of the saints. There is no growing out of or beyond the
ordinary motives and old truths of the faith even for
those who are most highly advanced, or are practising
the most disinterested love. There is no habitual state
in which the spiritual life can rest and stay itself up
in those thin atmospheres. Besides which, there can be
no bounds safely set to the self-distrust which the greatest saints should have, and are the most likely to have,
of themselves. This being so, it is extremely desirable
that even those who walk by love and are aiming at
perfection should bring frequently before their minds
the judgments of God in the terrific severities of hell.
There are times when we faint and are inclined to relax
our upward straining, our climbing of the steep mountain of God. Spiritual sweetnesses and periodical
absences of temptation often unnerve us for fresh
attacks of the Evil One. We come to do things in a
slovenly and remiss way from long habit. While we
grow in merits we are getting hugely into debt to the
greatness and the multitude of God's mercies, and this
at times unsobers us. Moreover sanctity cannot grow,

unless there be also a growing appreciation of the
possible extremities of God's justice. Neither is it
an uncommon delusion to think that we are beyond
the fears and impressions of the senses, though our
softness in mortification ought to teach us better.
Next to a very clear and penetrating contemplation
of the attributes of God, nothing enables us to get a
true hatred of sin more than the horrible nature of its
eternal punishments. In all these conjunctures the
frequent thought of hell is nothing less than an impulse heavenwards. The false delicacy of modern times
in keeping back the scaring images of hell, while in
the case of children it has often marred a whole education, is a formidable danger to the sanctity as well as to
the faith of men.

If the terrors of the Lord contribute largely to the
easiness of salvation, the attractiveness of His rewards
has also saved its thousands and its tens of thousands.
It is hard to disentangle the influence of the thought
of heaven from the purity of disinterested love, and it is
most undesirable even to attempt it. We want something to put out the beautiful light of earth, and to
sully its fair shining. We need a disenchanting power
in the midst of a creation so lovely, winning, and
specially alluring to our own particular selves, lest it
should rob us of our hearts and leave us nothing to
give to God. We covet some unfading ideal so to
possess our souls, that we may walk the world in the
pure cold chastity of perfect detachment, so that God
may be our all. The coruscations of His throne are
sometimes too blinding to our eyes. That lofty region
of perpetual thunders will sometimes stun us, when
littleness and imperfection have unstrung our spiritual
nerves. If we see God now through a glass darkly,

sometimes it must be through many earth-tinted glasses
that our weak eyes must look at Him. Hence the
need to us of familiarizing ourselves with all that the
schools teach us of the joys of heaven. Hence the power
which a simple soul acquires from reposing even on the
undeveloped thought of the greatness of his Creator's
recompense. And what are all the joys of heaven,
but the accidents, the corollaries, the overflows, of the
radiant Beatific Vision? So that pure love mingles
with our blameless thoughts of self, and heaven is
already a power on earth drawing us with magnetic
force into the spheres of its own abounding light; and
what is heaven but the locality we give to that dear
glory of our Incomprehensible and Omnipresent Father,
in whose embrace we long to hide ourselves for very
love?

I conclude therefore that God is bent on saving us,
that salvation is easy in itself, easy because of its helps,
easy because of the terrors of being lost, and easy because of the attractiveness of its own rewards. This
is my answer to those who object to the picture I have
drawn of God's creative love. It is founded upon
common truths which everybody knows, truths which
strike us the more, the more by assiduous contemplation of His attributes we come to know the God to
whom we belong. It is drawn from the distinct statements of Scripture. It is in harmony with the teaching
of the saints. It is the doctrine most full of consolation
for creatures. It is the belief most honourable to the
Creator.

CHAPTER II.

THE GREAT MASS OF BELIEVERS.

O Israel! quam magna est domus Dei.—*Baruch.*

It is sweet to think of the web of love which God is
hourly weaving round every soul He has created on tho
earth. If we bring the world before us with all its
picturesque geography, the many indentations of its
coasts, the long courses of its fertile rivers, its outspread
plains, its wide forests, its blue mountain chains, its
aromatic islands, and its verdant archipelagos, it en-
larges the heart to think how round every soul of man
God is weaving that web of love. The busy European,
the silent Oriental, the venturous American, the gross
Hottentot, the bewildered Australian, the dark-souled
Malay,—He comes to all. He has His own way with
each; but with all it is a way of tenderness, forbearance,
and lavish generosity. The variety of their circumstances, and those are well nigh numberless, are not so
many as the varieties of His sedulous affection. The
biography of each of those souls is a miraculous history
of God's goodness. If we could read them, as probably
the Blessed can, they would teach us almost a new
science of God, so wonderfully and inexhaustibly would
they illuminate His different perfections. We should
see Him winding invisible threads of light and love
even round the ferocious idolater. We should behold
Him dealing with cases of the most brutal wickedness,
tho most fanatical delusion, the most stolid insensibility,

22

and, even for these, arranging all things with the exquisite delicacy of creative love. But so astonishing, so
overwhelming is the flood of divine light, such and so
vast the very ocean of eternal predilection, which He
has poured upon His Church, that all outside looks like
utter darkness because of the dazzling excess of her
magnificence. This blinds us so that we cannot see
how what looks so dark to us is after all a true light,
lightening every man that comes into the world.

Let us turn our thoughts then to the Church. What
a comfort it is to think of the vastness of the Church,
and of her holiness! There is the incessant action of
those mighty Sacraments, and the whole planet trans-
figured with the daily Mass. There is all heaven busy,
as if time were too short for it, with a hundred occupations for each Christian soul, set in motion at that
soul's request, or self-moved by gratuitous love and
pity. Mary, Angels, Saints, and suffering Souls in
purgatory, all are hard at work. God is employed, as if
His Sabbath after creation were long since past. There
are sorrows to be soothed, temptations to be banished,
sins to be forgiven, tears to be dried, pains to be healed,
good works to be assisted, death-beds to be attended;
and the bright throngs in heaven, like some religious
Order of Mercy, are busy at them all. O happy we!
on whom all this dear diligence is thus perpetually
expended!

What is the fruit of it all? If salvation is easy,
and salvation is preached in the Church of Christ,
then it ought to follow that the great majority of
catholics are saved. We need speak only of catholics. We will not advert, however distantly, to those
outside the Church. People tempt themselves about
them, and play tricks with their gift of faith, for

which they ought to be thanking God their whole lives long. We have no business to concern ourselves with God's relations to others: however wistfully the ties of love may make us gaze upon that dark abyss. We are catholics. Let us be content with speculating about ourselves. We will suppose, therefore, the objection to be made, that if salvation is easy, then practically we ought to find that most catholics are saved. It is not enough to say that though salvation is easy, the corruption of man is so tremendous that little comes of it; for then it seems a question of words to call salvation easy. Salvation is the saving of *fallen* man, and, therefore, to be really easy, it must far more than counterbalance his corruption. The question is one of too momentous a character, of too thrilling an interest, for us to be content with mere rhetoric. We repeat, if salvation is easy, most catholics must be saved. Can we venture to say that such is our belief?

Before answering so abrupt a question, we must be allowed a few words of prelude. You are asking us what we think about one of God's secrets, a secret which He has reserved to Himself. It is one of those questions into which we may venture reverently to enquire, in the hope of finding fresh traces of His omnipresent love: but for no other reason than this. We may enquire that we may love; we may not enquire that we may know. It does not seem that we anger Him by such an investigation, provided we are humble. But we must remember we can decide nothing. After all our surmises, inferences, and guesses, the truth remains, as it was before, hidden with God. We have, however, in spite of much natural reluctance, a reason for entering into it, which seems to constrain us to it

as to a work of mercy.   Outside the Church the dreadful error of the day, which is ravaging the hearts of
men, is a forgetfulness that they are creatures.   They
seem in a certain way to remember the Creator, but,
as was said in the first chapter, in politics, in science,
in literature, in all the departments of the world's
greatness, they seem not to realize that they are creatures.   Now this error reaches faintly and feebly into
the hearts of true believers.   There is always in the
Church a kind of evil echo of the noise which the
world is making without.   But it is not more than
an echo.   Hence the spiritual physicians of the times
come across an unusual amount of suffering, which
good souls feel, from doubts about their relations with
God, questionings of His justice and His goodness which
will hardly be silenced, and which it were wild work,
and almost ruin, to try to silence by main force.   Such
men find a difficulty in their most intimate religious
life, for which we can think of no name.   It is not
simply temptation against the faith.   It is not a disgust
with the spiritual life.   It does not seem to rest in the
will at all, but in some perversity of the mind which is
so humble that it is a shame to call it by so hard a name
as perversity.   We believe it to be an habitual inca-
pacity of realizing that they are creatures, in the full
truth and in all the bearings of that idea.   This inability
might be brought on in these days by much and incau-
tious reading of newspapers, or by an absorbing interest
in the politics of the day, or by being mixed up with
the existing commercial system of the world, or by not
having always been catholics, or by having misused the
first graces of conversion, or from sheer want of generosity with God.   But it is a shadow, or an echo, or a
taint in the believer's heart, of the prevailing pestilence

of modern society. Just as in the presence of a cognizable plague we have frequently a mild form of some congenial disease, so does the sickness of the times infect even many of the faithful with a languor of a somewhat similar description. It is because I have been called to so many cases of this sort, that I have composed the present Treatise, happy if I may be allowed to console one afflicted brother, or to ease one tempted soul, or to enlighten one bewildered mind,—more happy than I can say if I can get from one of the creatures, whom He loves so well, an additional degree of love for our compassionate Creator.

It may be said that the view contained in the preceding chapters is taking God's side exclusively, and putting forward only a one-sided statement. But this is not really true; however, we are not concerned to argue the point. We look only to a practical result. But what in truth is it which forms the chief part of the suffering to the souls just now described? It is that they will obstinately look only at one side of the question, and the side which concerns them least instead of that which concerns them most, as that which God puts before them; and that they will pertinaciously extend the difficulty by bringing in a number of problems, in the solution of which they individually have no interest at all, and which they can hardly investigate, at least in their temper of mind, without forgetting what is due to God. They seem to have no eye, except for dark possibilities. They have a morbid hankering to climb giddy heights, to loiter on the edge of precipices, to balance themselves on the craters of volcanoes. They who love danger shall perish in it. We had better let God's thunderbolts alone, and not meddle with them, were it even to feel the sharp-

ness of their fiery points. We only ask these poor
sufferers now to look at the other side of the question ;
and not only to look at it, but to pray about it, and
meditate on it, and familiarize themselves with it.
Mere reading is nothing. A religious inquiry without
prayer is a mockery of God. We can define nothing.
We can unriddle none of God's secrets. But these
souls have fed on gloomy considerations until they are
almost poisoned. Now let us invite them to follow us
patiently through the brighter considerations which
commend themselves to an opposite temper and disposition, and which if not of greater weight than their
own views, are at least of equal authority with theirs,
besides the additional recommendation of their sunshine.

It will not be too much to ask of our readers to pay
an accurate attention to the language of a chapter on a
subject so capable of misunderstanding as the present.
When we treat of each consideration separately, we
seem to be exaggerating, from the mere fact that we
do not mention other, and perhaps opposite, considerations in the same breath, which is obviously impossible.
Let us bear in mind then that this inquiry is in no
respect a matter of theology. It teaches no doctrine
of contrition. Its facts have no doctrinal bearing. It
is a view of human conduct, combined with a view of
God's dealings with men, which must necessarily bear
upon it the impress of particular personal experience, as
well as of particular personal character and disposition.
But above all things we must bear in mind what has
been abundantly manifest in the preceding chapter,
namely, that salvation is easy, not because of any of the
requirements of God's sanctity being abated, but because
of the abundance and vigour of His grace. Thus when
we speak of deathbed graces, it is not that, because of

the pitifulness of the pains of death, God consents to be
reconciled to us on easier terms than when we are strong
and well, or that it is consistent with His perfections
to restore us to His favour without that inward vital
change of the sin-loving or world-loving heart, that
radical work in the soul, implied in real interior repentance. But we judge from what we see that it frequently
pleases Him in that great hour so to reinforce the operations of grace as to counterbalance, and more than
counterbalance, the physical disadvantages under which
the spiritual processes of the soul would otherwise have
laboured in the trial of such a terrific moment. So
again, when we speak of the Sacraments, we speak of
them accurately, that is, as implying certain earnest,
vigorous, inward dispositions on our parts, no less than
a peculiar gracious intervention on the part of God.
It is plain we cannot keep repeating all this in every
sentence. We must therefore ask our readers to read
the whole chapter in the abiding thought, that along
with every compassionate intervention of God there
remains, heightened rather than abated, the essential
necessity of real, solid, inward repentance and actual
transformation of heart, on the part of those who may
be favoured with His extraordinary graces. Nay, the
extraordinariness of a grace consists *precisely* in the
penitent having these dispositions at such a moment and
under such circumstances. To a thoughtful reader the
result of the enquiry must be to deepen his sacred fear
and to stimulate him to greater earnestness. All exhi-
bitions of the excesses of God's love produce these
results, else would the very Bloodshedding upon Calvary
be an encouragement to men to sin. I believe no man
would be less likely to trust to a death-bed conversion,
than one who had witnessed such a conversion. He

would so tremble to see so much resting on so little, such a peculiar, dubious, intricate, abnormal strife, such a terrible swinging of eternal interests on such an unsteady balance, such a miraculous rescue of a soul hanging more than half over the edge of such abysses, that he would be the most likely of all men to fulfil afterwards the apostle's injunction of passing the time of his sojourning here in fear. If any of us therefore rise up from the enquiry now before us only more hopeful, and not also more strict, I believe the fault will be in our own want of seriousness and honesty with God.

With this prefatory caution and admonition we may proceed therefore to answer the question before us thus: —We are inclined to believe, that most catholics are ultimately saved. Of course we do not know it, and we do not wish to know it. But as the objection is started, we look attentively at the Church as far as we have the power, and the result of our observations is, that to the best of our belief the great majority of her children save their souls. We will give our reasons, one by one, for this conclusion, begging the reader once more to remember that we are not laying down the law, and that the necessities of many souls have beguiled us into an enquiry, upon which of ourselves we should never have dreamed of entering.*

---

* Lest it should be supposed that there was anything unusual in discussing this question in a practical and popular book, I would venture to remind the reader that it has been the common practice of catholic writers, both in Italy, France, and England. Among preachers we have Massillon, Bourdaloue, Le Jeune, Lacordaire, Segneri, the Blessed Leonard of Port Maurice, and indeed almost all Italian Quaresimali, treating of this alarming subject. In practical and popular treatises, for reading, we have Drexelius, Bellarmine, Lecupitus, D'Argentan, Bossuet in his Meditations, Bail, Da Ponte, and our own Challoner, whose meditations have been translated into various languages. In Catechisms we have Lipsin, Turlot, who is translated into various languages, and the excellent Dr. Hay. Turlot asks why preachers do not often teach, often explain, often inculcate this? And he remarks,

There seems to be a sort of dishonesty in putting forward the view which is to occupy this chapter, without confessing that the authority of theologians, so far as there can be any authority in a question of this nature, is upon the whole, though not greatly, on the other side, while the authority of Scripture seems to be with us. Very many writers appear to hold that the number of the reprobate very far exceeds the number of the saved, not only taking the heathen into account, but taking heretics into account also—and not only taking heretics into account, but also the baptized infants of the faithful, whose deaths are said nearly to equal those of adult catholics, and also the infants of heretics who have received baptism ; so that, in their view, the question is narrowed to adult Catholics, and of these, perhaps most writers, though hardly those of the greatest weight, venture to say that only a minority are saved. Recupitus, the Jesuit, in his treatise on the Number of the Predestinate, enumerates Lyra, Denys the Carthusian, Maldonatus, Cajetan, Bellarmine, Fasolus, Alvarez, Ruiz, Smising, Drexelius, and perhaps Molina, as holding this opinion, together with most of the Fathers of the Church.[*] Sylvester, Carthagena, Granadus, Franciscus de Christo, are quoted on the other side. Suarez, who on the whole seems to be on the milder

Quæstio hæc (de numero salvandorum) non minus est utilis quam curiosa. Also the Tesori di confidenza in Dio, published at Rome by the Propaganda press, in 1840, discusses the question at great length. Parte Seconda, p. 316. This last book, it is important to add, is on the side of the question urged in this chapter; it is important, considering 1. the date of the book, 2. the place of its publication, 3. the press from which it issues, 4. its scriptural character, and 5. its popular style, and its being written in the vernacular.

[*] Yet an eminent patristic scholar informs me that this is by no means the case with the Fathers, especially as to the interpretation of the contested passages of Scripture.

side, in one place expressly includes the infants, and so does Lorinus, in his commentary on the hundred and thirty-eighth psalm.*

Cajetan, expounding the parable of the Virgins, teaches that even of those who live moderately well in the Church, and take a certain amount of care of their consciences, one half are lost. Suarez stigmatizes this opinion as " exceedingly rigorous." He then says, " It is a doubtful matter; but I think a distinction should be made. By the name of Christian we may understand all those who glory in the name of Christ, and profess to believe in Him, although many of them are heretics, apostates, and schismatics. Now speaking in this way it seems to me probable that the greater part of them are reprobate, and it is in this general way that I understand the less mild opinion. Now, as heretics and apostates have always been very numerous, if we add to them the number of the faithful who make bad deaths, the two together will plainly exceed the number of those who die well. But if by Christians we understand those only who die in the Catholic Church, it seems to me more likely, in the law of grace, that the greater number of them are saved. The reason is, because, first of all, of those who die before they are adults, the great multitude die baptized; and as to the adults, although the majority of men often sin mortally, yet they often rise again from sin, and thus pass their lives rising and falling. Then again there are but few, who are not prepared for death by the Sacraments, and grieve for their sins at least by attrition; and this is enough to justify them at that time, and after their justification, the time left them is so short that they can easily persevere, and do so, without any fresh mortal

* Recupitus de num. prædes. cap. ii. iii.

sin. Therefore, all things considered, it is probable that the majority of Christians in this stricter sense are saved."*

Vasquez considers it clear from Scripture that the number of the lost is greater than the number of the saved; but he adds that there may be a doubt about the faithful, and that some piously think that the majority of them are saved, and that the Sacraments of the Church, as well as the parable of the wedding garment, look that way. He himself however refuses to take either side.† Even Billuart will not allow to the Theologians quoted by Recupitus any more certain foundations for their opinion than for that of their adversaries.‡ Cornelius à Lapide argues at length against the benignant conclusion of Suarez, and says that the greater number of living theologians at Rome in his day thought the general laxity of morals in the world a strong proof that the sterner opinion was also the more correct.§ The Blessed Leonard of Port Maurice maintains, in his sermon for the third Sunday in Lent, that a great number of Christians are lost, because their confessions are null through want of true sorrow.‖ St. Alphonso on the contrary says, in his Istruzione ai predicatori, that he holds it for certain that of all those who come to the sermons at a mission, whosoever should die within a year, would with difficulty be lost.¶

According to the rigid view, if the deceased baptized

* Suarez lib. 6. De Comparat. prædest. cap. 3. n. 6.
† Vasq. in primam partem disp. 101. cap. 4.
‡ Billuart, De certitud. prædest. diss. 9. art. 7.
§ For the argument of the fewness of the saved taken from the Fathers, see a dismal work published at Rome in 1752, entitled Foggiuius de paucitate adultorum fidelium salvandorum.
‖ Quaresimale p. 195.
¶ *Difficilmente si danna*, lettera seconda.

infants of the faithful, together with the deceased baptized infants of heretics, added to the adult Catholics
who are saved, do not make a majority, and if also the
statement be true* that the deaths of the children of
catholics nearly equal in number, as Ruiz says, the
deaths of adult catholics, then must the number of adults
who are saved be so small, that it follows that the
Church of the redeemed in heaven, the conquest of our
Blessed Saviour's Precious Blood, is chiefly composed of
children, of those who on earth never merited, never
loved, never used their reason at all. Is not this a
conclusion so repugnant as to be inadmissible? I think
this consideration of very great weight.

F. Lacordaire has treated the subject with his usual
power, and also with great delicacy, in his discourse on
the results of the Divine Government, which forms part
of his Conferences of 1851. He inclines to believe that
a majority of mankind are saved, and dwells especially
on children, women, and the poor. His exposition of
the Scripture argument is very remarkable and ingenious,
especially his view of the words, " Few are chosen,"
from the light shed upon them by the context in the
two places in which that passage occurs. Bergier,
speaking of the number of the elect, says, " A solid
and sufficiently instructed mind will not allow itself to
be shaken by a problematical opinion ;" and again, after
describing the disagreement of the Fathers and commentators on the subject, he adds, " If the parables of
the Gospel might be taken as proofs, we should rather
conclude that the greater, not the less, number would
be saved. Jesus Christ compares the separation of the

---

* Le tiers des enfans meurt entre la première et la septième année de sa
naissance, plus de la moitié entre la première et la quatorzième année.—
Annuaire du Bureau des Longitudes.

good and bad at the last judgment, to the division of
the good grain from the cockle. Now, in a field culti-
vated with care, the cockle is never more abundant
than the wheat. He compares it to the separation of
the bad fish from the good ; now to what fisher did it
ever happen to take fewer good fish than bad ? Of ten
virgins called to the marriage five are admitted to the
company of the spouse. In the parable of the talents
two servants are recompensed, one only is punished ; in
that of the feast, only one of the guests is rejected." *
Da Ponte, in his treatise on Christian Perfection, seems
also to lean to the milder opinion ; and Lipsin, the
Franciscan, in his catechism maintains that the opinion
in favour of the majority of Catholics being saved is the
" more probable," and more " consonant to the glory of
God, the merits of Christ, and the hopes of men;"† and
Lipsin says expressly that he is speaking only of adults.

The interpretation given by F. Lacordaire of the
words, Many are called, but few are chosen, rests entirely on the two contexts in which the passage occurs.
In the twentieth chapter of St. Matthew the kingdom
of heaven is compared to a father of a family who hires
labourers into his vineyard at successive hours of the day,
and then when the evening comes, all are rewarded,
and all receive the same reward, notwithstanding the
inequalities of their time of labour. Those, who came
early in the day, complain, and the master answers
that he has given them what he agreed to give, that he
has a right to do what he likes with his own, that the
last shall be first, and the first last, and that many are

* Bergier. Dist. Theol. au mot. *Elus.* Traité de la Vraie Religion, t. 10,
p. 355. Lacordaire Conférences iv. 168.

† Da Ponte, De Perfect. Christiana. tr. 1. Lipsin. Catech. Histor. Theolog.
Dogmat. p. 446. De numero salvandorum.

called, but few chosen. Now it is clear that the difficulty of this parable does not consist in the small number who are recompensed, for all are recompensed, but
in the inequality of the recompense. The conclusion,
that there are but few who are saved, would have no
connection whatever with the parable. It seems rather
to mean that many, who are called by a common grace,
from being the first become the last, while a few, who
are chosen by a special grace, from being last become
first. In the twenty-second chapter of the same Gospel
the kingdom of heaven is compared to a king who
makes a marriage-feast for his son. The guests refuse to
come. Whereupon the king sends his servants out into
the highways and byeways to bring in a mixed multitude to the feast. Of all these only one is rejected; and
that, because he has not on a wedding garment. Cast
him out, says the king, into the darkness where there is
weeping and gnashing of teeth, for many are called but
few are chosen. Now here again the difficulty of the
parable cannot consist in the few who are definitely
admitted and remain to enjoy the feast; for, miscella-
neous multitude as they are, there is but one rejected.
If in such circumstances as these, it is said that many
are called, but few chosen, what can it mean but
that there are few who receive such a special grace as
permits them to behave with more familiarity than
others in divine things, or to count on an unusual favour
of God in their regard? It is the temptation of some,
says the great Dominican, who are called as it were by
chance upon the highway of life to replace other guests
who were invited and have not come, to persuade themselves that they are the objects of God's special predilection, and to neglect to make their calling sure by an
exact fidelity; and it is our Lord's object in this para-

ble to teach them, that if on the one hand there are last who become first, on the other hand no man must dare to presume it of himself.*

Here is a whole mass of conflicting opinions, not perhaps very clear. Let us now do the best we can to collect the suffrages of theologians in this matter. The controversy seems to stand in some such attitude as this :—

1. Many writers hold that the majority of mankind will be lost, because heathen, and unbelievers, and heretics make up a majority.

2. Some hold that a majority of all mankind, taking heathen, heretics, and Christians in one mass, will be saved.

* Salmeron (t. vll. tr. 33) and Cornelius à Lapide (on Matt. xx.) give simi-lar interpretations. Cornelius à Lapide says many are called to ordinary grace and the observance of the commandments, and few to the observance of the counsels. Bergier in his treatise de la Religion, quoted as a note in Migne's edition of the same author's dictionary, says, "Parmi les commenta-teurs, point d'uniformité. Pour ne parler que des catholiques. Cajetan, Mariana, Tostat, Luc de Bruges, Maldonat, Corneille de la Pierre, Ménochius, le père de Picquigny, admettent l'une et l'autre explication ; entendent par *elus* ou les hommes sauvés, ou les fidèles. Jansenius de Gand pense que ce dernier sens est le plus naturel : Stapleton le soutient contre Calvin ; Sacy dans ses *Commentaires*, juge que c'est le sens littéral ; dom Calmet semble lui donner la préférence. Euthymius n' en donne point d'autre ; il suivait S. Jean Chrysostome. Le père Hardouin soutient que c'est le seul sens qui s'accorde avec la suite du texte ; le père Berruyer exclut aussi tout autre sens ; c'est pour cela qu'il a été condamné, mais la faculté de theologie n'a certainement pas voulu censurer les interprètes catholiques que nous venons de citer, et ils sont suivis par beaucoup d'autres. Quel dogme peut on fonder sur un passage susceptible de deux sens si différents? And again he says, Pour fixer un peu plus cette discussion, nous disons qu'il y'a trois opinions sur le nombre des catholiques prédestinés. Quelques docteurs pensent qu'il y'aura plus de catholiques élus que de réprouvés ; ils se fondent sur ce qu'il n'y a eu qu'un seul convive exclu du banquet nuptial. D'autres croient qu'il y aura autant de réprouvés que d'élus. Ils se fondent sur la parable des Vierges, dont cinq etaient sages et cinq folles.—La plupart des theologiens enseignent qu'il y aura plus de réprouvés que d'élus. Ils s'appulent sur ces paroles : *Pauci vero electi.* Il n'y a donc rien de certain à ce sujet. Le savant Suarès regarde la première comme plus probable."

3. Some, to enhance their rigorous view, maintain that the children are to be taken into the account, and yet even so a majority of mankind will be lost, or, in other words, that very few adults will be saved.

4. Some, to enhance their mild views, maintain that the children may be put out of the reckoning, and yet that even so a majority of mankind will be saved.

5. None of these views regard Catholics exclusively.

6. Of those writers who regard Catholics exclusively, some maintain, that even taking the children into account, the majority will be lost.

7. Others maintain, that the majority will be saved, but the majority is only to be reached by reckoning in the children: this is perhaps the most common view of all. *

8. Others hold, that looking at adult Catholics only, as many will be lost as are saved: this opinion is founded on the Parable of the Virgins.

9. Others teach, that the far greater majority of adult catholics will be lost.

10. Others think, that a small majority of adult catholics will be saved.

11. Others finally, to whose opinion I strongly adhere myself, believe that the great majority of adult catholics, perhaps nearly all of them, will be saved.

12. In point of theologians, the rigorous opinions regarding the whole mass of mankind have an overwhelming authority.

13. The rigorous opinions concerning the damnation of the majority of adult catholics have, as far as my reading has gone, numerically more theologians on their side than the milder view.

14. But if we subtract moral, ascetical, and hortatory authors, who write to rouse and to impress their readers,

and retain only pure theologians in the stricter sense, I
think the authorities on the two sides will be not far
from evenly balanced, the excess being however in favour
of the rigorous views, so far as numbers are concerned,
and in favour of the milder views, so far as weight is
concerned.

15. The more recent theologians also exhibit a leaning
to the milder view; and in many cases the rigorous
views are held in conjunction with opinions on the
ultimate state of unbaptized infants, which probably
no single Catholic in the Church now-a-days would
hesitate to disclaim.

16. Some of the authorities on the milder side are of
very great weight.

17. In the use of the Scripture argument the triumph
is completely, and most remarkably, on the milder side.
Indeed the Scripture proof seems quite unmanageable in
the hands of the rigorists.

Thus then it appears, that the question is completely
an open one, and that the view, which is to occupy this
chapter, is not only lawful, but pious. Nevertheless, if
I could persuade myself that the discussion had but
little practical bearing on a holy life, or were likely in
any way to lead to a disesteem of strictness, I should
eagerly avoid entering upon it. It seems however as
if the inquisitive infidelity of the day had so far touched
the faith of many good men, that questions have been
started in their thoughts which mere contempt cannot
now put to silence, and that in order to restore to their
diseased minds a more true view of the fatherly character
of God, it is necessary to bring before them distinct
considerations, founded upon what we know of Him, in
opposition to those darker reflections which keep them
back from a cordial surrender of themselves to God, and

23 †

which even when they are true, become untrue by claiming to be exclusive. Begging then of God to bless this enquiry concerning a secret, which for our good as well as His own glory He has hidden from us, let us proceed reluctantly upon our way.

We know well that when men judge others, whether individuals or multitudes, they generally come to an erroneous conclusion from the mere fact that they judge over-harshly. It is part of the evil that is in us to put the worst construction upon what we see, and to make no allowance for the hidden good. Moreover we, unwittingly almost, judge by the worst parts of our own disposition, not by the best. We believe our evil to be common to all, and our good peculiar to ourselves. We consider evil a decisive test, while good is only allowed to establish a possibility. This is our rule for others: we reverse it for ourselves. We also find that our judgments get milder in proportion to the increase of our own strictness. The judgments of holy men sometimes astonish us by their laxity, while men, not even frequenting the sacraments, or in any way professing to be religious, will be scandalized by the least look of worldliness in a priest or a religious. They will detect with the most amazing sensitiveness the slightest inconsistency in the practice of an openly devout person. Thus we may lay it down as a rule, that the severity of our judgments of others, even where judgments are legitimate and unavoidable, is an infallible index of the lowness of our own spiritual state. The more severe we are, the lower we are. We must therefore be on our guard against this well-known infirmity in the present enquiry. There is something in the adorable compassion of God which looks like voluntary blindness. He seems either not to see, or not to appreciate, the utter unworthiness of men; at least He goes on His way with men as thoug'. He did not see it. The Bible is full of instances of this. Now the more we are with God, and the closer our union with Him is, the more shall we catch something of a similar spirit, which will destroy the natural keenness of our detection of evil, and control more materially our judgments of our fellow-men.

We must be careful also to make a distinction which is often forgotten, and which bears directly upon the present question. What we see around us among catholics may be far from satisfactory, and the authentic statistics which reach us from catholic countries may contain much that is unhappy and disheartening. Yet we must distinguish at any given moment between catholics not living so as to be saved, and their not being ultimately saved at last. In other words we cannot go altogether by what we see. Immense numbers are converted, and go to the sacraments, and persevere in their new life ; and then they are less prominent. We do not hear of them. The statistics of Easters, jubilees, retreats, missions, and the like, come less under our notice than statistics of crime or misery. Sin strikes us, and is startling, whereas ordinary goodness is a tame affair, and passes unobserved. Then there are multitudes of men who have an exceedingly bad chapter in their lives, some ten or twenty years of wickedness, and then change, as if the volcanic matter in them had burned out. This is what men lightly call sowing their wild oats. As one set of these men passes into a better state, another is succeeding them, so that the appearance of things is an incessant current of headstrong sin sweeping all before it, unredeemed by the hopeful features of the case, which the succession of sinners hides effectually from our view. Moreover old

age withdraws its thousands of actors from the stage of
sin, and so they disappear from view. It is wretched
enough to think of these conversions of old age, which
seem to have more of nature in them than of grace. A
man's passions are worked out. He becomes a moral
wreck. The avenues of sensual pleasure are closed to
him by the aches and pains and dull insensibilities of
age. In a number of cases the very powers of sinning
are diminished. And so, what with fear, what with
disgust, and what with making a virtue of necessity, the
old man gives himself to God, such little of him as is
left, and God accepts the gift, because along with all
these self-interested motives there is in the man's heart,
by His grace, a real inward repentance for sin, and
a saving faith in the atoning Blood of Christ. It is
not for us to criticize this amazing forbearance of God;
who knows if we may not one day stand in need of
it ourselves? But so it is. It is God's affair; and in
His infinite wisdom He is pleased to take the offering,
and to save the soul. Multitudes again, even before
old age, fall into sickness in the prime of life and the
middle of their sins, and they pass out of the outer
world of men into the inner world of the priest, that
world half visible and half invisible, where daily miracles of grace are wrought, and where the weary minister
of God is for ever drawing those earthly consolations
which are more to him than the dearness of domestic
affections, and support him sweetly in his incessant
toils. God partly admits him to His secrets, and takes
him into the inner room of sickness, and shows him
the machinery of salvation doing its finest and most
hidden work.

While we are gazing at this picture, we must not
forget to realize, and it is no easy matter, what we

have seen in a former chapter, how little God actually
requires as absolutely indispensable to salvation.   One
confession at the hour of death, ordinary fidelity in confessing, a purpose of amendment which has no temptation then to be insincere, a sorrow which is within easy
reach of any one who is in earnest, with huge allowances made for the clouded weariness and distracting
unsettlements of pain, which interfere with the sensible
fervour of prayer, but not with the grace of true interior
repentance,—and the soul that has spent close upon a
century of sin is saved, saved because God puts the
requisites for absolution so low, saved because He gives
the grand gift of repentance so gratuitously, and changes
hearts so swiftly, saved because by His merciful ordinance faith survived grace for all those years, saved
because the Precious Blood of Jesus is such a superabundant ransom, such a mighty conqueror of souls.
When a man is converted, he has to make little outward
change, so far as the eyes of men are concerned, in his
ordinary life.   Few will notice that he has begun to go
to mass.   Few see him enter the confessional, or kneel
at the altar rail.   Men are never very sedulous in finding out good, and it will even be some time before it is
perceived that habits of swearing, or lying, or intemperance are gone, or that violence of temper has passed
away.   Moreover the convert has relapses, and somehow these are always very much seen and noticed, and
they conceal completely the gradual formation of a
virtuous habit; and besides this, a great deal which
is externally disagreeable and also morally unworthy
will remain, and almost hide a man's conversion even
from his wife and child.   It is not generally mortal sin
which makes men so unbearable to others.   It is more
often selfishness, and temper, and churlishness, and

ferocity, and coarseness, and such like, which may all
be far short of mortal sin, or, perhaps in the cases of
rude persons, of any sin at all.   There is also much in
the demeanour of a converted sinner which is very puz-
zling.   He has had certain habits of sin ; and though
he no longer falls into the mortal sins in question, he
has ways about him which simulate the old habit of
sin. He talks as if he was still under its dominion.   He
omits things which a man   would characteristically
omit, if he had such a habit.   He even falls into venial
sins congenial to the old habit ; and it may often happen
that it shall look as if outward circumstances alone pre-
vented his positively committing the old mortal sin.
But it would be endless to enumerate all the things
which baffle our judgment of the insincerity of a man's
conversion. We may depend upon it that in a thousand
spots, which look desert, waste, and fire-blackened,
God's mercy is finding pasture for His glory.

It is very observable that evil is of its own nature
much more visible than good, while goodness is invisible like God.   Evil, like the world, is loud, rude,
anxious, hurried, and ever acting on the defensive;
while goodness partakes of the nature of Him who
alone is truly good.   It imitates His ways of secrecy
and concealment, and is impregnated with His Spirit
of unostentatious tranquillity and self-sufficient contentment.   The infuriated mob that burns down a
church, and tramples the Blessed Sacrament under foot,
is a much more obvious and obtrusive phenomenon
than the dozen Carmelite nuns who have been doing
the world's hardest work for it before that tabernacle
door for years.   The whole priesthood of the Church,
busy at its work of mercy, catches the eye much less
than a single regiment in scarlet marching down upon

its fellow Christians. Even in the individual this invisible character of goodness is perceptible, and that
not merely in the shy spirit and instinctive bashfulness
of great sanctity, but even without a man's intending
it, or being aware of it, or taking any pains about it.
When we know and love a man, and are in habits of
daily familiar intercourse with him, we know his faults
almost in a week. We learn where to distrust him,
and where he is not unlikely to fail. But the revelation of his goodness is a very slow process. He is
continually taking us by surprise with disclosures of
virtues which we never dreamed that he possessed.
He comes out on great occasions much better than we
expected. In little things too, and the ordinary wear
and tear of life, it is only by degrees that we become
conscious how much real humility, patience, sweetness,
and unselfishness there is about him. There are very
few men whom we do not come by experience to respect, if only we continue to love them. If, as Words-
worth says, all things are less dreadful than they seem,
so is it true that all men are better than they seem.
We must allow very largely for this, when we look
at the lives of catholics, and pass a judgment on the
likelihood of their salvation.

The visible character of evil also brings strongly
before us one of the most frightening features of the
world, and one which it is hard to dwell upon for any
length of time without some amount of gloom passing
on our spirits. It is the ceaseless activity of Satan.
His activity is appalling: his presence almost ubiquitous: his tyranny universal, overwhelming, and successful. Of a truth he needs no repose. To go and
lie down upon his bed of fire would be no rest to him.
Thus the world seems to be always in a storm of his

creating. One while he is persecuting the good, even in the cloister. Another while he is bent on ruining some man who is doing a notable work for God. Now he is urging on the multitudes of a whole country, and making them drunk with the spirit of anarchy and sacrilege. Now he is quietly weaving webs of unholy diplomacy, with a fair show of equity or patriotism, around the Holy See, that he may cramp its energies for good, and demoralize whole nations. Here he is getting up an intricate slander which shall throw discredit on God's servants, and dishonour the cause of religion. There he is sapping the foundations of a religious order by the insidious prudence of relaxation, or destroying the stability of some grand work of mercy by leading the founders to seek their own reputation and honour in it instead of God's glory. One while he is inspiring the press, and hiding the poison that he spreads under the rhetoric of morality and right. Another while he is artfully providing for coldness, dissension, and misunderstanding among those whose power for God consisted in the cordiality of their union. Even the chosen of the earth, the holy and the good, are running to and fro upon the earth, till they are weary, doing Satan's work and dreaming it is God's. Who can look on such a scene without disquiet and dismay? But then we must remember the prominent visible character of evil. Satan is active: can we suppose that God is not ten thousand times more active, even though we see Him less? The very reason why we see Him so little is because we do not follow Him, and search out His ways, and trace the footprints of His operations. If we did we should be astonished at the immensity, the vigour, and the versatility of the magnificent spiritual work which He is

doing all over the world in every year. Just as science
tells us that the earth's surface is never still, but that
some portion of it somewhere all day and night is
quaking and vibrating with the pulsations of the forces
bound up within the centre of the planet, so to the
observant and discerning eye of faith the whole natural
world of created wills and ways is tremulous and
troubled by the forces of the supernatural world, now
forcing their way to the surface, now engulfing whole
regions, now raising lofty summits of new mountains
out of deep valleys, and now altering the very features
of civilization by diverting the mighty currents of the
mind and purpose of humanity.

If the vigour of God abides with such intensity in
every particle of the inanimate world, everywhere wedding strength to beauty, so that the union might capti-
vate with its exquisite niceties the intelligence of angels,
if in every mineral atom He abides intimately by His
presence, His essence, and His power, how much more
shall we believe that He informs and controls the
world of men by the energies of an allwise providence,
whose majestic operations have all of them the one
single scope and end of love for their blissful accomplishment! We have already seen enough of the doctrine of grace to be aware to what an almost incredible extent it discloses the divine activity. Temptation
is feeble, languid, intermittent, and inert, compared with
this. Satan grows weary, even though he cannot rest,
while the perseverance of grace is incomparable, like
the freshness of that eternal mercy from which it eman-
ates. Moreover we know that Satan is bound by the
coming of our Lord. The little Babe of Bethlehem
circumscribed his monstrous empire. If he is as wild
and fierce as ever, he has now found the length of his

chain, and beyond that his fury is unavailing. Even
within his greatly lessened sphere, the Cross of Christ
is a perpetual torture, an endless defeat to his malicious
wiles. The very presence of the Church is an unbroken exorcism to the baffled prince of darkness. Her
benedictions keep extruding him from one corner of creation after another. Her exorcisms dispossess him even
of the hidden spiritual strongholds in which he craves
to keep his court. Her holy presences are tortures to
him, worse, some of them at least, than the fires of
that abyss which is the fallen creature's home. Up
and down all lands St. Raphael is for ever binding
him in the upper uninhabitable parts of the spiritual
Egypt. Who then can believe that in God's own
cloistered dwelling-place, the sanctuary of His Church,
Satan's activity will prevail against His, and that He
will be defeated even where His choice most loves to
dwell? Satan broke into the first paradise of God,
when he was young, and before the Cross of Christ had
bound him, and what followed? The saving of Adam
and of Eve by a more copious salvation, the superabundance of redeeming grace, the glorious reign of the
Queen of the Immaculate Conception, and the total
triumph of the Incarnate Word! Much more will like
consequences follow now. We must not tremble too
much at Satan's power. He is under our feet already.
We are stronger far than he. We must remember
the story of the servant of Eliseus in the fourth book
of Kings. The servant of the man of God, rising early,
went out, and saw an army round about the city, and
horses, and chariots; and he told him, saying, Alas,
alas, alas, my lord, what shall we do? But he answered, Fear not: for there are more with us than with
them. And Eliseus prayed, and said, Lord, open his

eyes that he may see. And the Lord opened the eyes of the servant, and he saw, and behold the mountain was full of horses and chariots of fire, round about Eliseus.

The very inconceivable magnificence of God would lead us to suppose that the number of the saved, which is one of the greatest glories of His creation, would be something far beyond our utmost expectations.* Has it not been so in every experience we have ever had of God? Has He not always outdone His own promises, as well as outstripped our imaginations? Have not His gifts always come in an embarrassing abundance? Have we ever formed an expectation of mercy or of grace, which has not been fulfilled far beyond our hopes, as if not even our necessities, much less our merits, but His own liberality, were the rule of answered prayer? Is it likely to be less so, or are we likely to find God changed all at once, in a matter, in which not only our happiness, but the honour of His dear Son and the interests of His own wonderful glory, are so exceedingly involved? There is something so uncongenial in the thought, that it surely cannot be received unless it be revealed. There is no word which describes His love of us as our Creator so faithfully as magnificence, and will His love as our Last End be less magnificent, less efficacious in the triumph of its glorious attractions? There is no word to express His prodigal expenditure in our redemption, except magnificence; can we conceive, in a divine work, of a magnificence in the design which shall not be equalled by magnificence in the execution? No one doubts that hell will be unspeakably more dreadful than we expected; because no one doubts but that our little views will be found foolishly narrow when compared with the

* See the note from Lessius at page 125.

transcendant realities of God. So will it be found with
our notions of the number of the saved. Yet, when
we think of what the catholic church is and of all the
privileges involved in being a catholic, it seems only
reasonable to expect that on the whole far more of them
would be saved than lost. There is no magnificence in
this idea. There would be a sense of failure and incompleteness in the opposite opinion. No one surely
can think steadily and continuously on the matter
without coming to this conclusion. But of necessity,
because He is Himself, God will go far out of sight of
our beliefs in the actual splendour of His accomplish-
ments. So that, from what we know of God, we should
augur that very few catholics, comparatively speaking,
would be lost. The salvation of almost all of them
seems to be claimed by the very magnificence of God.
He is a bold man, who, without the Church to back
him, believes that God's own gift of free will, which He
has mysteriously allowed to do Him so much injury in
time, shall have a final and complete victory over Him
for eternity; and if God is love, which is of faith, then
hell will be no victory to Him.

The honour of the Precious Blood would imply and require all this as much as the magnificence of God. It is a
hard saying that the majority of those for whom it was
shed, and on whose souls it has been actually sprinkled,
should be lost eternally. We are purposely turning our
eyes away from all without the Church, saying nothing,
defining nothing, hinting nothing, guessing nothing. It
is not our concern. But how hard will it be to say that
of those souls, who have been actually washed in it
again and again, the majority are lost. It has cleansed
them in baptism, and printed an ineffaceable character
upon their brows. It has absolved them again and

again. It has run through them with thrills of fervour
and fortitude in confirmation. Its red living pulses have
beaten with their human life within the heart at communion. Are we then to say, that of those, who of all
mankind have most trusted the Blood of Jesus, and
have made most use of it, the majority are lost? What
ground is there in dogmatic theology for an assertion so
little to the honour of our dearest Lord ? One drop is
more than enough to redeem all the possible sins of all
possible worlds, and yet oceans of it do not succeed in
redeeming the majority of the members of His Church!
Who would hesitate at anything which the Church
taught him to believe, and who would believe this unless
the Church should teach it?

Then again, the action of the sacraments is probably
much greater than we have any notion of. We learn a
great deal that is very surprising from theology, enough
to set us gratefully wondering at the ingenious excesses
of our Creator's love. But what we learn there rather
shows us the extent of our ignorance than furnishes us
with anything like a complete science. We may follow, first the school which teaches that the operation of
the sacraments is moral, then the school which teaches
that it is physical, and we are better and holier, because
more loving, men for our researches. But have they
not left us at a point beyond which, though we could
get no further, we saw that sacramental grace was
advancing far beyond us with an operation we could not
comprehend, into recesses of which mystical theologians
speak in grandiloquent words and with abstrusest terms ?
When we discuss the deep of the soul, or the point of
the spirit, or whether the character of a sacrament is set
as a signet on the soul or on the faculties of the soul, we
are at the end of our mind's tether, and grace has shot

miles ahead, and is working grandly out of sight. All God's works are greater when we get to look into them, than they seemed at first. Especially must it be so with such supernatural works as His sacraments. It is conceivable that a clear view of the operation of the sacraments, both in themselves, and also retrospectively in our own souls, may be a not insignificant item in our future blessedness. One good communion is enough, they say, to make a saint. Now think what goes to the making of a saint, the numberless things, their inexhaustible variety, their positive contradictoriness, their unlikely combinations, the intricate wide-spreading possibilities of their perseverance; and what can the axiom mean, except that, not only the inward power of a sacrament, but its actual operation, goes farther and deeper than we can follow it?* Look then at the numberless receptions of sacraments, which there are daily in the Church, and can you seriously believe that the result of it all is, that the majority of catholics are not saved? O be sure you are estimating far too low the glorious efficacy of the divine interventions, the successful majesty of creative love!

Our ignorance of the last inward processes of deathbeds leaves one of the most spacious portions of our

---

* As it is the tendency of the modern mind to eliminate the supernatural, believers must be on their guard against an inevitable temptation, which will beset themselves, to make little of the more supernatural agencies in the Church. Any departure from the old language about the wonderworking powers and peculiar privileges of the Sacraments would be a most suspicious feature in any modern theology. Upon the universally admitted principle of moral theology, Stat pro facto, the least that we can say about the sacraments is, that where they have been received, the probability is always in favour of their validity; and, if they were valid, then the right inward dispositions went along with them. For the sacraments do not take the place of a real inward change of heart, or do instead of it. It is their office to produce it by their marvellous reinforcements of grace.

lives inaccessible to our notice. Life is not counted
only by material time. The world, and all its sights
and sounds, too often leave little room for God in the
hearts of men. But the hour of death is very spacious.
It gives God room. It turns minutes into years. It
redoubles and redoubles the swift processes of the mind
just on the eve of its ejection from the body. It is an
hour of truth, and an hour of truth is longer than a century of falsehood. Heaven draws near to it, to help as
well as to behold. It is God's last chance with His
creature, and divine wisdom must know well how to use
its chances. A man is freed from many laws, when
time and space are visibly melting away in the white
light of eternity, or rather he himself is being brought
under wider and larger laws. He can live many lives
within the compass of his agony. We know very little
of what goes on then. The thick curtains of the glazed
eye, of the expressionless or only pain-furrowed face,
and of the inarticulate voice, are drawn round the last
earthly audience between the Creator and the creature.
But observation and psychology combine to teach us
that much does go on, and of a far more intelligent
character, than we should otherwise conceive. "Really,
according to my observations," says Sir Benjamin
Brodie,* " the mere act of dying is seldom, in any sense
of the word, a very painful process. It is true that
some persons die in a state of bodily torture, as in cases
of tetanus ; that the drunkard, dying of *delirium tremens,*
is haunted by terrific visions ; and that the victim of
that most horrible of all diseases, hydrophobia, in addition to those peculiar bodily sufferings from which the
disease has derived its name, may be in a state of terror
from the supposed presence of frightful objects—which

* Psychological Enquiries, p. 150.

are presented to him as realities, even to the last.   But
these and some other instances which I might adduce
are exceptions to the general rule, which is, that both
mental and bodily sufferings terminate long before the
scene is finally closed.   Then, as to the actual fear of
death ; it seems to me that the Author of our existence,
for the most part, gives it to us when it is intended
that we should live, and takes it away from us when it
is intended that we should die.   Those who have been
long tormented by bodily pain are generally as anxious
to die as they ever were to live.   So it often is with
those whose life has been protracted to an extreme old
age, beyond the usual period of mortality, even when
they labour under no actual disease.   It is not very
common for any one to die merely of old age ;—

> ‘ Like ripe fruit to drop
> Into his mother's lap.’

But I have known this to happen ; and a happy conclusion it has seemed to be of worldly cares and joys.   It
was like falling to sleep, never to awake again in this
state of existence.   Some die retaining all their faculties, and quite aware that their dissolution is at hand.
Others offer no signs of recognition of external objects,
so that it is impossible for us to form any positive
opinion whether they do or do not retain their sensibility ; and others again, as I have already stated, who
appear to be insensible and unconscious, when carefully
watched, are found not to be so in reality ; but they
die contentedly.   I have myself never known but two
instances in which, in the act of dying, there were
manifest indications of the fear of death.”

In the life of Condren there is a very remarkable
passage urging on us the duty of thanksgiving to God

for the graces He bestows on the dying, inasmuch as
" His compassion for them is inexplicable, and He
seems to distribute His favours to them all the more
willingly, because they are hardly now in danger of
profaning them." Beautiful thought! O how much of
the beauty of God's love is gathered round the dying
bed, how much more than we can see, how much more
than we believe! We grant that it is unknown ground;
but because mercy is so much needed then, because
mercy has had so many antecedents with the soul, because it is God's will it should be saved, and finally
because God is such a God as we know Him well to be,
we boldly claim all that unknown land of catholic death-
beds for the simple sovereignty of the divine compassion.
That hour may explain many inexplicable salvations.
The gloomiest mind must admit, that it may have
shrouded in it endless possibilities of salvation; and
with such a God at such an hour the possibilities grow
miraculously into probabilities, and forthwith disappear
in those sweet sudden certainties with which the dying
child of Jesus has fallen asleep upon its Father's
bosom.*

* I would *earnestly* beg of the reader to turn back here, and read again
our Blessed Lord's own revelation to S. Gertrude about deathbed mercies,
page 275. In the consideration of this matter there are two things to be
observed, and also to be kept studiously apart:—opinions based on theological teaching, and opinions gathered from the observation of mankind
and the experience of life. The last chapter, on the Easiness of Salvation,
was theology, the present chapter on the number of the saved rests mainly
on inferences from the character of God, and on a hopeful view of human
conduct. All consistent views of God's dealings with His creatures must
rest the fixed point of the compass either on His revealed character or on
our own personal observation of mankind. From our ignorance, neither
will give us certain results. But, on the one hand, the inferences drawn
from the revealed character of God are decidedly in favour of the mild
view of the number of the saved, while, on the other, personal observation
of mankind is a most uncertain affair, can only produce very precarious
results, and is by no means so decidedly on the rigorous side as the re-

24

When we see a man sinning, we see his sin, but we can seldom see the excuses of his sin. This is a very important consideration in the present discussion, and has already been partially adverted to. The depths of invincible ignorance may underlie no inconsiderable region of a man's moral nature, and each individual character has an invincible ignorance belonging to itself. It is a thing we cannot possibly presume upon for ourselves, because a suspicion destroys it: but we may put much to its account in our neighbour's favour. Again, the violence of the temptation is invisible ; and even if we saw it, we could not see the peculiar oppressiveness of it to another's heart, or its almost irresistible tyranny because of previous habits. Yet surely there are many cases in which the vehemence of the temptation is a

vealed character of God is on the milder side. We know more of God than we know of men, and what we know of Him we know more surely than what we know of them. It is the very object of this chapter to prove that.

With regard to the hopeful view of human conduct, my own observation in the priesthood, and that of others eminent in age and of wide experience, whom I have consulted, is that the great majority of catholics lead lives of *more or less* struggle. It is too often little enough. Yet missions, general confessions, and the like, reveal for the most part this feature of struggle. Now this is a most important feature. Combattasi pure, che qui sta il *tutto,* says Scupoli. (But read all his chapter 6.) The grace of a good deathbed, maintained in the text to be so common, is not the *ordinary* conclusion of a probation spent in life-long neglect of God, or in obdurate sin, but the final giving of the victory by a great and decisive mercy to the side in a struggle, which hitherto had been dubious and unsatisfactory. Meanwhile no one can deny that a good death as the end of a bad life is both a theological possibility, and an *occasional* mercy. But such are not the deathbed graces which I speak of as being common. Still, those other marvellous deathbed conversions, though they are rare phenomena, must necessarily be taken into the account, when we are occupied in fathoming the incredible depths of God's love. It has become proverbial that a *principle* is best tested by an extreme case. Thus even of sinners, as well as of martyrs, does God's love at times make these words true, true it may be even to the passing over of Purgatory,

Mortis sacræ *compendio*
Vitam beatam possident.

mitigating circumstance in punishment, even if it be not
an actual plea of mercy. We must also have a thorough
acquaintance with a man's peculiar turn of mind, the
bent of his disposition, the circumstances of his past
life, and, most of all, his early education, before we are
at all in a condition to form an estimate of what his
guilt is in the sight of God.* Also men often fall, when
they are in a good state, from a momentary self-trust,
or a sudden assault of Satan, God permitting it for their
greater good and more entire humility; and then a
man's sin is an exceptional case, and we cannot argue
from it to his habitual state. All these considerations,
and many more which might be adduced, very much
detract from the value of our observations on the sins of
catholics, as proofs that by far the greater number of
them are not ultimately saved.

This leads us to a further consideration. It can
hardly be denied that men's actions are often worse
than their hearts, even when they proceed from the
heart; and they have often less heart in them than
they seem to have. For instance, a man commits a
sin in a sudden outburst of passion; that passion may
have felt some peculiar sting in the provocation which
another would not feel, and it may have fallen upon
him when he was physically agitated or when his nerves

---

* Lacordaire says beautifully of the sinner as he is in the sight of God,—
Dieu y reconnaît encore sa main. Comme une statue mutilée sort de la
terre où les siècles l'avaient enfouie, ainsi l'âme dégradée par le péché appa-
raît aux regards de son père; c'est un marbre déshonoré, mais où respire
encore la vie, et auquel l'artiste suprême peut rendre sa première beauté.
Il y travaille avec ardeur; il aime ce débris; il y frappe des coups qui ém-
euvent son espérance et attendrissent ses regrets. Ce n'est qu'à la mort que
le mal persévérant prend une consistance à l'épreuve de l'amour divin, et
que Dieu le voit comme un impardonnable ennemi. Jusquelà, il appartient
encore à l'architecture du bien; il est une pierre espérable de la sainte cité,
et peut-être y entrera-t-il en un lieu magnifique, qui étonnera l'innocence
sans la décourager. *Conférences de* 1851.

were unstrung. For all this, the sin may remain a sin, and yet be no fair index of the sinner's heart. Or, again, men are propelled into sin not unfrequently by false shame, by human respect, by bad company; and a man's heart may be far better all the while than its outward actions testify. Many a man looks to his neighbours a very monster of depravity, while the priest, who heard his general confession, has been almost touched to tears by the spots of green verdure, the almost feminine sensibilities, the refined kindnesses, but above all by the moral shyness, the ground of so many virtues, which he found in that great rough nature. Are we not learning every day to be less surprised at finding how so very much good can dwell with so very much evil? Then, again, many have so many odd crossings in their minds which tell upon their motives, and hamper the free action of their moral sense; and thus it is that cruelty in war, agrarian murders, and the like, are not on the whole such conclusive proofs of a depraved heart as they are commonly taken to be. Much crime lies at the door of a warped mind; and how much of that crime is sin can be known to God alone. The heart is the jewel which He covets for His crown, and if the heart which we do not see is better than the actions that we see, God be praised! for then the world is a trifle less dismal than it seems.

It was perhaps these and similar considerations of human charity, almost infinitely magnified by His Sacred Heart which made Jesus, when on earth, such a lover of sinners. We know well that His predilection was for them. He came to seek and to save what was lost, and the more lost a soul was, the more especially He came to seek it and to save it. He seemed to prefer

the society of sinners to any other; and all-holy as He
was, it is wonderful how He contrived at once to exhibit
His holiness and also to put sinners into so interesting
a light: and He, which is much to be remembered,
is the Judge at last. Those sinners, who came near
Him in the Gospel and had intercourse with Him, seem
to be almost His chosen souls. There is a poetry
thrown around their memories, even in the case of the
poor young man who did not follow Him, which is
nothing else but the lustre of the Saviour's love. So
is it always with the saints of Jesus. They are characterized by a hopeful view of sinners.* They have a
positive devotion to them, as our Lord had. The very
power of the religious communities, which have to deal
with the reformation of sinners, consists at once in
their tender love of them and their supernatural respect for them. Without this last quality even the
charity of the spouses of Christ will be but intermittent, and lose the perfection of its beauty, the uniformity of its sweetness, and the power from God to
accomplish and bring to a happy persevering issue
the glorious work of conversion in the soul. In the
place of the steadiness of grace, their works of mercy
will have all the characteristics of capricious nature.
Truly it is a Christlike thing to love sinners. But is not
our love of them a piteous horror rather than a true love,
if our view of them is to be so depressing and over-
clouded, that we are to believe that the greater number
even of catholics are not to be saved? Does not this
peculiar tenderness, this almost devotion of our Blessed

* Great stress should be laid on the almost invariable characteristic of
the saints, that they took a hopeful view of human conduct; for the
saints are precisely men whose dispositions approach to the dispositions
of God.

Lord, point to a far more cheering view? Pray, said the Carmelite prioress of Beaune to Margaret of the Blessed Sacrament, pray for this soul, though I cannot hope for its conversion. O Mother, replied Margaret, wherefore doubt the goodness of our God? Is not this to do Him a dishonour? Who has ever invoked the Holy Child Jesus without being heard? Now let us go and implore of Him the grace which you desire, and three days shall not pass before your wishes shall be gratified.

The saints look at sinners as saints themselves in possibility. Their hopefulness is the secret of their charity. Their humility also, which gives them a clear view of the excess of God's grace over the amount of their own correspondence, makes them slow to believe that others, even with less grace, will not surpass their attainments. Thus they come to believe, what the experience of those versed in the affairs of souls abundantly establishes, that conversion is one of the most common phenomena of grace. It is the sort of thing to be expected of grace, the ordinary occurrence which comes as a matter of course, just as the sun warms, or the frost chills, or the water wets us, or the fire burns us. Now we have already seen the immense abundance of grace, with which heaven inundates the earth, and if conversion is quite an ordinary occurrence with it, and sinners alone can strictly speaking be the subjects of conversion, it follows that the great mass of apparently unworthy catholics is the chosen theatre of one of the strongest as well as the commonest of the operations of grace. Thus it is that apostolic zeal, with its enlightened love, looks at sinners as the materials for the future triumphs of Jesus, as the harvest yet ungarnered of His passion and His Cross. Bad

catholics, those who appear bad to us, are but a proportion of all catholics, and if redeeming grace has yet
got to invade that proportion, and according to all its
laws must triumphantly invade it, we can hardly think
otherwise than that the majority of catholics will be
saved. If we put all our data together, conversion can
hardly be common in the Church, unless salvation is
common too.

There is another point, which has already been adverted to, but which must not be omitted in the present enumeration. When men look at a country, or a
neighbourhood, or a town, and pass a judgment on its
religious condition, not only must they necessarily
have insufficient data, but they are very liable to fall
into an inaccuracy which seriously affects the value of
their observations. They do not distinguish between
the sinfulness of sin and the deformity of sin, which
last spreads out and covers a greater extent of ground
than the guilt, infecting the manners, tainting the
whole tone and atmosphere, and altogether making a
much greater show than the real sin. Much that is
morally unlovely is not sin, certainly not mortal sin.
And yet it catches the eye, and offends our moral sense,
and is extremely odious in the sight of religion. It
is of a truth an evidence of the existence of sin, but
by no means a measure of its quantity. Very often a
newly converted man is almost as disagreeable and
repulsive as he was when in his sins. His moral appearance is not improved all at once. The mellowing,
softening, beautifying powers of grace are long in their
operation, and follow with slow steps the sharp decisive
movements which effect conversion at the first. As it
is absurd for protestants to measure the truth of the
religions of two countries by the success of conquest,

the perfection of the monetary system, the extension of
commerce, or scientific improvements in agriculture,*
so is it equally a mistake to decide on the religiousness
of a population by the offensive prominences of national
character, or by the reigning foibles and unworthinesses
of a population, or even by a low standard of moral
integrity in some one or other department, peculiar to
the country, place, or time.   In judging of individuals
it is still more important to distinguish between moral
unloveliness and downright sin.   Goodness tends to be
graceful; but in this life there are always to each man
a thousand causes which hinder its development.

The extreme severity of the punishments of purgatory
is another consideration which leads the mind to contemplate the immense multitude of the saved, and of
those saved with very imperfect dispositions, as the
only solution of these chastisements.   Purgatory goes as
near to the unriddling the riddle of the world, as any
one ordinance of God which can be named.   Difficulties
are perpetually drifting that way to find their explanation;
and the saints of God have turned so full a light upon
those fields of fire, that the geography of them seems
almost as familiar to us as the well-known features of
the surface of the earth.   The charitable practices of
catholic devotion lead us to spend so much of our day
amid the patience of that beautiful suffering, that it has
become to us like the wards of a favourite hospital with
its familiar faces brightening at the welcome words of
consolation.   It is the same fire as hell.   That in itself
is a terrible reflection.   The revelations of the saints

* Yet the more thoughtful protestant writers are beginning to see now,
what political geography might have taught them before, that these developments of material grandeur are due to the amount of popular liberty
rather than to the dominance of any religious opinions.

depict the tortures of it as fearful in the extreme. There
is a consent of them, as to the immense lengths of time
which souls average under that punishment, a consent
fully bearing out the practice of the Church in anniver-
saries and foundations for masses for ever. The very
slightest infidelities to grace seem to be visted there
with the acutest sufferings. God Himself has bidden
His saints to honour with chaste fear and exceeding
awe the rigours of His justice, and the requirements of
His purity, in that land of bitter long delay. Now
does it come natural to us to look at all this system,
this terrible eighth sacrament of fire, which is the home
of those souls whom the seven real sacraments of earth
have not been allowed to purify completely, does it come
natural to us to look at it all as simply a penal
machinery invented for the saints and those most like
the saints, to cut away with its vindictive sharpness the
little imperfections which come of human frailty? That
it should fulfil this office is most intelligible, most
accordant with God's perfections, and most consolatory
to souls themselves. But does not the view at once
recommend itself to us that it was an invention of God
to multiply the fruit of our Saviour's Passion, that it
was intended for the great multitudes who should die
in charity with God, but in imperfect charity, and
therefore that it is as it were the continuance of deathbed
mercies beyond the grave, and that, as such, it throws
no uncertain light on the cheering supposition that most
catholics are saved, especially of the poor who sorrow
and suffer here?

Mention has been made in previous chapters of God's
unaccountable contentment with so little, as requisite
for salvation. Of course purgatory goes some way
towards accounting for it, but very far from the whole

way. Purgatory seems too good for ungenerous souls,
and yet they are crowding into it by thousands, and
become beautiful amid its flames.   The merits and
satisfactions of our dearest Lord seem our only refuge,
when we see how low it has pleased God to put the
terms of our redemption.   The charity of Jesus covers
the multitude of the sins of His people.   God sees the
world through Him, not simply by a fiction imputing to
us the holiness that is our Lord's, but, for His sake and
by the efficacy of His Blood, actually ennobling our
unworthiness, and giving a real greatness to our littleness, and a solid value to the merest intentions of our
love.   It is the daily delight of His justice to be limited
in the operations of its righteous anger by the adorable
Sacrifice of the Mass ; and the glory of Jesus is the
grand fundamental law of all creation.   Yet even so,
God's contentment with so little is an inscrutable mercy,
one of those bright lights that are dark because they
are so bright, and which are rising up perpetually from
the abysses of creative love.   Who shall tell the thousands
of souls in heaven at this hour, whom, almost to their
own surprise, that marvellous contentment has exalted
there?

Are any two angels exactly in the same degree of
glory ?   Theologians say that the graces of each radiant
spirit are unlike.   Perhaps then their glories are unequal also, and even where not unequal, at least unlike.
If so, what innumerable degrees of bliss there must be
in the angelic hierarchies!   The saints we know are
ranged in countless ranks.   We are not told that those
who are in the same rank have all an equal vision.   It
is of faith that the rewards of heaven differ in degree.
It is revealed to us in the parables of the talents
and the cities.   In my Father's house are many

mansions, said our Lord. Star differeth from star in
glory, is the doctrine of St. Paul. Now there can be
no exaggeration in supposing that there are at least as
many different degrees of happiness in heaven as there
are degrees of happiness on earth. We know that there
are as many different degrees of glory hereafter, as there
are different degrees of grace here ; and as far as we can
read the phenomena of grace, it would really seem as
if those differences were as numerous as the individual
nearts in which it dwells. This would admit of an
immense variety of scales of goodness upon earth, the
very lowest of which should reach heaven. And would
it not be in accordance with what we know of the works
of God, if heaven stooped almost down to earth, and
wellnigh blended with it, only, which is truly difference
enough, that the lowest there would have God's clear
light full upon him, and therefore be bathed in joys
which eye has not seen, nor ear heard, nor heart of
man conceived? This view would swiftly reach, and
that by no circuitous route, the sweet conclusion for
which we plead, that the great majority of catholics are
saved.

Hell teaches the same comfortable doctrine as heaven,
although in a rougher strain. Finite evil is almost infinitely punished, limited sin almost illimitably tormented. One mortal sin is chastised eternally. There
may be many in hell who have committed a less amount
of sin than many who are in heaven, only they would
not lay hold of the Cross of Christ, and do penance, and
have easy absolution. There is no life of self denying
virtue, however long and however laborious, but if it
ends in impenitence and mortal sin, must be continued
among the unending pains of hell. One mortal sin,
and straightway a death without contrition, and ever-

lasting despair alone remains. Now will evil be more
punished than good is rewarded? Will they even be
on equal terms? Theology teaches that the chastisements of hell are for the sake of Christ far less than the
wretched sufferers deserve. There is mercy even there,
whence hope has long since fled, compassion even there
where its tenderness seems so wholly out of place, and
its forbearance thankless and unavailing. Hell is less
than sin deserves. Then is there no corner of creation
where the divine justice enjoys all its rights? At least
it is not in hell; for hell is less than sin deserves. O
beautiful ubiquity of mercy! The Gospel nowhere tells
us that sinners shall be punished up to the plenitude of
their demerits; but it does tell us about the reward of
virtue, that it shall be "good measure, and pressed
down, and shaken together, and running over." You
see it is in heaven only that justice shall enjoy its royalties! Shall not then God's rewarding of good be in
all respects far beyond, in fulness and completeness, His
punishment of evil? Shall not a little good, a very
little good, be much rewarded? And is not the number
who are rewarded a chief feature in the magnificence of
the reward? Surely not only will heaven be unspeakably beyond our deservings, but many will go there,
whom only the generosity of divine love and the determination of persisting grace could have made deserving.
These are things which we cannot know, and they are
not put forward as amounting to arguments; but there
seems something easy in the process by which the very
existence and extremity of hell leads to the conclusion
that most catholics are saved.

The providence of God in the lives of men is to each
one in particular a private revelation of His love. The
biography of every one of us is to ourselves as luminously

supernatural, as palpably full of divine interferences, as
if it were a page out of the Old Testament history.
Moreover all that is providential is also merciful.
The interferences are all on the side of love. Stern-
looking accidents, when they turn their full face to us,
beam with the look of love. Even our very faults are
so strangely over-ruled, that mercy can draw materials
for its blessings even out of them. It is true we may
easily delude ourselves. But the natural tendency to
find a meaning in what happens to ourselves, and to
exaggerate its significance, cannot altogether, or even
nearly, account for the providential aspect which our
past lives present to us, when we reflect upon them in
the faith and fear of God. Our merciful Creator seems
to have led us very gently, as knowing how weak and
ill we are ; yet He has led us plainly towards Himself.
If it is not speaking of Him too familiarly, He seems to
have done everything just at the right time, and in the
right place, to have put nothing before us till we were
ready for it and could make the most of it, to have timed
His grace and apportioned it, so that we might have
as little as possible the guilt of resisting grace, to have
weighed even our crosses before He laid them upon us,
and to have waited an auspicious moment each time He
would persuade us to something fresh. He has combined events with the most consummate skill, and
brought out the most wonderful results, and they have
always been in our favour. There are difficulties and
seeming exceptions to the ordinary course of this genial
providence. But it is only at first sight that they
perplex us. These very exceptions on closer investigation, or longer experience, turn out to be the most striking examples of the general rule of benevolence and
love. If we ask each man separately, this is what he

will tell us. We have all of us had this private revelation. But are not God's works for the most part
remarkable for their efficacy? Do not all these secret
biographies of men, with their beautiful disclosures of
His assiduous ministering love, bear upon this question
of salvation? Has He so waited upon each of us, that
we might at any time have mistaken Him for our Guardian Angel, instead of our God, and yet is not His
solicitude in far the greater number of cases to have the
one issue which His glory so earnestly desires? God
is infinitely just, and He executes His justice upon the
sons of men. But Scripture does not put His vindictive
justice forward as coming in floods and inundations and
unheard-of wonders, as His mercy does, but rather as a
reserve, an interference, an exceptional visitation, and
as taking the room left for it in the world by previously
rejected mercy.

Let us dwell on one feature of His providence, the
way in which He vouchsafes to time things. Think
of the hour of death, of its surpassing importance, of
its thrilling risks, of all those inward processes of
which we have already spoken. Now may we not
conclude, or at least with reasonable hope infer, that
to most, if not to all, men, the hour of their death is
seasonably timed? They die when it is best for them
to die. There are some dangers in advance which they
avoid by dying then. They die when they are in the
best state for dying. Even the deaths of those who are
lost may be mercifully timed. When men die young,
t is perhaps because they would have lost themselves if
they had lived to be old. When men die late, it is
perhaps to give them time to correspond to grace, to do
penance for the past, and especially that they may get
rid of some evil habit which would else be their per-

dition, and which the mere infirmity of age will help them to abandon. When men die just as they are coming into the possession of riches, or at the outset of a smiling career of laudable ambition, it is perhaps because God sees in their natural character, or in their personal circumstances some seeds of future evil, and so He takes them while all that evil lies innocently undeveloped in their souls. Who can think of what death is, and yet doubt that God's wisdom and His love are brought to bear with inexpressible sweetness both on its manner and its time? If God were pleased to tell us, we should probably be amazed at the numbers of convincing reasons that there are why each of us should die when, and where, and how we do. The very sight of so much legislation and arrangement, on the part of God, about this one final act of our probation is doubtless pouring into the souls of the Blessed at all hours delightful streams of wondering adoration and extatic love. Is all this true of each Christian deathbed, and are not then the great majority of Christians saved?

But what is it which most obviously distinguishes catholics from all other men? Surely it is the gift of faith. This, next to the Beatific Vision of Himself in heaven, is the greatest gift which God can give to His creatures; for in some respects it may be said to be greater than sanctifying grace, because it is its indispensable foundation. It is hard to realize the greatness of a gift which is so intimate to every operation of our lives. But we may gain some idea of its importance when we remember that without faith no sacraments avail, and that with the loss of faith we lose almost all the capabilities of setting ourselves right when we have sinned. It is a gift therefore which we should not only guard most jealously, but which we should increase by exercise; for that it is capable of increase by our own, correspondence is one of those many really startling disclosures of divine love, at which nobody is startled because they are so common. We see or hear of souls wandering in the darkness, reading, arguing, writing, commenting, collating manuscripts, all in perplexity because they cannot perceive the Divinity of our Blessed Lord, while to every catholic child that sweet convert-ing truth is plainer than the sunshine on the trees. The little fellow could not doubt it, if he would. He is so sure of it, that he would be beaten to death rather than say it was not true. To others the mystery of the Most Holy Trinity presents difficulties of the most insuperable kind, how God can be One God yet Three Persons, how the Son can be evermore coequally begotten of the Father, and the Holy Ghost be evermore coequally pro-ceeding from the Father and the Son. The catholic finds nothing hard in it. He cannot explain it, even so far as theology arrives towards an explanation. But he knows it and sees it as distinctly as the writing of a letter or the pages of a book. Bewilder him as you will, you cannot inject a doubt into his mind. He can-not help himself; he is more certain of the Holy Trinity, than he is of your existence who are standing by him and questioning him. O glorious necessity of believing, which is hardly faith, but actual contact with a supernatural world, as if the prerogative of heaven was only to see God, while earth's privilege was to touch Him in the dark with fearless venture and with thrilling love! Heaven must indeed be beautiful, if the saints can part there with their gift of faith, and not pine to have it back again! Yet this gift every catholic re-ceives, not the faith of devils who believe and tremble, but the supernatural gift of divine faith. It is faith by

which so many, after years of sin, quietly and as it were
naturally, swing round to their anchors, and die well.
By this gift the catholic sees far up into the unbegin-
ning eternity of God, and beholds his own soul lying
there in the lap of that eternal love. By faith he sees
the unspeakable operations of the Holy Trinity with its
Innascibility, Generation, and Procession. By faith he
scans the numberless perfections of God. By faith he
sees Jesus, God and Man, in the Blessed Sacrament.
By faith he beholds Mary on her mediatorial throne.
By faith the joys of heaven, the delays of purgatory,
the pains of hell, are familiar to him as the hills
and streams and groves where his childhood played.
By faith he sees the lineaments of Jesus in His priests,
and beholds the Precious Blood dropping from the hand
that is raised to give him absolution. This gift is com-.
mon to all, so common that it stays with us even when
grace has left us, so persevering and so secure of itself
that it will lodge with sin and fear no evil; and is there
one sign of predestination of which so much can be said
as of this transcendent gift, which of its sole self makes
a creature of God into a catholic, and writes upon his
brow this plain inscription of his Creator, It is My
especial Will that this creature should be saved, and live
with Me for ever ?.

The Church militant on earth is the foreshadowing
of the Church triumphant in heaven. The destinies of
the heavenly Church are glassed and mirrored on the
earthly Church, and are in some sense anticipated there.
The end of the earthly Church is to be transplanted into
the heavenly. Is it not a difficulty, unless authority
should teach it, to think that less than the great majority of the earthly plants will not be worth transplant-
ing? Seed is wasted in sowing; yet the earthly
25. †

husbandman garners the produce of by far the greatest portion of what he sows, even when birds, and blight, and lawless footpaths, and uncertain weather, and waste, and theft, have done their worst. Shall the heavenly Husbandman be worse off than they? The Church may seem a failure; but is it likely to be so in reality? God has His little flock of saints, of eminent souls whom we technically call saints. These He leads by extraordinary paths. He introduces them into a mystical world. He furnishes them with peculiar graces, and endows them with miraculous powers. He inspires them with unearthly tastes for suffering and abjection, deluges them with the most unparalleled afflictions and trials, consigns them for years to the intimate assaults, not unfrequently to the bodily possession, of demons, constantly suspends their common life by mysterious extasies, and then again plunges them into such pitchy darkness that they hardly know if they are in a state of grace. He transfigures all their senses, He drives them to the most appalling austerities, He animates them to the most heroic deeds of charitable daring for the good of others, He renews in them supernatural likenesses to His Blessed Son. This is not the way of salvation, nor even the way of perfection. It is the way of the saints. No one is introduced into it except by God Himself. He takes the initiative. Every one should aspire to perfection; no one can lawfully aspire to what is technically the way of the saints, namely, the extatic.*

---

* Many mystical theologians, especially among the Germans, maintain that extasy is the natural state of unfallen man, that Adam was in an extatic state until the fall, and by consequence our Blessed Lady all her life. The passage in the text is not meant to express so much as this. I suppose that the ascetical life can produce what are technically called saints, without the predominance of the mystical element. S. Vincent of Paul looks like an instance of this. But is there any example of a canonized saint, in whom there was not a considerable admixture of the mystical life? Anyhow it is a doctrine

Now of this little flock some, as appears from the records of hagiology, fail and come to an evil end. But they are, comparatively speaking, few in number, and chiefly notable, not so much because they are so rare, as because the phenomenon is so terrific. He has two other little flocks, composed of religious, priests, laity, and many simple souls, who by love have worked themselves beyond the common way of precepts into that of counsels and of the inwardly perfect observance of the precepts. These are two ways of perfection, often combining, often converging, the way of counsels, and the way of perfect interior observance of precepts. Neither of them are like the way of the saints. We know from the lives of good people, and especially the chronicles of religious orders, that many out of these little flocks go wrong and frustrate the sweet purposes of God. Some fall back into the common way, and others find no way of salvation because they refuse the way in which God has put them. But surely by far the greater number, as far as we can judge from books, persevere, and not only save their souls, but avoid purgatory, or are high in heaven. Then God has a fourth little flock, the great multitude of catholics. It is a very little one compared with the great mass of men on earth, and it is yet more divinely distinguished from them, than even the saints or the perfect are from itself. A catholic has more marks of special love multiplied upon him as compared

of great importance in the theology of the spiritual life, that no man has any right to aspire to be what is technically called a saint, still less that he has any obligation to do so, or that the pursuit of perfection in any way involves it. I venture to think that the whole controversy about the obligation of aiming at perfection would be put on a plainer footing, if the fourfold division of good people, given in the text, were attended to: 1. the saints, who tread the extatic or mystical way; 2. those who aim at perfection through the counsels; 3. those who aim at perfection through the perfect interior observance of the precepts: 4. ordinarily good catholics, saving themselves by the frequentation of the sacraments, and by obedience.

with other men, than a saint has as compared with an
ordinary catholic. Why may we not think of this fourth
little flock, as we think of the others, that the failures
are few, and the successes overwhelmingly numerous,
especially as we have more grounds to go upon in this
last case than in any of the others, both because the
failure cannot be short of eternal misery, and because
an equal, if not a greater, amount of divine predilection
has been shown? Of those who were compelled to come
to the banquet in the Gospel, there was only one who
was without the wedding garment.*

It may be urged, that some of the considerations,
which have been here adduced, apply also to persons
who are not catholics. God be praised if it is so! The
overflow of mercy is surely not an argument against its
existence. That were strange logic. Doubtless the
mercy of God covers the whole earth as the waters
cover the sea. It is one of our best joys to know that
its abundance is beyond our gaze, and above our comprehension. But again we turn to those who are before
us, to catholics. If any of these considerations apply to
those outside the Church, and if moreover they are true,
then *a fortiori*, as logicians say, that is, with tenfold
greater force, will they apply to catholics. And so

* Since the publication of the first edition of this work the venerated Presi-
dent of Ushaw has kindly brought under my notice a Censura by the Franciscan, Dominic Lossada, prefixed to the Revelations of Brother Joseph of
St. Benedict, a Spanish Benedictine of Monserrato. Brother Joseph asserted
that the truth of the great majority of catholics being saved, (and he expresses
his view almost in the terms of this chapter,) was revealed to him, and he declares that he is "divinely certain" of it. Part of Lossada's Censura is occupied with a comment on this, and I confess I was surprised at the array of
proof and authority which he brings in favour of this view. I might have
spoken less guardedly, and with fewer restrictions, had I seen it before I
wrote my book. I hoped to have added that part of the Censura, either in a
translation or in the original, as an Appendix, but it was found that it would
add to the price and thickness of the volume.

whichever way we turn, the same benignant conclusion
looks us always in the face.

No one can meditate without very solemn apprehen-
sions upon his final judgment. Yet it is the deliberate
conviction of our best thoughts and most mature reflection, that we had rather leave our final doom in the
hands of the all-holy God than in those of the most
merciful of sinful men. Our knowledge of God does
not leave us room for a moment's hesitation. Strange
to say ! intimately as we know our own wretchedness,
and appalled as we often are by the vision of our own
sins, our sense of security in the hands of God rises in
great measure from the fact that He knows us better
than any one else can know us. There are so many
things by which God will not judge us, and by which
men would judge us, that it seems as if our deliverance
from these was already half a verdict in our favour.
How often in life are we accused wrongly and mis-
takenly ! How are motives imputed to us which we
never had ! We lose our temper for a moment, and
are judged by that fact for years to come. When we
do wrong, we often struggle manfully before we give
way, but men put not these invisible struggles to our
account. Full of want of simplicity as we are, and far
from perfect truth, we are on the whole always more
sincere than we seem. We frequently have good motives for imprudent and ill-looking actions. When we
often appear careless and unkind, some secret sorrow is
oppressing us, or anxiety disturbing us, or responsibility harassing us. Now God sees all this rightly, and
man cannot. God does not judge us by any of these
things; man must. Hence it is,—a strange conclusion
for sinners to come to!—that God loves us better than
men do because He knows us better.

He judges us by our inward religious acts, which necessarily go for nothing with men. He judges us by the fructifying of His own gifts within us, a very slight portion of which ever becomes visible to men, and even that portion only partially visible. Moreover He judges us as He sees us in His Son. He judges us by the love which Mary, angels, and saints have for us. And finally He judges us with all our good ever collec· tively before Him, while our evil is interrupted by frequent absolutions, and our sins supernaturally effaced by the Precious Blood, so that by the laws of His own redeeming love He cannot see them in the same way that men see them. Thus we are most reasonable in preferring rather to be judged by God than by men. The actueness of their criticism are far more to be dreaded than the niceties of His justice, when omnipotent love sits by as its assessor. Now if we judge that the great majority of catholics will not be saved, it is a human judgment; and like all human judgments it is more rigorous than the divine, because of the ignorance and the temper of the judge. Therefore we may modestly hope that God's judgment is otherwise, and that the great majority of catholics are saved. It is only applying to the case of the multitude what we each of us find true in our own, that largeness and allowance in the Creator's judgment, which it is hopeless to look for at the tribunal of the creature.

Let us conclude with the same protest with which we began. This is not theology; it is divination, divination from what we know of God and from what experience has taught us to hope of men. This is what may be said on the bright side of a question, which can have no demonstration either way on this side the grave. We do not enunciate it as certainly true, but we claim

to say it as lawful to be said. Moreover it must be
especially observed that the force of the proof, so far as
it is a proof, is cumulative. The arguments are many,
but it is not asserted that any of them are sufficient
by themselves to prove so much. The proof does not
rest on any one, or any two or three of them, but on the
cumulus. Thus to pull the proof to pieces, and attack
each consideration by itself, would be what is called in
logic the "fallacy of division." The strength of the
view is not in each separate member of the proof, but
in the huge improbability that so many considerations
should converge upon one point, should combine in one
cumulus, and yet the conclusion from them be untrue.
An adversary must meet it as a cumulative proof, or
he will not touch the question at all. This then is what
may be said on the bright side of this great mystery
and difficulty. It is the bright side, not only because it
is the most cheerful, but because it most invites to holiness. Had I not thought so, I would not have been
at the pains to draw out the proof. I am deliberately
convinced that this view will make men more conscientious, more austere, more strict, more spiritual,
more lovingly exact with God, than the opposite view;
and I speak from experience, and not merely from speculation. The other view, as I have seen, repels men from
common attainments, disheartens them in even necessary
struggles, and is almost fatal to all the higher kinds of
mortification, and so to the pursuit of perfection. The
soul-destroying laxity of rigorism is a phenomenon as
common as it is melancholy. Next to heresy, there is
nothing I should so much deplore as to give currency to
any opinions which should seem, however indirectly, to
make light of strictness, penance, purity, and holiness
of life. I have dwelt on the view contained in this

chapter, precisely because I regard such a view as the most efficacious protest against the prevailing laxity.

We are speaking then of what we do not know. But it is at least allowable to put all these considerations in opposition to those which justly or not, give us hard and to our weakness dishonourable thoughts of God.[*] They are not doctrines. They are not certainties. They are inferences, they are hopes, they are speculations, which are surely more in harmony with what we know of our most righteous and most compassionate Creator, than the opposite view. Even if we are wrong, which the last day alone will show, we shall be better men for having tried to think such thoughts of God as get Him more honour among men, and more love from ourselves. God knows His own secret. Blessed be His inscrutable judgment! Let the secret rest with Him. Doubt is even better for us than knowledge, when He, who is pure love, has chosen to withhold it from us.

We are speaking of Catholics. If our thoughts break their bounds, and run out beyond the Church, nothing that has been said, has been said with any view to

---

[*] "He (Perè de Ravignan) then passed to a subject which was of peculiar interest to me, as touching the sorest place of a parish priest. 'Suarez,' said he, ' has a discussion on the fewness of the saved, whether this is said with reference to the world or the Church; and he applies it to the world, but not to the Church. I think he is right; *this is the result of a ministry of twenty years in which I have necessarily had large experience; it is the feeling also of our fathers generally.* You know that the Church teaches that attrition only, combined with the sacrament of penitence, avails to salvation, *attrition arising from motives of fear rather than of love. Contrition by itself,* one act of pure love by the soul, avails even without the Sacrament, if there be a firm purpose and desire to receive it. God has no desire for the sinner's death. Jansenism has done great harm to this subject, by inspiring a sort of despair which is most dangerous.' I observed that purgatory was the necessary complement of such a doctrine. ' It is so,' said he. ' and though God is alone the Judge of the sufficiency of those acts of the dying, yet we may hope that a great number come within the terms of salvation, whatever purifying process they may afterwards require.'" *Allies, Journal in France,* p. 279.

those without. I have no profession of faith to make about them, except that God is infinitely merciful to every soul, that no one ever has been, or ever can be, lost by surprise or trapped in his ignorance; and, as to those who may be lost, I confidently believe that our Heavenly Father threw His arms round each created spirit. and looked it full in the face with bright eyes of love, in the darkness of its mortal life, and that of its own deliberate will it would not have Him.

CHAPTER III.

THE WORLD.

Linquenda tellus, et domus, et placens
Uxor: neque harum, quas colis, arborum
Te, præter invisas cupressos,
Ulla brevem dominum sequetur.

Horace.

THE question of worldliness is a very difficult one,
and one which we would gladly have avoided, had it
been in our power to do so. But it is in too many ways
connected with our subject, to allow of its being passed
over in silence. In the first place, a thoughtful objector
will naturally say, If the relation between the Creator
and the creature is such as has been laid down in the
first eight chapters, and furthermore if it is as manifest
and undeniable as it is urged to be, how comes it to
pass that it is not more universally, or at least more
readily, admitted than it is? Almost all the phenomena
of the world betray a totally opposite conviction, and
reveal to us an almost unanimous belief in men, that
they are on quite a different footing with God from that
one, which is here proclaimed to be the only true and
tenable one. There must at least be some attempt to
explain this discrepancy between what we see and what
we are taught. The explanation, we reply, is to be
found in what Christians call worldliness. It is this
which stands in the way of God's honour, this which
defrauds Him of the tribute due to Him from His creatures, this which even blinds their eyes to His undeni-

able rights and prerogatives. How God's own world comes to stand between Himself and the rational soul, how friendship with it is enmity with Him,—indeed an account of the whole matter must be gone into, in order to show, first, that the influence of the world does account for the non-reception of right views about God, and, secondly, that the world is in no condition to be called as a witness, because of the essential falsehood of its character. This identical falsehood about God is its very life, energy, significance, and condemnation. The right view of God is not unreal, because the world ignores it. On the contrary, it is because it is real that the unreal world ignores it, and the world's ignoring it is, so farforth, an argument in favour of the view.

But not only does this question of worldliness present itself to us in connection with the whole teaching of the first eight chapters; it is implicated in the two objections which have already been considered, namely, the difficulty of salvation and the fewness of the saved. If it is easy to be saved, whence the grave semblance of its difficulty? If the majority of adult catholics are actually saved, because salvation is easy, why is it necessary to draw so largely on the unknown regions of the deathbed, in order to make up our majority? Why should not salvation be almost universal, if the pardon of sin is so easy, grace so abundant, and all that is wanted is a real earnestness about the interests of our souls? If you acknowledge, as you do, that the look of men's lives, even of the lives of believers, is not as if they were going to be saved, and that they are going to be saved in reality in spite of appearances, what is the explanation of these appearances, when the whole process is so plain and easy? To all this the answer is,

that sin is a partial explanation, and the devil is a partial explanation, but that the grand secret lies in worldliness.   That is the chief disturbing force, the prime
counteracting power.   It is this mainly, which keeps
down the number of the saved; it is this which makes
the matter seem so difficult which is intrinsically so
easy ; nay, it is this which is a real difficulty, though
not such an overwhelming one as to make salvation
positively difficult as a whole.   Plainly then the phenomenon of worldliness must be considered here, else
it will seem as if an evident objection, and truly the
weightiest of all objections, had not been taken into
account, and thus an air of insecurity will be thrown,
not only over the answer to the two preceding objections,
but also over the whole argument of the first eight
chapters.

   This enquiry into worldliness will, in the third place,
truthfully and naturally prepare us for the great conclusion of the whole enquiry, namely, the truth that
personal love of God is the only legitimate development
of our position as creatures, and at the same time the
means by which salvation is rendered easy, and the
multitude of the saved augmented.   For it will be found
that the dangers of worldliness are at once so great and
so peculiar, that nothing but a personal love of our
Creator will rescue us from them, enable us to break
with the world, and to enter into the actual possession of
the liberty of the sons of God.

   O it is a radiant land,—this wide, outspread, many-
coloured mercy of our Creator !   But we must be content for awhile now to pass out of its kindling sunshine
into another land of most ungenial darkness, in the
hope that we shall come back heavyladen with booty for
God's glory, and knowing how to prize the sunshine

more than ever. There is a hell already upon earth ; there is something which is excommunicated from God's smile. It is not altogether matter, nor yet altogether spirit. It is not man only, nor Satan only, nor is it exactly sin. It is an infection, an inspiration, an atmosphere, a life, a colouring matter, a pageantry, a fashion, a taste, a witchery, an impersonal but a very recognizable system. None of these names suit it, and all of them suit it. Scripture calls it, " The World." God's mercy does not enter into it. All hope of its reconciliation with Him is absolutely and eternally precluded. Repentance is incompatible with its existence. The sovereignty of God has laid the ban of the empire upon it; and a holy horror ought to seize us when we think of it. Meanwhile its power over the human creation is terrific, its presence ubiquitous, its deceitfulness incredible. It can find a home under every heart beneath the poles, and it embraces with impartial affection both happiness and misery. It is wider than the catholic Church, and is masterful, lawless, and intrusive within it. It cannot be damned, because it is not a person, but it will perish in the general conflagration, and so its tyranny be over, and its place know it no more. We are living in it, breathing it, acting under its influences, being cheated by its appearances, and unwarily admitting its principles. Is it not of the last importance to us that we should know something of this huge evil creature, this monstrous sea-bird of evil, which flaps its wings from pole to pole, and frightens the nations into obedience by its discordant cries ?

But we must not be deceived by this description. The transformations of the spirit of the world are among its most wonderful characteristics. It has its gentle voice, its winning manners, its insinuating address, its

aspect of beauty and attraction; and the lighter its foot
and the softer its voice, the more dreadful its approach. It is by the firesides of rich and poor, in happy
homes where Jesus is named, in gay hearts which fain
would never sin. In the chastest domestic affections
it can hide its poison. In the very sunshine of external
nature, in the combinations of the beautiful elements,—
it is somehow even there. The glory of the wind-
swept forest and the virgin frost of the alpine summits
have a taint in them of the spirit of the world. It can
be dignified as well. It can call to order sin which is
not respectable. It can propound wise maxims of public
decency, and inspire wholesome regulations of police.
It can open the churches, and light the candles on the
altar, and entone Te Deums to the Majesty on high.
It is often prominently and almost pedantically on the
side of morality. Then again it has passed into the
beauty of art, into the splendour of dress, into the magnificence of furniture. Or again there it is, with high
principles on its lips, discussing the religious vocation
of some youth, and praising God and sanctity, while it
urges discreet delay, and less self-trust, and more considerate submissiveness to those who love him and have
natural rights to his obedience. It can sit on the benches
of senates and hide in the pages of good books. And
yet all the while it is the same huge evil creature
which was described above. Have we not reason to
fear it?

Let us try to learn more definitely what the world is,
the world in the scripture sense. A definition is too
short: a description is too vague. God never created
it: how then does it come here? There is no land
outside the creation of God, which could have harboured
the monster, who now usurps so much of this beautiful

planet on which Jesus was born and died, and from which He and His sinless Mother rose to heaven. It seems to be a sort of spirit which has risen up from a disobedient creation, as if the results and after-consequences of all the sins that ever were rested in the atmosphere, and loaded it with some imperceptible but highly powerful miasma. It cannot be a person, and yet it seems as if it possessed both a mind and a will, which on the whole are amazingly consistent, so as to disclose what might appear to be a very perfect self-consciousness. It is painless in its operations, and unerring too ; and just as the sun bids the lily be white and the rose red, and they obey without an effort, standing side by side with the same aspect and in the same soil, so this spirit of the world brings forth colours and shapes and sense in our different actions without the process being cognizable to ourselves. The power of mesmerism on the reluctant will is a good type of the power of this spirit of the world upon ourselves. It is like grace only that it is its contradictory.

But it has not always the same power. If the expression may be forgiven, there have been times when the world was less worldly than usual ; and this looks as if it were something which the existing generation of men always gave out from itself, a kind of magnetism of varying strengths and different properties. As Satan is sometimes bound, so it pleases God to bind the world sometimes. Or He thunders, and the atmosphere is cleared for awhile, and the times are healthy, and the Church lifts her head and walks quicker. But on the whole its power appears to be increasing with time. In other words the world is getting more worldly. Civilization develops it immensely, and progress helps it on, and multiplies its capabilities. In the matter of

worldliness, a highly civilized time is to a comparatively
ruder time what the days of machinery are to those of
hand-labour. We are not speaking of sin; that is
another idea, and brings in fresh considerations: we are
speaking only of worldliness. If the characteristics of
modern times go on developing with the extreme velocity
and herculean strength, which they promise now, we
may expect, just what prophecy would lead us to anticipate, that the end of the world and the reign of
antichrist will be times of the most tyrannical worldliness.

This spirit also has its characteristics of time and
place. The worldliness of one century is different from
that of another. Now it runs towards ambition in the
upper classes and discontent in the lower. Now to
money-making, luxury, and lavish expenditure. One
while it sets towards grosser sins, another while towards
wickedness of a more refined description; and another
while it will tolerate nothing but educated sin. It also
has periodical epidemics and accessions of madness,
though at what intervals, or whether by the operation of
any law, must be left to the philosophy of history to
decide, as soon as statistics have had time to become
more like a science. Certain it is, that ages have
manias, the source of which it is difficult to trace, but
under which whole communities, and sometimes nations,
exhibit symptoms of diabolical possession. Indeed, on
looking back, it would appear that every age, as if an
age were an individual and gifted with an individual
life, had been subject to some vertigo of its own by
which it may be almost known in history. Very often
the phenomena, such as those of the French Revolution,
seem to open out new depths in human nature, or to
betoken the presence of some preternatural spiritual

influences. Then, again, ages have panics, as if some
Attribute of God came near to the world and cast a
deep shadow over its spirit, making men's hearts quail
for fear.

This spirit is further distinguished by the evidences
which it presents of a fixed view and a settled purpose.
It is capricious, but, for all that, there is nothing about
it casual, accidental, fortuitous. It is well instructed
for its end, inflexible in its logic, and making directly,
no matter through what opposing medium, to its ultimate results. Indeed, it is obviously informed with the
wisdom and the subtlety of Satan. It is his greatest
capability of carrying on his war against God. Like a
parasite disease, it fixes on the weak places in men, pan-
dering both to mind and flesh, but chiefly to the former.
It is one of those three powers* to whom such dark
pre-eminence is given, the world, the flesh, and the
devil; and among these three it seems to have a kind
of precedence accorded to it by the way in which our
Lord speaks of it in the Gospel, though the line of its
diplomacy has been to have itself less thought of and
less dreaded than the other two ; and, unhappily for the
interests of God and the welfare of souls, it has succeeded. It is then pre-eminent among the enemies of
God. Hence the place which it occupies in Holy Scripture. It is the world which hated Christ, the world
which cannot receive the Spirit, the world that loves
its own, the world that rejoices because Christ has gone
away, the world which He overcame, the world for
which He would not pray, the world that by wisdom
knew not God, the world whose spirit Christians were

---

* Modi tentationum varii sunt, communiter vero ad tria genera reducuntur, carne, mundo, et dæmone. *Suarez de Gratia*, lib. i. c. xxiii. n. 3.

26 †

not to receive, the world that was not worthy of the
saints, the world whose friendship is enmity with God,
the world that passeth away with its lusts, the world
which they who are born of God overcome, or, as the
Apocalypse calls it, the world that goes wondering after
the beast. Well then might St. James come to his
energetic conclusion, Whosoever therefore will be a
friend of this world, becometh an enemy of God.* It
is remarkable also that St. John, the chosen friend of
the Incarnate Word, and the evangelist of His Divinity,
should be the one of the inspired writers who speaks
most often and most emphatically about the world, as if
the spirit of Jesus found something especially revolting
to it in the spirit of the world.

It is this world which we have to fight against
throughout the whole of our Christian course. Our salvation depends upon our unforgiving enmity against it.
It is not so much that it is a sin, as that it is the capability of all sins, the air sin breathes, the light by which
it sees to do its work, the hot-bed which propagates and
forces it, the instinct which guides it, the power which
animates it. For a Christian to look at, it is disheart-
eningly complete. It is a sort of catholic church of the
powers of darkness. It has laws of its own, and tastes
and principles of its own, literature of its own, a missionary spirit, a compact system, and it is a consistent
whole. It is a counterfeit of the Church of God, and in
the most implacable antagonism to it. The doctrines of
the faith, the practices and devotions of pious persons,
the system of the interior life, the mystical and contemplative world of the Saints, with all these it is at deadly

* S. John vii. 7; also xiv. 17; also xv. 19; also xvi. 20; also xvi. 33; also
xvii. 9; also 1 Cor. i. 21; also ii. 12; also Heb. xi. 38; also S. James iv. 4;
also 1 John ii. 17; also v. 4; also Apoc. xiii. 3.

war. And so it must be. The view which the Church takes of the world is distinct and clear, and far from flattering to its pride. It considers the friendship of the world as enmity with God. It puts all the world's affairs under its feet, either as of no consequence, or at least of very secondary importance. It has great faults to find with the effeminacy of the literary character, with the churlishness of the mercantile character, with the servility of the political character, and even with the inordinateness of the domestic character. It provokes the world by looking on progress doubtingly, and with what appears a very inadequate interest; and there is a quiet faith in its contempt for the world extremely irritating to this latter power.

The world on the contrary thinks that it is going to last for ever. It almost assumes that there are no other interests but its own, or that if there are, they are either of no consequence, or troublesome and in the way. It thinks that there is nothing like itself anywhere, that religion was made for its convenience, merely to satisfy a want, and must not forget itself, or if it claims more, must be put down as a rebel, or chased away as a grumbling beggar; and finally it is of opinion, that of all contemptible things spirituality is the most contemptible, cowardly, and little. Thus the Church and the world are incompatible, and must remain so to the end.

We cannot have a better instance of the uncongeniality of the world with the spirit of the Gospel, than their difference in the estimate of prosperity. All those mysterious woes which our Lord denounced against wealth, have their explanation in the dangers of worldliness. It is the peculiar aptitude of wealth, and pomp, and power, to harbour the unholy spirit of the world, to combine with it, and transform themselves into it, which called forth the thrilling malediction of our Lord. Prosperity may be a blessing from God, but it may easily become the triumph of the world. For the most part the absence of chastisement is anything but a token of God's love. When prosperity is a blessing, it is generally a condescension to our weakness. Those are fearful words, Thou hast already received thy reward; yet how many prosperous men there are, the rest of whose lives will keep reminding us of them; the tendency of prosperity in itself is to wean the heart from God, and fix it on creatures. It gives us a most unsupernatural habit of esteeming others according to their success. As it increases, so anxiety to keep it increases also, and makes men restless, selfish, and irreligious; and at length it superinduces a kind of effeminacy of character, which unfits them for the higher and more heroic virtues of the Christian character. This is but a sample of the different way in which the Church and the world reason.

Now it is this world which, far more than the devil, far more than the flesh, yet in union with both, makes the difficulty we find in obeying God's commandments, or following His counsels. It is this which makes earth such a place of struggle and of exile. Proud, exclusive, anxious, hurried, fond of comforts, coveting popularity, with an offensive ostentation of prudence, it is this worldliness which hardens the hearts of men, stops their ears, blinds their eyes, vitiates their taste, and ties their hands, so far as the things of God are concerned. Let it be true that salvation be easy, and that by far the greater number of catholics are saved, it is still unhappily true that the relations of the Creator and the creature, as put forward in this treatise, are not so

universally or so practically acknowledged as they ought
to be. Why is this? Sin, as was said before, is a
partial answer. The devil is another partial answer.
But I believe worldliness has got to answer for a great
deal of sin, and for a great deal of devil, besides a whole
deluge of iniquity of its own, which is perpetually debasing good works, hindering perfection, preparing materials for sin, assisting the devil in his assaults, and
working with execrable assiduity against the sacraments
and grace. The world is for ever lowering the heavenly
life of the Church. If there ever was an age in which
this was true, it is the present. One of the most
frightening features of our condition is, that we are so
little frightened of the world. The world itself has
brought this about. Even spiritual books are chiefly
occupied with the devil and the flesh; and certain of
the capital sins, such as envy and sloth, no longer hold
the prominent places which they held in the systems of
the elder ascetics; and yet they are just those vices
which contain most of the ungodly spirit of the world.
The very essence of worldliness seems to consist in its
making us forget that we are creatures; and the more
this view is reflected upon, the more correct will it
appear.

When our Blessed Lord describes the days before the
Flood, and again those which shall precede the end of
the world, He portrays them rather as times of worldliness than open sin. Men were eating and drinking,
marrying and giving in marriage: and He says no more.
Now none of these things are wrong in themselves.
We can eat and drink, as the apostle teaches us, to the
glory of God, and marriage was a divine institution at
the time of the Flood, and is now a Christian Sacrament. In the same way when He describes the life of

the only person whom the gospel narrative follows into the abode of the lost, He sums it up as the being clothed in purple and fine linen, and feasting sumptuously every day. Here again there is nothing directly sinful in the actions which He names. It surely cannot be a mortal sin to have fine linen, nor will a man lose a state of grace because he feasts sumptuously every day, provided that no other sins follow in the train of this soft life. The malice of it all is in its worldliness, in the fact that this was all or nearly all the lives of those before the flood, of those before the days of anti-christ, and of the unhappy Dives. Life began and ended in worldliness. There was nothing for God. It was comprised in the pleasures of the world, it rested in them, it was satisfied by them. Its characteristic was sins of omission. Worldliness might almost be defined to be a state of habitual sins of omission. The devil urges men on to great positive breaches of the divine commandments. The passions of the flesh impel sin-ners to give way to their passions by such dreadful sins, as catch the eyes of men and startle them by their iniquity. Worldliness only leads to these things occa-sionally, and by accident. It neither scandalizes others, nor frightens the sinner himself. This is the very feature of it, which, rightly considered, ought to be so terrifying. The reaction of a great sin, or the shame which follows it, are often the pioneers of grace. They give self-love such a serious shock, that under the in-fluence of it men return to God. Worldliness hides from the soul its real malice, and thus keeps at arm's length from it some of the most persuasive motives to repentance. Thus the pharisees are depicted in the Gospel as being eminently worldly. It is worldliness, not immorality, which is put before us. There is even much of moral decency, much of respectable observance, much religious profession; and yet when our Blessed Saviour went among them, they were further from grace than the publicans and sinners. They had implicit hatred of God in their hearts already, which became explicit as soon as they saw Him. The Magdalen, the Samaritan, the woman taken in adultery,—it was these who gathered round Jesus, attracted by His sweetness, and touched by the grace which went out from Him. The pharisees only grew more cold, more haughty, more self-opinionated, until they ended by the greatest of all sins, the crucifixion of our Lord. For worldliness, when its selfish necessities drive it at last into open sin, for the most part sins more awfully and more impenitently than even the unbridled passions of our nature. So again there was the young man who had great possessions, and who loved Jesus when he saw Him, and wished to follow Him. He was a religious man, and with humble scrupulosity observed the commandments of God; but when our Lord told him to sell all and give the price to the poor and to follow Him, he turned away sorrowful, and was found unequal to such a blessed vocation. Now his refusing to sell his property was surely not a mortal sin. It does not appear that our Lord considered him to have sinned by his refusal. It was the operation of worldliness. We do not know what the young man's future was; but a sad cloud of misgivings must hang over the memory of him whom Jesus invited to follow Him, and who turned away. Is he looking now in heaven upon that Face, from whose mild beauty he so sadly turned away on earth?

Thus the outward aspect of worldliness is not sin. Its character is negative. It abounds in omissions. Yet throughout the Gospels our Saviour seems pur-

posely to point to it rather than to open sin. When
the young man turned away, His remark was, How
hard it is for those who have riches to enter into the
kingdom of heaven! But the very fact of our Lord's
thus branding worldliness with His especial reprobation is enough to show that it is in reality deeply
sinful, hatefully sinful. It is a life without God in the
world. It is a continual ignoring of God, a continual
quiet contempt of His rights, an insolent abatement
in the service which He claims from His creatures.
Self is set up instead of God. The canons of human
respect are more looked up to than the Divine Commandments. God is very little adverted to. He is
passed over. The very thought of Him soon ceases
to make the worldly man uncomfortable. Indeed all
his chief objections to religion, if he thought much
about the matter, would be found to repose on his
apprehension of it as restless and uncomfortable. But
all this surely must represent an immensity of interior
mortal sin. Can a man habitually forget God and be
in a state of habitual grace? Can he habitually prefer
purple garments and sumptuous fare to the service of
his Creator, and be free of mortal sin? Can he make
up a life for himself even of the world's sinless enjoyments, such as eating, drinking, and marrying, and will
not the mere omission of God from it be enough to con-
stitute him in a state of deadly sin? At that rate a
moral atheist is more acceptable to God than a poor
sinner honestly but feebly fighting with some habit of
vice, to which his nature and his past offences set so
strongly, that he can hardly lift himself up. At that
rate the Pharisees in the Gospel would be the patterns
for our imitation, rather than the publicans and sinners;
or at least they would be as safe to follow. Or shall

we say that faith is enough to save us without charity?
If a man only believes rightly, let him eat and drink
and be gaily clothed, and let him care for nothing else,
and at least that exclusive love of creatures, that
omission of the Creator, provided only it issues in no
other outward acts than his fine dinners and his expen-
sive clothes, shall never keep his soul from heaven.
His purple and his sumptuous feasting shall be his
beatific vision here, and then his outward morality shall
by God's mercy hand him on to his second beatific
Vision, the Vision of the beauty of God, and the eternal
ravishment of the Most Holy and Undivided Trinity!
Can this be true?

Yet on the other hand, we may not make into sins
what God has not made sins. How is this? O it is
the awful world of inward sin which is the horror of
all this worldliness! It is possession, worse far than
diabolical possession, because at once more hideous and
more complete. It is the interior irreligiousness, the
cold pride, the hardened heart, the depraved sense, the
real unbelief, the more than implicit hatred of God,
which makes the soul of the worldly man an actual
moral and intellectual hell on earth, hidden by an outward show of faultless proprieties, which only make it
more revolting to the Eye that penetrates the insulting disguise. The secret sins moreover of the worldly
are a very sea of iniquity. Their name is legion; they
cannot be counted. Almost every thought is sin, because of the inordinate worship of self that is in it.
Almost every step is sin, because it is treading underfoot some ordinance of God. It is a life without prayer,
a life without desire of heaven, a life without fear of
hell, a life without love of God, a life without any
supernatural habits at all. Is not hell the most natural

transition from such a life as this? Heaven is not a
sensual paradise. God is the joy, and the beauty, and
the contentment there: all is for God, all from God,
all to God, all in God, all round God as the beautiful
central fire about which His happy creatures cluster in
amazement and delight. Whereas in worldliness God
is the discomfort of the whole thing, an intrusion an
unseasonable thought, an inharmonious presence, like a
disagreeable uninvited guest, irritating and fatiguing us
by the simple demand His presence makes on our
sufferance and our courtesy. Surely such a man has sin
in his veins, instead of blood!

Worldliness then is a life of secret sins. It is such
an irresistible tendency to sin, such a successful encouragement of it, such a genial climate, such a collection
of favourable circumstances, such an amazing capability
of sin, that it breeds actual sins, regularly formed and
with all the theological requirements, by millions and
millions. If we read what the catechism of the Council
of Trent says of sins of thought, we shall see how marvellously prolific sins can be, and what a preeminently
devastating power sins of thought in particular exercise within the soul. In numberless cases open and
crying sins must come at last. Still we must remember that on the whole there are two characteristics
which always distinguish sins of worldliness from sins
of the passions, or sins of direct diabolical temptation.
The respectability which worldliness affects leads it
rather to satisfy itself in secret sins. Indeed its worship of self, its predilection for an easy life, would
hinder its embarking in sins which take trouble, time,
and forethought, or which run risks of disagreeable consequences, and therefore would keep it confined within
a sphere of secret sins. And in the next place its love

of comfort makes it so habitually disinclined to listen to
the reproaches of conscience, or the teasing solicitations
of grace, that it passes into the state of a seared conscience, a deadened moral sense, with a speed which
is unknown even to cruelty or sensuality.

A seared conscience!* This is a fearful possibility,
and yet to use the apostle's expression, "the Spirit
manifestly saith" that there is such a thing. It is
according to St. Paul one of the marks of heresy. It
belongs also peculiarly to worldliness. To have gone
on for such a length of time doing wrong that we have at
last ceased to advert to its being wrong, to sin and for
the monitor within to be silent, to forget God and not
to remember that we are forgetting Him,—all this is
surely far worse than to be a savage or an idolator.
But this is to have a seared conscience. This is the
tendency of worldliness, a tendency which it can develop with incomparable swiftness. And then where
is the power of coming right again? We have drifted
away from all the sweet facilities of repentance. We
have hardened ourselves against the ordinary impetus
of grace. We have made ourselves so unlovely that
grace would shun us if it could. We have sold ourselves to the devil, and he has got us safe before the
proper time. With most men it is enough to say that
if they erred, at least they had a good conscience about
it, or that their conscience told them it was wrong,
and they are sorry they gave way. But if we have a
seared conscience, neither of these things avail. We
have forgotten and pretermitted God: we did so con-
tumeliously at first; but now our habitual contempt
has superinduced oblivion : it seems as if He were going
to retaliate, to pay us back in our own coin, and for the

* I Tim. iv.

present at least to pretermit us. We no longer know
when we are in danger. We have lost our chart. We
can tell nothing of our latitude and longitude. No land
is in sight : nothing but a waste of boundless waters.
The sun is hidden, and we can take no observations, and
have taken none for ever so long a time. The night is
so grim and murky, that not a star will give us an indistinct notion where we are; and the needle is snapped
and we know neither north nor south, nor east, nor
west. What are our chances of safety now? There
has come upon us the fatal woe of Isaias,* Woe to you
that call evil good, and good evil, that put darkness for
light, and light for darkness, that put bitter for sweet,
and sweet for bitter. There is nothing to compare with
worldliness for vitiating the moral taste. There are some
possibilities on earth which we cannot bear to think of
without shuddering. It is generally God's merciful
ordinance that we should not know them in the individual cases, even when we see them. One of these is
the possibility of a man's going hopelessly out of his
mind, when he is in a state of mortal sin. If he is to
have no intermission of his madness, no lucid interval
before his death, if he was actually in mortal sin when
the last step of his abberration was completed, and reason
had abdicated her throne entirely, then he is as it were
damned already. He walks about the earth a living
part of hell. His fate is sealed while the sun still shines
upon his head, and the flowers grow beneath his feet,
and the birds sing as he passes. He smiles, but he is
lost. He sings, but he is the hopeless property of God's
great enemy. Kindness touches his heart, but grace
has ebbed from it for ever. He belongs to the dismal
centre of the earth ; it is only by accident that he is

* Cap. v.

walking on its radiant surface. This is one of earth's fearful possibilities. And the seared conscience of worldliness is a desperately near approach to this. Faith is still there, and reason also, and a miracle of grace can rouse them both. But are worldly people the likely subjects of God's miracles? The sweet miracle of conversion haunts the company of publicans and sinners, not the undoubting self-sufficiency of this world's pharisees. O poor worldling, maliciously and guiltily unsuspecting now of thy real state, that man who went mad in mortal sin is thy shadow, thy brother, and thy type!

Now every one of these phenomena of worldliness may be resolved into a forgetfulness that we are creatures. There is no look about the life of Dives that he remembered he was a creature. There might be mingled with his characteristic good nature which made him love his brothers so much and give alms to Lazarus, some confused notions of duty to a Creator; but any abiding sense of his being a creature there was none. He solved the problem of the possibility of these two forgetfulnesses being separated, that of having a Creator and that of being a creature. It is this forgetfulness which is the fountain of almost all sins of omission. A worldly man never looks like a man who so lives as having to give an account of himself to a higher power. Anything, which should evince a sense of an invisible world, would be incongruous in his ordinary conduct; and if from early associations or natural timorousness of character he should betray any such sense, it would instantly take the form of superstition rather than that of religion. When the devil tempts a man to a great sin of passion, such as murder, or sensuality at last beguiles a man to relapse into his intemperance, in neither of these cases does he forget that he is a creature. Indeed it is his advertence to the law of his Creator which gives the malice to his sin. But there is no struggle in worldliness. It is a false faith, a false religion. It does not recognize the rights of the Creator, nor occupy itself with the duties of the creature. It begins with self and ends with self, and if compelled to lodge an appeal outside itself, it appeals to the judgments of human respect. Where-ever there is worldliness, there is the forgetfulness that we are creatures; and wherever there is this forgetfulness that we are creatures, there also is world-liness.

When a man's sympathies are with a disloyal State rather than with the Holy See, there is worldliness. The world is preferred before the Church. When men object to the doctrine of religious vocation, and without other reasons than a certain instinct try to hinder their children from entering religious orders, there is worldliness. The one work of the creature to do the Creator's will is overlooked or unacknowledged. When men are ashamed of their religion before here-tics, especially of its distinctive practices and unpopular doctrines, there is worldliness. The creature forgets himself, and makes himself the standard of truth. Wherever men, who are not to their own sensible cost taking up the cross daily and following Christ, inveigh against religious enthusiasm or the want of moderation in piety, there is worldliness. The creature wants to limit the service of the Creator. When men do not give alms, or give them scantily, or give them in an eccentric and peculiar way, there is worldliness. The creature either claims as his own what he only holds at the good pleasure of his Creator, or he claims to satisfy his own whim and caprice in the way in which he pays

it back to his Creator. Indeed all developments of
worldliness exhibit some obliquity in a man's perception of the true relations between the Creator and the
creature. Ought we not then seriously to ask ourselves if we have any right to be so little afraid of
worldliness as we are? If an evil is universal, if it is
almost imperceptible, if it is generally fatal, if we know
it to be in the middle of us, and if the not suspecting
that we have it, is, or may be, one of the worst symptoms of our having it, does not prudence suggest to us
almost an excess in caution, almost a nervousness of
fear, almost a fancifulness of apprehension? Is it well
that we should be so calm and cool? Is it certain that
our calmness and our coolness are not actual proofs of
the disease? Worldliness only requires one condition
for its success,—that we should not fear it. He who
fears God, must also fear the world, and he who fears
the world need never fear that he has lost the fear of
God.

It is hard to live in a place and avoid the spirit of it.
It is hard to live in the world and avoid worldliness.
Yet this is what we have to do. The world we cannot
leave till God summons us: but worldliness, which is the
spirit of the world, should not be allowed to infect us.
As the smell of fire had not passed upon the garments
of the three children in the burning fiery furnace, so
must the odour of worldliness not pass upon our souls.
But to. the avoiding of worldliness no help is more
efficacious than having a right and fixed view of the
world. There are two views of the world which Christians may take, two views which are actually taken by
those who are striving to serve God and to love Him
purely. Which of the two views a man takes depends
partly upon his early associations, partly upon his

natural character, and partly upon the circumstances of his vocation; and his spiritual life will be
found to be considerably modified by the particular
view which he is led to take. Some take a very
gloomy view of the world. To them it seems altogether
bad, wholly evil, irredeemably lost. Everything is
danger; for there is sin everywhere. All its roses have
thorns under the leaves. There is a curse upon everything belonging to it. Its joys are only other forms of
melancholy. Its sunshine is a mockery : its beautiful
scenery a deceit: the soothingness of its domestic affections a snare. Its life is an incessant death. We have
no right to smile at anything. The world is so dark that
it is even a perpetual partial eclipse of God. If the present is miserable, let us delay upon it; for in misery we
shall find food for our souls. If it is joyous, let us rush
from it into the forebodings of a future, when all this world
and the fashion of it will be burned up with fire. Let
us speak low lest the devil hear us, and use his knowledge to our destruction. Let us live as ancient monarchs
lived, in daily fear of poison in every dish. A funeral
on a wet day in a disconsolate churchyard, this is the
type of the minds who take this view.

The other view is the very opposite of all this. It is
the bright view. Those who take it see all creation
lying before them with the lustre of God's benediction
on it. It is the earth on which Jesus was born, and
where Mary lived. They marvel at the number of exquisite pleasures with which it is strewn, so very few of
which comparatively are sins. The innocent attach-
ments of earthly love are to such men helps to love
God better. Natural beauty supernaturalizes their
minds. The sunshine makes them better men. God's
perfections are seen everywhere written in hieroglyphics

over the world. Kindness is so abundant, nobility of
heart so plentiful, the joys of home so pure yet so
attractive, the successes of the Gospel so infinitely consoling, all things in fact so much better on trial than
they seemed, that the world appears a happy place, and
missing but a little, so little it is sad to think how
little, of being a holy place also, holy from the very
abundance of its pure happiness. At every turn there
are radiant fountains of joy leaping up to meet us.
Each day, like the cystus, has a thousand new blossoms to show; it lays them down when evening comes,
and the next morning it has as gay a show of flowers as
ever. Even adverse things are wonderfully tempered
in the present, while in the past they have such a
pathetic golden light upon them, that the memory of
them is one of our best treasures, and we would not for
worlds have missed the suffering of them ; and as to any
evil in the future, there is such an inextinguishable light
of joy within us, that we simply disbelieve it. The
clouds fly before us as we go. Music sounds about our
path. And as to cares, they find themselves so little at
home with us, that when we come to the night "they
fold up their tents like the Arabs, and as silently steal
away."

St. Bernard may be called the prophet of the first
view: St. Francis of Sales of the second. The first
seems more safe for human presumption; the second
more cheering to discouragement. One leads through
holy fear to love ; the other through holy love to fear.
The one disenchants more from the world ; the other
enchants us more with God. The one subdues ; the
other gives elasticity. The one seems more admoni-
tory to man ; the other more honourable to God. Both
can make saints; but saints of different kinds Both

27 †

are true; yet both are untrue. Both arc true as far
as they go, and both are untrue when they exclude the
other. They are partial views; and one is more true
to a man than the other, because it is more suitable for
his character and temper to dwell upon what is prominently dark, or prominently bright, as the case may
be. The great thing is, whichever view we take, to
have it clearly before us and keep to it consistently,
because of the irresistible influence which these views
exercise upon the spiritual life. They make men pray
differently, and act differently in their secret relations
with God. They foster different graces. They give
birth to different vocations. They supply different
motives. The subjects for meditation, the subjects for
particular examination of conscience, have to do with
the dark or bright view men habitually take of the
world. The question between an active or a contemplative life is often decided by them. They have each
their own class of temptations, and their own rocks on
which they may strike and go down. They have each
also their own graces, their own beauties, their own
attractions, their own blessings, and their own short
roads to heaven. The strange thing is that no one
seems to be able to take in impartially the whole view
of the world, the true view, the bright and dark together.
Intellectually they may do so; but practically they
must lean either to the dark or bright, exaggerate their
own view, and do the other view injustice. No mind
leaves things uncoloured. It is our necessity; we cannot help ourselves. The grand thing is to turn it all
to God, and to begin straightway to manufacture
heavenly love both out of our darkness and our light.

It is dangerous to talk of general rules in such subject matters. But as upon the whole we find the

darker view taken by cloistered saints, and the brighter view by secular saints, it may not be an error to suppose that the brighter view of the world is the best for those who live in the world. The dark view may readily become gloomy, and gloom leads to inaction, to concentration upon self, to the judging of others, to a discontentment with the state of things around us; and the fruit of all this is pride, sourness, want of zeal, and self-righteousness. Men with a frustrated vocation to religion, and living in the world, where they have no right to be, are mostly uncharitable men. Reformers, good and bad, have for the most part emanated from the cloister. Luther was an Augustinian: Savonarola a Dominican. A monk has beautiful examples of the highest virtue constantly before him, which not only urge him on in his heroic love of God, but also counteract what there might be depressing or unnerving in his melancholy view of the world. To him in his circumstances it is a powerful stimulus to sanctity. But it would require very peculiar circumstances indeed to make it such to persons aiming at perfection in the world. They are good; they love God; they frequent the Sacraments; they make mental prayer; they practice voluntary mortifications; they live under spiritual direction; their interests and tastes are in spiritual things. Yet for all this they enjoy the world. Many of its blameless pleasures are real pleasures to them. They love many persons, and many persons love them. Their home-circle is bright and tender; and if it does not lead to God, there is no appearance of its leading away from Him. Now what will happen if we force them to believe that all is misery around them, and that they ought to be miserable themselves, and that it is very imperfect of them

not to be so ? The fact is, they are not miserable, and
they cannot see why they should be so: and moreover
they actually cannot be miserable, even if they try.
Consequently if we persist in forcing upon them a view
which does not suit them, and is against the grain,
they either become perplexed and scrupulous, seeing
sin where there is no sin, and believing the detection
of sin to be the highest spiritual discernment, and so
farewell to their serving God for love ; or they start
away from a devout life altogether, in disgust and impatience, as an unreality, which is based upon a false
theory, and so worth nothing at all, or as an inflated
pedantic imposture, which even those who talk big
about it do not themselves believe. Then, as a matter
of fact, the number of things which are sinful is much
less than this view would lead us to suppose; and a
man aiming at perfection in the world is much more
exposed than others to occasions of sin. Indeed this
is one of his chief difficulties, the difficulty which in all
ages has so blessedly filled the cloisters and recruited
the congregations of apostolic men. But this very
fact makes any exaggeration of the matter extremely
dangerous, as both discouraging and unsettling ; and
every one knows that in the world, where there are
neither rules nor vows, discouragement and unsettle-
ment are the two most fatal enemies of the spiritual
life. The bright view is doubtless a better basis for
perfection in the world. Meanwhile it must guard
itself against laxity, and love of pleasure, and an inadequate notion of sin, as much as the darker view must
shun discouragement, self-exaltation, and uncharitable-
ness, to which of its own nature it is prone. The dark
view must not be querulous with God, nor the bright
view make too free with His perfections.

Whatever view we take of the world, we must be upon our guard against its spirit. Of that spirit Christians can have but one view. Inspiration has fixed it for ever; it is the enemy of God. No cloisters can hope to keep it out; for it has the gift of subtlety. There is air enough in one heart for it to live, and thrive amazingly. But much more are those who live in the world exposed to its dangers. It looks so moral, and sometimes, but not often, even generous, in order to deceive us. It can talk most reasonably and well. It can praise religion, and take its side, though there is always an ulterior purpose in view. We see its influence in society. Faith deciphers it for us there. We behold a system of proprieties with no self-denial in them, a number of axioms of doubtful morality gaining ground and passing current, a humility which consists in our ruling ourselves by the opinions of others, an inventiveness of amusements which bewilder our notions of right and wrong; and in all this we can prophecy evil and suspect dangers, while it is hard for us to name the evil and to put our finger on the danger. When we look at people outside the Church, we see how insinuatingly worldliness prevents their coming into it. We can see clearly, what the sufferers themselves cannot see at all. We can watch its influence on sinners, how artfully it entices them into the deep places, how strongly it holds them down, how cleverly it throws suspicion upon the advances and offers of grace, how variously it contrives delays, and when it fails, how hypocritically it can rejoice in a man's conversion, how successfully it can lay hold of his fresh vigour and high spirits, and how mercilessly it can lead him backwards and blindfold into a relapse! But the sinner sees nothing of this himself. If it were told him, it would sound in his ears as a romance.

We can trace the influence of worldliness upon pious people. Their frequentation of the sacraments, their church-going, their alms-giving, their interest in catholic plans, contrast strangely with their anxiety to get into society, with their hankering after great people, with their excitement about marriages, with the perpetual running of their conversation on connections, wealth, influence and the like, and their unconscious but almost gross respect for those who are very much richer than themselves, or very much higher than themselves. It would never do for them to sit for a picture of catholic devotion.   Yet they do not see all this, and they are really full of God, always talking of Him, always planning for Him, always fidgetty about His glory.   Sometimes a step further is taken, and we see a most portentous union of piety and worldliness, really as if one person were two persons, one person in church, and another person out of church, one person with priest and religious, and another person with worldly company. These people make the oddest compensations to themselves for their pious self-denials, and again with such grotesque earnestness penance their worldliness in revenge for its inroads upon their piety, that they remind us of the stories protestants tell us of the Italian bravos, who, before they commit a murder, most devoutly recommend it to the Madonna. Yet God and the world keep the peace so unbrokenly in their hearts, that they have hardly a suspicion of the incongruous appearance they present to others, still less of the horrible reality of their spiritual condition. Now if we can see all this in others, is it at all likely that we are free from it ourselves ? Depend upon it

there is no freedom but in excessive fear, no security
but in a weary vigilance! It is heavy work always to
be keeping guard. But there is no sleep in the enemy's
camp, and we are in a war which knows neither peace
nor truce. The night is both cold and long, and if
divine love keeps us not awake, what else is there that
will?

It may very naturally be now objected that the conclusion of this chapter tends to destroy the conclusion
of the last, that if worldliness accounts for the widely
spread denial of those relations of Creator and creature
which have been shown to be true, so it will not allow
us to suppose that the majority of Catholics are saved,
when worldliness is at once so universal, and so deadly
to the soul. But this by no means follows. What
has been said of the obtrusiveness of evil and the hiddenness of good, and of the graces which visit old age,
sickness, and death, applies as well to worldliness as to
sin. No! the conclusion, which might seem to follow
from this doctrine of worldliness, would be, that very
far from a majority of the rich among catholics would
be saved. But the rich are a mere handful compared
to the multitudinous poor. So that, even allowing the
stern conclusion to be drawn that very few rich persons
are saved, even among catholics, the conclusion of the
preceding chapter would remain unshaken. Many
writers have taken this startling view. Lacordaire, in
making up his majority of the saved, lays the chief
stress on children, women, and the countless poor.*
Bossuet, commenting on the words of the seventy-first
psalm, He shall judge the poor of the people and He
shall save the children of the poor, draws a picture
similar to that of Lacordaire.† Fromond, in his com-

* Conferences, iv. 178, et seqq.   † Œuvres, vii. 442.

mentary on the catholic epistles, enters upon the question of the number of the saved when he is explaining
the thirteenth verse of the second chapter of St. James,
and one of the arguments which he brings forward in
support of the more gloomy view is, that "although
perhaps the majority of the faithful do not die without
the sacrament of penance, yet very many worldly
people (plerique mundani) do not receive the fruit of
the sacrament;" and the reason he gives for this opinion
is, that their appreciation of riches, honours, pleasures,
and other earthly goods is too high and fixed for their
sorrow for sin easily to rise to that appreciation of its
malignity, which theology requires even in the adequate
attrition for absolution.*   Palafox also, in his book on
Devotion to St. Peter, teaches the same doctrine in his
comparison of the prodigal son, and the young man who
went away sorrowful. It was his appreciation of
riches which hindered his appreciation of God, and it
was the prodigal's freedom from this which on the other
hand facilitated his conversion.†   There is no doubt
that our Lord's woes pronounced upon the rich are
among the most painful and terrific mysteries of the
Gospel, and should drive rich men into that facile,
prompt, various, unasked, abundant, and self-denying
almsgiving for the love of God, in which alone their
safety consists.   But, so far as the present question is
concerned, I express no opinion as to whether a very
small minority of rich catholics are saved; I do not
know enough of the world to form a judgment, and my
little experience of the rich would go the other way: I
only say that even if this melancholy belief be true, it by

* Migne, Cursus Sacræ Scripturæ, Tom. xxv. col. 682.
† Palafox, Excellencias de San Pedro, lib. iii. cap. 9.

no means destroys the previous conclusion that the numerical majority of catholics are saved.

But to conclude, there are certain things which it is important to note with regard to worldliness, and which cannot be too often repeated. The first is, that even spiritual persons for the most part greatly under-estimate its danger. They have not a sufficiently intelligent belief in its universality, in its subtlety, in its power of combining with good in the most imperceptible quantities, and then spoiling it, or in its peculiar aptness for fixing itself just upon the very persons who consider themselves decidedly free from it. Spiritual discernment is a rare gift, and one which belongs only to those whose hearts are all for God. It is the great art of the world to persuade men that it is not so dangerous as it is described, and that with monks it is a sort of pious fashion to abuse the world, while with preachers it is simply an affair of rhetoric. This persuasion is its triumph. Nothing more is needed. When you have under-estimated its dangers, you are already its victim.

In the second place, as men are very apt not to know worldliness even when they see it, and as it is not an easy matter always to be paying attention to the atmosphere we breathe, it is of great importance to have well-ascertained principles. It is astonishing how few men are in possession of such. An almost incredible amount of excellent effort comes to nothing great, because it is at random, and by fits and starts, and operating inconsistently with its antecedents. The really powerful man in the world is the consistent man, the man of ascertained principles and of adjusted views. The world, like a suspicious potentate, is always proposing concordats. We are asked first for one compromise,

then for another. We do not know when we have
passed the line which involved a principle, and so we
discover, that we have committed ourselves to something, in which it is impossible for us to keep our word
without surrendering our independence altogether.
Now with ascertained principles we have settled all this
at the outset.   Even when we get beyond the extent of
our knowledge, or the sphere of our experience, we
know what to suspect and where to be upon our guard.
Our instincts are right, and, what is practically of
greater importance, they are consistent also.   Thus we
do not fall into the world's power, and are never taken
unawares, and have not to give offence by having to
retrace our steps.   Thus when we change our state of
life, or enter upon a new department of duty, or come
to a crisis in life, our relations with the world are more
or less altered ; and if we have then to hesitate and
linger, settling our future mode of operations and map-
ping out the country before us, because we have no
ascertained princples, every step we take, (and we cannot stand still, this is not a world for that work,) we are
putting on record some precedent against ourselves.
An inconsistent great man is an impotent creature in
practical matters, while a consistent moderate man does
the work of a great one.   Above all, a man should have
ascertained principles of practical religion, if religion
is to be the business of his life.   It is deplorable
for the cause of God on earth, that such men are so
few.

In the third place, if ascertained principles are of
such importance to us in this respect, and if the power
of our faith depends materially either on its simplicity
or its intelligence, and if our faith is " the victory
which overcometh the world," it is of great consequence

that we should know and study our religion well. In
these days there is an immense amount of information,
floating in society, regarding the controversies of the
Church and the world. They are now daily coming
more into collision, in questions of politics, in systems
of beneficence, in the statistics of crime, in the doctrines
of progress, in the discoveries of science, in the quarrels
of the metaphysical schools, and in the new shapes of
old controversies between the Church and the dissident
sects around her. The world has a power and a purchase in the anti-church side of all these questions ; and
it is so tempting to be moderate, so pleasant to yield,
so hard to prove, so weary to argue, so unnatural to
confess our own ignorance, that an educated modern
catholic who does not study the doctrines of his religion,
as carefully as the subject-matter of his profession, will
hardly escape betraying God sometimes, and getting on
the wrong side without intending it. Even a study of
theology, at least to some extent, is of considerable
utility, in this particular light, as a safeguard against
worldliness. It is proverbial that a little knowledge is
a dangerous thing ; but this is less true of theology than
it is of any other science, because the least acquaintance
with it deepens our view of our own ignorance, and it
breathes such an odour of God that intellectual bashfulness would seem to be its special gift, increasing as our
studies penetrate nearer and nearer to those divine
abysses, into which knowledge may not descend until
it has been metamorphosed into love. A man, who has
finished his education in these days without having
acquired a profound intellectual respect for his religion,
is the most likely of all men to become the prey of an
unbelieving and ungodly world, and to betray his Lord
without intending it, and then to grow angry, and turn

away in proud dislike from Him whom he has thus betrayed.

In the last place, it is honestly to be confessed, that all these things do but form an armour against the spirit of the world. They are not a victory over it. Moreover it is an armour which is by no means invulnerable. The weight of the arms and the weariness of the fight have laid many a warrior low from whom no blood had flowed, but whose very bones the heavy fall had cruelly broken. Many a spear, that could not penetrate the cunning joints of the suit of mail, has unseated the rider, and left him lifeless beneath his charger's feet. So all these helps, which have been here suggested, are not infallible ; nay, they are but auxiliaries for a season, and for all their worth, the world may, and most likely will, if we have no other resources, take us captive in the end. There is no redemption for the creature but in the service of the Creator. There is no power to counteract the manifold spirit of evil but one, and that is the desire of God, the craving to see His face, the yearning for His beauty. There is no specific against worldliness but God.

CHAPTER IV.

OUR OWN GOD.

Διὸ δὴ καὶ εἰς αὐτὸν ἐπίστραπται τὰ σύμπαντα, ἀσχέτῳ τινι πόθῳ καὶ ἀρρήτῳ στοργῇ πρὸς τὸν ἀρχηγὸν τῆς ζωῆς καὶ χορηγὸν ἀποβλέποντα.

S. Basil.

THE Creator is the creature's home. Neither spirit of angel nor soul of man can rest short of God. They can anchor nowhere save in the capacious harbour of His infinite perfections. All things teach us this beautiful truth. All things that find us wandering lead us home again, to the Bosom of our Eternal Father. The three distinct orders of nature, grace, and glory, if the two last may indeed be called distinct, all in their own respective ways, at once teach us this comforting and saving truth, and help us also to practice what they teach. The natural joy of beautiful scenery, the strong grace of Christian holiness, and the thrill of glory which passes through our souls from the unveiled Face of God, all, in degrees almost infinitely apart, draw us home to God, or keep us there. God is our Last End as well as our First Cause. O that the day were come when we shall be securely at His Feet for ever!

God is included in the idea of creation as our Last End as well as our First Cause. It is as our Creator that He is both the one and the other. We have seen that creation was simply love, a love which called our natures out of nothing, a love which gave them all that was due to them, a love which gave them grace which was not due for them, a love which in matter of fact destined them to a glory which is far beyond our natural capacities. All the three orders of nature, grace, and glory were represented in the act of creation, nature from the very necessity of the case, grace because as a matter of fact God created both angels and men in a state of grace,* glory because it was for His glory that we were necessarily created, and, as a matter of fact, in the exuberant goodness of His decrees, for the special, but not necessary, glory of the Beatific Vision.

The angels were created all at once, and because of their excellent perfections, and especially the perfect knowledge which they had of themselves, they rapidly exercised their free will, completed the course of their probation, and entered into the rest and enjoyment of the Creator's beauty. Men are created slowly and by successive generations, and from the great inferiority of their rational nature to the vast intelligences of the angels, they require the revolution of many centuries before their numbers are completed, their destinies fulfilled, and the whole of the elect enter into the everlasting joy of God. The world of men is a world of slower rotation. Both these creations of angels and men were created simply for God's own glory; but His glory was the creature's bliss, because His glory was to have rational children who should be like Himself and be made participators of His beatitude. But as we cannot be participators of His joy by any natural beatitude, however exquisite and satisfying, and as His very first intention in creation was that we should participate in His own beatitude, it follows that His very first intention in creation already involved both grace and glory; and this is the explanation of the beautiful and touching

* Throughout the whole Treatise the opinion of St. Bonaventure as to the creation of the angels has been assumed to be incorrect.

mystery of our being created in a state of grace originally. So nature involved grace, not necessarily, but in the designs of creative love, and grace looked on to glory, and prophecied of it to free-will, and more than prophecied of it, for it was the capacity of glory and its beginning.

Because God is infinitely good and infinitely perfect, He is by His nature, so to speak, bent upon the communication of Himself; and this communication of Himself is, as theologians tell us, twofold, a natural communication, and a free communication. The natural one, as it is altogether necessary, is eternal. It is that by which the Father communicates to the Son His whole essence, power, wisdom, goodness, and beatitude, and the Father and the Son to the eternally proceeding Spirit. It takes place in the production of the Word through the intellect, and of the Spirit through the will; and each of these processions is so perfect and full, that by it the whole good, which is communicated, is as perfectly possessed by Him who receives as by Him who communicates it. The free communication of God is temporal, and takes place in creation, and creation is in order to it, and it takes place first, and foremost, and eminently, in the Hypostatic Union, and then in the gifts of grace and glory ; and God's communication of Himself, which in the act of creation was not supernatural, was with a view to what was supernatural, and as a matter of fact, was not disjoined from it in act. To this, therefore, says Lessius, did God of Himself incline, that is, of His own goodness, setting aside all merit and all necessity of the creature. This communication begins in this life by the gifts of grace, especially faith, hope, and charity ; by which virtues we are not only made like to God, but God also is united to us. It is per-

fected however in the next life by the gifts of glory,
namely, the light of glory, the vision of the Divinity,
beatific love, and beatific joy. For by these we attain
our highest possible similitude to God, and become perfectly the sons of God, and deiform, shining like the
Divinity, and exhibiting in ourselves the most excellent
image of the Holy Trinity. For by the light of glory
we are made like the Father ; by the vision of the
divine Essence and divine Persons we become like the
Son ; by beatific love we are made like the Holy Ghost ;
by joy we become like the Godhead in beatitude, and
the participation of the divine beatitude is completed in
us.*

When we speak of God's glory we may mean one or
more of four things. First of all, His glory may be
either intrinsic or external ; and then each of those may
be of two kinds also. God's own excellence, His own
beauty, the infinity of His perfections in Himself, is as
it were the objective glory of God, which is intrinsic to
Himself; whereas His own knowledge of Himself, His
own love of Himself, and His own joy in Himself, which
are also intrinsic, are what theology terms His formal
glory. The beauty of creation, the perfections of creatures, their loveliness, their number, their adaptations,
even their colour and form, are the external glory of
God, represented objectively, whereas the knowledge of
Him, the love of Him, and the joy in Him, which His
rational creatures have, is His formal external glory.
It is necessary to put these hard words together in order
to understand the practical conclusions to which we
shall be coming presently.

Now we say that God is necessitated to do everything
for His own glory, and that through the creation of the

* Lessius de Perfect. Divin. lib. xiv.

world was perfectly free, yet, granting that it was to be created by God, it must of necessity be created for His glory. This is almost venturing to say that He could not help Himself, at least as to the end for which He created. But oh! what joy the creature will find at last in this very necessity, which God is under, of doing everything for His own glory! That God has created the world is a fact. It is contradictory not to His wisdom only, but to every one of His perfections, that He should have created it without an object at all. It is impossible to Him, as God, to have any other end but Himself. It is contrary to the plenitude of His self-sufficiency, that He should have created it in order to gain from it conveniences which He has not now, or joys which He does not already possess; for these are intrinsic to Himself. But it is possible for Him to have a glory extrinsic to Himself, over and above that which is intrinsic. On the other hand, it is impossible for Him to have anything else extrinsic to Himself, which creation could give Him, except glory. Even then the glory is not necessary to Him, and does not make Him more blessed or more self-sufficient than He was; at best it is only congruous to His divine Majesty to have it. Thus it is that God is necessitated to do all things for His own glory. He is limited to this by the very plenitude of His perfections. As nothing exists in the world without the influx of His omnipresence, supporting it and keeping it above the abyss of nothingness, into which of itself it is falling back evermore, so also nothing exists in the world, which is not involved in and depending upon God's glory. Even the permissions of sin glorify Him, for without them according to the present laws the wills of His creatures would not be free.

While God was thus under the necessity of creating
28 †

all things for His glory, if He created at all, much more
is the creature under the necessity of glorifying God in
all things. But it was not necessary for God to raise
the creature to the special glory of the Beatific Vision.
It was not due to his nature, not to the highest angelic
nature. It was beyond it; and it was beyond it, not
in degree only, but in kind also. It belonged to another
order than that of nature. It was superadded to nature. Nature had to receive another order, that of
grace, before it could be capable of the third order, that
of glory. Wonderful things had to be done to it, in
order to habilitate it for such a possibility as the sight
of God. But the remarkable thing is, that these things
were done in the act of creation. The orders both of
nature and of grace started in that one act of divine
benignity. It was sin only, which separated what God
had put together. The rebellious angels sinned, and so
lost their primal grace, and having no fresh trial given
them, forfeited thereby for ever the order of glory.
Man sinned, and in him also the two orders became
separated, and the whole magnificent apparatus of redeeming love is God's invention to unite them again, so
that men may become capable of the order of glory.
Not that this is the sole reason or the whole explanation of the Incarnation, but only of Redemption. Thus
it is absolutely necessary, when we are thinking of creation, to bear in mind the fact that God created angels
and men in a state of grace, and not in a state of pure
nature. We are not concerned with other possible creations, but only with our own creation; and the creations
of both those angelic and human families of rational
creatures, united in the church under the single headship
of Jesus, were accomplished in a state of grace; and
they were so, because glory, and the especial supernatu-

ral glory of a participation in His own beatitude, entered
into God's first intention and original idea, as Creator.
We shall never understand creation, if we let this fact
out of sight for a moment.*

The inanimate and irrational creations glorify God
by the very splendour of the beauty in which He has
clothed them. They glorify Him by their adaptation
and subservience to man. Their abundance in their
kinds, and their many kinds which are over and above
what are necessary to man, is another glory of their
Creator by being in some sort a picture of His copious
magnificence. They glorify Him also by bearing on
themselves the seal and signet of His Divinity, and even
of His Trinity and Unity, and their degree of goodness
depends on the degree in which they adumbrate the
divine perfections. But much more does the rational
creation glorify its Creator. By its very existence it
represents God, as the inanimate and irrational creations do. But by its intelligence it knows God, and
with its knowledge loves Him; and by its will it loves
Him, and with its love enjoys Him. Thus the knowledge, love, and joy of the rational creatures, the three
things by which they chiefly shadow forth the Holy
Trinity, praise and admire and worship the Divine
Nature, all which is the rendering glory to Him. By
these three things they as it were enter into God and
rest in Him, through the gifts of grace and glory. But
let us hear Lessius. In these three acts resides God's
chiefest glory, which He Himself intended in all His
works; and so likewise in the same acts reside the
highest good and formal beatitude of men and angels.
By these acts the blessed spirits are elevated infinitely

* Charitas est ergo causa effixiens creaturæ rationalis, et participatio divinæ
bonitatis est causa finalis.—*Harphius.*

above themselves, and, in their union with God, become
deiform, by a most lofty and super-eminent similitude
with God, so that the mind can conceive no greater
similitude.　Thus, like very Gods, they shine to all
eternity as the sons of glory and the divine brightness.
By those same acts they expand themselves into immensity so as to be coequal and coextensive, as far as may
be, to so great a good, that they may take it in and
comprehend it all.　They will not linger outside, as it
were upon the surface of it, but they go down into its
profound depths, and enter into the joy of their Lord:
some more, some less, according to the magnitude of
the light of glory which is communicated to each.
Immersed in this abyss, they lose themselves and all
created things; for all other goods and joys seem to
them as nothing by the side of this ocean of goods and
joys.　In this abyss there is to them no darkness, no
obscurity, such as hangs about the Divinity to us now:
but all is light and immense serenity, although they are
not able fully to comprehend it.　There is their eternal
mansion, with a tranquil security that they shall never
fail.　There is the heaven of heavens, in comparison
with which all creation is but dross.　There is the fulfilling of all their desires; there the possession and
fruition of all things that are desirable.　There nothing
will remain to be longed for, or sought for more: for all
will firmly possess and exquisitely enjoy every good
thing in God.　There the whole occupation of the saints
will be to contemplate the infinite beauty of God, to
love His infinite goodness, to enjoy His infinite sweetness, to be filled to overflowing with the torrent of His
pleasures, and to exult with an unspeakable delight in
His infinite glory, and in all the goods which He and
they possess.　Hence comes perpetual praise, and bene-

diction, and thanksgiving; and thus all the Blessed, arrived at the consummation of their desires, and, knowing not what more to crave, rest in God as their Last End.*

Thus does creation come home, like a weary bird to its roost, to rest in its Creator. And then all movements cease, all vicissitudes, changes, progresses, aspirations, discoveries; and all is rest within, without, around, the kingdom of eternal peace. Then the Son gives up the kingdom to His Father, as the Apostle speaks;† and the subjection of His Human Nature, which had been as it were veiled in the government of the Church and in the pomp of judgment, becomes more apparent; and then, as if this last act of unspeakable subjection on the part of that Created Nature, which is the Head and First-born of all creatures, were the crowning beauty of creation, God the Creator becomes all in all, and the chronicles of this creation close. Beyond that, all is lost in the indistinguishable radiance of eternity. Such is the history of creation, as theology ventures to conceive it lying in the divine mind. It is a work of simple love, of gigantic dimensions, with the most beautiful proportion in all its parts, and the most exquisite finish in every detail. Love is the life of it from first to last, and its result is an abiding, immortal, created counterpart of the eternal, uncreated, and undivided Trinity.

If we have taken pains to master this somewhat difficult account of creation, we shall see that it is as it were the frame within which all the relations of the Creator and the creature, which have occupied the preceding chapters, are enclosed. It will make some things plain, which perhaps were not plain before; and it will

* Lessius lib. xiv.   † 1 Cor. xv.

itself be the easier to understand from what has gone before. Even the horror of worldliness will now become more apparent, and its danger more alarming. But what is the conclusion to which it all leads? That religion must necessarily be a service of love, that the easiness of salvation comes of its being a personal love of God, and that the only security from worldliness is also in a personal love of God. It is neither the wonderful character of its doctrines, nor the pure simplicity of its precepts, nor the supernatural power of its assistances, which make religion what it is, but the fact of its being the creature's personal love of the Creator. This is an obvious thing to say; and yet such consequences flow from it that it must be still more insisted on.

That all holiness should consist in a personal love of God flows out of the very tie of creation. Creation was an act of love, forestalling or including all other loves whatever. The creature was at once put by the act of creation into various personal relations to the Creator, all of which were of the very tenderest and most intimate description. It flows also out of the knowledge which the creature has of the Creator, and the motives for his personal love of Him increase with the amount of that knowledge. Each perfection pleads for love. Each puts a price on love, and on nothing else but love. Love is the one want of all God's attributes, if we may call it want, and the supplying of that one want is the sole worship of the creature. The easiness of salvation showed that all religion must be a personal love of God. It was easy just because this was all. The end of all its sacraments and graces was to infuse or to elicit that love, and the more of it they infused and the more of it they elicited, the more did they contribute to the facility of the triumph. Sin

teaches us that all is nothing-worth but personal love
of God, both because its forgiveness is the sweetest
preacher of divine love on earth, and because the horror of its punishment is the total loss of love in that
dark godless hell which is its end. The personality of
the evil spirit drives us also into personal love of God,
as our security and refuge. The dangers of the world,
are to be met in no other way than by the personal
love of God. It is only the love of Him which can
kill unworthy loves. It is only the desire of Him
which can turn the soul away sick, and dispirited, with
the perishable goods of earth. It is only the light of
His beauty which can dim and dishonour the flaunting,
garish beauty of the world, or make us secretly and
sweetly discontented with its lawful, natural, and
blameless loveliness. But most of all does this necessity of a personal love of God flow out of the fact, that
God Himself, and not any of His created rewards, is
our Last End. God Possessed, our own God, that is
creation's home, that is our last end, there only is our
rest. O that the winds of grace would blow that we
might sail more swiftly over this broad sea to our
eternal home! Another day is gone, another week is
passed, another year is told. Blessed be God then, we
are nearer to the end. It comes swiftly; yet it comes
slowly too. Come it must, and then it will all be but
a dream to look back upon. But there are stern things
to pass through; and to the getting well through them,
there goes more than we can say. One thing we know,
that personal love of God is the only thing which
reaches God at last. Other things,—they look wise,
they begin well, they sound good—but they wander;
they are on no path; they go aside, or they fall behind, but home they never come. To love, the way is

neither hard to find, nor hard to tread; for so it is that love never comes home tired. It gets to God through the longest life more fresh, more eager, more venturous, more full of youth, more brimming with expectation, than the day it started amid the excesses and inexperiences of its first conversion.

No one denies this doctrine of the necessity of personal love of God. It could not be denied without heresy. But there are two different schools of spirituality which treat it very differently; indeed whose difference consists in their different treatment of it.*
All are agreed that as the proof of love is the keeping of the commandments, so the sense of duty, the brave determination to do always and only what is right, and because it is right, must go along with and be a part of personal love of God.† Personal love of God without this would be a falsehood and a mockery. They who dwell most strongly on the sense of duty do not omit personal love of God; and they who lay the greatest stress on love both imply and secure the keen sense of rightfulness and duty. But much depends on which of the two we put foremost. It is possible by dwelling exclusively on love to make religion too much a matter of mere devotions, an affair of sentiments and feelings, highly strung and therefore brittle, overstrained and so shortlived. It is possible on the other

---

* A whole string of consequences seem to follow in ascetical theology from the doctrine of Vasquez, Naturam rationalem esse regulam honestatis. The common teaching however is against him. See Vasq. 1. 2. disp. 58. 2. and disp. 97. 3.

† To the doctrine that a good action is essentially and intrinsically good, Medina objects, Si quis velit amare Deum, et non ex motivo, quod hoc sit conforme legi divinæ id præcipienti, adhuc ponit actum honestum et bonum. Viva replies, Qui amat Deum, et non ex motivo honestatis, ponit actum honestum sed non ponit actum honestum honestè. De Actibus Humanis qu. ii.

hand, that by laying all the stress on duty, especially
with young persons or again with sinners, the true
motive of duty may not have fair play, and the peculiar character of the Gospel be overlooked or inade-
quately remembered. We must pursue such and such
a line of conduct because it is commanded, because it
is right, because it will win us respect, because it will
enable us to form habits of virtue, because it will edify,
because we cannot otherwise go to communion, because
we shall be lost eternally if we do not pursue it. This
is quite intelligible, and it is all very true, but not particularly persuasive, especially to those whom youth
makes ardent, or those whom sin has made invalids.
We must pursue such and such a line of conduct because it is the one which God loves, and God loves us
most tenderly and has loved us from all eternity, and
God yearns that we should love Him, and He catches
at our love as if it were a prize, and repays it with a
fondness which is beyond human comprehension, and it
grieves His Love; and He makes it a personal matter, if
we swerve from such conduct, while if we only love, all
will be easy. This also is intelligible, and very true,
and also very persuasive, and has a wonderful root of
perseverance in it. But it comes to pass that, while
both views are very true, they nevertheless form quite
different characters. So that it is one of the most important practical questions of our whole lives, to settle
whether we will love God because it is right, or whether
we will do right because God loves us and we love Him.

Strange to say, while both these views are true, they
look as we examine the working out of them, like two
different religions. The fact is, that for some reason
or other it is very hard to persuade a man, or for him to
persuade himself, that God loves him. The moment that

fact becomes a part of his own sensible convictions, a
perfect revolution has been worked in his soul. Everything appears different to him. He has new lights,
and feels new powers. Faculties in him, which were
well nigh dormant, wake up and do great things. He
is a new man. It is a kind of conversion. However
good he was before, however regular, however conscientious, however devotional, he feels that the change
which has passed over him is in some sense a veritable
conversion. He is on a new line, and will henceforth
move differently. Many go to their graves without at
all realizing practically the immense love which God
has for them. It has been a want in them all through
their lives, and they would have been higher in heaven
had they known on earth what heaven has now taught
them. A theologian says, that it is one of the weaknesses even of the saints, that they cannot believe in
the greatness of God's love for them. It is related in
the chronicles of the Franciscans, that until her direc-
tor with some difficulty undeceived her, St. Elizabeth
of Hungary thought that she loved God more than He
loved her. In truth the very immensity, the excesses,
the apparent extravagancies of God's love, stand in its
own light, and hinder men from believing it as they
should. They hardly dare to do so; for it seems incredible that God should love us as He is said to do.
It is the grand crisis in everybody's life, an era to date
from, when the knowledge that his Creator loves him
passes into a sensible conviction.

If all the evil that is in the world arises from the
want of a practical acknowledgment of the true relations between the Creator and the creature, it is
equally true, that from the same want comes all that is
deficient in our spiritual lives; and furthermore, the

true relations between the Creator and the creature
are more readily appreciated, more lovingly embraced,
and more perseveringly acted out, on the system which
puts love first and duty second, which does right because God loves us, rather than loves God because it
is right. Religion,, no doubt, comes to persons, in
different ways. Different parts of it attract different
minds. Men begin in various places in religion. There
is not exactly any one normal beginning of being pious.
We should never think therefore of condemning, or
throwing the slightest slur, on any method which
succeeded in securing the continuous keeping of God's
commandments upon supernatural motives. This must
be borne in mind, together with the full admission both
of the safety and soundness of the other principle,
while we state the reasons for preferring that school
of spirituality, which puts forward most prominently
the personal love of God, and dwells upon it to all
persons and at every turn. It seems of the two the
most likely to advance the Creator's glory, first by
saving a great number of souls, and secondly by
swelling the ranks of those who generously aim at perfection.

Love sharpens our eyes, and quickens all the senses
of our souls. Now when we dwell very exclusively
on the sense of duty, and urge people to learn to do
right just because it is right, we seem often to be want-
ing in the delicacy and fineness of our spiritual discernment. We are not always on God's side, because
we do not instantaneously and instinctively apprehend
on which side He is. We do not prophetically see the
evil, which is as yet invisible and implicit in some line
of action. Our spiritual tastes are blunt, sometimes
inclining to be gross. We do not at once detect world-

liness in its first insidious aggressions. Love has a
specialty for all these things; and conscientiousness
often runs aground in shallow places, where love sails
through, finding deep water with an almost supernatural
skill. The duty principle, if it is allowable so to name
it shortly for convenience sake, is more apt to grow
weary than love. It is always against the grain of our
corrupt nature, and consequently we are obliged to be
always making efforts, in order to keep ourselves up
to the mark; and when times of dryness or seasons of
temptation come, these efforts are not easy to sustain.
Love on the contrary is a stimulant. It has a patent
for making things easy. It invigorates us, and enables
us to do hard things with a sensible sweetness and a
religious pleasure, when mere conscientiousness would
fail through the infirmity of its own nature. Thus perseverance is more congruous to the conduct which proceeds on the principle of love, than to that which looks
prominently to duty. Moreover where there is effort,
there is seldom abundance, while it is the characteristic
of love to be prolific.

It is necessary for us when we act entirely from a
sense of duty to go through many more intellectual
processes than when we act from love. We have to
investigate the character of the action, to ascertain its
bearings, to inform ourselves of its circumstances, to
guess its consequences. All this takes time and makes
a man slow, and as life runs rapidly, he is apt to be
taken by surprise, and either be guilty of some omission, or act in a hurry at the last. This is the reason
why slow men are often so precipitate. Any one who
observes will see instances of this daily, in the habitual
impetuosities of timid men. The duty principle, also,
only sails well in fine weather. It does not do for

storms. It wants elasticity and buoyancy, and so, when it has fallen into sin, it recovers itself with great difficulty, and is awkward in its repentance, as if it were in a position for which it never was intended. It soon despairs. Sin seems a necessity, and a few serious relapses are enough to make it give up the spiritual life altogether. There are cases of men who never could recover one mortal sin; and we should be inclined to suspect that they were mostly cases of men who acted from conscience in preference to love.*

It also has a propensity to concentrate us upon ourselves, and so to hinder charity. Self must come in, when we are always looking at self and self's behaviour, and when even the Object of faith presents itself habitually to us in the light of self's rule. In this way it not unfrequently hinders the more beautiful exercises of charity; for charity is not the doing only our duty to our neighbour. That does not take us much beyond justice. The habit of mind of mere conscientiousness seems different from the habit of mind of exuberant charity. It is not moreover genial to high spiritual things, such as voluntary austerities, the love of suffering, the practice of the evangelical counsels, the sorrow because God is so little loved and so much offended, and the willing renunciation of spiritual consolations and sensible sweetnesses. A merely conscientious man may be intellectually convinced that he ought to aim at perfection, but the chances are immensely against his succeeding;

---

* Even conscience acts rather by love of the beauty of virtue than by hatred of the malice of vice. Antoine says, Voluntas aversari non potest objectum malum propter solam ejus malitiam tanquam unicum motivum, quia odium malitiæ vitii necessario fundatur in amore objectivæ bonitatis virtutis oppositæ, illumque necessario supponit. Uude nemo odit malitiam alicujus vitii propter se, nisi amet, et quia amat, bonitatem et pulchritudinem virtutis oppositæ, De Act. Hum. cap. iii. art. i.

and for this reason, that he has not sufficient momentum. His impulse dies out, and he stops short of the aim. Doing what is right because it is right is not a sufficiently perfect or robust motive to carry a man all the way to perfection. Love alone can do that. It sounds almost like an absurdity to talk of observing the counsels from a sense of duty, or of aiming at a more perfect interior observance of the precepts than it is our duty to aim at, because we have determined to make a duty of it.

This principle, too, although it is thoroughly Christian, and leans on Christ, appears to have but a weak tendency to produce that nameless indescribable likeness to Christ, which is the characteristic of the saints. It has not enough of self-oblivion in it, and is very deficient in its sympathies with the mystical operations of grace. Moreover it has not the same blessings as love; not that it is not an ordinance of God, and one which no one can with safety forget or depreciate; but there is an air about it of the Old Testament rather than the New. It likewise keeps men back by leading to scruples. It never lets conscience alone. It wastes in a fruitless post-mortem examination of its actions the time that might have been spent in acts of heroic contrition or of disinterested love. Nay, it will even disinter again and again those actions, which have already passed the ordeal of so many examinations, and it will dissect, and meddle, until it has acquired an inveterate habit of stooping, and contracted a disease of the eyes. This is its immoderation, the excess to which it tends, and to which it must tend with all the more determination the higher it rises in the spiritual life, where common rules are less clear in their application, and the processes of grace more intricate and unusual. Yet

while it breeds scruples, this same principle also minis-
ters to self-trust, because of its habit of examining
actions for itself, and then of going by what it sees.
it is very rare to find a man, who habitually does what
is right only because it is right, who is not at the same
time quietly self-opinionated, and dangerously free from
all distrust of his own decisions.

Then again there seems in such a principle of action
no real rehearsal for heaven. The Blessed in heaven
do not act from a sense of duty. They contemplate and
love. Surely there must have been some habit formed
on earth, to correspond to and anticipate that celestial
habit of keeping the gaze fixed on the beautiful object
of faith. A conscientious seraph is a very difficult idea
to realize. In truth there is nothing supernatural about
this principle, except the amount of love which it contains. It borrows from love all about it that is worth
much, and yet keeps love in the lowest place, as if it
were a dependent and inferior. Thus we are not surprised to find those who habitually act upon it, somewhat out of harmony with the lives of the saints, with
new miracles, with popular devotions, with apparitions,
pilgrimages, taking vows, and other supernatural things.
For the principle does not take kindly to the supernatural, grasps it nervously, and so is perpetually letting
it slip because it cannot hold it.

Neither is it an attractive principle to others. It
deprives goodness of much of its missionary character
and of many of its converting influences. It does not
draw people round it, or make sinners wonder enviously
at the sweetness of Christian sanctity. Is is dry. It
repels. It speaks shortly, and makes no allowances.
It is unseasonable, and is proud of disregarding circumstances. Time and place are out of time and place to

448   OUR OWN GOD.

it. It has a propensity to preach, and dictate, and be tiresome. In all these respects it plays into the hands of the natural foibles of those to whose character this principle is most likely to commend itself. Then, which sounds a privilege but is in truth a disability, it is a rarer gift than love. It is often a growth of natural character, whereas God pours love out on every one. It thus embraces fewer souls: because fewer are capable of walking by it. It is love, it is walking by love, that swells the grand multitude of the number who are saved. Conscientiousness could never fill heaven half so fast as love. So that it neither manufactures the high saints, nor yet throngs with happy crowds the outer courts of heaven.

It is also less directly connected with the gift of final perseverance than love. As was said, it is a life of efforts, and it is the nature of efforts to be complete in themselves, and not enchained one with another; and the doctrine of habit is a poor thing to trust to in the supernatural affairs of grace. God Himself acts from love, that is, from conformity to Himself, and not from a sense of duty.* God's life is love; and thus love has the blessing of exuberance, of fruitfulness, of speed. It is venturesome, overflowing, divine.

All that is good about the other principle is liable to constant error from a want of moderation; and in pointing out the reasons for preferring the principle of love to the principle of duty, as an habitual motive-

---

* In Deo operationes moraliter bonæ, honestæ, ac laudabiles dicuntur quæ sunt conformes fini ipsius Dei, ut est amor suimet. And again, Deus, quia non habet finem ultimum a se distinctum, quando operatur honeste, hoc est conformiter ad proprium finem, et juxta exigentiam, quam habet a propria natura, non obligatur rigorose a regula honestatis, sed physice, imo et metaphysice, necessitatur a Seipso. Viva, p. ii. disp. vii. q. i. de prima regula moralitatis.

power in the spiritual life, it has been necessary to touch upon some of the exaggerations to which the exclusive principle of duty may lead, but does not necessarily lead. This must not be misunderstood. The principle of duty is holy and strong. The principle of love disjoined from the principle of duty is a thing which will save no man. Doing right because it is right is a course which every one ought to pursue, a habit which all should cultivate. All that we have been maintaining is, that the spiritual man who looks at love primarily and prominently, and at duty secondarily and subordinately, will sooner be a thoroughly converted man, or a saint, or a higher kind of saint, than the spiritual man who reverses the process, and looks at duty primarily and prominently, as the solid part of his devotion, and love secondarily and subordinately, as the sweetening of his duty.

Personal love of God! this then is the conclusion of the whole. To love God because He desires our love, to love Him because He first loved us, to love Him because He loves us with such a surpassing love, to love our Creator because He redeemed us and our Redeemer because He created us, to love Him as our Creator in all the orders of nature, grace, and glory, and finally to love Him for His own sake because of His infinite perfections, because He is what He is,—this, and this alone is religion; this is what flows from the ties between the Creator and His redeemed creature; for what is redemption but the restoring, repairing, and ennobling of creation? To love our Creator as our First Cause, as our Last End, and as our Abiding Possession, —this is the whole matter. He in His mercy has made the love of Him a precept, and therefore those who do right because it is right really love Him, and

29

go to Him at last, as well as those who only love Him
or chiefly love Him out of love. But this last way is
the most easy for ourselves, and the most honourable
for Him. This is why I said at the outset that the
beginning of the whole process was rather in God's
touching and mysterious desire for our love than in His
love of us. That desire of His seems the handle by
which loving souls take hold of their religion, and in
which they find the key of their own position of
creatures, and to the rights and attractions of the Creator; and this desire of God for our love leads straight
to our desire for Him, our desire not so much for His
love as for Himself, that gift of Himself, which, though
inseparable from His love, is yet much more than love,
more precious and more tender.

What then is life, but the possession of God, and the
beauty of God, drawing us ever more and more powerfully to the fuller possession of Him, until at length in
heaven we come to the fulness of our possession? Let
us emancipate ourselves for awhile from earthly
thoughts, and look up to heaven, while the angels, who
rejoice over one sinner that does penance, are keeping the feast of All Saints. That day might be called
the Feast of the Magnificence of Jesus; for the spirit
of the feast is a spirit of magnificence; it is the feast of
the heavenly court of the great King of our salvation.
Yet what is the sight which we behold there? Ah!
if we look into heaven, we shall learn much about
creation! Let us put aside, not in forgetfulness, still
less for lack of burning love, the empire of the angels,
our elder brothers, and look only at the human family
which is there. Around the altar of the Lamb, by
Mary's maternal throne, there are various rings and
choirs and glorious hierarchies of the saints. They lie

bathed in splendour, beautiful to look upon, but it is a
splendour which is not their own. Each soul is beau-
tified with an infinite variety of graces, the particular
combination of which is distinctive of that particular
soul, and is a separate ornament of heaven, so that not
one saint could be spared without heaven missing a
portion of its beauty. Yet those graces are not their
own. They were gifts to begin with, and they must
remain gifts to the end. Their exceeding joy is such a
vision of delight that we could not see it now, and live.
In truth there is not one of their gifts, not the least and
lowest of their rewards but they might well joy in it
with a surpassing joy. But it is not so. Their joy is
not in their own beauty, or their own perfections, or
their bright rewards. It is entirely in something which
is not their own. It is the beauty of Jesus which is
their magnificence and joy. The eternity of their joy
depends, not on any inward possibility of their own to
fall away, but on the ceaseless attraction of that unfading beauty. O look at the tranquillity of that vast
scene, outspread before our eyes! It is creation in its
Father's house, creation in its home of glory. Its wanderings are over, its problems solved, its consummation
gloriously accomplished. Yet the completion and elevation of its nature, the expansion and coronation of its
graces, and no less also the actual exuberant and joyous
life of its eternal glory, is not in itself, but in its possession of the Creator. It has left itself, and taken up
with something else, and so it is perfect, complete, at
home, at rest; for that something else is God, its all in
all, its own God.

But let us look back again to earth, into the ages
past, and see the processes by which God made His
saints, by which He drew all these multitudinous rings

and choirs and hierarchies of the saints, out of the thick
of the world into His Bosom, where just now we saw
them lying. The same beauty, which, seen, is their
eternal life, unseen and believed in drew them over
earth to heaven. The ways were many, the ways were
strange, the ways were unlike each other, but this was
the one invariable process. It was not a mere sense
of duty, nor a grand conscientiousness, however bright
and strong, which carried them heroically through
opposing obstacles, right up to the highest seats in
heaven. It was a secret attraction, a drawing at their
hearts, a current sucking them in, at first faint and
feeble, slow and uncertain, then steadier, and now
swifter, and at last turbulent, and then suddenly they
were drawn under and engulfed for ever in the beautiful vision of their Creator. It is the characteristic of
God's greatest operations on earth to be invisible. So
is it for the most part with His process of making
saints. When it does come to view, it is so unlike
what we should have expected that it scandalizes us by
its strangeness. Can we point to the life of any one
saint, at whom people did not take scandal, while he
was being sanctified? Why do we not remember more
continually this fact, and the lesson it teaches us?
When men saw Jesus too near and too openly, they
judged Him worthy of death. So it is with ourselves.
When His shadow crosses us in a saint, we judge him
to be anything rather than a saint, and worthy of condemnation.

The immense variety of ways in which the saints
are drawn to God is greatly to be noted. Climate,
rank, date in the world's history, sufferings, circumstances, education, vocation, national character, all
these have had so much to do with it, and yet so little.

They account for much, yet not for all, and for the main thing not in the least; for the same things, which seem to be helping saints forward, are visibly keeping other souls back. There is plainly a secret spell at work, a spell on the world, on life, on sorrow, on darkness, on trial, and even on sin. It is working in them. It is strengthening itself in different souls by contradictory circumstances. But it is a spell, nothing else than a spell. It is none other than the beauty of Jesus, which is the life and light of heaven. Heaven is heaven, because God is so beautiful in the light; and earth is the factory of saints, because God is so beautiful in the darkness.

See how the spell acts, even against the huge, almost resistless, power of the world. Who are they whom it affects? Ah! look at them, lying on God's breast, gleaming there, bright trophies of redeeming grace. They are young delicate highborn virgins, in the fires, under the pincers, among the teeth of lions, boy and girl martyrs, like Venantius, Agatha, Agnes, Lucy, Catherine, and Cecilia. They are children, saints in childhood, whose reason was anticipated that they might love Jesus; they were little things who tore their flesh with scourges, who prayed hours at a time, who had extasies and worked miracles, who had mysterious sufferings, and lived in a mystical world, and were incomprehensibly like Jesus. They were kings and queens, who put away their crowns, took up the cross, and bared their feet, and went off after God. They were gallant soldiers, like St. Ignatius, or lawyers like St. Alphonso. They were freshly converted sinners, with all their habits of sin still strong upon them. Or they were ordinarily good men in the world who loved permitted liberty and blameless pleasure, but

over whom by degrees a sort of dream seemed to pass;
and noiselessly they were led out of the crowd dreaming of the beautiful God; and there was a cold touch
of death; and they woke up and found it more than true.

These were the persons on whom the spell worked.
Now see from what it drew them. There were first
of all the exquisite sinless pleasures of all the senses.
The saints are so far from being insensible persons,
that none can rival them in the keen susceptibilities of
pleasure, or in the refined vivacity of their sensitiveness. It is this which enables them to suffer so acutely,
as if they had first been flayed alive, and then bid to
walk through the thorny world. There was the external beauty of the earth, in which they could read
more plainly than other men the sweet enticing loveliness of God's perfections. There were the ties of the
most holy and tender love. Children deserted their
parents, who loved those parents with such a love as
common children do not know. There were mothers
walking into convents over the bodies of their sons.
There were mothers watching their sons writhing in
the excruciating agonies of a ferocious martyrdom, and
encouraging them with tearless eyes to suffer more and
more. There were fond husbands and doting wives
parting of their own accord for all the term of life, and
the cloister door closing upon well-known faces as if it
had been the hard cold slab of the very tomb. There
were joys from which the saints voluntarily turned in
order that they might indulge in sorrow, and so catch
just a little look of Christ. And under their sorrows,
when heaven rained crosses on their heads, and earth
burned their feet as they walked,—O then was the
magic of the potent spell! with what elasticity they
rose up under their load, and now they sang, like angels,

as they went! And it was liberty which they all gave
up, the liberty out of which God gets all His creature's
love, the liberty which alas! refuses Him so much!
They gave up their liberty for the sweet captivity of
personal love of God ; but it was the free surrender of
their liberty which made it beautiful to God's eye, and
sweetness to His taste, and music in His ear. What a
spell to have drawn such myriads of souls from such
attractions, what power, what pleading, what persua-
siveness, what versatility, and yet withal tranquil as the
beautiful God Himself!

All these wonders are done by the beauty of God
acting on the soul. In heaven it is more intelligible ;
for there the blessed Vision is eternal, unchanging, and
in the full blaze of glory. But the strange and touching
thing is, that on earth it is the merest glimpses of
God which work all these wonders. A chance text of
scripture falls upon the ear, in church or out of it, and
a touch of power comes with it, and with the power a
flash of light, and a saint is made. There are brief
sweetnesses in prayer, which come now and then in
life, like shooting moonbeams through rents on close-
packed cloudy nights. They lit up the cross upon the
steeple and were gone. But the soul fed on them for
days. There are the first moments after communion,
an unearthly time, when we are like Mary carrying the
Lord of heaven and earth within her, and we feel Him,
and have so much to say that we do not speak at all,
and the time passes, and we seem to have missed an
opportunity. But the work was done, and a supernatural health is dancing in our blood, and straightway we climb a mountain on the road to heaven. Then
there are sudden gushes of love, and along with the
love light also; and we know not why they come nor

whence. Heaven is all quiet above us, and makes no
sign. Circumstances are going on around us in the old
tame languid way. What can it be? Certainly it
came from within as if a depth of the soul had broken
up, and flooded the surface; and we remember that,
within us, in one of those depths, in which perhaps we
have never been ourselves, and till eternity dawns never
shall be, God deigns to dwell, and now we understand
the secret. Then there are momentary unions with
Him in times of sorrow, which were so swift that they
looked like possibilities rather than actual visitations.
But they were true embraces from our Heavenly Father,
and they have healed us of diseases, and they have infused a new strength into us, and they were so close
that we have been tingling ever since, and feel the
pressure at this moment still. Then there were flashes
from the monstrance, which showed us we know not
what and told us we know not what. Only they made
the darkness of the world very thick and palpable, like
lightning on a moonless night. But they did a work;
for we felt ourselves laid hold of in the solid darkness
which followed the sudden light, and hurried on over
stocks and stones and up high places, and then we were
left, lonely, but behold! so much nearer than we had
ever seen it before, a pale streak, which was the dawn-
ing of the heavenly day. Nay, one sight of God's
beauty at death, such a sight as the dying have sometimes, and which we cannot explain, is enough in the
way of sanctity, to do all life's work in one short hour.
If God be all this in time, what must eternity be like?
O happy, happy saints! for awhile longer you shall be
in His beautiful light, and we be far, far away: for
awhile—yet but for awhile, and then we also shall be

with you, with the same glad light of that Divine Face
shining full upon our ransomed souls!

Meanwhile even upon earth God is our possession,
and we are entering upon our inheritance by degrees.
Jesus is the Creator clad in the garments of redeeming
love, and we have Him here on earth already all our
own, while we are sadly but sweetly striving to be all
for Him. Already the attributes of the Creator are
fountains of joy and salvation to the creature. Why do
we not gaze upon them more intently? There is no
earthly science which can compete in interest with the
science of God. It is a knowledge which quickly leads
to love, and love is at once conversion, perseverance, and
salvation. The divine perfections support us by their
contrast with what we see on earth. They relieve our
minds. They increase our trust. They actually out of
their own abundance supply our deficiencies. They
feed our souls by their grandeur, and exercise an awful
mysterious attraction upon us, drawing us towards
themselves, yea, into themselves. They affect our souls
variously and medicinally. Justice gives us the gift of
fear, while mercy emboldens us to the grace of familiarity. Omnipotence is what our weakness wants, and
omnipresence what our discouragement requires. Our
ignorance consoles itself in omniscience, and our fears
lean and rest themselves on providence. All our wants
and all our weaknesses and all our wrongnesses carry
their manifold burdens to God's fidelity, full certain that
they will be lightened there. All these perfections are
deeps, into which we are ever descending now with most
surpassing contentment both of mind and will, and in
which we shall be ever sinking delightfully deeper
through all eternity. They satisfy us, and they delight
by satisfying; and again they do not satisfy, and by not

satisfying, they delight still more, because of the delightful hunger which they leave behind, and which is
in itself a marvellous, insatiable contentment. They
are a rest, and out of them there is no rest; they are a
home, and short of them, all is wandering and banish-
ment. They are our own. They belong to us. The
Creator has made them all over to us to be our possession and our joy, as if He kept them Himself only to
bear the weight of them, so that to us they might be
nothing else but joys.* Even His eternity is ours; and
though we are but sons of time, yet, possessing God, we
enjoy in Him eternity, and our religious minds even
now, much more our glorified spirits hereafter, run forth
up the backward ages and again down the countless ages
yet untold, and ever lose themselves, and ever find
themselves, in that ocean of everlasting life. Surely
there is no devotion like devotion to the attributes of
God. O blessed, O beautiful inheritance of the creature! They are eternal, and will never fail us, immutable and will never change, immense and always leave
us room. O space! thou must widen thy gigantic

---

* Nieremberg in the eighth chapter of the seventh book of his Prodigy of
Divine love, while dwelling on the way in which God vouchsafes to put His
attributes at our disposal, uses language which might seem nearly to fall under
the condemnation passed by Innocent XI. in 1679, twenty-one years after
Nieremberg's death, on the theses de omnipotentia donata. But it must be
remembered that those propositions had nothing whatever to do with God's
being the last end and enjoyment of men. They concerned the concurrence
of His omnipotence to our actions, and our free use of that concurrence in
sinning, and they implied the conclusion that God's dominion over His free
creatures was imperfect because of their freedom. These propositions were
condemned as " at the least temerarious and novel." Viva has a short commentary on them. (Opera Omnia: tom. vii. p. 194. Ferrara edition. 1757.)
They are also given by Philippus de Carboneano, the friend of Benedict XIV.,
in his treatise on condemned propositions, but he does not name their author;
nor does Denzinger in his Enchiridion; and Berrino does not give them at all
among the propositions of Innocent XI., perhaps because they were not condemned as " heretical."

shadowy limits, else wilt thou be a very prison for our immortal joys!

If earth be such a heaven to believing souls, what sort of heaven must the real heaven be? What is that incomparable beauty which the Blessed are gazing on this very hour? We have no words to tell, no thoughts to think it. What is it that that beauty is doing to their capacious, serene, and glory-strengthened souls? We have no words to tell, no thoughts to think it. What is that divine torrent of love which bursts forth from it, and threatens to submerge and overwhelm their separate created lives? We have no words to tell, no thoughts to think it. Whither reaches that white glistening eternity through which it will endure, and which seems to brighten in the far-off prospect rather than to fade away,—whither does it reach? We have no words to tell, no thoughts to think it.

Look how the Splendours of the Divine Nature gleam far and wide, nay infinitely, while the trumpets of heaven blow, and the loud acclaims of the untiring creatures greet with jubilant amazement the Living Vision! See how Eternity and Immensity entwine their arms in inexplicable embrace, the one filling all space, the other outliving all time; the one without quantity or limit, the other without beginning, end, or duration. See how Mercy and Justice mingle with and magnify each other, how they put on each other's look, and fill each other's offices. Behold the Divine Understanding and the Will, the one for ever lightening up with such meridian glory the profound abysses of God's uncircumscribed Truth and illimitable Wisdom, the other enfolding for ever in its unconsuming fires the incomprehensible Life of God, His infinite oceanlike expanse of being, and every creature of the countless worlds that from His life draw their own. Look at the Divine Immutability and Liberty, how they sit together like sisters, deep enthroned in that marvellous Life, and how God is free because He is immutable, and immutable because He is so free. See how the Son and the Holy Ghost know all the Father's knowledge, and yet He alone by His understanding produces that coeternal Word who is His Son. See how the Holy Ghost has all the love both of the Father and the Son; and yet They alone by Their will produced that blessed Limit of Themselves, that uncreated Sigh, that sacred Jubilee of Theirs, that everlasting Bond of union, who is the Holy Ghost. Thus is the loving Light of the Divine Understanding ever on fire with Love ; and thus is the living Love of the divine Will ever gleaming with the magnificence of uncreated Light. All this life, and all this assemblage of perfections, and all this royal vision, and all this eternal intertwining of uncreated beauties, is itself a simple act, and its simplicity and its actuality are the crowning beauties of it all. God is. He possesses actually all the plenitude of being, without admixture of privation, without dilution of possibility ; for not only are all things possible in Him but all possibilities are actual to Him. He never yet has been able to be: He never will be able to be : He never will be able not to be. He simply is. Beginning, end, succession, change—they come not nigh Him. They breathe no breath upon Him. He is a Pure Act. As St. Gregory Nazianzen says, He is all things, and yet He is nothing, because He does not belong to things at all. He is, and He is eternally, and He is necessarily, and He is of Himself. It is this Simplicity, this Actuality, which passes over the Grand Vision with incessant soft flashes from end to end and again from end to end, of that endless Nature, and which is to the Face 'of God what expression is to the face of man, at once its charm and its identity, its beauty and its truth. As we know each other by our looks, so we know God by His Simplicity.

O happy souls of the Blessed, and what of you? It is all written in the Holy Book;* and it needs no commenting. On the third day she laid away the garments she wore, and put on her glorious apparel. And glittering in royal robes, after she had called upon God, the Ruler and Saviour of all, she took two maids with her. And upon one of them she leaned, as if, for delicateness and over-much tenderness, she were not able to bear up her own body. And the other maid followed her lady, bearing up her train flowing on the ground. But she with a rosy colour in her face, and with gracious and bright eyes, hid a mind full of exceeding great fear. In going in she passed through all the doors in order, and stood before the King, where He sat upon His royal throne, clothed with His royal robes, and glittering with gold and precious stones, and He was terrible to behold. And when He had lifted up His countenance, the queen sank down, and her colour turned pale, and she rested her weary head upon her hand-maid. And the King's spirit was changed into mildness, and all in haste He leaped from His throne, and holding her up in His arms till she came to herself, caressed her with these words: What is the matter, Esther? I am thy Brother, fear not. Thou shalt not die: for this law is not made for thee, but for all others. Come near then, and touch the sceptre. And as she held her peace, He took the golden sceptre, and laid it upon her

* Esther xv.

neck, and kissed her, and said, Why dost thou not speak
to Me? And she answered, I saw Thee, my Lord, as
an angel of God, and my heart was troubled for fear of
Thy majesty. For Thou, my Lord, art very admirable,
as Thy Face is full of graces! And while she was
speaking she fell down again, and was almost in a
swoon. But the King was troubled, and all His servants comforted her.

Such is the picture of the Creator and the creature.
It is a history of the truest love that ever was: nay of
the only love that was ever truly true. And what is
the end of all? We are God's own creatures, and God
is our own God. All else will fail us, but He never
will. All is love with Him, love in light and love in
darkness, love always and everywhere. There are many
difficulties left unexplained, many problems yet unsolv-
ed. Would it not be strange, if it were not so, seeing
that He is infinite and we finite, He is Creator and we
but creatures? But the difficulties are only difficulties
of love. There is nothing cold in them, nothing
frightening, nothing which goes one step towards dis-
proving that sweet proof that He is our own God, our
very own. There is no difficulty in wondering why we
are not in heaven already. The wonder and the difficulty are, that such as we know ourselves to be should
ever enter there at all. This is the great difficulty, and
it is a difficulty for tears. Yet when that difficulty
looks up into the face of God's Fidelity, then that
sweetest and most soothing of all our Creator's grandeurs wipes the tears from our eyes, and hope comes
out from behind her cloud, and shines softly, and the
heart is still. Our own God? And so beautiful! A
theologian said that if one lost soul could reunite in
itself all the rage and hatred of all the lost against God,

and that it could root, fortify, and confirm all this gigantic rage and hatred in itself for millions and millions of years, until it had become a new, ineradicable, and preternatural nature to him, one little ray of God's beauty falling gently on him for a single moment would change his whole being that instant into such respectful love and utter adoration, that he would not feel the fires that burned him, because of the greater fires of his transported love. But we are free, and we are in earth's fair sunshine, and our heart is full of a little but most true love of God, and a whole world of God's blessed love is resting on our single heart,—and shall we doubt, shall we hesitate, shall we tremble, shall we be chilled in the midst of all these fires of love? O my Creator, my Eternal Love! O my Father, my Heavenly Father! weary yet full of trust, worthless but truly loving Thee, on earth still and very far from heaven, my home and my rest are still in Thy Fidelity! In te, Domine! speravi, non confundar in æternum!

THE END.

INDEX.

Printed in Great
Britain
by Amazon

31913730R00267